D1415172

The Postmodern Military

The Postmodern Military

ARMED FORCES AFTER THE COLD WAR

Edited by

Charles C. Moskos
Northwestern University

John Allen Williams
Loyola University Chicago

David R. Segal
University of Maryland

New York   Oxford

OXFORD UNIVERSITY PRESS

Oxford University Press

Oxford   New York
Athens   Auckland   Bangkok   Bogotá   Buenos Aires   Calcutta
Cape Town   Chennai   Dar es Salaam   Delhi   Florence   Hong Kong   Istanbul
Karachi   Kuala Lumpur   Madrid   Melbourne   Mexico City   Mumbai
Nairobi   Paris   São Paulo   Singapore   Taipei   Tokyo   Toronto   Warsaw

and associated companies in
Berlin   Ibadan

Published by Oxford University Press, Inc.,
198 Madison Avenue, New York, New York, 10016
http://www.oup-usa.org

Library of Congress Cataloging-in Publication Data
The postmodern military : armed forces after the Cold War / edited by Charles C.
Moskos, John Allen Williams, David R. Segal.
     p. cm.
   Includes bibliographical references and index.
      ISBN 978-0-19-513328-8
    1. Armed Forces. 2. World politics—1989- I. Moskos, Charles C. II. Wlliams, John
Allen, 1945- III. Segal, David R.

UA15 .P673 1999
355'.009045—dc21

                                                                99-048791

Printed in the United States of America
on acid-free paper

Dedicated to

Morris Janowitz
A scholar who understood soldiers

Sam C. Sarkesian
A soldier-scholar

Contents

Acknowledgments

Studies on armed forces and society are enjoying an unprecedented renaissance, which is all the more remarkable considering the state of such scholarship just a decade and a half ago. A post–World War II generation was approaching retirement, and interest in the field was undermined by the post-Vietnam mood. Yet, the contemporary period has been the most productive on a variety of dimensions: intellectual activity, topical relevance, citizenship education, increasing minority and female participation, as well as international collaboration among scholars in diverse countries.

It is not an exaggeration to say that this renaissance is largely due to the Inter-University Seminar on Armed Forces and Society (IUS). The IUS today constitutes an "invisible college" of some 700 fellows representing over forty-five countries. The fellows who make up the IUS include academics, students, military officers, and researchers in a variety of settings, both public and private. The fellows of the IUS differ widely in their strategic and political outlooks, but they hold in common the view that objective research on military institutions is a most worthy goal for which we should continually strive.

It is no coincidence that the three editors of this volume are current officers of the IUS and all the contributors are IUS fellows. The original *raison d'etre* of the IUS— stimulating independent research and scholarship in armed forces and society in an academic environment—is even more important today than it was when the IUS was founded in 1960 by Morris Janowitz. A World War II veteran, Janowitz, long associated with the University of Chicago, was—and remains even after his death—the giant figure in military sociology.

Sam C. Sarkesian, currently professor emeritus of political science at Loyola University Chicago, succeeded Janowitz as head of the IUS and did much to institutionalize the charismatic organization Janowitz founded. Sarkesian, a retired army lieutenant colonel of infantry, enhanced the IUS role of connecting individual scholars of diverse disciplines, organizations, and countries. He continues to make significant scholarly contributions to the field, both directly through his own writings and indirectly through his many students at Loyola.

The IUS is unique because its influence is based on scholarly soundness and professional responsibility rather than political connections or working under government auspices. This ensures its independence and immeasurably enhances its special credibility throughout the world.

Our gratitude is deep to Morris Janowitz and Sam Sarkesian, whose founding roles in the IUS kept studies of military organization alive in academia during some very trying years. That we remain in this enviable position is due to the core support we have received from the Robert R. McCormick Tribune Foundation and The Ford Foundation. The continuing core support of the Robert R. McCormick Tribune Foundation is gratefully acknowledged, with particular thanks to Neal Creighton and Richard Behrenhausen. The Ford Foundation, with the support of Christine Wing, also provided significant conference support and continued outreach support for scholars from soft-currency countries.

We are indebted to The John M. Olin Foundation, which sponsored the original international conference on which this volume is based. We thank program manager William Voegeli especially for his appreciation of our work and his support of it.

We also wish to thank Henry S. Bienen, president of Northwestern University and an IUS fellow since its inception, who has maintained the organization's secretariat on the Northwestern campus. With the support of President Bienen, two superb graduate assistants served as IUS office manager: Hatoshi Kawano and Dean Schloyer. Their contribution to the IUS cannot be overstated.

The editors would like to take this opportunity to note our indebtedness to a number of talented individuals who have helped us along the way. Not all were associated with this project directly, of course, but all contributed to our professional development in meaningful ways. Surely each of our authors—whose research is the real focus of this edited book—would have his or her own list. This is ours.

Charles Moskos would like to acknowledge those whose insights on the American military he has especially relied upon: Richard Behrenhausen, Martin Binkin, James Burk, John Sibley Butler, John Campbell, Neal Creighton, Mark Eitelberg, Robert Gifford, William Hauser, W. Darryl Henderson, Edward C. Meyer, David Ohle, Dennis Reimer, Stephen Rippe, John M. Shalikashvili, Jay Stanley, Theodore Stroup, Gordon Sullivan, and Arnold Weber. He would also like to list those military officers who, although technically his graduate students, were in reality his teachers: Robert Carroll, Robert DeMange, Karen Dunivin, John Hurley, Charles Johnson, Robert P. Kane, Exequiel Sevilla, and Frank R. Wood. This is also the opportunity to recognize the intellectual brilliance of Maxwell R. Thurman (1931–95), who turned the all-volunteer force around through the use of social scientists to inform army policy.

Moskos would also like to make special mention of those individuals to whom he owes special debts. The incomparable editing skills of Karen Feinberg were called upon in this book as well as in his previous ones. Dear friends accompanied him on arduous field trips, including zones of hostile fire: Ernest Degenhardt, Tom Kelly, Angela Manos, Laura Miller, John Wattendorf, and Leonard Wong. Without the moral and practical help of these individuals, his knowledge of the American military would be greatly impoverished. He joins his coeditors in thanking Sandra Carson Stanley for her own work and for making the biannual IUS meetings in Baltimore, Maryland, the premier event in the study of military organizations around the world.

Jay Williams's greatest intellectual debt is to Sam C. Sarkesian: soldier, scholar, and an extraordinary example of an officer and a gentleman. No one outside Jay's family has influenced him more. Professor Sarkesian has been a continuing source of intellectual and personal inspiration, as he continues to be for yet another generation of his students. Williams has also learned much about the military and its relationship with society from Alexander A. Belkin, Andrei I. Cherkasenko, Donald C. Daniel, Stephen M. Duncan, Frank Harness, John Hillen, Irving Louis Horowitz, Morris Janowitz, Robert Killebrew, James R. Kurth, Morris I. Liebman, John J. Mearsheimer, Michael Pocalyko, Thomas E. Ricks, Alvin Z. Rubinstein, Larry Seaquist, Peter Swartz, and Robert S. Wood.

He thanks those former graduate and military students, now friends, who continue to be a source of pride, including Stephen J. Guerra, James E. McPherson, and IUS treasurer Robert A. Vitas. Special thanks go to his graduate assistants, Brian Endless, Steven Michels, Michael P. Noonan, and Mark Souva. Each of them provided invaluable assistance at various phases of the project, and all are well on their way to distinguished careers. Mike Noonan's keen insights and his help in pulling the threads of the book together are particularly noted.

David Segal notes that many of the military people he would acknowledge are already on Charles Moskos's list. He would like to highlight the important contributions of David Ohle, Theodore Stroup, Gordon Sullivan, Angela Manos, and Leonard Wong to his professional work. In addition, he would thank Steve Mirr, Joe Jones, Sara Lister, and Morton Ender as individuals who extended themselves greatly to be of professional assistance to him.

He expresses particular gratitude for the outstanding work of two of his graduate students, Brian Reed and Bradford Booth, who worked with him teaching the military sociology course in which the manuscript of this book was used. The success of that course (repeated once) convinced him that the audience for sound, comparative scholarship on civil-military relations is even wider than he supposed.

We are grateful to dozens of students at the University of Maryland and Loyola University Chicago who read and critiqued drafts of these chapters in military sociology and political science classes in 1997 and 1998.

We gratefully acknowledge the support of the U.S. Army Research Institute for the Behavioral and Social Sciences (ARI). This unique organization is the lineal descendant from the army research group that was established by George C. Marshall in World War II. It has consistently shown that doing good for the army and doing good social research can be one and the same. With the strong support of Edgar M. Johnson, Michael Drillings, and Zita Simutis, ARI underwrote a substantial portion of the conference at which the final versions of these chapters were presented, through Contract Number DASW 0195K005 to the Center for Research on Military Organization at the University of Maryland.

Our greatest debt of gratitude is due to our authors, who shared their special insights as social scientists and keen observers of their societies. Their patience and cheerful assistance during the long period of gestation for this book is much appreciated. We are grateful for their personal friendship, as well as their excellence as professional collaborators.

Finally, because parts of this book are likely to be controversial—or at least we hope so—the usual caveat is especially relevant: The authors and editors alone, and not ARI, the Department of the Army, the Department of Defense, or any other organization with which any of us have ever been affiliated are responsible for the findings and interpretations presented here.

C.C.M.   J.A.W.   D.R.S.
Evanston, Illinois   Chicago, Illinois   College Park, Maryland

August 1999

About the Editors and Contributors

The Editors

Charles C. Moskos, a former draftee, is professor of sociology at Northwestern University, where he holds the Harold H. and Virginia Anderson Chair in the Weinberg College of Arts and Sciences. He is chair of the board of the Inter-University Seminar on Armed Forces and Society. Professor Moskos has conducted field research with American troops in Vietnam, Panama, Saudi Arabia, Somalia, Haiti, and Bosnia. His most recent books include *A Call to Civic Service; The New Conscientious Objection;* and *All That We Can Be: Black Leadership and Racial Integration the Army Way.* His writings on military sociology have been translated into sixteen languages.

John Allen (Jay) Williams, executive director of the Inter-University Seminar on Armed Forces and Society, is associate professor of political science at Loyola University Chicago, where he specializes in national and international security policy and civil-military relations. He is a captain in the U.S. Naval Reserve with extensive Pentagon staff experience. He is chair of the Academic Advisory Council of the National Strategy Forum and serves on the U.S. General Accounting Office Expert Panel on the Quality of Military Life. His previous work (with Sam C. Sarkesian) includes *Soldiers, Society and National Security; The U.S. Army in a New Security Era;* and (with Robert A. Vitas) *U.S. National Security Policy and Strategy: 1987–1994.*

David R. Segal, president of the Inter-University Seminar on Armed Forces and Society, is distinguished scholar-teacher, professor of sociology and of government and politics, and director of the Center for Research on Military Organization at the University of Maryland. He has been a distinguished visiting professor at the United States Military Academy, and serves on the Board of Visitors of the U.S. Army War College, the Defense Science Board Task Force on Human Resources Strategy, and on the U.S. General Accounting Office Expert Panel on the Quality of Military Life. His research focuses on human resource management issues in the military.

The Contributors

Bernard Boëne is professor of sociology at the University of Toulouse-II and has served as vice president of Research Committee 01 (Armed Forces & Conflict Resolution) of the International Sociological Association since 1994. Previously he taught for twenty years at the Military Academy Saint Cyr (1977–97). In 1995 he defended a Habilitation thesis on a history and sociology of military sociology (broadly defined) in the United States, 1892–1992. A graduate of the Sorbonne (1971) and the Paris Institute for Political Studies (1977), he has published books and monographs in the field of military studies in English and French. Notable among his publications are "How Unique Should the Military Be?" *European Journal of Sociology*, *La specificite militaire*, and *Conscription & armee de metier*. "The Armed Forces' 'New' Missions: An European View," *The Tocqueville Review*, vol. XVI, No. 1, 1995, pp. 145–165, and (with Christopher Dandeker) *Les Armées en Europe*.

Jakkie Cilliers holds an Hons. BA, MA (*cum laude*), and DLitt et Phil from the University of South Africa (UNISA). He also holds holds a diploma in operations management from the UNISA School of Business Leadership. Following his resignation from the South African military in 1988, he co-founded the Institute for Defence Policy, which became the Institute for Security Studies (ISS)—the largest independent institute for security studies in southern Africa. The Institute played a leading role in the transformation of the South African military in support of the transition to democracy of his country in the 1990s. Dr. Cilliers has been the Executive Director of the ISS since 1993. His awards include the Bronze Medal from the South African Society for the Advancement of Science and the H. Bradlow Research Bursary. Dr. Cilliers has presented numerous papers at conferences and seminars, is a regular commentator on local and international radio and television, and has attended numerous international conferences. He regularly lectures on security and defense issues and is widely published in South Africa and abroad. He serves on the Civic Education Monitoring Committee, the Defence Rationalisation Strategy Committee, and the Equal Opportunity Advisory Board of the South African Department of Defence.

Stuart A. Cohen is professor of political studies and senior research fellow of the BESA Center for Strategic Studies at Bar-Ilan University Israel. His principal research interests are the Jewish political tradition, Zionist thought, and civil-military relations in Israel.

Christopher Dandeker is professor of military sociology and head of the Department of War Studies at King's College London. He is joint founder and secretariat member of the British Military Studies Group, which is affiliated with the Inter-University Seminar on Armed Forces and Society (IUS). Professor Dandeker's publications include (with C. Ashworth and T. Johnson) *The Structure of Social Theory, Surveillance Power and Modernity, Nationalism and Violence*, and (with Bernard Boëne) *Les armees en Europe*. In addition, he has published numerous articles in the field of military sociology.

Cathy Downes is a senior defense official of the New Zealand Defence Force. She has held research appointments at Harvard University's Center for International

Affairs, the University of Melbourne, and Australian National University's Strategic and Defence Studies Centre. Her published works include *Special Trust and Confidence: The Making of an Officer*; (with Desmond Ball, eds.) *Security and Defence: Global and Pacific Prospectis*; *High Personnel Turnover*; and *Senior Officer Professional Development*. Dr. Downes is a fellow of the 21st Century Trust (U.K.) and of the Inter-University Seminar on Armed Forces and Society. Her recent work focuses on strategic security and resource planning in Western democracies, military leadership and ethos for the new millenium, and the impact of military technology developments on future war and doctrine.

Bernhard Fleckenstein, director and professor, is a sociologist and political scientist. He has served with the Parliamentary Commissioner for the Federal Armed Forces, with the planning staff of the Ministry of Defense, and with Joint Services Command. Before he took his present position in the office of the president of the Bundeswehr University Munich, he directed the German Armed Forces Institute for Social Research (SOWI) for twelve years. He holds degrees from the University of Frankfurt and from Harvard University.

Reuven Gal serves as the director of the Carmel Institute for Social Studies and the Israeli Institute for Military Studies. He formerly served as the chief psychologist of the Israeli Defense Force (IDF). He received his BA and MA degrees in psychology and sociology from the Hebrew University and his PhD in psychology from the University of California at Berkeley. Dr. Gal has taught at various universities and academies, both in Israel and abroad, and has published numerous articles, papers, and books.

Karl W. Haltiner is a senior lecturer in military sociology in the Department of Military Studies at the Swiss Federal Institute of Technology in Zurich (ETHZ). His current research is on the relation of armed forces and society. He focuses mainly on the effects of social changes on the military and the officer profession in Switzerland. He directs the annual study *Swiss Public Opinion and Security Policy*. His books include (in German) *The Citizen Army—Still a Model for Citizenship or an Antiquated Ideal?* He has published in national and international journals.

Lindy Heinecken is a military researcher and deputy director of the Centre for Military Studies (Cernis), located at the South African Military Academy. She holds a master's degree in sociology from the University of Cape Town, is a research associate of the Institute of Security Studies, a fellow of the Inter-University Seminar on Armed Forces and Society, and serves on the council of the South African Sociological Association. The main focus of her research is defense human resources, with a specific focus on defense labor relations, military professionalism, and the management of diversity. She has delivered numerous conference papers and presentations, and has published several articles in the field. She lectures at the various South African National Defense Force (SANDF) staff colleges, and serves on a number of Department of Defense transformation project teams.

Eduard Hirt was formerly a teacher at the secondary education level, and is now a professional military officer. He serves in the Division for Mechanized Troops within the Federal Office for Combat Troops and in the Swiss Military College from 1992 to 1995. His contribution to the article in this book grew out of his diploma paper, "Post-Modern Armed Forces—The Case of Switzerland."

Michel Louis Martin is professor of political science at the Institute for Political Studies at the University of Toulouse 1. He is the director of the Morris Janowitz Center for the Study of Armed Forces and International Security. He has written extensively on the military in France, including *Warriors to Managers: the French Military Establishment since 1945*, and in Africa, with *Le Soldat Africain et le Politique: Essais sur Le Militarisme et L'État Pretorien au Sud du Sahara*. He has also written on constitutional issues, with *L'Histoire Politique et Constitutionnelle de la France depuis 1789*, *Les Constitutions Africaines: Évolutions Récentes*, and international relations. He is member of the IUS Council and the editorial board of *Armed Forces & Society* and other journals. For many years he was visiting scholar at the University of Chicago, where he worked with Morris Janowitz and Edward Shils.

Marina Nuciari is professor of sociology at the Department of Social Sciences, Torino University. She also teaches military sociology at the Italian Army Academy. She is a member of many international associations, and was chairperson of the European Research Group on Military and Society (ERGOMAS). For many years she has taken an active part in various cross-national research programs dealing with military and society matters. Her recent publications include (in Italian) *Armed Forces and Effectiveness, The Italian Officership: Present and Future of the Military Profession in Europe*, coauthored with G. Caforio, "The Military Profession, Models of Change Considered," *Current Sociology*, Vol. 42 (1996), and "Value Orientations and Political Attitudes of Cadets in a Comparative View," in G. Caforio, ed., *The European Cadets: Professional Socialisation in Military Academies*, pp. 74–91.

Franklin C. Pinch is principal, FCP Human Resources Consulting, Gloucester, Ontario; professor, Military Psychology and Leadership Department, Royal Military College of Canada, Kingston, Ontario; adjunct research professor (sociology) at Carleton University, Ottawa; and faculty member of the Lester B. Pearson Canadian International Peacekeeping Training Centre, Cornwalis Park, Nova Scotia. Formerly the senior behavioral scientist of the Canadian Forces, Dr. Pinch also has been a human resources policy advisor and change management consultant on armed forces in and outside Canada. He is past chair and current cochair of the Inter-University Seminar on Armed Forces and Society, Canada Region. His previous work includes a number of major reports, journal articles, and book chapters on military social, organizational, and personnel change issues. The most recent of these is *Lessons from Canadian Peacekeeping Experience: A Human Resources Perspective*.

Henning Sorensen, PhD, MPA, MBA, is director of the Institute for Sociological Research (ISF), a private consulting company in Copenhagen. He is a fellow of the Inter-University Seminar on Armed Forces and Society and a member of the European Research Group on Armed Forces and Society (ERGOMAS). He serves on the executive board of the International Sociological Association Research Committee 1 on Armed Forces and Conflict Resolution.

Jan S. van der Meulen is the director of the Dutch Society and Armed Forces Foundation in The Hague. He holds functions in the IUS as well as in the European Research Group on Armed Forces and Society (ERGOMAS). He is a sociologist whose research and publications relate to (the end of) conscription, public opinion, and civil-military relations. His essays include "Homosexuality and the Armed Forces in The Netherlands," with Marion Anderson, in Wilbur J. Scott and Sandra Carson Stanley (eds.), *Gays and Lesbians in the Military*; "Post-Modern Societies and Future Support for Military Missions," in Gert de Nooy (ed.), *The Clausewitzian Dictum and the Future of Western Military Strategy* (1997); and, "Zero-Draft in the Low Countries" (with Philippe Manigart), *Armed Forces & Society* (Winter, 1998).

1

Armed Forces after the Cold War

CHARLES C. MOSKOS
JOHN ALLEN WILLIAMS
DAVID R. SEGAL

The armed forces of the United States and those of other Western developed democracies are moving from what can be termed *Modern* to *Postmodern* forms of military organization. This is the core argument of this volume. The Modern military that fully emerged in the nineteenth century was inextricably associated with the rise of the nation-state.[1] Though the Modern military organization was, of course, never a pure type, its basic format was a combination of conscripted lower ranks or militia and a professional officer corps, war-oriented in mission, masculine in makeup and ethos, and sharply differentiated in structure and culture from civilian society. The Postmodern military, by contrast, undergoes a loosening of the ties with the nation-state. The basic format shifts toward a volunteer force, more multipurpose in mission, increasingly androgynous in makeup and ethos, and with greater permeability with civilian society.

The term *Postmodern* as applied to the armed forces must imply some significant departure from Modern forms of military organization. Otherwise *Postmodern* is just another misapplication of an overworked adjective. Drawing heavily on the historical experience of the United States and Western European nations, we present a threefold typology of the military and society.

The first is the *Modern* type, which we can date from the nineteenth century to end of World War II. Of course, the Modern era can be traced as far back as the Treaty of Westphalia in 1648 signed by the Holy Roman Empire, France, Sweden, and various German principalities. The treaty not only ended the Thirty Years War, but proclaimed the principle of national sovereignty, one that has echoed down the three and a half centuries since. But the hallmark of the Modern military is better traced to the *levee en masse* of the French Revolution in 1793, when the concept of citizen soldier enters the European continent.[2]

The second is the *Late Modern* type that prevailed from the mid–twentieth century into the early 1990s and is essentially coterminous with the Cold War. Along with the mass-conscripted armies, the Late Modern

1

military was accompanied by an accentuation of military professionalism in the officer class. Prior to that time, military officership in Europe—and to some extent in the United States as well— was primarily determined by lineage rather than the professional military education associated with academies and war colleges.

The *Postmodern* type is ascendant in the contemporary era.[3] Although antecedents predate the end of the Cold War, the collapse of communism in the Soviet Union and Eastern Europe provided the major thrust to move the military toward the Postmodern model. Without the threat of invasion, Western states no longer needed to buttress armed forces so distinctive from the social values of the larger society. While the military in such countries continues to emphasize national patriotism, the globalization of finance, trade, communication, and other vital human activities steadily erodes much of the traditional basis of national sovereignty.

Why these three periods and not others? Primarily, they make sense of the direction of societal-military relations at the conclusion of a watershed period, one in which the fear of total annihilation was present. Nuclear weaponry imposed an ultimate reality that forced both sides to accommodate—whether at the building of the Berlin Wall in 1961, during the Cuban missile crisis of 1962, or in surrogate wars in Korea, Vietnam, and Afghanistan. The power to destroy civilizations was the defining quality of the Cold War. Though the nuclear threat has not vanished, it has receded greatly as a possible instrument of war between major states. The core thesis of this volume is that the end of the Cold War has ushered in a period of transition in which the conventional Modern forms of military organization are giving way to new Postmodern forms.

The Postmodern military is characterized by five major organizational changes. One is the increasing interpenetrability of civilian and military spheres, both structurally and culturally. The second is the diminution of differences within the armed services based on branch of service, rank, and combat versus support roles. The third is the change in the military purpose from fighting wars to missions that would not be considered military in the traditional sense. The fourth change is that the military forces are used more in international missions authorized (or at least legitimated) by entities beyond the nation state. A final change is the internationalization of military forces themselves. Here we have in mind the emergence of the Eurocorps, and multinational and binational divisions in NATO countries.[4]

Debate over the state of armed forces and society at the end of the twentieth century pits a kind of naive optimism against a deep pessimism. Among the optimists, the end of large-scale war was captured in such visions as the "new world order" proclaimed by President George Bush following the Gulf War, or in Frances Fukuyama's seminal phrase "the end of history."[5] The notion of a future without major war was a reincarnation of the beliefs of the founders of modern social thought. Immanuel Kant, Adam Smith, Auguste Comte, Herbert Spencer, and Karl Marx, among many others, held in common (about the only thing such a diverse group did hold in common) the notion that industrial societies were evolving toward greater pacification, even toward a warless world.

Taking a darker view of the post–Cold War era are those who see post–Cold War anarchy. In this perspective, the very tools of war are slipping out of control of central states as the employment of organized violence become more and more the characteristic of armed bands, terrorists, and gangsters. Martin Van Creveld moves away from the Clausewitzian assumption that war is rational in the sense it reflects national interests to posit the blurring of existing distinctions between civilian and soldier, between individual crime and organized violence.[6] Robert Kaplan evokes this mood in the title of his influential essay, "The Coming Anarchy and the Nation State Under Siege."[7] In a more muted but still essentially pessimistic tone is the influential thesis of the ultimately insoluble "clash of civilizations" advanced by Samuel Huntington.[8]

But whether or not one takes the more pessimistic or optimistic viewpoint, it's a fact that the missions of the armed forces will be structured in ways fundamentally different from the relative certainties of the Cold War.[9] A distinguishing feature of the contemporary period is the decline of wars between states and the rise of war within states, sometimes resulting in state collapse. Separating belligerents, resettling of refugees, delivering of food and medical supplies, providing security for humanitarian organizations, and so forth, create demands that, if not entirely new, are certainly of a larger scale than those with which the military has traditionally contended.[10] Peacekeeping and humanitarian missions have come to occupy a more central position in military doctrine than ever before. Indeed, the term "military humanitarianism" enters the new vocabulary and strikes few as an oxymoron.[11]

Although many of these changes can be traced back to before the end of the Cold War, they have become more prominent since the tearing down of the Berlin Wall in November of 1989 and the end of the Soviet Union two years later. It is incontestable that the demise of the Soviet Union has ushered in a new era in international relations and with it concomitant changes in the structure and culture of the armed forces. Very importantly, the very missions of the military shift from primarily war fighting or war deterrence to military deployments for peace and humanitarian purposes. The Appendix lists over fifty military operations by Western nations since the end of the Gulf War in 1991, and is by no means a complete accounting. In the vast majority of these missions, the main purpose was of a peacekeeping or humanitarian nature.

The changes taking place, of course, are not simply confined to the military or to the realm of war. On the contrary, we are dealing with a general reorganization of postindustrial societies. There are several indicators that sweeping change is taking place. Of special relevance for us is the relative weakening of central forms of social organization that have been the hall-marks of the modern age: the nation-state and national markets. The sub-stantial growth of global social organizations has altered the conditions un-der which modern nation-states can expect to exercise their power, maintain the loyalty of their citizens, or raise and deploy their military might.

Social commentators who conceptualized the shift away from the para-digm of the old industrial state to something new are as diverse as David Reisman, Marshall McLuhan, Alvin Toffler, and Robert Reich.[12] Respec-tively, these observers pointed to the shift from inner-directed to other-directed societies, from print to electronic media, from industrial to information-based economies, and from producers of goods to symbolic analysts as the dominant occupation. These macro-organizational shifts also correspond with the demographic transition from high- to low-fertility societies.

As important as these structural changes is the cultural shift in public attitudes and opinion. Old verities are questioned rather than accepted. There are fewer overarching authorities to whom people are willing to de-fer. There is a shrinking consensus about what values constitute the public good, and little confidence that we know how, by the use of reason, to de-termine what the public good might be. The eighteenth century's faith in reason, the nineteenth century's faith in the nation-state, and our own cen-tury's confidence in science and technology have all lost their hold on our imagination, despite their considerable accomplishments. It is precisely this transition which social theorists mean when they refer to ours as a Post-modern age.[13]

The Postmodern movement began as a whimsical architectural style around 1960 in reaction to the dominant "international" style. In the 1970s Postmodernism became a fashionable form of literary criticism in which all "texts" (pronouncements, novels, historical events, etc.) are indeterminate, subject to endless interpretation and reinterpretation. Postmodernism began to infiltrate social theory by the early 1980s and to subvert absolute values and metaphysical foundations. This is not the place to render a full treat-ment of Postmodernism; it is sufficient for our purpose to note that Post-modernism subverts absolute values and introduces a profound relativism into discourse. The operative terms are pluralism, fragmentation, hetero-geneity, deconstruction, permeability, and ambiguity.

Citizenship is a distinctively Modern institution, depending as it does on the conception of an autonomous individual, capable of free choice and self-regulation, participating in public affairs with expectations of affecting the outcome of political decisions. The boundaries creating separate sover-eign domains (which made the Modern nation-state possible at the global level and made the autonomous individual possible within the state) are blurred and disintegrated by the transnational character of cultural, eco-nomic, and even military organizations. And so the sense of identity with and loyalty to the nation-state is "decomposed" in Postmodern society. Inasmuch as the nation-state is the *sine qua non* of the Modern military, such developments fundamentally change civil-military relations.

The advent of information technologies and their impact on armed forces has been described as the Revolution in Military Affairs, or RMA for short. Proponents of the RMA point to the accelerated integration of computer-age technologies into weapon systems and military command and control networks. The RMA carries the promise of greater military agility, precision, and potency, but it also requires large force reductions to finance the new technology. A corollary of the RMA is the lessening of the distinctions between warrior and non-warrior, between officers and other ranks, and between the branches of the military.[14] Although not quite congruent with our concept of the Postmodern military, the RMA vision does point to a qualitative break with the patterns of warfare characteristic of the Modern era.[15]

An even more striking parallel to our concept of the Postmodern military is the duality between the contemporary armed forces' tendency to decouple from national structures and the increasing convergence between humanitarian and military operations. Consider the following.

- *Item.* 1998 marked the first time more civilians working for the United Nations were killed in peacekeeping and humanitarian missions than were military personnel serving under the United Nations flag.[16]

- *Item.* A more martial attitude begins to characterize hitherto pacifist-inclined nongovernment organizations. The secretary general of Doctors Without Borders argues for an international force to break the grip of Hutu gangs in refugee camps in Zaire.[17] Similarly, the humanitarian agency Oxfam states UN troops should secure refugee areas in Rwanda.[18]

- *Item.* Secretary General Boutros Boutros-Ghali proposes a permanent military force that the United Nations can call upon for peacekeeping and peacemaking operations.[19] Though no concrete action results, the proposal receives serious debate in many Western capitals.

- *Item.* Executive Outcomes (EO) is a South African enterprise that offers to train soldiers for governments with ineffective militaries. In practice, the soldiers of EO lead troops and fly combat missions against rebels and outlaws. For these services, the firm pays its infantrymen around $2,000 a month, while specialists like pilots earn $5,000 monthly and up. Executive Outcomes can point to some striking successes in assisting the governments of Angola, Sierra Leone, and Papua New Guinea.[20] Whether private military corporations are war profiteers or representative of the future of peacekeeping has become a serious question.[21]

- *Item.* The German government allows male German citizens of the Danish minority living in Schlesweg-Holstein the option of serving in either the German or the Danish army to fulfill their military obligation.

- *Item.* In 1997, the United States secretary of the army hired as a temporary consultant an advocate of replacing a "masculinist" with an "ungendered vision" of military culture.[22]

- *Item.* After interviewing Italian soldiers who served in Somalia and Albania, a researcher detects a new type of inducement for military service. A "Postmodern motivation" characterizes soldiers who enter the military more for the desire to have a meaningful personal experience than out of either national patriotism or an occupational incentive.[23]

- *Item.* The 1998 movie *Wag the Dog* portrayed an American president concocting a war to displace public attention from a sexual scandal with a young girl. On December 16, 1998, the eve of the congressional vote on his impeachment, President Clinton sent American warplanes and missiles to attack Iraq. Whatever the president's motives for the timing of the bombings, connections with the movie were immediately drawn.[24] The term "wag the dog" entered the Postmodern lexicon as fiction seemingly became reality and vice versa.

As this volume went to press, the warfare phase of the Kosovo crisis had concluded with no combat-related casualties on the NATO side during its air attacks against Yugoslavia. Peace in Kosovo is far from assured, with scores continuing to be settled on both sides. Still, it is clear that the conflict there can fairly be called the first Postmodern war. It was a war where "everything is turned on its head, soldiers build refugee camps, aid workers clamor for war, and a guerrilla army seeks to do what the world's most powerful military alliance will not."[25] In a front page news story, the *New York Times* described "a calibrated war, enabled by high-tech weaponry, guided by the flickering light of opinion polls."[26]

With respect to formal social organizations such as the military, a Postmodern critique sees increasing permeability between civil and military structures and the erosion of martial values (which traditionally have been seen as masculine). From the vantage point of Postmodern theory, we can illumine and, perhaps, forecast key changes in military organization and civil-military relations.

For this volume, the international contributors were asked to discuss the relationship between the military and their society along a series of dimensions discussed in greater detail in the next chapter. This book is not simply a merging of conference papers. Rather, a distinguished group of military sociologists followed a common paradigm to describe and analyze their own countries' experience in the post–Cold War era. We seek here to capture the commonalty as well as the uniqueness of each nation's civil-military changes.

Chapter authors were asked to address the categories of the Postmodern model as they apply to their countries over time, although they were given wide latitude in how they did so. The goal of the editors was to impose some structure on the contributions to ensure comparability and the coverage of theoretical issues we think important. It was not our goal to make the contributions identical in format (a difficult prospect in any case), but to make them equivalent insofar as they addressed the same issues.

We use the comparative case study method, choosing the richness of detail provided by expert observers of the armed forces in their own societies. Our approach is case-based rather than variable-based. This decision differs from the dominant methodology of empirical social science based on the language of hypothesis testing, in which researchers develop theories that specify relationships among variables and then collect data to determine the extent to which the relationships hold. The corresponding methodology deals largely with measurement questions, determining the reliability of the data, and with statistical manipulation. Statistical analyses tend to break cases into parts and require many simplifying assumptions, while qualitative comparisons allow examination of constellations and configurations.

The problem is that in the course of satisfying the demands of statistical techniques, the connection between the findings and substantive reality can become stretched. Context and complexity are slighted to fit the Procrustean bed of the methodology. This is why most cross-national studies often have an unreal quality, since the data examined have little meaningful connection to an actual historical process.

Comparative analysis has no logical affinity with the variable-based approach, and is often better pursued with case studies. Thus, variable-based analysis generally starts simply with one independent variable, then adds more independent variables, usually one by one, to deduce the variance in explaining a dependent variable. Case-based analysis, on the other hand, starts out complicated and then begins to discard extraneous independent variables that do not affect the dependent variable, while remaining sensitive to organizational complexity and historical specificity. This kind of analysis assumes that causal relations are complex, and allows the judgment of knowledgeable observers to be taken more fully into account.

The plan of this book is straightforward. Charles C. Moskos sets the stage by presenting a conceptual framework that posits three stages of armed forces and society: Modern, Late Modern, and Postmodern. These are roughly coterminous with the century and a half preceding the end of World War II, the Cold War era, and the post–Cold War era (since 1990). The basic reference point for the Postmodern paradigm is the United States. The analytical method draws heavily upon the "developmental construct" introduced by Harold Lasswell as early as 1935 and developed more recently in the futuristic studies of Wendell Bell.[27] A developmental construct posits an ideal-type at some future point by which past and present trends can be identified and appraised. The Postmodern military is a developmental construct based upon observation of the past.

The bulk of the volume consists of comparative perspectives predominantly representing twelve Western countries: Great Britain, France, Germany, The Netherlands, Denmark, Italy, Canada, Australia, New Zealand, Switzerland, Israel, and South Africa. While the historical background in each country is not neglected, the primary focus is on recent developments in armed forces and society.

Many of the traditions of the military forces of English-speaking nations have been adopted from the armed forces of the United Kingdom, which has probably been a more enthusiastic keeper of these traditions than her former colonies or fellow members of the Commonwealth. Christopher Dandeker points out that as the British armed forces move into the post–Cold War world, they bring with them elements of earlier periods as well. Thus, while new missions are being faced by smaller, more flexible forces that are more dependent on civilian personnel and contractor support, and while these forces are moving toward full integration of women, preparations for traditional military missions have not been excluded. The roles of soldier-statesman and soldier-scholar have not as yet supplanted the role of warrior.

If the long-term trend is in the direction of a new Postmodern form of military organization, this development has nowhere been as dramatically illustrated in the mid-1990s as it has been in France. As Bernard Boëne and Michel Martin demonstrate, as recently as 1994, although colonial wars and deterrence of Warsaw Pact aggression had faded into the past, nuclear deterrence was still central to the French military mission. Most significantly, the birthplace of the mass armed forces still clung to a conscription-based army. By contrast, during the late 1990s, the decay of the public service tradition was evident, conscientious objection had increased, and France was moving rapidly toward a smaller, more professional, volunteer military focused on peacekeeping and humanitarian operations. The roles of soldier-scholar, soldier-diplomat, and soldier-communicator were on the ascent.

Germany's armed forces are deeply rooted in alliances, initially NATO and now the European Union as well. As Bernhard Fleckenstein suggests, the Bundeswehr may be forerunner of a postnational military in advanced democratic societies. Germany is also a forerunner toward a Postmodern military in another way. During the 1990s, conscientious objection had reached such levels that about one in three draftable men chose civilian service over military service. These conscientious objectors enjoy good standing in German society as they serve in medical and institutional facilities and deliver services to elderly or handicapped people. Ironically enough, with the end of the Cold War and the possible end of conscription, Germans seem more concerned over losing the conscientious objectors who perform alternative service than over the loss of draftees who would fight in the eventuality of war. In one key feature, however, the German military does not accord with the Postmodern paradigm. Almost nowhere else in the West do women play such a minor role in the armed forces.

The Netherlands is crossing a historic threshold. Its centuries old conscription system for the active force has come to an end. This development—along with military unionization, acceptance of homosexuals, placement of women in combat assignments, and a strong commitment to peacekeeping missions—would seem to have launched the Dutch armed forces well into Postmodernity. Yet, as Jan S. van der Meulen points out, the military may be becoming more marginalized rather than Postmodern; marginalized in the sense that it is no longer a major institution in Dutch society. Also, the move toward professionalization may see some backtracking on liberal social policies within the rank and file. Most significantly, there is deep soul-searching on the utility of the military in the wake of the Dutch contingent's lamentable failure to stop the killing of 7,000 Moslems in the Srebrenica area of Bosnia, in its role as part of the United Nations peacekeeping force in the former Yugoslavia.

In overall terms, the Danish armed forces fit the Postmodern paradigm remarkably well. Security policies are influenced more by national desire than by actual threats to the nation. The downsizing of the Danish armed forces reduces the significance of conscription as a rite of passage for adult males. Or as Henning Sorensen phrases it, the armed forces have gone from national defense to selective defense. Data gathered from Danish surveys show a marked tendency toward individualization rather than broader identities. The major departure from the Postmodern model is that there has been no decline in the positive attitude the Danish public holds of its military. This may be because the Danish military has yet to undergo a serious scrutiny or investigation by the media or other groups.

The Italian military, as with most other Western armed forces, is in the throes of a massive drawdown and a shrinking military budget. Indeed, the army chief of staff in protesting the budgetary cuts was quoted as saying, "It would be better to abolish the Army." As described by Marina Nuciari, however, the Italian armed forces remain relatively traditional with regard to restrictions on homosexuals, limits on the role of women, and an almost invisible conscientious objectors program. A strong Postmodern element does appear in the dramatic transformation of the military purpose, however. The traditional concerns of territorial defense have given way to the new perceived threats of terrorism and uncontrolled immigration. This has led to a fundamental questioning in Italy about the purpose of military service.

Among the Anglo-American nations (with due acknowledgment of the centrality of Quebec in the Canadian fabric), Canada has probably moved earliest and farthest from a traditional military model. The armed forces themselves have been increasingly democratized, liberalized, and civilianized. Canada's military posture is increasingly driven by internal rather than external considerations. A high value is placed on military integration with the larger society and transparency of the civil-military interface. As Franklin Pinch notes, while there is continued involvement in global activities such as peacekeeping, public support for the military is ambivalent. Defense spending is at its lowest point since the 1930s and the active Canadian Forces receive less support from a reserve structure than is the case in most other Western countries. The dominant professional roles in the Canadian military are becoming the soldier-diplomat and the corporate manager. As elements of a more general societal concern with human rights, both gender integration and sexual orientation integration have progressed further in the Canadian Forces than in any other Anglo-American nation.

Australia and New Zealand were on the periphery of the Cold War, but as Cathy Downes notes, they were clearly influenced by it. Like England and Canada, they have used conscription only rarely. In the post–Cold War era, they have experienced an accumulation of new missions. With new alliance arrangements, they are reorienting themselves toward the Asia-Pacific region just as information-age dynamics weave them more tightly into the global community. Australia and New Zealand have maintained a high ratio of officers to enlisted personnel, reflecting the recognition that for mobilization purposes it takes more time to "grow" officers. As the enlisted ranks have been reduced, the two countries' armed forces have become more dependent on defense civilians and contractors. At the officer level, the role of combat leader, which dominated until recently, is now being accompanied by the role of military entrepreneur as corporate culture spreads through the military, and by that of military diplomat as the force structure is shaped by contemporary contingencies.

Switzerland defines itself as a special and unique case: without war for a century and a half, with neutrality and nonalliance as national policy, and with a militia conscription system whose universality for males is not approached by any other European country. Karl Haltiner describes how the age-old Swiss system is now being increasingly undermined. Advanced military technology cannot be maintained by a part-time militia. Military service for young men, formerly seen as entry into an important reference group, is now becoming more likely to be regarded as a nuisance to be avoided. While it is unlikely that Switzerland will abandon its militia system entirely, it will find itself relying increasingly on more volunteers and long-term professionals.

Israel, unlike many states, confronts genuine threats to its national survival. This is the overriding reality that shapes the format of the Israel Defense Force and civil-military relations. Since the inception of the nation in 1948, the Israeli military has also been the great melting pot for Jews coming from the various diasporas. Israel is the only country that conscripts women, although the role of female soldiers is circumscribed. Reuven Gal and Stuart A. Cohen see some signs of Postmodern trends in the Israeli Defense Force, notably in suggestions to widen the definition of service to include civilian service, perhaps even incorporating non-Jewish Israelis. But the authors argue basically that Israel does not fit a Postmodern paradigm. For the foreseeable future, Israel will remain "a nation in arms."

South Africa's military, like the country as a whole, has undergone perhaps the most dramatic changes experienced by any democracy in contemporary times. The end of white rule in 1993 was followed a year later by the end of conscription (which had applied only to whites). The new South African National Defense Force consists of white officers in the former military and newly integrated soldiers from the armed wings of antiapartheid groups. Jakkie Cilliers and Lindy Heinecken describe these and a host of other dramatic changes in both force composition and definition of military purpose. In a manner of speaking, the South African military is making the leap from a very traditional armed force to one that is looking more and more like a Postmodern one.

The final chapter, by John Allen Williams, is a summary perspective that evaluates the Postmodern paradigm as it is supported, modified, or refuted by the essays on the various countries.

We finish with a caveat, a speculation, and a conclusion. The caveat is not to take for granted that the movement toward a Postmodern military will continue into the future. The speculation is that we may be moving into an era in which conflict would occur between a military system anchored in traditional social forms (with relatively low technology) and one more Postmodern, with high technology. The form of social organization might become more important than the level of technology.

The conclusion of this book is that whatever the future holds, we can, for now, confidently state that the dominant trend is a blurring of the lines between the military and civilian entities, both in structure and in culture. This permeability between military and civilian structures is a major new historical phenomenon. Armed forces are part and parcel of the evolution of other postindustrial entities in the West. Events since the end of the Cold War augur that some meaningful, even momentous, and not illusionary change is occurring within armed forces in Western societies. The purpose of this volume is clarification of this change.

NOTES

1. The literature on how the military and war laid the basis for the modern state is quite extensive. See especially Stanislav Andreski, *Military Organization and Society* (London: Routledge & Kegan Paul, 1954); Brian M. Downing, *The Military Revolution and Political Change* (Princeton, N.J.: Princeton University Press, 1990), Charles Tilly, ed., *Coercion, Capital, and European States* (Cambridge, Mass.: Basil Blackwood, 1990), Anthony Giddens, *The Nation-State and Violence* (Berkeley: University of California Press, 1987); Michael Mann, *The Sources of Social Power* (New York: Cambridge University Press, 1986); Bruce D. Porter, *War and the Rise of the State* (New York: Free Press, 1994).
2. Predating the French Revolution was the militia obligation for men in the British colonies in North America.
3. Earlier formulations of the "Postmodern military" thesis are found in Charles

Moskos, "Armed Forces in a Warless Society," in Juergen Kuhlmann and Christopher Dandeker, eds., *Armed Forces After the Cold War* (Munich: SOWI, 1992), pp. 1–19; Charles Moskos and James Burk, "The Postmodern Military," in James Burk, ed., *The Military in New Times* (Boulder, Colo.: Westview, 1994), pp. 117–140; and John Allen Williams and Charles Moskos, "Civil-Military Relations After the Cold War," in Anton A. Bebler, ed., *Civil-Military Relations in Post-Communist States* (Westport, Conn.: Praeger, 1997), pp. 25–35.

4. The EUROCORPS consists of German, French, Spanish, and Belgian troops. The NATO multinational division in Rheindalen includes Dutch, British, German, and Belgian soldiers. The First German-Dutch Army Corps represents a binational military organization. The degree of internationalism in various western European armies is examined in J. Soeters and R. Recht, "Culture and Discipline in Military Academies: An International Comparison," *Journal of Political and Military Sociology*, Vol. 26, No. 2 (winter 1998), pp. 169–190.

5. Frances Fukuyama, *The End of History and the Last Man* (New York: Free Press, 1992). See also Martin Shaw, *Post-Military Society* (Philadelphia: Temple University Press, 1991).

6. Martin Van Creveld, *The Transformation of War* (New York: Free Press, 1991). For another highly readable perspective see Ralph Peters, *Fighting for the Future* (Mechanicsburg, Pa.: Stackpole, 1999).

7. See, notably, Robert Kaplan, "The Coming Anarchy and the Nation State Under Siege," *Sources of Conflict* (Washington, D.C.: U.S. Institute of Peace, 1995), pp. 7–11.

8. Samuel P. Huntington, *The Clash of Civilizations and the Remaking of World Order* (New York: Simon & Schuster, 1996). Interestingly enough, Huntington had advanced a more optimistic appraisal of historical trends just a few years earlier. See his *The Third Wave: Democratization in the Late Twentieth Century* (Norman, Okla.: University of Oklahoma Press, 1991).

9. On the nature of future warfare and its contrasts with the Modern period, see Martin Van Creveld, *The Transformation of War* (New York Free Press, 1991); John Keegan, *War and Our World* (London: Hutchinson, 1998); and Chris Hables Gray, *Postmodern War* (New York: Guilford Press, 1998).

10. For a critical assessment of the use of the military in humanitarian operations, see Michael Mandelbaum, "Foreign Policy as Social Work," *Foreign Affairs*, Vol. 75, No. 1 (Jan./Feb. 1996), pp. 16–32. For a somewhat more positive appraisal, see Edward N. Luttwak, "A Post-Heroic Military Policy," *Foreign Affairs*, Vol. 75, No. 4 (Jul./Aug. 1996), pp. 33–44.

11. Thomas G. Weiss and Kurt M. Campbell, "Military Humanitarianism," *Survival*, Vol. 33, No. 5, Sept./Oct. 1991, pp. 451–465.

12. David Reisman, *The Lonely Crowd* (New Haven, Conn.: Yale University Press, 1952); Marshall McLuhan, *Understanding Media* (New York: McGraw-Hill, 1964); Alvin Toffler, *The Third Wave* (New York: William Morrow, 1980); and Robert B. Reich, *The Work of Nations* (New York: Alfred A. Knopf, 1991).

13. The literature on Postmodernism grows rapidly. Useful reviews for social scientists are David Harvey, *The Conditions of Postmodernity* (Cambridge, Mass.: Basil Blackwell, 1989); Anthony Giddens, *The Consequences of Modernity* (Stanford, Conn.: Stanford University Press, 1990); Scott Lash, *Sociology of Postmodernism* (New York: Routledge, 1990); Bryan S. Turner, *Theories of Modernity and Post-*

modernity (Newbury Park, Calif.: Sage, 1990); Pauline Marie Rosenau, *Post-Modernism and the Social Sciences* (Princeton, N.J.: Princeton University Press, 1992); and Zygmunt Bauman, *Postmodernity and Its Discontents* (Oxford, England: Polity, 1996).

14. For a concise discussion of the factors affecting the emerging military, see Andrew J. Bacevich, "Tradition Abandoned: America's Military in a New Era," *The National Interest*, No. 48 (summer 1997), pp. 16–25.

15. The literature of the Revolution in Military Affairs is quite extensive. For a concise guide, see James R. Blaker and Robert A. Mannin, eds., *Understanding the Revolution in Military Affairs: A Guide to America's 21st Century Defense* (Washington, D.C.: Progressive Policy Institute, 1997). See also James Adams, *The Next World War: Computers Are the Weapons and the Front Line Is Everywhere* (New York: Simon & Schuster, 1998). For a critique of the RMA, see William Murray, "Clausewitz Out, Computer In," *The National Interest*, No. 48 (summer 1997), pp. 57–64.

16. Georgie Ann Geyer, "Passive Mode at the U.N.," *Washington Times*, Nov. 19, 1998, p. 18.

17. Alain Destxhe, "We Can't Be a Party to Slaughter in Rwanda," *New York Times*, Feb. 9, 1995, p. A15. See also Thomas G. Weiss and Kurt M. Campbell, "Military Humanitarianism," *Survival*, Vol. 33, No. 5 (Sept./Oct. 1991), pp. 451–465; and Larry Minear and Thomas G. Weiss, *Mercy Under Fire* (Boulder, Colo.: Westview, 1995).

18. Reuters, April 24, 1995.

19. Boutros Boutros-Ghali, *An Agenda for Peace* (New York: United Nations, 1992).

20. "Have Gun, Will Prop Up Regime," *U.S. News & World Report*, Jan. 20, 1997, pp. 46–48.

21. David Shearar, "Outsourcing War," *Foreign Policy*, Fall 1998, pp. 68–81.

22. See Madeline Morris, "By Force of Arms: Rape, War and Military Culture," *Duke Law Journal*, Vol. 45, No. 4 (1996), pp. 651–781.

23. Fabrizio Battistelli, "Peacekeeping and the Postmodern Soldier," *Armed Forces & Society*, Vol. 23, No. 3 (Spring 1997), pp. 467–484.

24. For a most thoughtful commentary on President Clinton and the December 1998 bombing of Iraq , see Ralph Peters, "A Question of Leadership," *Wall Street Journal*, Dec. 17, 1998, p. A22.

25. David Rieff, "Lost Kosovo," *The New Republic*, May 31, 1999, pp. 26–32.

26. *New York Times*, May 22, 1999, p. A1.

27. For a contemporary appraisal and reprinting of his core articles, see Harold Lasswell, *Essays on the Garrison State*, edited and with an introduction by Jay Stanley (New Brunswick, N.J.: Transaction, 1997). The definitive work on the social science of the future is Wendell Bell, *Foundations of Futures Studies* (New Brunswick, N.J.: Transaction, 1997). Bell sees future studies as intrinsically involved with values as one's image of the future affects the likelihood of change moving in that direction.

2

Toward a Postmodern Military: The United States as a Paradigm

CHARLES C. MOSKOS

Changes in military organization reflect, as they sometimes affect, large-scale social changes in the broader society. Comprehensive analysis of these reciprocal relations requires a clear specification of the dimensions along which change is expected to occur. As a practical matter, we rely on typologies of military organization to accomplish this task, even though we are fully aware that any typology does an injustice to reality. Drawing heavily on the historical experience of the United States and Western European nations, it is possible to describe and contrast Modern, Late Modern, and Postmodern military organizations, and to speculate about the factors facilitating movement from one type to the other.

A developmental construct posits an ideal-type at some future point by which past and present trends can be identified and appraised. The Postmodern military is a developmental construct based upon observation of the past. What is presented is a model, not a prophecy, and may help explain what has happened and predict what is likely to happen. By positing a Postmodern military we are thus able to recognize trends among a variety of dimensions, trends that differ substantially between Modern, Late Modern, and Postmodern armed forces. These trends within the three basic types are summarized in Table 2.1.

Our concern is to grasp the whole, to place the salient facts within a framework that will enable us to study the main trends of institutional development in military organization. The typology, in other words, is offered as a guide to systematize current research findings. We must avoid using it mechanically to bring artificial closure to our thinking about these matters. Its use, rather, is to help bring focus to ongoing research and, if need be, to set the stage for revising the analytic framework we are about to present.

The discussion in this chapter depends heavily on the American experience, but the essential observable features of the Postmodern military are phrased in terms suitable for cross-national research in Western advanced democracies.[1] Indeed, it is the cross-national comparisons that are the substantive and conceptual heart of this volume. Still, the American case pre-

Table 2.1.
Armed Forces in the Three Eras: The United States

Forces Variable	Modern (Pre–Cold War) 1900–1945	Late Modern (Cold War) 1945–1990	Postmodern (Post–Cold War) Since 1990
Perceived Threat	Enemy invasion	Nuclear war	Subnational (e.g., ethnic violence, terrorism)
Force Structure	Mass army, conscription	Large professional army	Small professional army
Major Mission Definition	Defense of homeland	Support of alliance	New missions (e.g., peacekeeping, humanitarian)
Dominant Military Professional	Combat leader	Manager or technician	Soldier-statesman; soldier-scholar
Public Attitude toward Military	Supportive	Ambivalent	Indifferent
Media Relations	Incorporated	Manipulated	Courted
Civilian Employees	Minor component	Medium component	Major component
Women's Role	Separate corps or excluded	Partial integration	Full integration
Spouse and Military	Integral part	Partial involvement	Removed
Homosexuals in Military	Punished	Discharged	Accepted
Conscientious Objection	Limited or prohibited	Routinely permitted	Subsumed under civilian service

sents itself as a good reference point not only for the intrinsic interest that inheres in the world's foremost military power, but also because its military occupies somewhat of a midposition on the spectrum of Postmodern developments.

PERCEIVED THREAT

We begin with the simple idea that the probability of war and the perception of threats shape the basic relations between armed forces and society. One key difference between Modern and Postmodern societies lies in the character of the threats they face and the ways they perceive them. Charles Tilly has argued that the rise of the Modern nation-state in Europe rested on success in meeting these threats.[2] Over the last two centuries, an important factor accounting for a state's survival has been its ability to mobilize and deploy a mass armed force, relying typically on a system of military conscription to prepare its population for war. In the Modern era, the threat of war, and so the justification for armed forces engaged in border defense, was close at hand. Mobilization to meet this threat, at least since the end of the eighteenth century, was one of the main sources of nationalist fervor.

What are the threats against which the military is suppose to defend society? These change in time and character, as well as in specifics. In the pre–Cold War period the primary concern was invasion either of a nation or its allies. Although the source of an invasion might change and the technology of an attack certainly would change, the primary concern still remained that of invasion. Once both sides in the Cold War acquired nuclear weapons, the older threat of invasion gave way to the primary fear of nuclear war. For the West, this began with the 1949 acquisition of the atomic bomb by the Soviet Union and reached full force by the mid-1950s, when the Soviets demonstrated both thermonuclear weapons and methods of delivering them.

The 1991 Gulf War, although not a Cold War conflict, nevertheless was a war involving states against state and in that sense was a throwback to the early Modern period, albeit at unprecedented levels of high technology on the winning side. The threat, however, was not one of invasion to the West (although Kuwait was invaded), but to oil interests that were deemed vital to national security.

In the post–Cold War era, Western democracies are not typically concerned with invasion or of nuclear war initiated by enemy states; instead the greatest tension and violence are occurring within states—such as the former Yugoslavia with its ethnic conflicts, or African states, such as Somalia, Congo, and Rwanda—with starvation and ethnic struggles veering into genocide. Advanced Western states feel vulnerable to terrorism that may be augmented by nuclear, chemical, or biological means of destruction. Indeed, in 1998, Secretary of State Madeline Albright called terrorism conducted by non-state entities as "the war of the future."[3]

MAJOR MISSION DEFINITION

With the demise of the Soviet Union and the resultant lessened threat of a world war, the American military underwent something of an identity crisis. While seeking to maintain its conventional war-fighting capabilities, the American military rapidly created new training exercises and manuals to incorporate lessons learned from deployments since the end of the Cold War.

New buzzwords entered the Pentagon lexicon: "operations other than war," "other military operations," and "sustainment and stability operations." (Likewise, the predictable acronyms are OOTW, OMO, and SASO.) Whatever these kinds of missions are called, they reflect a fundamental shift in the emphasis of armed forces from defense of the homeland to multinational peacekeeping and humanitarian missions. Indeed, one of the growing internal debates within military circles is the degree to which "operations other than war" detract from the "warrior" capabilities of the armed forces.[4]

In addition to intrastate violence, other matters come to occupy the attention of armed forces in Western states, and many of these tend to be non-military in any traditional sense. Edward Luttwak argues that geo-economics rather than geopolitics will dominate the use of military force.[5] Threats to national security increasingly have transnational dimensions, such as the drug trade, uncontrolled immigration, and environmental degradation.[6] A few examples suffice to make the point. In 1991, the army constructed a ten-foot-high steel-panel fence on the Mexican border to close off a popular route for smugglers who were bringing drugs and illegal aliens into the United States. In 1992 and 1993, the U.S. Navy and Coast Guard picked up thousands of Haitians at sea seeking to enter the United States and placed them in refugee camps at the American naval base in Cuba. In fact, the American invasion of Haiti in 1994 was motivated in part by the desire to stop illegal Haitian immigration to the United States.

A "greening" of the definitions of national security was also clearly evident in the 1990s. A State Department official in 1995 put the new thinking succinctly: "During the Cold War, most security threats stemmed from state-to-state aggression. . . . Now we're focusing more on internal factors that can stabilize governments. Now we're paying much more attention to early warning factors, like famine and the environment."[7]

FORCE STRUCTURE

As the perceived threat changes, so also does the force structure to deal with it.[8] From the early Modern era to well into the Cold War, countries relied on mass armies, typically of conscripted able-bodied men. These mass armies were based on conscripts with a cadre of professional military officers, non-commissioned officers, and certain technical specialists. The United States relied on a large standing army of conscripts from the early years of the Cold War until 1973, when the draft ended and the all-volunteer force (AVF) came into being.[9] From that time until the end of the Cold War, the military was increasingly professional, although still large. Throughout the Cold War, all continental European states relied on conscription (Britain being the exception, having done away with the draft in 1963). But during the Late Modern period, volunteer components in technical specialties had become the rule. Still, the move toward a volunteer force came more quickly than expected once the Cold War was over. In 1995, both France and Spain announced they would end the draft and the Netherlands planned to phase out conscription by the close of the century. Other northern European countries were experiencing similar debates. The overriding fact was that the end of conscription meant the shrinking of the military forces.

In the American case, the active duty force of 2.6 million in the peacetime draft years of the Cold War was down to 1.4 million by 1999. Despite the manpower drawdown, recruitment for the AVF was becoming increasingly difficult by the end of the century. Spending on defense in the United States declined from 6 percent of the gross national product in the mid-1980s to slightly less than 3 percent a decade later. The end of the Cold War saw heightened budgetary debates on the relative sums to be spent on military versus nonmilitary expenditures in the federal budget. Within the military budget itself, there was sharpening contention as to whether priority should be given to personnel costs, readiness, or weapons modernization.

One outcome of the move to an AVF was a sharp rise in the compensation of entering soldiers. In 1999, a corporal in the United States military (two years of service) earned approximately $30,000 per year, a sum that included allowances for housing and subsistence as well as base pay.[10] This sum did not include medical insurance, enlistment bonuses, specialty pay, or postservice educational benefits. In real buying power, the junior enlisted soldier earned more than double that of his drafted counterpart. The comparable figure for a sergeant major (twenty-five years of service) was $70,000 per year, a sum whose buying power was about the same for the senior NCO of the draft era. In other words, enlisted pay scales in the AVF underwent a pronounced compression.

With a diminishing active-duty force, reserve components began to play an increasingly important role in the AVF. From being rather moribund during the Cold War period and virtually excluded from the Vietnam War, reserve forces became integral components of force deployment. Following the end of the Vietnam War and especially from the end of the Cold War, reserve units were particularly well integrated within the air force in a wide range of roles, including pilots. Reserve personnel were also heavily relied upon for support roles in all the services during the Persian Gulf War and in the humanitarian missions to Somalia, Haiti, and Bosnia. Still, the realities of a smaller military force and the increasing deployment of military personnel in peacekeeping and humanitarian operations leads to a heightened operation tempo or "OPTEMPO." The accompanying deterioration in morale becomes a command concern.

DOMINANT MILITARY PROFESSIONAL

The military's genetic self image is that of a specialist in violence, ready for combat. Certainly in pre–Cold War times, the primary military need was for the leader skilled in the arts of war and leadership. Increasingly, however, technological sophistication replaces brute force as the key to victory. Probably the most well-known finding in military sociology tells how the dominant type of military professional shifts from the combat leader in the early Modern period to the managerial technician in the Late Modern period. This shift was most clearly argued for in the American case by Morris Janowitz.[11]

In the Postmodern period, more than a residue of the warrior spirit will continue within the officer corps, but we can also expect to see the ascendancy of alternative professional types: the soldier-scholar, including the attainment of advanced civilian degrees; and the soldier-statesman, the officer skilled in handling the media and adept in the intricacies of international diplomacy. This is not to suggest that soldier-scholars were absent in earlier eras, but the relevant empirical question is which kind of officer will most likely be promoted into the military elite.[12] Of some note is that when Gen. Wesley K. Clark was selected as supreme commander of NATO and all American forces in Europe in 1997, he was described as "scholarly" and possessing the "diplomatic skill" that made him right for the job.[13] Likewise in the same year, when Gen. H. Hugh Shelton was selected to become the chairman of the Joint Chiefs of Staff, a key factor was "how he transformed from a warrior to a diplomat" during the 1994 American intervention in Haiti.[14]

PUBLIC ATTITUDES TOWARD THE MILITARY

One might expect public attitudes toward the military to shift over time, based on a diminution of perceived national threats. The picture is more complex. During both world wars the American public and media were extremely supportive of the military. This was especially the case during World War II in the all-out conflict against the Axis powers. In contrast, support was much less evident during the Korean War and, especially, during the Vietnam War. Yet, during the Cold War or Late Modern era, public attitudes were generally supportive of the military as an institution and of its budgetary demands, although there was some erosion of that support. A more nuanced and at times even critical attitude toward the armed forces appeared especially within the intelligentsia (a disproportionate number of whom seemed to evade conscription). Professional military personnel come to be characterized sometimes as buffoonish characters in the popular media. Thus, the public attitude in the Late Modern era can be characterized as ambivalent.[15]

In the post–Cold War era, the public mood toward the armed forces becomes more one of indifference. The end of conscription makes military service less salient to the general populace. The likelihood of volunteer recruitment drawing upon future elites and opinion leaders becomes increasingly remote.[16] I also suggest that the willingness of a country to accept casualties in wartime is positively related to the proportion of elite youth who are putting their lives on the line.[17]

Military cinema ceases to be a major genre and when the contemporary military is portrayed it can have a sinister edge. In *Broken Arrow* (1996), an air force major plots to steal two nuclear bombs for which he plans to hold Denver in ransom. In *The Rock* (1996), a marine general holds San Francisco hostage by threatening to use poison gas. In *Snake Eyes* (1998), a navy commander masterminds the assassination of the secretary of defense.

Yet, in counter to the prevailing trend, two 1998 box-office hits—*Saving Private Ryan* and *The Thin Red Line*—portrayed American soldiers in a positive light. These critically acclaimed movies gave gritty accounts of World War II battles, the former starting with the Normandy invasion, the latter set in Guadalcanal. Put in another way, both of these movies were firmly set in the Late Modern era.

It is of some note that since the end of conscription in the United States in 1973, not one major novel has been written about the all-volunteer force.

MEDIA RELATIONS

In the Modern period, the civilian media were typically an integral part of the military system. Through World War II, the American media were basically incorporated into the armed forces. Not only were journalists subject to censorship, but they also had formal status in the armed forces and were issued military uniforms. In essence, both the media and the military were "on the same team."

In the Late Modern period, the media, while no longer incorporated into the armed forces, were nevertheless subject to a high degree of control, as occurred during the American operations in Grenada, Panama, and the Gulf War. The defense establishment effectively controlled the media through the use of press "pools" in which only a small and select number of journalists was given access to the troops. The media saw themselves as being manipulated by the military, even though there was no formal censorship.[18]

The post–Cold War era, as represented by the operations in Somalia, Haiti, and Bosnia, presents an entirely different situation.[19] The media are frequently in country before the arrival of the military and take care of their own logistical needs. More important, the media were essentially autonomous entities as technological advances allow for direct transmission of news to the outside world. Whereas the media were manipulated by the armed forces in the Late Modern period, they are courted by the military in the Postmodern era. The ultimate in Postmodernism may well be the state of affairs in which commanders watch CNN commercial television to see what is happening in their areas of operation (as this writer observed in Somalia).

CIVILIAN EMPLOYEES

The civilian component of the defense establishment undergoes significant change as well.[20] In Modern military systems, civilians are a minor component of the operational side of the defense establishment. But, in the Late Modern period, an increasing number of civilian employees work in the defense establishment in operational roles. In part this is due to turning over many menial jobs to civilian workers on the grounds of cost-effectiveness and releasing soldiers from nontraining tasks. More important, the shift toward civilians is due to the military's greater reliance on technically complex weapons systems, with the corresponding need for technical experts, both contract and direct-hires, to work in the field and at sea. At least since the 1950s, the capabilities of American warships would have been severely handicapped without the civilian technicians—"tech reps"—who maintain their weapon systems.

In the buildup leading to the Gulf War, some 10,000 "emergency essential civilians" working for the U.S. military were sent to Saudi Arabia to help operate logistics systems. Interestingly enough, these civilian personnel had a lower rate of being returned back to the United States for physical and disciplinary reasons than regular military personnel.[21]

In the Postmodern period, civilians become even more intimately involved in military functions. Without the contractors who were responsible for much of the logistics and housekeeping duties, it would be hard to conceive the American missions to Somalia, Rwanda, Haiti, and Bosnia having taken place.[22] It is more than a historical footnote that the first American casualty in Operation Provide Comfort in Somalia was an Army civilian employee who died when the vehicle in which he was traveling hit a mine.[23]

WOMEN'S ROLE

A particularly revealing way to understand the trend toward Postmodernism in the armed force is to look at the role of women in the military.[24] In the mass army of the Modern period, women were typically excluded from service. In those cases where women did serve, they did so in separate corps. In the United States, the Women's Army Corps (WAC) and the navy's Women Accepted for Volunteer Emergency Service (WAVES) of World War II typified this form of utilization.

In the Late Modern period, separate corps were generally abolished in Western armies, though the numbers of women remained small. In the United States, women were formally integrated into many support roles starting in the 1970s. Women were allowed to join the officer commissioning programs on civilian campuses in 1972. A major threshold was crossed with the admission of women to the military academies in 1976. Through the Cold War period, however, American policy remained one of exclusion of military women from combat roles or even being assigned to areas of high risk.

In the Postmodern military, pressures have grown to incorporate women into all assignments, including combat roles. Although the United States was not in the forefront of the movement, by the 1990s steps in that direction were clearly evident, and though still excluded from ground combat assignments, the role of women in the American military has increased dramatically since the end of the Cold War. Starting in the early 1990s, basic training was gender-integrated in all of the armed forces except in the Marine Corps and in the ground combat arms of the army. Advanced individual training was largely gender-integrated. Starting in 1995, navy women were allowed to serve aboard warships (excluding submarines) and as combat pilots aboard aircraft carriers. Similarly, women pilots (albeit a small number) were assigned to bombers and fighter planes in the air force.

These changes came with both benefits and costs to the military's reputation. The sexual shenanigans of primarily navy fighter pilots in the 1991 convention of the Tailhook Association in Las Vegas, Nevada, became a national news story.[25] In 1996, incidents of sexual harassment at training camps rocked the army. Yet even these scandals could serve as an impetus for opening up the remaining proscribed roles for women. It had become an article of faith for feminist spokespersons to hold that sexual harassment would come under control only when women were no longer regarded a second-class members of the military—that is, no longer excluded from the combat arms.[26] Certainly the Tailhook scandal facilitated the opening up of virtually all navy assignments to women, including combat aircraft and warships.

SPOUSES AND THE MILITARY COMMUNITY

In the not-so-distant past—the 1950s—a junior enlisted man informing a superior of his wish to marry would be admonished: "If the Army wanted you to have a wife, it would have issued you one." And, in fact, fewer than one in ten draftees were married men. The advent of the all-volunteer force saw a sharp increase in the proportion of married soldiers. Thus, in 1998, at the pay-grade level of corporal, one in three were married. In a striking reversal of the draft pattern, soldiers in the AVF are more likely to be married than their civilian counterparts. The presence of large numbers of married junior enlisted personnel becomes an accepted reality. Indeed, the commandant of the Marine Corps was publicly rebuked in 1993 when he proposed that recruits be limited to single persons only.

For the career soldier, especially commissioned officers, military membership in a manner extended to his wife and family.[27] The military wife was expected to take part in numerous social functions and "volunteer" activities. Indeed, promotion to higher ranks might depend to some degree on how well one's wife performed in this role. These formal and informal requirements for officers' wives seemed more pronounced in the American than in European militaries.

In the Late Modern period, a discernible trend was the increasing reluctance of wives of military personnel at both the noncommissioned and officer levels to take part in customary military social functions. This trend became more pronounced in the Postmodern military, as military spouses became much more likely to have employment outside of the home. Fewer and fewer of them—and we are still speaking mainly of wives rather than of husbands—have either the time or the inclination to engage in the social life of military installations. Curiously enough, it appears that as demands on military spouses decrease, there is more resentment of those demands that remain.

HOMOSEXUALS IN THE MILITARY

The status of homosexuals in the military remains contentious, but the general movement is toward increased toleration and acceptance.[28] During the Modern period of the mass army, military personnel who were discovered to be homosexuals were frequently incarcerated during times of war, or dishonorably discharged during times of peace. Such punishment did not prevent homosexuals from performing military service or having covert forms of informal associations. In the Late Modern military of the Cold War, homosexuals were still not welcome, though the severity of punishment diminished. Gays and lesbians were typically given medical discharges, though even these could be coded in ways by which civilian employers could know the cause of discharge. The trend, however, was toward less stigmatizing discharges.

A key characteristic of Postmodernism is lack of consensus on absolute standards to inform moral judgments. As the status of homosexuals becomes increasingly accepted in society at large, similar pressures arise to allow open homosexuals to serve in the armed forces. The higher education establishment in the United States for some years has urged the Defense Department to remove the ban on homosexuals entering the military as a condition for maintaining Reserve Officer Training Corps (ROTC) detachments on campus. (Efforts to remove ROTC from several prestigious campuses stalled when Congress passed legislation prohibiting government contracts to universities that disestablished ROTC.) The United States occupies somewhat of a midposition on the issue of homosexuals in the military. It is more lenient than the United Kingdom and certain Mediterranean countries, but much more restrictive than the policies found in Scandinavia, the Netherlands, or Canada.

The controversy surrounding President Bill Clinton's effort to lift the gay ban in 1993 dominated much of the news coverage of the new administration. After much negotiation between service chiefs, the Congress, and the administration, the new policy announced in 1994 forbade the military to inquiry as to a service member's sexual orientation, but if the service member declared his or her homosexuality, then that person was to be discharged. In other words, the "don't ask, don't tell" policy meant in effect that a discrete homosexual could remain in the service (as, de facto, he or she could always do).

In point of fact, the number of homosexual discharges increased by about 40 percent following the implementation of the "don't ask, don't tell" policy. In the late 1990s, the great preponderance of homosexual discharges for either sex—over 80 percent—were for "statements" (i.e., "telling") rather than for persons caught in "acts." Women soldiers (especially white) were much more likely to be discharged for homosexuality than men. This reflected not only the increasing number of women in the military, but probably as well the lesser stigma homosexuality has for women than for men.

Only time will tell whether "don't ask, don't tell" will hold firm or be only a way station to the full integration of open homosexuals into the American armed forces. Although the early lifting of the full ban seemed unlikely as of this writing, the United States has clearly moved toward greater acceptance of homosexuality than would have been imagined a decade or so earlier.

CONSCIENTIOUS OBJECTION

In most Modern Western societies, the state formally recognized conscientious objection, but limited such recognition to traditional "peace churches," such as the Mennonites, Brethren, Quakers, Seventh Day Adventists, and, with less consistency, the Jehovah's Witnesses. Screening is fairly severe. Conscientious objectors (COs), if not outright allowed, were often given the option of going to prison or serving in a noncombatant role in the military. This was basically the case in the United States up to World War II. In the Late Modern period, the state accepted broad religiously based objection as a criterion; thus objector status was granted to COs from mainline Protestant denominations, Roman Catholicism, and other religious—but nonpacifist—bodies. This stage saw the appearance of alternative civilian service, as occurred in America during World War II.

In Postmodern Western societies, the definition of conscientious objection vastly expands to include secular and humanitarian motives.[29] In effect, religion is no longer a defining factor. This secularization of conscience is accompanied by a definite movement toward regarding civilian service as the civic equivalent of military service. With the advent of all-volunteer forces, conscientious objection appears even among serving military members. During the Gulf War, several hundred American servicemen claimed CO status. Almost surely the first female CO appeared at that time, though her name, up to now at least, has been lost to history.

THE POSTMODERN PARADIGM

The three-stage paradigm can be applied to other phenomena. Consider the following. The first Muslim chaplain entered the American armed forces in 1993, thus ending the monopoly of the chaplaincy by Christians and Jews. Starting in 1997, in another symbol of growing religious diversity, soldiers of Native American Indian descent were allowed to use the hallucinogenic plant peyote in religious services. Perhaps even more striking, in 1999 the U.S. Army chaplaincy recognized the neo-pagan Wicca as a legitimate faith. More than 40 active-duty "witches," male and female, celebrated the Rite of Spring at Ford Hood, Texas.[30]

A particularly sharp example of the conflict between a Modern and a Postmodern conception of military service occurred in the case of Michael New. A lower-ranking enlisted man with a heretofore unblemished military record, New refused to deploy with his unit when it was sent to Macedonia in 1995. New told his superiors he would refuse to wear the United Nations blue helmet and shoulder insignia, the standard uniform of all the soldiers, including Americans, in the peacekeeping force in that country. The case was taken up on the talk-show circuit and New was supported by conservative critics of the United States' willingness to put some of its troops under United Nations command. From the military's viewpoint, New was disobeying a direct order. Although New could have been subject to confinement, he was eventually given a bad-conduct discharge. The New case highlighted the growing gap between the Modern military's total allegiance to the nation-state and the Postmodern conception of transnational command of a military force.

One of the most telling illustrations of the shift to a Postmodern military was the case of Lt. Kelly Flinn, the first female B-52 pilot. In May 1997, the nation was transfixed when charges of an adulterous affair with a civilian married to an airwoman (along with charges of insubordination and making a false statement) led to her removal from the air force. The anti-adultery regulations of the military justice system came under heavy attack from the establishment press. Thus, the *New York Times* castigated the "antiquated adultery rules" of the armed forces.[31] The salient point was that the very idea that the moral codes of the military and those of civilian society should be different was now coming under Postmodern criticism.

Another sign of the permeability between civilian life and military service occurred in 1993. In that year, AmeriCorps, a national youth service program, was introduced by President Bill Clinton. AmeriCorps offered its enrollees an educational benefit of $4,725 for each year of service. The educational benefit was explicitly modeled after the G.I. Bill principle first introduced for veterans of World War II. The amount of the AmeriCorps educational benefit was a subject of much haggling. The armed forces and veterans associations were concerned that a civilian postservice educational benefits would siphon off possible military recruits. The final AmeriCorps figure was equal to 80 percent of the minimum postservice educational benefit that a member of the military could earn. Still, that a civilian variant of the G.I. Bill was now codified into law was clearly a Postmodern trend.[32]

Yet another contemporary sign of the interpenatrability between armed forces and civilian spheres is the closer cooperation between armed forces and nongovernmental organizations (NGOs) in humanitarian operations. Though we are accustomed to thinking of the military and the NGOs as contrasting types of organizations, even contrasting character types—the tough-minded and the high-minded—this is becoming increasingly wrong. At the very time the military becomes more nuanced in its dealings with local populaces in peace and humanitarian missions, the NGOs become more reliant and even more supportive of the military.[33]

The Postmodern military also finds itself working more closely with various governmental entities. Western military forces have collaborated with the United Nations High Commission for Refugees in Africa and supported the Organization for Security and Cooperation in Europe in monitoring elections in the former Yugoslavia. The United States military has worked closely with American governmental interagency personnel in training and setting up local police forces in Haiti. The head of the National Defense Panel set up by the Department of Defense in 1996 to assess the future of the armed forces reported to Congress that future military forces would "require different forces and more cooperation with other agencies of government and private agencies."[34]

The hallmark of the Modern military was that of an institution legitimated in terms of values and norms based on a purpose transcending individual self-interest in favor of a presumed higher good. Members of the American military were often seen as following a calling captured in words like "duty, honor, and country." With the end of conscription and the advent of an all-volunteer force, marketplace factors began to play an increasing role in the recruitment of armed forces. Distinctive military values still predominate, but occupational incentives of the marketplace came to compete with normative considerations of an institution.[35]

The Postmodern model, however, implies much more. The structure, makeup, and purpose of the armed forces changes as well as the values. The basic point is that a Postmodern military ultimately derives from the decline in the level of threat to the nation and, in the American case certainly, the rise in identity politics based on ethnicity, gender, and sexual orientation.

The social sciences can come to grips with constantly changing realities only by recasting conceptual frameworks. Of course, experience teaches us that it would be unwise to claim an indefinite life expectancy for any new paradigm. But when reality makes the Postmodern framework obsolete, so be it. For the foreseeable future, however, it appears to be a good guidepost to armed forces after the Cold War.

NOTES

1. A pioneer work to make systematic predictive statements about the armed forces was Morris Janowitz, ed., *The New Military: Changing Patterns of Organization* (New York: Russell Sage Foundation, 1964). More recent works using predictive vocabulary are Gwyn Harries-Jenkins, *Armed Forces and the Welfare Societies: Challenges in the 1980s* (London: Macmillan, 1982); Martin Edmonds, *Armed Services and Society* (Leicester: Leicester University Press, 1988 [reprinted as Martin Edmonds, IUS Special Editions on Armed Forces and Society, No. 2: *Armed Services and Society* (Boulder, Colo.: Westview Press, 1990)]); David R. Segal, *Organizational Designs for the Future Army* (Alexandria, Va.: U.S. Army Research Institute for the Behavioral and Social Sciences, 1993); Mark J. Eitelberg and Stephen L. Mehay, eds., *Marching Toward the 21st Century* (Westport, Conn.: Greenwood, 1994); Christopher Dandeker, "New Times for the Military," *British Journal of Sociology*, Vol. 45, No. 4 (Dec. 1994), pp. 637–654; James Burk, ed., *The Military in New Times* (Boulder, Colo.: Westview, 1994); Sam C. Sarkesian, John Allen Williams, and Fred B. Bryant, eds., *Soldiers, Society and National Security* (Boulder, Colo.: Lynne Reinner, 1995); Gwyn Harries-Jenkins, *The Western European*

Military Establishment: A Re-Assessment (London: European Research Office of the U.S. Army, 1996); and James Burk, ed., *The Adaptive Military* (New Brunswick, N.J.: Transaction, 1998).

2. Charles Tilly, *Coercion, Capital, and European States, AD 990–1990* (Oxford and Cambridge, Mass.: Basil Blackwell, 1990). See also Christopher Dandeker, *Surveillance, Power and Modernity: Bureaucracy and Discipline from 1700 to the Present Day* (New York: St. Martin's Press, 1990).

3. *New York Times*, Aug. 21, 1998, p. A1.

4. An early empirical study on the potential contradictions been the warrior and the peacekeeping roles, based on the UN contingent in Cyprus, is Charles Moskos, *Peace Soldiers: The Sociology of a United Nations Military Force* (Chicago: University of Chicago Press, 1976). My conclusion was that "Peacekeeping is not a soldier's job, but only a soldier can do it." For more recent empirical studies of military attitudes in peacekeeping missions, see David R. Segal and Mady Wechsler Segal, *Peacekeepers and Their Wives* (Westport, Conn.: Greenwood Press, 1993); Laura L. Miller and Charles Moskos, "Humanitarians or Warriors? Race, Gender and Combat Status in Operation Restore Hope," *Armed Forces & Society*, Vol. 21, No. 4 (summer 1995), pp. 615–637; David R. Segal and Dana P. Eyre, *The U.S. Army in Peace Operations at the Dawning of the Twentieth Century* (Alexandria, Va.: U.S. Army Research Institute for the Behavioral and Social Sciences, 1996); Laura L. Miller, "Do Soldiers Hate Peacekeeping? The Case of Preventive Diplomacy Operations in Macedonia," *Armed Forces & Society*, Vol. 23, No. 3 (spring 1997), pp. 415–450; and Eva Johansson, "The Role of Peacekeepers in the 1990s: Swedish Experience in UNPROFOR," *Armed Forces & Society*, Vol. 23, No. 3 (spring 1997), pp. 451–466.

5. Edward N. Luttwak, *The Endangered American Dream* (New York: Simon & Schuster, 1993).

6. The elevation of environmental concerns in the national security agenda is reflected in *Environmental Diplomacy* (Washington, D.C.: Department of State, 1997). The forewords are by Vice President Al Gore and Secretary of State Madeline Albright.

7. "The Greening of American Diplomacy," *New York Times*, Oct. 9, 1995, p. A4. See also Donald N. Zillman, "Environmental Protection and the Mission of the Armed Forces," *George Washington University Law Review*, Vol. 64, No. 2 (January 1997), pp. 309–327.

8. For discussion of changes in the recruitment and force structure of U.S. forces, see David R. Segal, *Recruiting for Uncle Sam* (Lawrence, Kans.: University Press of Kansas, 1989); and Sam Sarkesian and Robert E. Connor, Jr., *America's Armed Forces* (Westport, Conn.: Greenwood, 1996).

9. The early years of the all-volunteer force were characterized by low morale and extreme recruitment difficulties. See William L. Hauser, *America's Army in Crisis* (Baltimore, Md.: Johns Hopkins University Press, 1973); John B. Keeley, ed., *The All-Volunteer Force and American Society* (Charlottesville, Va.: University Press of Virginia, 1978); Richard A. Gabriel and Paul L. Savage, *Crisis in Command* (New York: Hill and Wang, 1978). This gave way to much more positive accounts. See for example Frederic J. Brown, *The US Army in Transition II* (McLean, Va.: Brassey's, 1993); and James Kitfield, *Prodigal Soldiers* (New York: Simon & Schuster, 1995). An exception to the favorable portrayals of the contemporary all-

volunteer force is W. Darryl Henderson, *The Hollow Army* (New York: Green-wood Press, 1990).

10. These compensation figures are given in *Army Times*, Jan. 11, 1999, p. 13.

11. Morris Janowitz, *The Professional Soldier: A Social and Political Portrait* (Glencoe, Ill.: Free Press, 1960). Where Janowitz saw the need for the professional officer corps to have greater civilian interaction, Samuel P. Huntington saw an inevitable, and not necessarily bad, disjuncture between the conservative ethos of the officer corps and the liberal society. See Huntington, *The Soldier and the State* (Cambridge, Mass.: Harvard University Press, 1957). A middle position is found in Sam C. Sarkesian, *The Professional Army Officer in a Changing Society* (Chicago: Nelson-Hall, 1975). A recent analysis of the contemporary officer corps is Edward C. Meyer and R. Manning Ancell with Jane Mahaffey, *Who Will Lead? Senior Leadership in the United States Army* (Westport, Conn.: Greenwood, 1995).

12. For a discussion of the soldier-scholar in the period between the two world wars, see Timothy Nenninger, "Leavenworth and Its Critics: The U.S. Army Command and General Staff School, 1920–1940," *The Journal of Military History*, Vol. 58 (Apr. 1994), pp. 199–231.

13. "Clinton Picks Army General for NATO Post," *New York Times*, Apr. 1, 1997, p. A3.

14. "Cohen Gets One Right," *Time*, July 28, 1997, p. 52.

15. David R. Segal and John D. Blair, "Public Confidence in the U.S. Military," *Armed Forces & Society*, Vol. 3, No. 1 (fall 1976), pp. 3–11.

16. See Don M. Snider, ed., *U.S. Civil-Military Relations: In Crisis or Transition?* (Washington, D.C.: Center for Strategic and International Studies, 1995); and Michael Desch, *Soldiers, States and Structure* (Baltimore, Md.: Johns Hopkins University Press, 1998). Thomas E. Ricks, in *Making the Corps* (New York: Scribner, 1997), documents a growing gap between young marines and the prevailing youth culture in the larger American society.

17. Charles Moskos, "Grave Decisions: When Americans Feel More at Ease Accepting the Casualties of War," *Chicago Tribune*, Dec. 12, 1995, p. 25. A counter viewpoint on acceptance of combat casualties is that the small family size of postindustrial societies makes such societies' populations loath to suffer wartime casualties. See Edward N. Luttwak, "Where Are the Great Powers?," *Foreign Affairs*, Vol. 73, No. 4, (Jul./Aug. 1994), pp. 23–29. Another viewpoint holds that national interests must be clearly articulated by the civilian leadership for the country to accept casualties. See E. V. Larson, *Ends and Means in the Democratic Conversation: Understanding the Role of Casualties in U.S. Military Operations* (Santa Monica, Calif.: RAND Corporation, 1996).

18. A caustic account of how journalists covered the Persian Gulf War is John J. Fialka, *Hotel Warriors* (Washington, D.C.: Woodrow Wilson Center Press, 1992).

19. See Peter R. Young, ed., *Defence and the Media in Time of Limited War* (London: Frank Cass, 1992); Larry Minear, Colin Scott, and Thomas G. Weiss, *The News Media, Civil War, and Humanitarian Action* (Boulder, Colo.: Lynne Rienner, 1994); and Charles Moskos with Thomas E. Ricks, *Reporting War When There Is No War: The Media and the Military in Peace and Humanitarian Operations* (Chicago, Ill.: Robert R. McCormick Tribune Foundation, 1996).

20. There is little research on the subject of civilians who work for the military. For one of the few analytical treatments, see Martin Binkin, *Shaping the Defense Civilian Work Force* (Washington, D.C.: Brookings Institution, 1978).

21. Of the 2,297 Department of Army civilians assigned to Desert Shield/Storm, five would not go and four were sent back after arrival in Saudi Arabia. Personal communication (1994) to author by a Department of Army official.

22. Thomas E. Ricks, "U.S. Military Turns to Civilian Workers for Support Services," *Wall St. Journal*, May 1, 1995, p. 1. For a critical view of this trend, see R. Philip Deavel, "The Political Economy of Privatization for the American Military, " *Air Force Journal of Logistics*, Summer 1998, pp. 3–9.

23. *New York Times*, Dec. 24, 1992, p. A1.

24. The literature on women in the armed forces is vast and growing. See especially Cynthia Enloe, *Does Khaki Become You?* (Boston: South End, 1983); Brian Mitchell, *Weak Link* (Washington, D.C.: Regnery Gateway, 1989); Jeanne Holm, *Women in the Military: An Unfinished Revolution* (Novato, Calif.: Presidio, 1992); Sandra Carson Stanley, *Women in the Military* (New York: Julian Messner, 1993); Judith Hicks Stiehm, ed., *It's Our Military, Too* (Philadelphia, Penn.: Temple University Press, 1996); Laura L. Miller, "Not Just Weapons of the Weak: Gender Harassment as a Form of Protest for Army Men," *Social Psychological Quarterly*, Vol. 60, No. 1 (Mar. 1997), pp. 32–51; Linda Bird Francke, *Ground Zero: The Gender Wars in the Military* (New York: Simon & Schuster, 1997); and Brian Mitchell, *Women in the Military: Flirting with Disaster* (New York: Regnery, 1998). A useful comparative examination is Mady Wechsler Segal, "Women's Military Roles Cross-Nationally: Past Present, and Future," *Gender and Society*, Vol. 9, No. 6 (Dec. 1995), pp. 757–775.

25. William H. McMichael, *The Mother of All Hooks: The Story of the U.S. Navy's Tailhook Scandal* (New Brunswick, N.J.: Transaction, 1997).

26. For an insightful treatment of this issue, see Laura L. Miller, "Feminism and the Exclusion of Army Women from Combat," *Gender Issues*, Vol. 16, No. 3 (summer 1998), pp. 33–64.

27. For a concise summary of the literature, see Mady Wechsler Segal and Jesse J. Harris, *What We Know About Army Families* (Alexandria, Va.: U.S. Army Research Institute for the Behavioral and Social Science, 1993).

28. A balanced compendium on homosexuals in the armed forces is Wilbur J. Scott and Sandra Carson Stanley, eds., *Gays and Lesbians in the Military* (New York: Aldine de Gruyter, 1994).

29. A full discussion of conscientious objection across Western democracies is found in Charles C. Moskos and John W. Chambers, eds., *The New Conscientious Objection: From Sacred to Secular Resistance* (New York: Oxford University Press, 1993).

30. *Washington Times*, National Weekly Edition, May 17–23, 1999, p. 19.

31. "The Discharge of Kelly Flinn," *New York Times*, May 23, 1997, p. A18. Contrary to popular understanding, adultery in the American military is not a "stand-alone" offense. Adultery is punishable when it is "directly prejudicial to good order and discipline and not to acts which are prejudicial only in a remote or indirect sense. . . . It is confined to cases in which the prejudice is reasonably direct and palpable." Article 134, *Manual for Courts-Martial* (Washington, D.C.: Government Printing Office, 1995), p. IV-93.

32. For a fuller treatment of the analogies between civilian and military service, see Charles Moskos, *A Call to Civic Service* (New York: Free Press, 1988); and Charles Moskos and John Sibley Butler, *All That We Can Be: Black Leadership and Racial Integration the Army Way* (New York: Basic Books, 1996), pp. 143–169.

33. See Chris Seiple, *The U.S. Military/NGO Relationship in Humanitarian Interventions* (Carlisle, Penn.: U.S. Army War College, 1996).
34. Remarks of Philip A. Odeen, *AUSA News*, June 1997, p. 9.
35. For a full discussion of institutional versus occupation norms in the armed forces, see Charles C. Moskos and Frank R. Wood eds., *The Military: More Than Just a Job?* (McLean, Va.: Pergamon-Brassey's, 1988).

3

The United Kingdom:
The Overstretched Military

CHRISTOPHER DANDEKER

Since the end of the Cold War the British armed forces have reduced their military establishments by about 30 percent; meanwhile, the range of missions to which they are expected to contribute has widened to encompass new forms of peace-support operations as well as more traditional warfighting missions. At the same time, they have confronted a series of domestic challenges from the wider society, some of which have been directly encouraged or sponsored by government. These range from debates about the relevance of new civilian models of business management for the armed forces to demands for the military to abandon other elements of its traditional institutional status.

The following analysis reveals that although the British armed forces are moving toward the model of a Postmodern military, they retain elements of the Modern and Late Modern periods.

DEFENSE ROLES AND MISSIONS

The post–Cold War world is more uncertain and more turbulent than that of the preceding four decades.[1] Accordingly, during the course of the 1990s the British government sought to reorder its priorities in terms of three defense roles. These can be viewed in ascending order of optionality (but not necessarily of priority).[2]

Defense Role 1 is "to ensure the protection and security of the U.K. and our Dependent Territories, even when there is no external threat."[3] This entails the routine practice of sovereignty—without the performance of this role, the United Kingdom could not be recognized as a sovereign state. There might well be internal threats to national sovereignty; in such cases it would be legitimate to deploy force in support of the civil authority, as for example in counterterrorism.

Defense Role 2—insuring against any major threat to the U.K. and its allies—brings into play additional obligations and indeed rights, such as that of self-defense under Article 51 of the UN Charter.

Defense Role 3—promoting the United Kingdom's wider security interests through maintenance of international peace and stability by acting under mandates issued by the U.N.—provides the clearest scope for discretion or choice, depending on what the government perceives the U.K.'s interests to be and what resources it believes can be made available to pursue them.[4]

Although discretion or optionality is greatest in Defense Role 3, one can argue that the U.K.'s involvement in military operations in support of this role is quite likely. This is partly because of U.K. economic interests in an interdependent global economy and the continuing issues and connections arising from its imperial past. Not least of these are the interests of 8.6 million British citizens who live outside U.K. borders.[5] In addition, one must consider the impact of modern means of communication on the relationships between public opinion and security policy. The "something must be done" factor has placed additional pressure on governments to become involved in humanitarian and peacemaking efforts, pressures they find difficult to ignore.[6]

Indeed, some evidence suggests that in light of the Gulf War and the peace-support operations in Bosnia, priority is shifting to Defense Role 3 rather than Defense Roles 1 and 2.[7] Yet in view of the uncertainty of the current security picture, the government thinks it would be most imprudent to discount the continuing relevance of Defense Roles 1 and 2. In short, the Modern and Late Modern roles have persisted.[8]

STRUCTURE OF FORCES

Smaller, More Flexible Forces

The U.K. armed forces (which have been volunteer forces since 1963) were reduced from 326,000 in the mid-1980s to about 250,000 in the mid-1990s, following an overall reduction of between 30 and 40 percent since the Cold War era.[9] In 1995, it was anticipated that they would be reduced further to approximately 210,000 in 2010.[10] With the 1997 figure of 211,000, this calculation may understate the future position given nonmilitary pressures on the defense budget (such as health and social welfare) and further efficiency gains from the rationalization of military technologies. Between 1985–86 and 1995–96, the defense budget declined by 27 percent; the proportion of gross domestic product devoted to defense was reduced from 5.2 percent in 1984–85 to the 2.8 percent projected for 1997–98.[11]

Despite cuts in military establishments, the armed forces must be prepared for a wide spectrum of missions arising from the three defense roles outlined above. These include military aid to the civil power in the United Kingdom; meeting challenges to the internal or external security of a dependent territory; general war arising from a large-scale attack on NATO; a limited regional war involving a NATO ally who asks for assistance under Article 5 of the NATO Treaty; and providing military support for measures designed to contribute to international peace and stability and to the maintenance of humanitarian principles—activities normally under the auspices of the UN but possibly under another, regional organization legitimized by the U.N.[12]

To provide forces for these missions, the armed forces are considered in terms of three categories: "forces for general war" requiring general mobilization; "permanently committed forces" such as those in garrisons and the Trident nuclear deterrent force; and the "national contingency forces." The latter, including the Joint Rapid Deployment Force [JRDF]

> . . . are thus intended to provide a "golf bag" of forces held at graduated levels of readiness from which we can assemble force packages to meet the specific needs of those missions and the contribution we wish to make alongside those of other nations, and a pool of capability for conducting a number of different but concurrent operations.[13]
>
> This "golf bag" contains the capability for regional intervention as well as the means for meeting NATO commitments under Defense Role 2—in army terms, up to a reinforced division.[14]

The Cadre/Reserve Concept

The cadre/reserve concept is useful in illustrating how the armed forces are organized. The British army, for example, is based on two divisions: one armored and based in Germany, and the other mechanized and based in the U.K. Both are reduced to a cadre to a significant extent; that is, there is a gap between their war and peace establishments. These two cadre divisions provide a basis for mixing and matching packets of force to meet various contingencies.[15]

The model is designed to meet the twin challenges of major war with longer warning times, and lesser conflicts with warning times of only weeks or days. Thus the two-division system provides a basis for a brigade-sized maximum force at high readiness with sea and air support, and for regenerating a reinforced division with the possibility that such a force might be light, heavy, or mixed. These arrangements reflect a current preference for a regeneration capability rather than for a smaller army at a higher level of readiness.[16]

Two cadre-ized divisions can be regenerated by using regulars in backfilling as others are deployed in operations, and (assuming that one does not decrease the cadre) by seeking to make greater use of the reservists in the cadre. The reserves are to be used to provide units and subunits to complete the services' capability in case of a major war; in addition, according to the plan, they are to provide

> ... specialist capabilities for which there is little need in peacetime, and which therefore are available only on a limited basis in the regular forces. . . . [Also] they would supplement existing regular capability on a broader front to meet temporary increases in commitments.[17]

Thus, a number of individuals will be required at very short notice to fill gaps in the regular forces when operations short of war occur.

This more flexible use of reserves will be facilitated by creating a two-tier reserve. The High Readiness Reserve (about 4,000 in number, of which 1,500 will be in the army) will serve in areas of scarce skills such as linguists, intelligence, and public relations; medical, air-movement support staff, and technical specialists to look after equipment; and air crew, special forces, and civil affairs for Defense Role 3 duties.[18]

The other tier of the reserve will be concerned with mobilization for more general war. In addition, there will be a sponsored reserve comprising key individuals who work in support functions contracted out to civilian companies. In case of general war the reserves will be needed even more than before to complete the army order of battle, especially in support and logistics.

Certain constraints, however, limit the use of reserves in operations short of major war. If the most likely operations involve no clear threat to national survival and indeed if the national interest may not be obvious, politicians and public might be reluctant to accept the callout of reserves.[19] In addition, employers' support of the new system is open to question. For the present, reservists in the army will be used as individuals and in small packets, not as units formed to fill gaps in the regular forces. The effectiveness of these reserve packets will depend on their close working relations with regular units. The trend towards focusing reservists on combat support and combat service support is likely to continue. Finally, the cost of smaller, flexible forces being asked to do more with less is a case of "overstretch," with consequent morale and retention problems.[20]

Civilianization and Increasing Use of Contractors

The development of a smaller military establishment and the cadre/reserve concept are connected with a broader theme: the application of market mechanisms to the public sector, and especially the use of civilians, market testing, and the increasing use of contractors. These trends are likely to continue for the foreseeable future.[21] The number of civilians employed by the Ministry of Defence has been reduced radically. Between 1979 and 1990 this number was cut by 40 percent, with significant decreases in the number of civil servants in the ministry. More than one-third of the reduction was due to privatization of the Royal Ordnance Factories and Royal Dockyards; a further 20 percent cut was scheduled in 1996.[22] In addition, the proportion of civilian employees to military personnel has been reduced from about 75 percent to 46 percent since 1980, and efforts have been made to cut central staffs and to place more civilians in direct support of the military commands.[23]

Yet there is also a trend toward substituting civilians for military personnel, with 2,000 posts having been civilianized. Civilians are cheaper to employ than military personnel and often stay longer in their posts. The objective is to "civilianise posts and so release valuable military resources to the front line wherever it makes operational and economic sense to do so."[24]

The desire to cut costs has led to market testing—submitting a function to a competition in order to learn whether a private enterprise can perform it more cheaply without a reduction in quality—and to the contracting out of defense functions such as the maintenance of military equipment and installations.[25] The challenge facing the military is to identify the core requirement for uniformed regular military personnel, beyond which functions could be performed by civilians employed either by the Ministry of Defence or by private companies under contract. Further civilianizing of noncore functions can be anticipated,[26] not least because of the savings in costs.[27]

NEW PROFESSIONAL MILITARY ROLES: THE SOLDIER-STATESMAN AND THE SOLDIER-SCHOLAR

In a Postmodern military, in which armed forces are required to perform a broad spectrum of increasingly multifunctional and multinational missions, and where media scrutiny of operations is intense, professional roles other than those focused on war-fighting become significant, not as substitutes but as supplements.

In the U.K. we see some evidence for the emergence of soldier-scholar and soldier-statesman roles. The soldier-scholar is required to think through the conditions for applying force in the new security context—for example, in those operations which lie midway between classical peacekeeping operations and war, where the defeat of an enemy is sought. The most likely military operations probably lie at this midpoint; experience and doctrine are relatively undeveloped here, although much has been learned during the last few years.[28]

The soldier-scholar's role is promoted not only by new strategic conditions but also by political and technological conditions. With the decline in the military experience of the political elite, both inside and outside government, politicians are less well versed than they used to be in the conditions under which force can usefully be applied in pursuit of security policy. Yet the situation is complicated not only by the need to deal with new types of mission but also by the revolution in communications. This revolution has compressed the time in which political and military decisions must be made, while exposing the consequences to immediate media scrutiny. Thus it is increasingly risky to give the armed forces missions without the appropriate means and to use technology to micromanage operations; the consequences harm the operation as well as civilian-military relations.

Both new peace-support missions and more familiar operations, such as peace enforcement in Desert Storm, have promoted the development of the soldier-statesman, the military professional who is adept at handling the media and international diplomacy. Political skills are becoming increasingly important. In connection with the Gulf conflict, for example, Gen. Sir Peter De la Billiere remarked on

> . . . one of the basic principles of high command, which I was learning as I went along: that a senior commander must bring together everyone concerned, not only in theatre, but outside as well, and that often he must act almost more as a diplomat than as a soldier.[29]

The soldier-statesman's role is becoming more significant because of the complexity of political problems in coalition warfare. This is the case especially in missions where threats to national interests fall well short of the threat to national survival that characterized war planning during the Cold War. Also, as mentioned above, the pace of events and their reporting made possible by the modern electronic media telescopes the decision time available to political and military decision-makers. Therefore, much closer cooperation between them is required; the result is a blurring of the divide between political and military skills and a challenge to traditional ideas of the military professional as an apolitical technician.[30] Finally, because of the delicate nature of a mission, mandates may well change during an operation. Again, in such a case military commanders must be politically sensitive to the changing diplomatic context.[31] As alluded to earlier, the projected involvement of service personnel in tasks of "defense diplomacy" such as arms-control inspection, and "outreach" activities involving the education and training of other armed forces on such matters as defense management and systems of civilian control of the military, will raise the profile of both the soldier-statesman and the soldier-scholar roles.[32]

Preparing military professionals for the roles of soldier-statesman and soldier-scholar requires innovation in education and organization—for example, arranging for the efficient management of complex joint opera-

tions involving components from all three services and from other countries as well.[33]

PUBLIC OPINION, THE MEDIA, AND THE MILITARY

Relationships connecting public opinion, the media, and the military develop in three situations: in time of peace, when the military seeks to secure
public support of the armed forces; in time of crisis, when government seeks
public support for the possible use of force; and during the conduct of operations, when government seeks to retain public support for its actions. In
each of these situations, we can observe some movement by the military toward courtship of the media.

In time of peace, the armed forces must retain the support of public opinion in order to recruit, retain, and resettle their personnel. They must ensure
that the public knows what armed forces are for and why they are organized as they are, with a culture that must continue to differ, in important
respects, from the ways of the civilian world. Public support is also needed
to defend the defense budget now that the "sacred canopy" of the Cold War
Soviet threat has been supplanted by a more diffuse world of risk, and when
the Treasury is always seeking further reductions in public-sector costs.

The key problem for the armed forces is to identify those elements of
their institutional culture that must be retained for operational effectiveness
and those traditions that can be eliminated, though reluctantly, in the light
of contemporary values. Examples include economic issues such as the areas of service life that require uniformed rather than civilian personnel or
contractors, and social issues such as the controversial current ban on homosexuality in the armed forces (see below).

In dealing with these problems, the armed forces must take account of
a postdeferential society in which—like other traditional institutions including the church and the monarchy—they are accountable to the public
for their mission and how it is performed.[34] Furthermore, the proportion of
the population with direct knowledge and experience of military affairs has
declined. Perhaps more telling, there has been a decline in the proportion
of the political elite with such expertise—for example, in the House of Com-
mons and in the cabinet.[35]

In seeking ways of reinforcing the supportive links between public opinion and the armed forces, the media play a crucial role, providing the indirect knowledge and experience on which most people rely for their information on the military. The armed forces must invest more heavily in the
public-relations function if their structures are to be effective. To perform
that function effectively, the forces must be clear about, and satisfied with,
the message that they are sending out to the public; they must be confident
that the remaining elements of military uniqueness will command legiti-

macy. Mere assertion of tradition or a plea to be spared from public scrutiny and questioning will not be successful.[36] There are indications that the military is taking a more proactive approach to public relations and public opinion regarding the purposes of defense and why armed forces have the structure and culture they have.[37]

This approach also will be required in times of crisis, especially in Defense Role 3 missions. Advanced societies will find it difficult to argue to their own publics that vital national interests are at stake in such military involvement. This task of legitimizing Defense Role 3 missions is not insuperable. Rather, in these cases, such missions have what I have called elsewhere a fragility of legitimacy: The commitment to a mission, especially a willingness to suffer casualties over a long period, is tenuous.[38] This does not mean that the public cannot be persuaded by political elites about the material and human price that might be worth paying for a mission in which an immediate national interest is lacking or obscure. Indeed, some evidence suggests that when missions are explained clearly, the public can be persuaded to support them. This is true even when the task is humanitarian relief rather than a matter related to immediate national interests.[39] On such questions of security policy, the public is more independent of elite and media manipulation and less fickle or irrational than some suppose.

In military operations, one can detect a drift away from manipulation of the media toward more courtship and a more proactive approach. These relations also can be more positive and more constructive despite inherent tensions between the military and the media. Such tensions are due to conflicts between the demands of operational secrecy on one hand and, on the other, journalists' right to publish and the public's right to know what is being done in their name.

Military/media relations no longer can be as manipulative as they were during the Falklands conflict.[40] Politically it is difficult to justify levels of censorship that normally would be associated with a war for national survival.[41] In any case, it is technically very difficult to impose censorship when the numbers of journalists in an operational theater and their access to the latest communications technology make them more independent than in the past. Because of these factors, together with the paucity of expertise and experience among many contemporary defense journalists and their profession's less deferential attitude toward political authority, it is in the interests of the military to cultivate a more constructive relationship with the media. As a result, the media could be a useful adjunct to military policy in sustaining public support for an operation (thus lessening the risks of micromanagement by politicians, who are extremely sensitive to public reactions) and in maintaining the morale of the forces themselves.

Although the military remains suspicious of and sensitive to negative reporting by the media, this attitude is unlikely to prevent the development of a more courting relationship with them. This is true especially if the necessary training, which is now recognized as genuinely important, is extended beyond its current modest level.[42] In developing a constructive relationship with the media in all three contexts discussed here—a relationship based on mutual trust and a proactive approach—the armed forces have an opportunity to provide a key focus for the soldier-scholar and soldier-statesman roles: to inform and educate the public about military affairs.

WOMEN IN THE MILITARY

In regard to the position of women in the military, over the past two decades the British armed forces have shifted significantly in a Postmodern direction, from exclusion toward full integration.[43]

In the army, women played a significant part in both world wars, as reflected in the formation of the separate Women's Royal Army Corps (WRAC) in 1949. Women were confined mainly to administrative work, however; they were excluded from combat roles and denied field training, and were only a small proportion of the total number employed in the army (about 2.5 percent in the late 1970s). While legislation against sex discrimination[44] facilitated the spread of equal opportunities for men and for women in civilian employment during the 1970s, the armed forces were exempt.

During the 1980s and early 1990s women became more fully integrated into the rest of the British army. By 1991, 100 of 134 trades in the army were open to women, although women were excluded from employment in the combat arms of infantry and armor (other than administrative positions such as adjutant). In 1992 the WRAC was disbanded and women were fully integrated into the army. Although the army has downsized, the proportion of women serving in the force is higher than during the Cold War (7.9 percent of the officers and 5.4 percent of the enlisted).

Deployment rules also have become less restrictive. During the Cold War women were not allowed farther forward than the rear boundary of the corps. During the early 1990s the rule was changed: Women would be employed in all arms or corps except armor and infantry (other than in administrative positions) but were not to serve in posts farther forward than the second echelon of a brigade in combat.[45] Although women are armed for self-defense rather than for direct offensive engagement with the enemy, the current exclusion from infantry and armor is under review.

The Royal Air Force contains a higher proportion of women than either of the other two services (about 8.8 percent), mainly because of its technology and its organizational structure: Women are more easily assimilated into noncombat roles, and the total number of personnel employed in combat roles is very small. A separate women's organization (the WRAF) was abolished in 1949; separate ranks were integrated in 1968; women began to be trained in the defensive use of firearms in 1980.

Nevertheless, women were excluded from air crews not only because of perceptions about their suitability for such roles but also because of concerns about adequate returns on high training costs: It was likely that women would wish to leave the service to have children. Yet change was facilitated by the evidence that women serve for longer periods—on average ten years—and that they bring a reliable return on training investment. This was the case especially when it was realized that high-quality candidates wished to join the service; the political context made it imperative to show that the service was an equal-opportunity employer. Thus women now can serve in fast jets and all other employments except with the RAF regiment in infantry roles.

In the Royal Navy, the most significant developments occurred after a review of the issue during 1988–89. This led to a trial "WRNS at sea" scheme and a subsequent policy of full integration. In September 1990 all women became eligible for service at sea, and currently almost all surface specializations, including fast jets, are open to women so long as they meet the technical criteria for the job in question. The exceptions are army-style direct combat employments such as the marines; commando helicopters; and small vessels such as minehunters, fisheries protection, and submarines, which cannot provide appropriate privacy for female personnel. (Now that the Royal Navy only has nuclear-powered submarines, the main reason for excluding women is its duty to ensure the safety of the fetuses of pregnant female service personnel.)

Four main factors have led to the integration of women in the British armed forces. The first concerns pressures from the wider society. These are due in part to demographic change and to consequent shortages of male recruits, but also to normative and legal changes. During the late 1980s major employers (including the late Cold War armed forces, especially the army) became concerned that shortages of male recruits would damage operational effectiveness; extending the recruitment pool to women would address that problem.

In addition, women's increased participation in the civilian labor market had facilitated changes in public perceptions about appropriate employment roles for women and had led to legislation on equal opportunities for men and for women (Sex Discrimination Act 1975). To these pressures were added further legal directives, especially those stemming from European law, which undermined the services' legal exemption from the Sex Discrimination Act. Because of the problems of proving that operational effectiveness, or even privacy, can be reasonable grounds for excluding women from employments, it is likely that all employments will become open to both men and women.

A second factor is that the armed forces have been responding to pressures for better career opportunities from women already in service. It is widely recognized in the services that women have been relatively underutilized, given their generally high quality.

Third, technological changes in the armed forces have led to a relative decline in the emphasis on physical prowess and aggressiveness as factors essential to effective military performance. (The extent of this process, however, is a matter of controversy in regard to the requirements of different services, particularly the combat arms of the army.)

Finally, the attitudes of policy makers, military and civilian officials, and politicians have played a significant role in the evolution of policy—not least a generation of policy-makers socialized in the less traditional atmosphere of the 1960s. They have been less resistant to the demands from sections of a postdeferential civilian society that the military conform to principles of equal opportunity well established in nonmilitary employment.

THE MILITARY COMMUNITY

Family life has important effects on military cohesion and effectiveness. Thus the armed forces are always concerned with problems that will arise because of the length of separation between military personnel and their families, due to unaccompanied military service and the turbulence associated with moving location and housing.[46]

Family problems can weaken the capacity of personnel to deal with the stresses of combat. Family ties, and especially a community of families, can provide social and psychological support to spouses and children of military personnel when they must deal with the loss of men and women killed in operations. This is especially the case in an organization such as the British army: Some regiments are still based on close-knit community ties rooted in a continuity of personnel and a history of families providing generations of recruits to the same regiment.[47]

These close ties of family and community are based on the collective provision of housing and welfare by the military. Together with the impact of the conflict in Northern Ireland and the threat of terrorism to military personnel, these arrangements have produced a military community set apart from wider society. This separation is reinforced by the ban on wearing uniforms in public and by the continuing fading, among civilians, of direct experience with military life. (In November 1998, the ban on wearing uniforms in public—at least in mainland U.K., while on duty—was lifted in order to raise the public profile of the armed services.)

In recent years, however, the basis of the separate military community has been eroded significantly, although the effects on operational effectiveness remain unclear.[48] This fact helps to explain why current plans for privatizing the armed forces' housing stock have created controversy.[49]

First, an increasing number of military spouses have become less content with their traditional role of providing informal welfare and community support, and have sought to enter the civilian labor market for economic gain as well as personal freedom. Such nonmilitary work commitments can cause marital and thus morale problems if a military posting leads to a spouse's refusal to give up a job. This is true especially when available work in the area of the posting is, or is perceived to be, markedly inferior to the existing job.

In addition, more military families have sought to own their own homes outside the military system so as to have an economic and domestic basis for postmilitary life, when second careers must be considered. Parents also need to consider housing in connection with schools—what they regard as the best school for a child may well require residence outside the military community.

Finally, some personnel prefer to establish a sharper dividing line between work and personal/domestic life, as is characteristic of wider civilian society. This trend is linked to a broader movement toward personal freedom and choice that began in the early 1980s. For example, officers tend to reject traditional mess life in favor of spending more time with family or friends, and use their own house or apartment as a base for doing so.[50]

Current plans are to sell the housing stock of the armed forces' married quarters, to charge military personnel market rates for accommodation, and to shift surplus stock to civilian use. These plans might be expected to accelerate the trend toward the erosion of the military community, especially if other forms of payment in kind, such as welfare services, are also cut in the continuing attempt to reduce the defense budget and improve cost-effectiveness.

Some critics of this scheme fear that it would erode the military community too far, removing a critical support mechanism of cohesion. For example, family and community support were important in sustaining the morale of service members' families during the Falkland War and the Gulf conflict; the knowledge that such support exists sustains the military personnel in combat. Military families may be more vulnerable in the more junior ranks, where financial stability and maturity may not be great enough to cope with a dispersal of military personnel into civilian society. Yet this may be no more than a failure to come to terms with the norms of individuality and choice. Others fear that erosion of the military community will lead to a decline in the distinct ethos of the services, which needs to be nurtured through social interaction apart from civilians, particularly the idea that the military contract is unconditional, as opposed to the "nine-to-fiveism" perceived to be the norm in civilian society. As Jessup has pointed out, erosion of the traditional military community will continue.

> The regrouping of the Army and the RAF in the UK will in all probability lead to the extension of home ownership among military families so that they come to resemble both the civilian and the naval pattern.[51]

That said, service housing is likely to be left with a higher proportion of young married couples, leading to a requirement for family support schemes not only within this community, but also for forms of outreach to assist those families who have become dispersed into the wider civilian society. Jessup shows how the welfare of military families will increasingly be shared between the armed services and the civilian community, echoing the American experience that it is a mistake to assume that community support mechanisms can be equated with those provided by the armed services, or indeed, that formal mechanisms are always superior to those informal networks forged by service personnel themselves.[52]

HOMOSEXUALS AND MILITARY SERVICE[53]

In regard to homosexuality, the British armed forces have not yet moved toward a Postmodern military; changes are limited to decriminalization and administrative discharge associated with the Late Modern type.

Homosexuality has been decriminalized in the armed forces in the sense that homosexual activities of a type that are legal in civilian law do not constitute an offense under service law. This concession, announced in June 1992, did not change the government's basic policy toward homosexuality in the armed forces, however: Overt homosexuality still is considered incompatible with military service. Homosexuals will continue to receive administrative discharges if they engage in homosexual activities, even if they have committed no offense under service law.

The rationale for continued exclusion of homosexuals from the armed forces remains as it was in 1991, when Archie Hamilton, then a junior defense minister, stated:

> [B]oth homosexual activity and orientation are incompatible with service in the armed forces. The main reason centres on the need to maintain discipline and morale. The services are hierarchical, close knit, overwhelmingly single sex and young communities. Units can work to full effectiveness only on the basis of mutual trust and the expectation of equal treatment among each rank. The formation within these units of sexually motivated relationships [is] potentially very disruptive of discipline and morale, particularly when they cross rank boundaries.[54]

The problem with these arguments is that they rely on anecdotal evidence or personal conviction rather than hard data. According to Stonewall, although the Ministry of Defence has consulted other countries' experience on the issue of homosexuality and the effectiveness of armed forces, it

> ... has never produced testimony from any of these countries to say that they have experienced any of the hypothetical difficulties which the MoD insist would follow if lesbians and gay men were allowed to serve.[55]

Nevertheless, further policy changes are likely. In 1991 the prime minister announced that because of changes in social attitudes, homosexuality would no longer preclude security clearance for members of the civil service. Since that time, pressure groups such as Stonewall have continued to work for extension of this policy to members of the armed forces. Recently, four homosexuals dismissed from the services lost their case in the British Court of Appeal and took their case to the European Court of Human Rights. European law might lead to a change in policy by the current Labour government. Although at least one government minister (in the last Conservative administration) restated his opposition to change, the current position looks untenable in the medium term.

It will be interesting to see if policy shifts towards the U.S. scheme of "don't ask, don't tell, don't pursue." Alternatively, the British armed forces might adopt the scheme of the Australian defense forces, which is based on a code of conduct that proscribes "inappropriate behaviour" (of whatever kind and whether heterosexual or homosexual) that damages the operational effectiveness of the unit. One issue associated with this approach is identifying and applying rules—both regulations and informal conventions—specifying "inappropriate behaviour." In any event, problems of implementing a different policy would need to be addressed.

CONCLUSION

During the 1990s, the British armed forces have shifted towards a Postmodern military in significant respects but have retained important elements of the Modern and Late Modern social structure. This is evident in the wide spectrum of defense roles and military missions allocated to the armed forces and in a force structure of regulars and reserves designed for those purposes—a force capable of war at various levels of intensity as well as a variety of peace-support missions. The soldier-statesman and soldier-scholar are viewed most appropriately as supplements to the combat leader and the management technician rather than substitutes. Also, with the continuing integration of business models into the armed forces, civilians and contractors are likely to play a more significant role in the management of defense.

Although the public remains attached to the military, there is concern that many civilians know little of military affairs or their importance. Thus the military is beginning to understand the value of courtship of the media as the chief access point to society. The military is also beginning to see the media as the context in which to determine which unique institutional elements of the military must be retained so that the armed forces can protect, not simply reflect, the society that pays for them.

Finally, the issue of homosexuality will be a key test of the balance between Late Modern and Postmodern elements in the armed forces.

NOTES

1. See J. Burk, ed., *The Military in New Times: Adjusting Armed Forces to a Turbulent World* (Boulder, Colo.: Westview, 1994).
2. See *Statement on Defence Estimates, 1995*, Cm 2800, Her Majesty's Stationer's Office (HMSO), p. 107; discussions by B. Robertson, "Joint Needs in 2010," in *British Security 2010: Proceedings of a Conference Held at Church House*, ed. G.A.S.C. Wilson (London: Westminster, 1995), pp. 271–292; D. Omand, "Future Defence Planning," in *British Security*, pp. 261–269; M. Clarke and P.A.G. Sabin, *British Defense Choices for the Twenty-First Century* (McLain, Va.: Brassey's, 1993).
3. *Statement on Defence Estimates, 1995*, p. 107.
4. Omand, *Future*, p. 263.
5. Omand, *Future*, p. 265.
6. See C. Dandeker, "New Times for the Military: Some Sociological Observations on the Changing Role and Structure of the Armed Forces of the Advanced Societies," *British Journal of Sociology* 45 (December 1994), 637–654, 642.
7. Robertson, "Joint Needs in 2010," p. 275.
8. The thinking underlying the three defense roles is not dissimilar to that found in other countries, such as The Netherlands, Argentina, or the United States. As for the U.K., while the three Defense Roles received a lower profile in the *Statement on the Defence Estimates, 1996* (Cm 3223), they continued to inform defense planning and are set out in an annex. Recent government thinking has been that the DR framework tends to overemphasize the importance of defending national sovereign territory, whereas the key priority is perceived to be the provision of flexible, home-based expeditionary forces, with the capacity to be configured for a variety of military tasks, to defend U.K. interests abroad. In 1997, military tasks comprised ensuring the security of the U.K. and its dependent territories (this includes supporting the civil authority—as, for example, in Northern Ireland); making contributions to new NATO as well as WEU missions, including provision of military assistance and training; providing military contributions to missions supporting international order and humanitarian principles; contributing forces to deal with serious conflicts outside the NATO area which could threaten British interests or affect European or international security; responding to limited crises involving a NATO ally seeking assistance under Article 5 of the NATO Treaty; and meeting the need to prepare for general war in case of a major attack on NATO. This approach now forms the basis of doctrine for all three services. The latest thinking, in 1998, gives explicit priority to intervention forces rather than preparation for major war defense of the U.K. and its allies in Europe—a reversal of Cold War thinking. (For some commentators this underplays the possible threats to U.K. national territory—for example, arising from terrorist responses to U.K. crisis intervention abroad, or from DR2 scenarios. The possibility of defense missions becoming an entirely optional matter is seen as a step too far.) The current approach also elevates "defense diplomacy" (the use of military personnel for arms control, outreach, and education and training as part of the U.K.'s attempt to help build democratically accountable armed forces), especially in central and eastern Europe. See the *Strategic Defence Review*, Cm 3999, July 1998, London, Stationary Office; and "The *Strategic Defence Review*: How Strategic? How Much of a Review?" *London Defence Studies*, No. 46, Center for

Defense Studies, for Brassey's London, 1998. Although no longer explicit, the defense roles can still be detected as underpinning, in broad terms, the main roles and tasks of the armed forces, with DR3 becoming more prominent.

9. These figures refer to regular uniformed personnel and exclude the significant numbers of civilian and reserve personnel, numbering, in 1997, 109,000 and 321,000, respectively.

10. *Independent Review of the Armed Forces' Manpower, Career and Remuneration Structures: Managing People in Tomorrow's Armed Forces.* Report to The Secretary of State for Defense, Chairman, Michael Bett CBE (London: HMSO, 1995), p. 2, para. 1.5. The approximate service manpower figures are likely to be army, 110,000; Royal Air Force, 55,000; Royal Navy, 45,000. The 1997 figure of 109,000 excludes 8,000 Gurkhas and the Home Service personnel of the Royal Irish Regiment. See "The *Strategic Defence Review.*" 1998.

11. K. Hartley, *Economic Premise and Resource Availability, British Security 2010,* (London, Westminster, 1995) p. 222. It would be unwise to deduce military capability from manpower figures alone; much depends on technology, training, and readiness.

12. See *Statement on the Defence Estimates, 1995,* p. 27 and the detailed analysis provided by E. Grove, "The Army and British Security after the Cold War," *The Occasional* 20 (1996), p. 17.

13. Grove, "The Army," p. 21; quoting from Cm 2800, p. 32.

14. Grove, "The Army," p. 24. As Grove notes, the other two services play key roles in the NCF: The navy provides two carrier groups for sea control and power projection, and twelve air force squadrons with defensive and offensive capabilities assume a shore-based infrastructure to support them (Grove, "The Army," p. 25).

15. On these points, see Gen. Sir Charles Guthrie, "The British Army at the Turn of the Century," *RUSI Journal* (June 1996), 5–9, 5.

16. Alternative schemes include a structure for one division fully manned with regulars and configured for use as a regional intervention force, leaving the second division with only a relatively thin framework provided by the regular component. This could be the basis for a British role specialization in expeditionary warfare; heavy armor, and indeed much of the role of national defense, would be left to the reserves and greater reliance would be placed on, for instance, Germany in an evolving European defense identity for that capability. (See Grove, "The Army," p. 23.) It is even conceivable that forces could be trimmed even more to fit the situation: One might have to shift to a near-militia system of part-timers for national defense and a small number of professional units, such as marines, paratroops, and special forces, for missions overseas. See C. Coker, "Defence Needs in 2010," in *British Security 2010,* p. 243. However, it has been argued that such schemes would incur financial costs in absolute terms (by keeping the first divisions at such a high level of readiness), create problems of sustainability, and limit the ability to adjust manpower and equipment in the light of future changes in the strategic context. See Guthrie, "The British Army," pp. 6–7.

17. *Britain's Reserve Forces,* (London: HMSO 1993), p. 5.

18. See *Strength in Reserve—Draft Reserve Forces Legislation,* Consultative Document (London: HMSO, 1995), p. 13; Guthrie, "The British Army," p. 7.

19. That said, the services, and the army in particular, rely on reservists (who volunteer rather than being called out), including those from the combat arms, to make up shortfalls in the regular components on operations, such as those of IFOR and SFOR in Bosnia.

20. The *Strategic Defence Review* referred to earlier has highlighted the two mutually reinforcing problems of undermanning and overstretch. The first is a gap between actual and planned strengths, and is one cause of overstretch. Personnel in undermanned units have to do more and have to be reinforced from other units, especially in operation. Unit overstretch is caused by a mismatch between available personnel numbers and commitments, leading to less time between tours and thus less time for training and family and personal time. Undermanning and unit overstretch produce individual overstretch, leading to early exit (i.e., poor retention). The problem is unevenly spread in the services, with overstretch being worst in logistics support. In recent years it has been complaints about these problems rather than complaints about the standard of service accommodation and other conditions that have been the most vociferous. This point emerged in recent discussions with MOD officials. See *Strategic Defence Review*, Cm 3999, July 1998, Supporting Essay Nine, 9–2; 9–3; paras 10–15.

21. See *Statement of Defence Estimates*, Cm 2800, 48.

22. *Statement on Defence Estimates, 1994*, Cm 2550, 77.

23. *Front Line First, Defense Costs Study*, 38, para 608. The proportion of civilian strength shifted from about 47 percent to 36 percent between 1975 and 1995. See *UK Defence Statistics 1995*, 18; *Statement of Defence Estimates, 1996*, 52.

24. *Statement of Defence Estimates, 1994*, Cm 2550, 77.

25. C. Coker, "Defence Needs in 2010," in *British Security 2010*, p. 242.

26. In establishing such core figures it is assumed that if a post is required in time of peace and war, a regular is needed; if a task is required in wartime only, it could be performed by a reservist; tasks required in peacetime only could be contracted out or civilianized. The trend thus is toward smaller forces with fewer regulars and more use of reservists, civilians, and contractors.

27. See Sir Christopher France, "Managing Defense: New Approaches to Old Problems," *RUSI Journal* (April 1994), 12–16, 14. In fact, by 1994, 68 percent of market testing in the public sector had been won by in-house teams with average savings of about 23 percent (see R. Mottram, "The Reform of Government: The Place of Market Testing," *RUSI Journal* [April 1994], 1–6, 4–5). Latest reports indicate that market testing in defense, focused on the support areas, achieve about 16 percent in savings. (See K. Hartley, "Economic Premise," p. 227.) However, any cost savings must be set against the concerns of the military about erosion of the service ethos due to processes of civilianization and contracting out; against questions about the reliability of contractors in time of emergency; and against problems of inflexibility caused by the smaller numbers of regulars.

28. See J. Gow and C. Dandeker, "Peace Support Operations: The Problem of Legitimation," *The World Today* Vol. 51 (Aug./Sept. 1995), pp. 171–174; C. Dandeker and J. Gow, "The Future of Peace Support Operations: Strategic Peacekeeping and Success," *Armed Forces & Society*, Vol. 23 (spring 1997), pp. 327–348.

29. Gen. Sir Peter De La Billiere, *Storm Command: A Personal Account of the Gulf War* (New York: HarperCollins, 1992), p. 104.

30. This point, we suggest, applies in all types of operation today, including various types of peace support as well as enforcement and war.
31. Thus, although it is reasonable for the military to request clear objectives and rules of engagement, it is unrealistic to ask that these change as little as possible while an operation is in progress. The latter request is an example of Late Modern, not Postmodern, thinking.
32. See *Strategic Defence Review*, p. 15, para. 49.
33. For example, the JRDF structure and Permanent Joint Headquarters 1996 and the establishment of Joint Services Command and Staff College are designed to develop the joint ethos required of future operations. This is linked with the possible development of a more robust central defense staff manned by officers whose ethos is to put defense above individual service interests. See the discussion on "jointery" by B. Robertson, "Joint Needs in 2010," 271–292, 284–285.
34. See C. Dandeker, "Trust: Lessons from the Military in the Reconstruction of Civic Culture," in *This Will Hurt: The Restoration of Virtue and Civic Order*, ed. D. Anderson (London: The Social Affairs Unit, 1995), pp. 115–130.
35. An erosion of the informal supportive links between military and political elites has led some people to argue for a federation for the armed forces to express its professional concerns. See Maj. M. J. Perry, "A Military Federation for Britain's Armed Forces," *British Army Review*, Vol. 107 (August 1994).
36. In Huntingtonian terms, such a view overemphasizes the functional imperative of protecting society at the expense of the societal imperative of conforming to dominant civilian values. For a recent example, see A. Roberts, "The Enemy a Great Army Must Beat," *The Sunday Times*, Apr. 8, 1996, Section 3, p. 5.
37. Recently, the British army has developed a position establishing the reasons why the army has the right to be different from civilian society, although need might be the more appropriate term. This will provide the basis for a more proactive position in debates on convergence and divergence between the military and society.
38. In Dandeker, "New Times for the Military," pp. 643–644.
39. I am indebted to discussions with James Burk for this point. For related arguments in connection with UN operations in Somalia, see W. Clarke and J. Herbst, "Somalia and the Future of Humanitarian Intervention," *Foreign Affairs*, Vol. 75 (Mar./Apr. 1996), pp. 70–85.
40. See Col. A. D. A. Duncan, "Mixing with the Media: Guidelines for Operational Commanders," *British Army Review*, Vol. 110, pp. 17–25.
41. In Bosnia, for example, Gen. Sir Michael Rose's attempt to mobilize the media as part of his operational plans did not receive enthusiastic support from that quarter. (From conversations with journalists and British officers.)
42. Duncan, "Mixing," p. 24.
43. This section draws on collaborative work with M. W. Segal. See C. Dandeker and M. W. Segal, "Gender Integration in Armed Forces: Recent Policy Developments in the United Kingdom," *Armed Forces & Society* 23 (Fall 1996), pp. 29–47.
44. The Sex Discrimination Act 1975.
45. This rule, however, would be applied flexibly in light of operational circumstances. If the job required it—supplying ammunition, for example—women would go forward.

46. See H. McManners, *The Scars of War* (New York: HarperCollins, 1993), p. 19; A. Beevor, *Inside the British Army* (London: Corgi, 1990), p. 55.

47. McManners, *Scars*, p. 19.

48. See the excellent work by C. Jessup, *Breaking Ranks: Social Change in Military Communities* (London: Brassey's, 1996).

49. The idea of contracting out housing to a nonprofit trust operating in the private sector was introduced in Cm 2550, 72.

50. R. Jolly, *Military Man, Family Man: Crown Property?*, 2nd ed. (McLean, Va.: Brassey's, 1992).

51. Jessup, p. 179.

52. Jessup, p. 180, and discussion with Professor M. W. Segal, University of Maryland at College Park, United States.

53. This section draws on collaborative work with Gwyn Harries-Jenkins. See C. Dandeker and G. Harries-Jenkins, "Sexual Orientation and Military Service: The British Case," in *Gays and Lesbians in the Military: Issues, Concerns and Contrasts*, ed. W. J. Scott and S. C. Stanley (New York: Aldine De Gruyter, 1994), pp. 191–204.

54. *Hansard*, Vol. 193, (June 17, 1991), c. 115–116.

55. Press release, Stonewall Group, June 14, 1993, p. 3.

4

France: In the Throes of Epoch-Making Change

BERNARD BOËNE
MICHEL LOUIS MARTIN

A decade ago, in describing French society, it was still conventional wisdom to emphasize its exceptionalism. Today, however, when comparing France with other countries in the West, pundits tend to point to emerging similarities. These are variously ascribed to factors such as European integration, the end of class-based politics, and the long-term "Anglo-Saxonization" of value systems (increased individualism, materialistic orientations, secularization, and the like). Though the term *Postmodern* is not widely used outside the intellectual circles in which it originated, its rhetorical equivalents in the media and public opinion attest to the increasing awareness, frequently tinged with frustration, of the country's declining uniqueness.

Yet until 1996, this trend was less apparent in the domain of security; continuities with the past were still in evidence. Noteworthy in this regard was the Defense White Paper (DWP) published in 1994, the first in more than twenty years. Its policy guidelines showed no enthusiasm for a possible sea change, however lucidly its authors analyzed the future consequences of a radically transformed situation. Whereas the post–Cold War era seems to call for a strategy of conventional action geared to collective security and world stability, nuclear deterrence retained political pride of place, as shown by the national controversy that followed President Mitterrand's freeze on testing nuclear devices. Similarly, although universal conscription was increasingly problematic, it had been confirmed repeatedly by successive ministers of defense as the cornerstone of a mixed format, even while other western European countries seemed to be phasing it out. Force levels had shrunk somewhat since 1990, though appreciably less than in comparable countries (and less than they had declined over the previous decades), but defense spending had yet to be affected by an absolute decrease. The political timidity revealed by such a conservative approach owed less to geostrategic blindness than to the domestic situation.[1]

This is not to say that nobody was aware of impending change; only its timing, scope, and modality were in doubt. Despite continued efforts to maintain international status, the old Gaullist tenets—autonomy, sanctuarization of national territory, and unilateralism—had been weakened over the past decade by a strong sense that France's relative weight in world affairs was diminishing. Multilateralism, regional or global, was the order of the day, and Europe was uppermost in the minds of mainstream politicians. Moreover, the consensus on defense issues was now less solid, and support for large defense expenditures more brittle. Although pressures for peace dividends have been considerably less evident in France than elsewhere in the West, President Chirac's political will to reduce ballooning public deficits created the temptation to reduce the defense budget's investment side. Meanwhile, low-key, in-depth transformations, discretionary (sometimes ahead of anticipated trends) or otherwise, were at work in the military. Yet it was not always easy to determine which of these changes were related to the new international configuration and which were a carryover from the previous period, notably those associated with decline of the mass armed force.

President Chirac put an end to these lukewarm, wait-and-see attitudes on February 22, 1996, when he addressed the nation in a prime-time telecast. France's military, he said, would do away with its traditional organizational format and would become all-volunteer by 2002. A national debate would be organized to determine the future of conscription. Should the citizen tradition be continued in the guise of mandatory national "civic" service to benefit society in France and overseas, or should such civilian forms of service become voluntary? Now that the link between service under arms and citizens' obligatory duty was to be severed, should national service be open to women?

This announcement, sensational as it was, was accompanied by others regarding a further 30 percent reduction in force, studies of restructuring modalities, and long-term savings of 15 percent on the investment side of the defense budget. (Because of resettlement and reorganization costs, few savings were expected initially.) No mandatory separation scheme would be imposed on career service members.

On May 28, on the heels of a new six-year military programming bill providing for a budget of 185 billion francs, fewer big-ticket items, and longer procurement schedules,[2] another televised presidential address signaled the end of the public debate. Men born after January 1, 1979, would no longer be conscripted into the forces. Male and female volunteers would serve in civilian capacities for as long as a year or more as part of an expanded national service scheme.

Nor was this all. During the previous summer, the new president's supercharged, voluntaristic style had caused a dramatic reaffirmation of the nation's nuclear status, as well as many diplomatic and public relations headaches. Much more discreet, but equally significant, was the rapprochement with NATO. In the previous few years, France had discovered that remaining on the sidelines had more drawbacks than advantages. With the end of the Cold War, it seemed to many that de Gaulle's legacy regarding the Alliance had become dysfunctional. The official policy line was not that France would rejoin the military arm of NATO after thirty years' absence, but that it would increase its participation in (it was hoped) a revamped transatlantic military structure allowing for the expression of a European defense identity.[3]

Together these policy changes created, in months, a substantially different doctrinal and organizational landscape, to which, remarkably, the more prudent leftist government elected in the spring of 1997 brought precious few alterations. They open a new chapter whose sources and consequences must be placed in perspective.

PERCEIVED THREATS

Except for the 1815–65 period, the Modern era in France was dominated by concerns about the security of national territory. In addition, until World War II, it was a time of empire-building and consolidation. Later, in a wrong-headed bid to restore national prestige after the debacle of 1940, long colonial wars occupied center stage. Thus France's Late Modern phase did not begin until the early 1960s. The empire had ended, and it was realized that security as well as status now depended on the careful management of alliance relationships (with the aim of making room for a solitary foreign policy) and on a complex system of mutual nuclear deterrence within the framework of a prolonged East-West standoff.

The Cold War's demise has meant that for the first time since the mid–nineteenth century, France has no designated foe posing an immediate, massive threat to the security of its territory. Yet the international environment is hardly free of risks or threats. In the 1994 Defense White Paper (DWP), the findings on these post–Cold War risks and threats did not differ greatly from those in comparable countries. These included a multipolar power structure; increased freedom of action for regional powers with substantial military capabilities; weak but insistent assertion of *Idealpolitik*; proliferation of nuclear, biological, and chemical (NBC) weapons and ballistic delivery vehicles; uncertain leadership by the only remaining superpower; a return of nationalism and religious fanaticism in some parts of the globe; ethnic tensions in central and eastern Europe; closer ties between external and internal security; real-time media coverage; globalization of trade, communications, and movements of people; growing interdependence; severe imbalance in the geographic distribution of population and economic growth; emergence of three trade blocs; and heightened importance of economic factors in the measure of power—in brief, increased instability and complexity in world affairs. On the strength of such considerations and on the basis of circumstantial evidence, the DWP outlined six scenarios for the use of military force.

A renewed threat from the East was not ruled out. Soon after the breakup of the Soviet Union into independent states questioning one another's borders, France feared the multiplication of nationalist conflicts and the risk of a politically conservative reaction in Russia, possibly under military rule. The possibility of Moscow's assuming the lead in a new imperial entity, capable of dictating the agenda in neighboring nations to the west, was not taken lightly. Russia, it was sometimes argued, had not forsaken the option of a nuclear first strike. Yet it is significant that such a scenario, the response to which called for a rebuilding of forces to Cold War strength and readiness, was listed last (as Scenario 6) in the White Paper's ranking of present and future dangers, both in terms of probability and in the advance notice allowed before risk became an actual threat.

A less remote concern focused on hegemonic regional powers with world-class conventional assets and the rudiments of NBC armories, capable of initiating military action conducive to world instability and therefore directly (Scenario 2) or indirectly (Scenario 1) antagonizing French interests. This eventuality, regarded as not unlikely throughout the Mediterranean area, in the Middle East, or even in eastern Europe, would entail a multilateral military response by status quo powers. Possibly it would require a new type of crisis-management involving the substitution of "strong to the mad" nuclear deterrence, designed to dissuade irrational dictators, for the "weak to the strong" stance of Cold War days.

Apart from these sizable risks, the most probable type of military action was regarded as low to medium in intensity, in response to rather minor threats to French overseas possessions, the security of black African states, or collective peace endeavors (Scenarios 3, 4, and 5 respectively).

It was recognized, however, that the more serious threats in the new environment might not be military in the pre-1990 definition of the term. Destabilization of the country from within is now a clear and present danger.[4] Although many have come to doubt the armed forces' relevance to risks such as terrorism, uncontrolled immigration, drug trafficking, internal violence spilling over from immigrant "no-go areas," or the internationalization of organized crime, the DWP emphasized the need for closer links between internal and external security; such connections would imply new, still unspecified roles for the military.

The Chirac administration, upon assuming power, did not formally disavow the DWP, though its more down-to-earth style has led it to simplify the analysis offered therein and to crucially modify the policy guidelines derived therefrom. This administration is less anxious than its predecessor to provide a rationale for the previous conservative approach to defense requirements; it has produced a strategic vision in which Scenario 6 and (to a lesser extent) Scenario 3 are all but discounted, and the other four have been collapsed into three main "assumptions for the use of force": (1) regional conflict calling for a major commitment as part of NATO or the Western European Union (WEU), inside or outside the area covered by treaty provisions; (2) multinational action under a UN mandate; and (3) national or multilateral intervention in minor crises in Africa or the Middle East.[5] Again, the new period of cohabitation, ushered in by the 1997 general election, between a president and cabinet of different political persuasions has not led to profound changes in what is emerging as a consensus of sorts on the new defense doctrine.

STRUCTURE OF FORCES

For many years the French military establishment epitomized the mass armed force: it was large and relied on conscripting a clear majority of military-age male cohorts into both active and reserve components. The various factors causing the decline of such a format throughout the West, beginning in the 1960s, affected France only partially. Despite the lower manpower requirements associated with mutual deterrence in the latter part of the Cold War, French force levels remained relatively high until the mid-1980s (slightly under 600,000 effective members). The draft, with conscript tours of duty reduced to a year, continued in force. Its legitimacy fed then, as previously, on the republican ideal of the citizen-soldier and on other, related arguments about its antipraetorian role, political socialization, and the like. Technological modernization, especially in the army, forced a reduction in service strength in the Cold War's final years; this reduction eroded the principle of universal service under arms, and hence its legitimacy.

In the Gulf War, the mixed format was shown to be dysfunctional in the new international context. France was forbidden by tradition and by political expediency to send draftees out of area unless they volunteered for such missions; the country deployed only 13,000, whereas Britain, with a military establishment half as large, fielded a force of well over 30,000. Thereafter the need for a sizable component of deployable troops, capable of meeting various complex contingencies, asserted itself and led to an acceleration of earlier trends away from the mass army.

Yet the situation in 1995 was one of only slightly steeper declines in force levels, and was partly offset in overall figures by a continuing long-term rise in the numbers of gendarmes (best left out of account for comparative purposes). Service strengths were then scheduled to further decrease by some 5 percent from 1995 to 2000. The army (227,000, as opposed to 320,000 in the early 1980s, 280,000 in the early 1990s, and 240,000 in 1995) and the air force (84,000, down from 104,000 in 1980 and 94,000 in 1990) would account for most of the loss; the navy (62,000) was meant to remain almost unaffected.

France had no plan yet to do away with conscription; the Defense White

Paper was unambiguous in that regard. As a sign of significant change, however, the citizen-soldier ideal, which linked conscription with democratic citizenship, was no longer evoked as forcefully as before the 1980s. The reasons officially advanced for keeping a mixed format were mostly pragmatic:
costs had to be kept within reasonable limits, the flow of true volunteer enlistments probably would have been too small to staff an all-volunteer force
(AVF) of the size desired, and the draft presumably enhanced the legitimacy
of the military establishment as a whole, even if conscripts were now a minority (40 percent). The role of the draft as a safeguard against praetorianism, a matter of practical import until 1962, was no longer relevant; also, the
idea of an AVF had been gaining ground among politicians over the previous decade. (A majority of officers rejected the AVF, however, fearing that
it would mean smaller forces, cause a powerful onslaught of cost-efficiency
considerations, and cramp style and initiative.)

The key trend of the previous years had been a significant rise in the
proportion of career/contract personnel. The number had increased by 17
percent since the mid-1980s and was projected to rise by an additional 10
percent before 2000. In 1995 the professional or volunteer component of military personnel had reached 44 percent in the army, 63 percent in the air
force, 71 percent in the navy, and 87 percent in the gendarmerie. Meanwhile
the very duration of mandatory citizen service under arms, curtailed to ten
months in 1990, tended to marginalize draftees, who were assigned increasingly to unskilled general-purpose slots unless they volunteered to extend their tour of duty and to be deployed overseas.

From the standpoint of personnel managers, a major drawback was that
the flow of such deployable citizen-soldiers could not reliably be planned
far in advance. In addition, the need to sort out those draftees who were
willing to be sent out of area for a given mission implied that some conscript units had to be "cannibalized" and others created or reinforced before the operation started. As a result, disorganization would be introduced
and a cohesion problem would arise when it was least needed. Ironically,
because of shortages of rank-and-file troops deployable at will, declining
service strengths, and rising proportions of professionals, the number of conscript slots now hardly exhausted the annual supply of young men declared
fit for service, even with allowance for a projected increase in civilian forms
of national service.

Conscription no longer could be said to be universal and egalitarian: For
the preceding five years up to 50,000 men a year had been exempted de
facto, with no rational justification except that the system did not know what
to do with them. Added to this number were the usual 25 percent or so who
were exempted for medical, mental, or family reasons; cases of legal evasion by graduate students; a few thousand draft dodgers, conscientious objectors, and the like. Fewer than 60 percent actually served under arms, and
evasion was high at both ends of the socioeconomic spectrum. Thus, social

representativeness was no longer assured among the draftees, and the legitimacy of conscription had gradually weakened to the point where it was questioned—though in muted tones, which contrasted strongly with the vocal protests of the early 1970s. Public opinion was deeply ambivalent: Surveys now regularly showed that two-thirds of respondents still favored citizen service, but even stronger majorities believed that the defense function would be performed more effectively by a fully professional force. The issue divided mainstream parties on both the left and the right.

In the face of surprisingly mild opposition, President Chirac decided that epoch-making change was the only solution: The country had to depart from a format that had served it well but was no longer adaptable.[6] To make sure that procurement of volunteers would meet its numerical target, the government set manpower requirements so low as to virtually guarantee success. Military sociologists earlier had estimated at about 150,000 the maximum feasible size[7] of an all-volunteer army—widely expected to be the problem child of the AVF, as in Britain and the United States. The new all-volunteer army will number only 136,000 (a 42 percent reduction); about half (up from 33 percent today) will be officers and NCOs, who are already on service payrolls. In the other two services, requirements have been set at 45,000 for the navy (down 29 percent) and 63,000 for the air force (also down 29 percent); the number of petty officers and noncoms will be reduced by a few thousand, while only half at most of the present minority of conscripts will be replaced by new volunteers. The gendarmerie, however, gains some 3,000 extra service members (up 3.5 percent). Thus, although the overall volunteer requirements for the rank and file—the issue that will determine success or failure—will more than double, from some 44,000 under the present mixed format to over 92,000 (two-thirds of these in the army), these rather low numbers probably will make the task of recruitment manageable.[8]

New ground was broken in the early 1990s by a new reserve personnel management plan (Réserves 2000); this will remain in force, with some modifications (listed below), under the all-volunteer system. Instead of the huge numbers that existed on paper in Cold War days but were seldom called up for training, the plan provided for the mobilization of at most a half-million reservists, hardly more than the number of active-duty forces set before the change-of-format announcement. The rank and file were to be recruited in the traditional way from among the last few age cohorts that had completed their mandatory tour of active duty under the draft law. Formerly, commissioned and noncommissioned officers served according to an informal arrangement: A small pool consisting of the most "activist," who were known to local military authorities, were assigned on a purely voluntary basis. Assignment was subject to their often uncertain availability for service, and to mobilization slots almost entirely separate from active-duty units. Under Réserves 2000, officers and noncoms must sign formal contracts; these are backed by guarantees that their civilian careers will not suffer, thanks to agreements reached by the Ministry of Defense with various confederations of employers. Touted as "part-time professionals," they are offered "career"-development schemes that parallel those of active-duty cadres, with whom closer organizational links have been established.

The reserve picture is altered in some important ways by the change to an all-volunteer mode of manpower procurement. To begin with, the rank and file will be recruited from among former active-duty service members as part of their normal contractual obligations, and will be supplemented by a minority of true volunteer reservists. Another innovation will be the distinction between a "first" and a "second" reserve, based on training and availability for service. The former is intended to be subsumed under a "total force" concept. Analysts have been surprised by the low figure (100,000) announced for the first reserve, which is designed to supplement the active-duty AVF in whole units, or individually under specialist programs.[9] The plan is especially surprising because 50,000 of those reservists will be assigned to the gendarmerie; the army will receive only 35,000, and the other two services will share the rest. Although this arrangement is consistent with a doctrine that downplays territorial defense (which is entrusted in part to the gendarmes), it raises a question: How sustainable will action by the new expeditionary force be?[10]

DEFINITION OF THE MAJOR MISSION

In the early days of the Cold War, under the Fourth Republic, the major mission of the French military was twofold: to fight the nation's colonial wars and, as part of NATO, to guard against invasion by communist armies. With de Gaulle's Fifth Republic and the end of colonial wars, the equation changed dramatically. Beginning in the early 1960s, the main body of conventional assets, geared to supporting the strategic status quo in central Europe, would have tested enemy intentions in time of war, delivered an ultimate warning in the form of a "prestrategic" nuclear strike, and bought time for the president to reach a final decision about pushing the button. A strategy of action was reserved for a small minority of forces earmarked to intervene for a limited time, and with limited objectives, outside the main central European theater—essentially in French-speaking black Africa or on odd peacekeeping missions. Conventional strategy then was subsumed almost entirely by a position of nuclear deterrence; the French military of the late Cold War conformed perfectly to the constabulary model outlined by Morris Janowitz.

Post–Cold War missions until now have included a high-intensity regional war, mild and muscular forms of peacekeeping, and humanitarian assistance, mostly multinational. Because of the success of the Gulf War, Saddam Hussein and others like him will probably think twice before initiating frontal military action of a type that status quo powers are bound to consider destabilizing. Thus, for the foreseeable future, peacekeeping and humanitarian operations will remain the most likely type of real action for the French services. Nuclear weapons are still regarded as an important source of political capital in world affairs and as a core component of a future European defense identity, in which France intends to play a central role along with Britain and Germany. Finally, armed forces have been used in surveillance or emergency border control during terrorist campaigns.[11]

Under DWP guidelines it was difficult to point to a single major mission as the principal function of armed forces in the new context. The only salient fact was that *practical* priorities had been reversed: Though they remained fundamental, the traditional military functions (protecting the nation's territorial integrity, population, discretionary sovereign prerogatives, and economic lifelines) and deterrence of nuclear war now were to be subordinated to new roles centering on collective security and designed to affirm international status. Central to French defense was a strategy of action designed to promote stability and world peace in conjunction with others. The picture was somewhat blurred, however, by lack of sufficient selectivity due to the desire to keep options open until firmer choices became politically feasible. High force levels and the goal of being able to transport up to 130,000 troops several thousand miles from home added up to an expensive proposition.

The Chirac administration's daring new policy provides a much clearer doctrinal outline and has removed any doubt or hesitancy on that score. Probably this is the case because it believes (and so does the new leftist cabinet) in accelerating the projection of old national ambitions onto a European defense identity and thereby increasing selectivity through a future division of labor. In keeping with the perception, recently emphasized by officials on numerous occasions, that "first lines of defense" are now located far beyond national borders, the new doctrine calls for the establishment of a smaller, more mobile, less expensive expeditionary force of some 50,000, which will become the centerpiece of the French military apparatus.[12] Such a force, complete with its associated support assets, should be able to sustain either a major commitment under assumption 1 (see above) for a year without replacement forces, or simultaneous interventions under assumptions 2 and 3. In the latter case, 30,000 troops would be committed to one theater for a year, backed if necessary by some 5,000 replacements. Five thousand troops would rotate in and out of action in a second theater every four months. This expeditionary concept, together with the fact that territorial defense has become secondary, makes the French military more similar, for the first time, to the British or U.S. "insular" model than to the old "continental" model.

Paradoxically, this long-delayed change in attitudes and posture has caused an enlargement and deepening of the constabulary trends that emerged in the late phase of the East-West standoff.

THE DOMINANT TYPE OF MILITARY PROFESSIONAL

In the colonial wars the heroic leader predominated over managers, at least symbolically. In those days the army was very much the senior service; it had a quasi-monopoly on low-intensity warfare, then the most visible function of armed forces. In 1962, after the final retreat from empire, the balance was evened by nuclear deterrence; the marginal position was reserved for a strategy of true conventional action. For about a quarter-century, the professional military was a stable mix of heroic leaders and managers or technicians. The former style remained central among officers and in the army, while the latter became the norm among noncoms and in the navy, the air force, and the gendarmerie.

The post-bipolar pattern of conflict, which has increased by a factor of seven or eight the probability of seeing action (albeit strongly constabulary action), is likely to bring back the tradition of panache, as exemplified by Lt. Gen. Morillon in Bosnia, as well as the long-forgotten hardships of life in the field under difficult operational conditions. The heroic leader is staging a comeback of sorts. Meanwhile, middle managers are being squeezed out of their former controlling role by (1) the short-circuits that the broadcast media are likely to cause in chains of command, and (2) the new influence wielded by field leaders: Instantly informed politicians and high-ranking commanders frequently make direct contact with junior officers. In an age when there is no time to write up full reports until the action is over, these lieutenants and captains often are the only ones in a position to size up a local situation and specify the details on which to base an urgent decision.

New professional role models have appeared recently, however. In the past decade officers have developed a keen sense of the political-military restraints surrounding the use of force. This has come in the wake of a general lengthening of military and civilian education at all levels, especially in the army. This branch of the service, after lagging behind for more than three decades, is now leading the way in a movement intended to broaden officers' intellectual horizons. Professionals now can fully appreciate a complexity based on technology and the close integration of military with extramilitary factors; the proportion of graduate degree holders has increased dramatically in this group. Consequently, the soldier-scholar is on the rise. This phenomenon is not new: Military intellectuals were active, visible, and influential at the turn of the century, in the 1920s and 1930s (de Gaulle was one of them), and again in the 1960s (including Beaufre, Gallois, and Poirier) and even later. One difference is that soldier-scholars in those days were a small, often uncharacteristic community of maverick authors; now, however, they tend to be more numerous and thus less visible individually. Another difference is that today they tend to work in teams, as part of research centers that have sprung up in academies, war colleges, or headquarters staffs, and they are developing increasingly effective links with their civilian counterparts.

The new context has also generated a breed of soldier-diplomats. These professionals cultivate political skills (especially in negotiation) that multinational, multifunctional missions of peacekeeping and humanitarian assistance have made necessary in dealing with belligerents, local populations, nongovernmental organizations, journalists, UN officials, and military contingents from other nations. This change in part reflects a return to an old colonial tradition in which local commanders had to allocate scarce resources and arbitrate between tribes or ethnic groups to keep imperial peace. The new game, to be sure, is much more complex than in the days of empire. The "new" missions originate from international mandates, but national authorities can always choose to withdraw their military contingents; orders come through multinational chains of command, but the careers of officers at the receiving end are still in the hands of their superiors at home. Crisscrossing lines of authority and divided loyalties have the potential to enlarge the latitude allowed military leaders in the field and to grant them independent legitimacy and political influence. This situation, together with the revolution of real-time media coverage, probably foreshadows a change in the equation of soldier-statesman relations if the present situation prevails long enough.[13]

By far the most impressive development is the emergence of soldier-communicators. Courses in public relations and the proper handling of press correspondents in the field have been introduced at all levels of military education. The Ministry of Defense information and public relations agency, created in the 1960s, was managed centrally for a long time; now, however, it has somewhat decentralized branches throughout the military. Officers have become extremely media-sensitive and adept at projecting the most favorable image—in many cases military action is not complete without a graphic video sequence, a still picture, or a sound bite. Highly visible events are employed to the best effect in anticipation of media interest.

Apart from a slight decrease in numbers (1,700 officer slots, 13,000 noncommissioned positions) out of proportion to the overall drawdown, the new organizational format is not expected to affect professionals beyond confirmation of the trends described here.

MEDIA RELATIONS AND PUBLIC ATTITUDES TOWARD THE MILITARY

In contrast to the period before 1945, when war correspondents were officially accredited and found a place in the defense establishment, the colonial wars saw the rise of an adversarial relationship between journalists and the military. Wariness, ideological differences, and resentment often led to mutual suspicion and distrust. Media coverage of defense issues in the late Cold War was largely indifferent except in denouncing disciplinary repression, abuses of rights, and inequities. The adversarial relationship usually resurfaced during operations, whenever media correspondents felt that they were being restricted or manipulated. This was the case, for instance, during the Gulf War, when the press had to be satisfied mostly with official briefings.

Such animus is largely absent today in the coverage of peacekeeping operations. One reason is that the media are now handled by military specialists in public relations, who go to great lengths to oblige them; another is that the new missions are now presented in an almost systematically favorable light.

Apart from divergences in functional imperatives and spans of ideological norms, the relations between media and military seem to reflect public attitudes toward the defense function. A generally supportive phase prevailed before 1950 (with periods of ambivalence, as between the world wars). This was followed, for about two decades, by a growing unpopularity due to postwar prosperity and to the nation's general desire to turn its back on the horrors of wars, total or otherwise. The military ethos passed through a period of profound devaluation; this helps to explain why public support for colonial wars eroded, and why the retreat from empire was followed by a general lack of interest in the military as a social institution (and by an almost complete media silence on the subject).[14]

Hedonistic individualism among the young after 1968 produced a cultural clash, greatly amplified by the media, which eventually forced the military (especially the army) to liberalize in the mid-1970s. After that point, the late–Cold War phase was marked by a consensus by default on the Gaullist legacy in defense matters; this consensus revealed a deep but generally muted ambivalence toward nuclear deterrence. From about the mid-1970s to 1990, the public image of the military gradually improved, less because of enthusiasm (though modernization and liberalization surely helped) than because of deterioration in the images of other public institutions.

The post–Cold War era has changed this situation. A dim awareness of the implications of the new context has earned the military a better public image in the populace. In today's Western societies, the cause of peace and suffering humanity is more popular than preparation for war in the name of purely national interests. Yearly general survey data collected by the Defense Public Relations Agency (SIRPA) show that the proportion of favorable opinions about the military, which had risen above two-thirds in the 1980s (from about three-fifths in the 1970s), is now close to 80 percent. These figures probably underestimate the qualitative change of climate: A young officer recently confided that wearing a military uniform on the street has been a new experience in the last few years, and the change is definitely for the better.[15]

It is possible, of course, that the services' present legitimacy and favorable public image will suffer due to the fading away of conscription. People may fear praetorianism (though there is very little evidence of that[16]) because far fewer people in the future will have firsthand experience of military life; consequently the general public would become apathetic toward the defense establishment.[17] Alternatively, the armed forces may come to resemble the foreign legion writ large.[18] Yet the only sign of change to date seems to point the other way: After the announcement of cutbacks, disbanded battalions, and the closing of armaments factories, the dominant reaction has been to treat service members as an endangered rare species.

CIVILIAN EMPLOYEES

Mainly because general-purpose support functions have been performed historically by cheap conscripted military labor in the services proper, their civilian component has never been as large as in the British and U.S. AVFs. In 1995, civilian employees numbered 32,000 in the army (12 percent of overall strength), 6,500 in the navy (10 percent), 5,000 in the air force (5.2 percent), and 1,000 in the gendarmerie (slightly over 1 percent). Over time these figures had been affected less strongly by the downward trends cited earlier than had those of conscript or career uniformed personnel. It was widely expected that a shift away from conscription would cause an abrupt rise in the numbers of civilian employees.

Much to the analysts' surprise, the projected increase in the services (as opposed to interservice agencies) will add fewer than 10,000 civilians to the 45,000 already on the payrolls. One would have thought that a mere 10,000 additional employees in the army, navy, and air force would be far too few to substitute for the 60,000 to 70,000 draftees presently filling service support slots, even considering that the latter need not be replaced head for head and allowing for the assignment of a few thousand uniformed volunteers to such roles. After all, the British and U.S. defense establishments, which reputedly are more ruthless in applying cost-efficiency principles than their French counterpart (and have far fewer state arsenal workers), include well over 30 percent civilians among their total manpower, in contrast to less than 20 percent (excluding industrial workers) in the French AVF project as it now stands. The conclusion seems to be that civilian manpower requirements have been seriously underestimated, or else that a policy (still undeclared) of relying heavily on outsourcing for service support will come into effect.

Most Ministry of Defense civilians, however (57,000 of a total of 102,000 in 1995), are found not in the services but in interservice agencies, notably in materiel research, development, and production. Most are industrial workers in state arsenals; without them the picture would be incomplete and inaccurate. These civilians are slated for a steep reduction in the coming years.

For about a quarter-century after 1960, France built up a significant defense industrial base[19] around a core of nationalized ordnance establishments and naval shipyards. This core was present in all segments of the arms market. Extensive exports lengthened production runs and made bearable the unit costs of equipping French forces. The assurance of independence in equipment supplied the basis for de Gaulle's "autonomy of decision" within the alliance. This arrangement, however, has reached a state of crisis and is now being overhauled.

Faced with increased competition from non-NATO countries for low- and medium-technology weapons (a logical outcome of transfers of expertise to customer nations over three decades), France no longer can count on exports to reduce the unit costs of such materiel for its own forces. Therefore it has abandoned the idea of remaining active in all segments of the arms market, and will consider leaving these production lines to the private sector (especially in regard to dual civilian/military technologies) or buying equipment off the shelf abroad. In concentrating on costly high-technology programs, French defense industries must take into account the possibilities offered by European cooperation and division of labor. The most difficult problems will reside in restructuring, with competitiveness in such narrow world markets as the medium-term goal. This process, which is likely to be gradual because of resistance by unions and local politicians, will entail reduction of excess capacity and the loss of jobs among one-third or one-half of those presently employed (some 30,000) in state armaments factories.[20]

Provided AVF policy parameters remain as announced, these increases and decreases in the numbers of civilian state employees in, respectively, support and industrial roles are likely to balance out over time. However, if the prognosis in relation to future reliance on outsourcing is correct, private sector workers are bound to enlarge the overall civilian component.

WOMEN'S ROLE

Although integration of women has been less extensive than in the American military, by European standards the French armed forces have not lagged. As recently as the mid-1970s, when segregated all-female schools and corps were eliminated, military women were regarded as somewhat out of place. They had to struggle individually for acceptance and recognition in a world obviously not meant for them. In the 1990s, with numbers stabilized at some 20,000 (4 percent overall, 7 percent of career and contract personnel), nobody seemed to notice their presence, though in relative terms it increased in proportion to the decline in total force levels. Such "progress" is even more remarkable because it has been achieved gradually, without a hint of controversy. In part this may be related to the fact that personnel managers appreciate women as a source of high-quality recruits: The rate of selection, which often hardly exceeds 1 in 2 or 1 in 3 among men, frequently rises as high as 1 in 10 or 1 in 15 for military women.

Female service members, in theory, have been almost fully integrated since the early 1980s; they are no longer limited to "traditional" jobs or to the lower levels of the hierarchy. Women represent some 8 percent of NCOs and other volunteer ranks.[21] Because the younger generation of women was granted access to service academies a decade ago, their representation and prospects in the officer corps have improved, and a handful of their predecessors have now reached general officer rank. Women are more numerous in the army and the air force than in the gendarmerie and the navy. Yet even in the tradition-oriented navy they make up 5 percent of the force; since 1992 they have been authorized to serve aboard ship, and one is a ship commander.

In practice, however, though the probability of inadvertent exposure to hypothetical combat risks has increased, females' access to combat units is restricted by very low quotas; almost three-quarters of military women are sergeants engaged in specialist jobs. Few of them are willing to quarrel with this situation, at least for the time being. Dissatisfaction is hardly evident, if only because (as surveys have shown) women's reasons for joining the services are job security, a highly structured environment, a military family background, and the desire to do something different from the routine jobs in which civilian women tend to concentrate.[22] Their conservative orientations may explain why feminist movements in France, which are characterized (unlike their American counterparts) by fairly strong antimilitary feeling, have neglected the armed forces as a possible symbolic battleground. External support for female emancipation in the services therefore is lacking. However, the dynamics of society[23] and of the military under an AVF format may well change the equation in the long term.

Quantitatively, because all women under the mixed format were volunteers, their numbers are not likely to decrease under the AVF; indeed, they will probably increase slightly. Meanwhile, force levels are slated to be reduced by 30 percent (38 percent if the gendarmerie is excluded), so women will become more visible, with their proportion approaching 10 percent overall. There is even talk about abolishing quotas in the longer term. Qualitatively, women are making quiet progress in access to male sanctuaries (as exemplified by the recent announcement that women now can become fighter pilots); this too will make them more central symbolically. If such is the case (and although complete equality is unlikely in defense establishments), French military women will be a prime example of emancipation achieved through nonadversarial gender relationships.

SPOUSES AND THE MILITARY COMMUNITY

Military spouses are essentially servicemen's wives because fewer than three-fifths of the 20,000 or so military women are married, and only half of those are married to civilians.[24] Over the last two decades, trends affecting military wives' behavior patterns have tended to bring them closer to those prevalent in the parent society. Except for geographic mobility and temporary separation, most family trends (such as lifestyles and average size) parallel those on the outside, with a time lag of about five to ten years. This is especially remarkable because until the 1960s civilian and military families diverged substantially in most respects. In those days very few military wives worked for pay, and most played an important (if informal and hardly recognized) part in local military communities.

With the partial relaxation of readiness standards that closely followed the end of the Cold War, some of the distinctive features of military life (24 hours' availability for service, nomadic lifestyle, separation from family) have become attenuated, at least for those who are not involved in the peacekeeping missions typical of the new times. Because of this development, as well as recent measures regarding service members' status and conditions of employment (pay, compensation in time or money for service during unusual hours, increasing lack of connection between geographic and functional mobility), spouses and families are more able to lead the "normal" lives to which surveys regularly show they aspire.

Especially notable is the number of wives gainfully employed or seeking jobs outside. This number has increased dramatically over the past decade. In 1985, 30 percent went out to work and an additional 4 percent were job seekers;[25] in 1994 those proportions had risen to 42 percent and 19 percent respectively.[26] Over the same period, the proportion of families living outside military compounds has risen significantly (from about 30 percent to some 45 percent). Houses or apartments offered for rent by the military (except in the Paris area, where the accommodation problem is acute) are now reported to be empty.

As another sign of change, even those military wives who are not gainfully employed outside the home are not tradition-oriented and eschew the kind of deep involvement in the life of the local military community that was common in former times. Even in geographically isolated installations, where civilian jobs are in short supply (and where one would expect informal social control to be stronger than elsewhere), few wives show up at female parties organized by the highest-ranking officers' wives, unless they feel for some reason that they must do so.

This conformity to civilian patterns also affects personal behavior. Cohabitation outside marriage is now socially acceptable, though it is less frequent than in civilian life (about 7 percent, in contrast to more than 10 percent outside). Divorce rates, though lower than civilians' rates, have been on the rise. This fact may help to explain why increasing numbers of military wives (who enjoy slightly higher educational levels than average) wish to be gainfully employed: for security, just in case. Conversely, these less dependent, more career-minded wives are less willing to accept the constraints placed on them by their husbands' nomadic lifestyle. Though the size of military families has been decreasing and is hardly distinguishable from the civilian norm,[27] "geographic bachelors" now account for more than 6 percent of married service members.

It is unlikely that the new organizational format will dramatically alter such trends. If anything, professionals will be made less secure by the notion of short military careers, alien to the French tradition but imposed by a reduction in the numbers of units to command, ships to sail, and aircraft to fly, and by a surplus of senior officers and noncoms. This situation will incite their spouses to go out to work in even larger proportions—almost three-quarters of military men, according to a recent survey,[28] favor the idea of outside gainful employment for their wives. Budgetary pressures (as well as the general dynamics of society) preclude the generous on-post benefits that would heighten interest in returning to the traditional prescribed sociability.

Spouses and families probably will persist in their desire for "normal" lives. They will be reluctant to accept the informal social control and the reproduction of the rank hierarchy in all spheres of life which are typical of isolated military communities. Because of the shift to an AVF, higher marriage rates among the rank and file (where concerns about financial security are most acute) probably will increase the rate of spouses' removal from the military community.

HOMOSEXUALS

In the past, military and civilian society did not differ much with regard to homosexuality. France was a normative society, but because of its Catholic sensibilities it tolerated deviant behavior at the margins, if only because it could be pardoned in confession. In addition, the idea that one must live in a glass house is alien to the French cultural tradition. This explains why one finds great military figures with known homosexual tendencies (such as Napoleon's secretary, General Caffarelli, or Marshal Lyautey) and even why, as illustrated in all sorts of legends, homosexuality was proverbial among colonial troops. After the French conquest and occupation of Algeria, Marshal de Saint-Arnaud said half-jokingly, "All of us had a taste of it, some have remained that way." Nevertheless, homosexuality at that time might not have had the same significance as in the late twentieth century.

Today, although homosexuality is recognized as "normal" in civilian society, the issue is rarely raised in the military. Indeed, it is shrouded in the kind of silence that signifies neither embarrassment nor a sense of taboo, but complete lack of interest. Out of 15,000 registered disciplinary incidents in 1992, only twenty were related to sexual matters; only five of these involved homosexuals.[29] Military gays and lesbians have yet to create the kind of *cause célèbre* seen in America and Britain in the last few years, and it is unlikely that they will do so.

Part of the reason, again, is cultural: Sexuality belongs to the realm of inviolable individual privacy. Nobody is required to declare his or her sexual orientation, or told that homosexuality is incompatible with military life. The norm is that sexual activity is off-limits in military precincts. Either this norm is followed strictly, or local military authorities handle things informally (if they do not turn a blind eye), as long as the service climate is not unduly disturbed. Because homosexuality is not illegal per se, gays and lesbians cannot suffer discrimination unless they commit a criminal offense. Thus they feel little pressure or incentive to vindicate their sexual conduct publicly. It is likely that gays are underrepresented in the services, if only because the virile image projected by the latter is bound to make many of them uncomfortable. Gay conscripts, when revealed as such (of their own accord) before induction, are often discharged informally by service doctors (with proper medical confidentiality), on the unproven but not unreasonable grounds that they may create problems of cohesiveness in their units. Probably few gays pass up the chance to be exempted from military duty at such a low cost. The gays who do serve, self-selected or otherwise, must be fairly conservative, because none so far has come forward with the burning desire to stir things up. This combination of minimal formal rules, at once tolerant and stringent, and informal arrangements in which the medical service generally plays the central role, apparently has worked so far to everybody's satisfaction.

The only short- or medium-term challenge to such a state of affairs could come from a European Court of Justice ruling in a case originating in another country, or from an outside group bent on public recognition of homosexuals' rights in the forces, as in the American or British scenario. Until recently, as in the case of feminist movements, the latter possibility was virtually precluded by antimilitary sentiments among such activist groups in France; these sentiments fed in part on resentment of conscription as a form of majoritarian tyranny.

In either case, the French military would have to abandon its informal traditions and make its norms explicit, thereby emphasizing equality between the heterosexual majority and homosexual minorities, and making the former uncomfortable. Formalization also would place the seal of approval on homosexuality, encourage litigation, and make the issue politically sensitive. This has not happened yet. Abolition of the draft and the general dynamics of society[30] are likely in the long run to change the equation toward fuller acceptance, but for now it is best to avoid predictions.

CONSCIENTIOUS OBJECTION

Over the long term, the status of conscientious objection in France has passed from strictly prohibited to a rather severely restricted alternative (1963) and then to a less than fully liberalized form of nonmilitary service (1983). Conscientious objectors (COs) today must serve for twenty months, twice as long as ordinary draftees. They may fulfill their legal obligation in various capacities in nonprofit organizations, including private associations not controlled by the state.

Until recently the overriding feature of conscientious objectors was their small numbers. Though now on the rise, the figures were exceedingly low in comparison (for example) with Germany or Spain. In 1992 there were only 4,933 COs, hardly more than 1 percent of eligible males in their age group. For purely cultural reasons, the image of conscientious objection in France remains negative except in extreme left-wing circles.

The latest figures, however, reveal a sudden, significant increase. In 1993 the number of COs rose by 42.3 percent to 7,265, and has now passed the 8,000 mark (2 percent of draft-age cohorts). Yet this may have occurred simply because civilian forms of national service were still underdeveloped. With the end of the Cold War and the slightly relaxed standards that have resulted, those who seek to escape the military draft for purely secular reasons may have been encouraged to take advantage of a status designed for genuine objectors.

In any case, the issue is settled by the option favoring an all-volunteer military format and a scheme of voluntary national civic service. In certain quarters, nostalgia is expressed for a state of affairs in which there was something to object to, and objectors enjoyed their hard-won recognition.

MEMBERSHIP IDENTIFICATION

In the mid-1980s it was rather difficult to say that the French military had shifted from institutional to occupational. Various studies showed that officers and the army generally retained institutional loyalties, while NCOs and large portions of the navy, air force, and gendarmerie were more occupationally oriented. A decade later, there are few indications that things have changed substantially.

As for the rise of civic orientations hypothesized in the model, this question is probably the most difficult to answer, if only because we seem to be at a crossroads without a clear map of the terrain ahead.

In the last fifteen years or so the French tradition of public service, which was strong in the monarchy and even stronger after the Revolution, has entered a period of decay. The decline of national sentiment, the death of millenarian utopias, the deep financial crisis affecting the welfare state, the rise of individualism, and market orientations have combined to depreciate public values. With the luster gone and public accounts in the red, government efforts to introduce cost-efficiency into state operations at all levels have met with stiff resistance, with civil servants and nationalized industry workers protesting their meager salaries and loss of societal respect. The rest of society now strongly suspects that striking government employees wish to defend their remaining privileges (job security, early retirement age, exploitation of captive publics and customers) rather than to uphold the true spirit of selfless public service. The French bureaucratic model is still alive, but by any measure it is not well. Reforming it appears to be problematic in the extreme: Witness the quasi-general public-sector strike of November–December 1995, in response to the announcement of drastic measures widely perceived as redolent of "Thatcherism."

Such a climate has reinforced the long-term effects, dating back to the 1960s, of a redefinition of citizenship in terms of rights rather than a balance of rights and duties. The rise of welfare caused the symbolic displacement of traditional institutions representing nationhood by new institutions emphasizing choice, opportunity, personal autonomy, and self-expression as well as the worth of socioeconomic well-being. In the 1980s, the willingness to enter public service on idealistic grounds appeared to be at an all-time low.

This situation has generated a deep moral and social crisis, as well as a fair measure of intellectual malaise.[31] As a result, national identity has been redefined at a time when Europe holds center stage. Before 1990, such malaise was analyzed as the symptom of a multifaceted transition from Late Modern to Postmodern; in the more optimistic assessments of the gradual "Anglo-Saxonization" of French society, this transition seemed to promise a better life and a more civilized age.[32] That was followed after 1990 by calls for a reaffirmation of citizenship:[33] a yearning for new formulations of the common interest, a mobilization of social energies geared to rational control of collective destiny, and the political will to turn individuals into citizens again through the imposition of abstract ideals, following the prescriptions of Rousseau and Kant. Some thinkers, such as Régis Debray, whom one could hardly suspect of reactionary feelings, advocated a return to the principles of the early (pre-1914) Third Republic.[34] In 1995 the presidential race was won, against all odds, by the candidate who campaigned for a renewal of the old "republican pact" of equal opportunity, social solidarity, and political purpose.

Such prescriptions fail to recognize that some of the basic social, economic, and external conditions for a return to strong norms of national citizenship are largely absent. Although these norms seduce through nostalgia, they tend to ignore the leading trends embodied in the concept of Postmodernism. These trends seem to be based on a fragmentation of personality, culture, and society, and therefore are hardly conducive to a voluntary renewal of civic orientations. It is symptomatic that, as in the United States, official support for new forms of national service so far has failed to stir the country's blood. Chirac's announcement of an expanded volunteer national service scheme has drawn reactions devoid of hostility but ranging from mild interest to muted skepticism.

Although the military cannot isolate itself entirely from society, it has managed to remain relatively free of the surrounding anomie. Military professionals still exhibit institutional orientations strong enough to rub off on draftees, who have a higher opinion of military service *after* they have fulfilled their draft obligations than before.[35] This can pass for an ex post facto affirmation of civic orientations. There is overwhelming enthusiasm for the AVF idea, however, among those of military age who expected to be drafted: over 80 percent approve of the move, which indeed is in tune with the spirit of the time. Sometimes the state no longer seems to command enough legitimacy resources to impose on its citizens (or exact from them) anything beyond taxes, welfare contributions, and the rule of law—if that.

Social representativeness, so important when society held integration in high regard, no longer seems an overriding requirement when multiculturalism is on the rise. The military has lost much of its influence as a major socializing agency; the "school of the nation" period is now a fading memory. If Postmodern logic blossoms one day as an all-pervasive societal pattern, the defense establishment will be legitimate if it completely renounces its societywide normative pretensions; if it is content with the status of a "lifestyle cum functional value" system (among many other statuses); and if, as far as possible, it reflects the diversity of a multicultural society (symbolically rather than quantitatively). Life in the armed forces is now a minority experience, and fewer than 30,000 slots (8 percent of the force level target for the AVF) are reserved for "citizen" short-timers. The result will be a drastic limitation on whatever role the armed forces could play in reaffirming civic consciousness.

For the same reasons, the government decided against mandatory forms of civic service; this was one of the rare points on which there was strong consensus in the public debate. Unlike in the German experience, alternative forms of service until now had remained marginal. The social legitimacy of such a scheme, if it had to be extended to those who did not expressly apply for these forms of service, was very much in doubt. It would have been far more problematic than that of the hallowed (if increasingly hollow) tradition of drafting young men into the forces. In addition, compulsory national service was fraught with technical difficulties. Legal problems probably would have been raised by the uncertainty of conformity to the 1950 European Convention on human rights, notably its provisions against forced labor.

Also, the "old" forms of civilian service, numbering fewer than 30,000 slots today, were designed to absorb surplus demographic resources not used by the armed services. Such service fulfilled social needs that neither the market (through lack of recipients' solvency) nor public bureaucracies (because of budget constraints) cared to meet. The "new" forms would have risked condemnation by union workers as unfair competition in more than one sector of activity, as well as by nonprofit humanitarian organizations, which disliked the prospect of bureaucratization of their craft.

Finally, if the ultimate rationale for civilian service was formal equality of citizenship duties, then the present high level of exemptions fell victim to the application of the civilian economy's norms, which are less exacting than physical military standards (and would thus have added another 100,000 servers). In addition, the exclusion of young women became unjustifiable. We were speaking of a proposition involving well over a half-million people, with the attendant complexity, bureaucratization, and (probably) greater numbers of discontented servers than under the well-worn—and recently fairly liberal—system in force for the past nine decades. In other words, civilian conscription is intrinsically more difficult to legitimate and implement than a military draft.

What will happen now, when the projected five-year transition period ends? To be successful, the new system must attract large numbers of male and female volunteers serving in civilian capacities for up to a year or more in three types of socially useful functions: security (police, the gendarmerie, fire brigades, customs and excise, environment, and emergency services), "social solidarity" at home (programs geared to narrowing the perceived widening gap between the disadvantaged and the mainstream segments of society), and service abroad (international cooperation and humanitarian action). The plan provides for incentives; the nature and amount of these incentives (monetary compensation, job or educational opportunities, symbolic recognition of civic merit) remains to be specified, though budgetary pressures will surely translate into substantial resource constraints.

One possibility is that middle-class youths, caught in fierce competition for education and jobs, will see no point in serving and will shun such civic schemes altogether. In the worst case, only a minority will be attracted; then "civic" service soon would assume a welfare quality (and possibly, at the other extreme, an elitist slant) that would both devalue and marginalize it, as in America. Then the French republican tradition of personal citizen service to the nation, dating back to the mass levy of revolutionary days and institutionalized gradually through military conscription between 1872 and 1905, would come to an end and would be difficult to revive.[36] This outcome is feared by many, and may explain why it took so long to adopt an all-volunteer military system in view of the draft's less than adequate fit with geopolitical factors and the attendant organizational requirements.

Yet, given the current nostalgia for an age in which the Republic could readily mobilize social energies in the name of the common interest, a shift away from conscription might trigger a countertrend back to stronger (but

voluntary) citizenship norms. After all, despite the slow erosion of its legitimacy, the draft, now in its final hour, is in much better condition in France
than in Germany, Spain, or elsewhere in Western Europe. Its resilient spirit
can be used as a foundation for new relationships between the citizen and
the state. Possibly the same factors that make military personnel analysts
rather optimistic about meeting the future AVF's quantitative and qualitative targets[37] will work in regard to civilian national service. The value of a
socially meaningful first work experience away from school and higher education establishments may attract majorities of young men and women to
temporary civic jobs. Such work could give scope to their idealism and could
enhance their future job prospects more fully than academic credentials,
whose utility and discriminating function are being eroded by "educational
inflation."[38]

Meanwhile there is no telling how "civic" the medium-term future will
be. Much will depend on the details of programs to be instituted beginning
in 2002, and it is idle to venture predictions.

CONCLUSIONS

How well does the French case fit the paradigm? The attributes hypothesized for the Modern variables (in France, pre-1960) qualify it for "very well,"
even if a few nuances must be considered. The armed forces' mission then
was defense of the homeland, but also (and most visibly in "peacetime") a
(re)affirmation of empire; homosexuals were punished only insofar as overt
behavior on duty, not latent preference, was involved; and public attitudes
in that era ranged from highly supportive (before World War I) through
somewhat ambivalent (during the interwar period) to more negative (after
1950)—if not consistently hostile, then apathetic at best.

Similarly, a few qualifications apply to the Late Modern (1960–90) phase.
Although professionalization had set in, France retained a mixed format in
which conscripts were a bare majority for most of the period. Also, the military establishment's major function, based on its nuclear capability, was a
symbolic instrument of choice for pursuing de Gaulle's active and independent foreign policy; support of the NATO alliance became apparent only
in times of acute East-West crisis. Finally, the shift in role models from combat leader to manager or technician, and the change in organizational identification from institutional to occupational, were observed but remained
very incomplete and uneven.

Until 1996, the post–Cold War situation presented much the same profile of partial adherence to the Postmodern construct. This was true largely
because the decline of the mass armed force, which had started later in France
than elsewhere, still had not reached its logical conclusion—for sociopolitical reasons, many people were reluctant to let go of the draft tradition. The

revolution introduced by President Chirac has hardened the trends bringing France closer to the model on a number of dimensions: perceived threat,
a smaller professional military, definition of mission, the dominant type
of military professional, media relations, and spouses and the military
community.

A few differences stand out, however. Contrary to the expectations of
the model, reserve forces—at least those enjoying operational status—are
smaller now than before 1990, at less than 30 percent of active-duty force
levels. The numbers of civilian Ministry of Defense employees in nationalized defense industries will decrease in the next few years. This decrease
will be so great that even the projected rise associated with the shift to an
AVF in the services proper cannot make them a much larger component
than they are at present (unless private sector workers are factored in, should
Defense resort to outsourcing in a big way).

An additional carryover from the Late Modern period, in terms of the
paradigm, is that France will become more supportive of NATO than in the
past. Similarly, though women have become more visible and more fully accepted, they are still denied unrestricted access to combat slots, and are not
yet completely integrated. Also, though homosexuals do not suffer discrimination, neither are they officially recognized. Conscientious objection
under an AVF and expanded voluntary national service is expected to van-
ish as an issue.

Other present features include supportive public attitudes (a major departure from the model) and a question: Can the president's voluntarism,
shared by the Socialist-led cabinet, and the future societal circumstances
counteract less-than-vigorous civic orientations and move France ahead in
a trend that will lead to civic revival, or does Postmodernism preclude such
a revival?

Indeed, on most variables examined here, the lines between the military
and the civilian have blurred further, in the manner viewed as characteristic of the post–Cold War era. In the indecisive 1990–96 period, the French
case remained so ambiguous that it was difficult to assess the relative weight
of cultural identity and cross-national trends. The dramatic decision to abolish conscription allows little doubt: The French military will conform more
closely than in the past to trends prevalent in the West. Even so, it is all too
easy to confuse military style (where exceptionalism is on the wane) with
political substance (in which France's loyal but contrarian mode within the
NATO alliance may not yet be at an end).

In reply to those who reason in terms of a sharp, Postmodern break with
the past (as against those who see an accentuation of past trends ushering
in a new Modern phase), recent developments permit neither proof nor dis-
proof. But perhaps the outcomes of the delicate, probably painful transition
from drafted to all-volunteer manpower procurement, with all the associated doctrinal, organizational, and societal changes, will clarify that point in
the first decade of the next century.

NOTES

1. Revising defense doctrine, a move likely to weaken or destroy a multipartisan consensus built over three decades of strenuous effort, was widely perceived as fraught with political risks. This was especially so when it became probable that a socialist head of state would be linked with a conservative cabinet in the last years of François Mitterrand's *fin de règne*. Also, it was clear that overhauling the defense system would produce dissent on both the right and the left, thereby confusing debate. Public opinion appeared deeply ambivalent about any move that would spare its young a burden of service viewed as increasingly ill-adapted, but that also would involve the end of a well-worn tradition, linking conscription and democratic citizenship, while depleting its conventional forces. After all, France's military history is full of ups and downs: The nation was invaded three times in three-quarters of a century. Thus, the idea that there is no such thing as a risk-free international environment, that conscription not only appears to be a perennial factor for societal cohesion but also is a time-tested hedge against more serious odds, still could be contemplated without seeming implausible. Finally, the prospect of dismantling a strong defense industrial base and adding to record unemployment levels was unappealing to many politicians of all persuasions.

2. See Jacques Isnard, "Le gouvernement veut attribuer à la défense 185 milliards de francs par an entre 1997 et 2002," *Le Monde*, May 14, 1996.

3. This writer's analysis on that score is consistent with that of William Pfaff, "The Ill-Grasped Logic Behind France's 'Return' to NATO," *International Herald Tribune*, Jan. 31, 1996.

4. The irredentist problems that had emerged in the 1970s on the outer fringes, in Britanny, Corsica, and the Basque country, have grown less acute. But the bombing campaign that took place in the summer of 1995 and frequent scenes of collective street violence in cities have dramatized the need for better integration and control of the now-large Islamic community. Furthermore, the dismantling of border controls in the wake of new European advances in integration has produced many undesirable consequences.

5. *Rapport d'orientation* presented to Parliament by Charles Millon, minister of defense. See Jacques Isnard, "Pour le gouvernement, la 'première ligne de défense' se situe loin du 'territoire national,'" *Le Monde*, Mar. 13, 1996.

6. The debate was short (it lasted only three months) and tepid at best. Of course, some people in both the populace and the political class worry about what will be lost when the draft comes to an end. In a country that has not had a true AVF for more than two centuries, and has relied on universal conscription as the hallmark of political citizenship, such a major shift has deep symbolic significance: The sociopolitical underpinnings of republican tradition are at stake. But everyone knows the impossibility of retaining meaningful conscription when the manpower levels required by the external situation are only a small fraction of the human resources supplied by annual age cohorts of youths. Some would have liked a territorial army or national guard, or some scheme of short universal military training. The government decided against such ideas, rejecting the first two because they are probably not needed in a nation that boasts more gendarmes or police forces per square mile than most in Europe, and the last because it would be both costly and ineffective.

7. François Cailleteau, "Le recrutement d'une armée de métier," in *Conscription et armée de métier,* ed. Bernard Boëne and Michel-Louis Martin (Paris: FEDN/ Documentation Française, 1991), pp. 252–266.

8. Depending on modal duration of contract, reenlistment, and nonprior service attrition rates, this will entail procuring 20,000 to 30,000 new volunteers annually, hardly twice as many as today. An improved public image, better pay for the rank and file, increasing technology-related attractiveness, more sophisticated resettlement aid policies, and record unemployment levels among the young should make that objective well within the recruiters' reach. The problem of quality should be resolved by the legitimacy of post–Cold War missions and the professionalism they require, and by educational inflation and the declining utility of credentialism on the outside. (Every youth in the nation, except for a minority of social misfits, now boasts a diploma or degree of some sort, and close to 30 percent of coming-age cohorts will have the equivalent of a master's degree. Thus, credentials will count for less in the job market than the experience described in the first few lines of résumés.) Another indication of success is the allocation to the armed forces proper of at least part of the yearly supply of citizen-soldiers (those opting for military rather than civilian voluntary national service).

9. Charles Millon, minister of defense, address to representatives of national associations of reserve officers and NCOs, Paris, Apr. 10, 1996.

10. Two interpretations are plausible here, which need not be mutually exclusive. Either the new concept implicitly rules out long and costly commitments entailing heavy casualties even in the more serious scenarios, or planning has proceeded from the beginning on the assumption that the new mobile force in most cases will act as one component of a larger European, allied, or UN force. A further problem is that the gendarmerie, overburdened in peacetime with a surfeit of missions under various government departments, appears unenthusiastic about maintaining a reserve force of 50,000 to meet the demands of yet another expensive and time-consuming mission that it will not relish, especially under strict resource constraints. Today, the gendarmerie has few reservists of its own; therefore transfers of army reserve cadres (of whom there are now too many) will be in order. The army's self-image (alien to the police work with which it equates the gendarmerie) promises to make this process somewhat problematic.

11. In fact, it has been used to back up police surveillance as part of the Vigipirate Plan, in the wake of Islamist terrorist actions in the summer and fall of 1995.

12. *Rapport d'orientation,* Ministry of Defense. See Isnard, "Pour le gouvernement."

13. A case in point—the first of its kind since the Algerian War—is the December 1995 recall of General Bachelet, UNPROFOR commander in Sarajevo, after he made public pronouncements on the Dayton accord which stirred international controversy and embarrassed the French government. Two years earlier, Gen. Jean Cot, the commander of UN forces in the Balkans, openly ignored or challenged the authority of UN Secretary General Boutros Boutros-Ghali.

14. Bernard Paqueteau, *Grande muette, petit écran* (Paris: FEDN, 1986).

15. Contrary to what has been observed in other countries (notably the United States and Germany), this enhanced legitimacy of the use of armed force in the recent period has not suffered from the relatively high level of casualties (more than sixty dead and 300 wounded in five years). This is probably the case, however,

because these casualties have been spread evenly over time. There is no telling how the public might have reacted if a large fraction of that total had been killed in a single day, as was the case with U.S. forces in Somalia or Belgian soldiers in Rwanda. (On differences between public attitudes on this point in France and in America, see Thomas L. Friedman, "Two Cultural Landscapes and Their Views of War," *International Herald Tribune*, Aug. 24, 1995.) Another factor is that those casualties are volunteers who are supposed to know the risks involved. This may help to explain why the number of candidates for peacekeeping action among conscripts has declined by more than half since 1992, even though their pay is considerably higher in Bosnia than at home. There is no reason to suppose that the public attitude toward casualties among volunteers will change with the advent of an AVF. (This attitude is inherited from the colonial past, when volunteers were regarded as adventurers recruited from among social misfits.) Change in attitude is not likely unless the social makeup of the AVF becomes minority-heavy; in that case, an American-style sensitivity to an unrepresentative distribution of those killed or wounded in action might well develop.

16. Though voiced occasionally without much conviction during the recent debate, the old fear of a praetorian professional force did not play a major role. People seem to understand that such a force would constitute a danger only if there was a wide social and ideological gap between the military and society, and a large political segment willing to use the armed forces as a rallying point to topple the government or regime, as at the turn of the century. This clearly is not the case. People intuitively accept the Janowitzian idea that an effective high-tech force tends to be pragmatic in outlook, and cannot long afford to draw its personnel mainly from outside the mainstream. They also know that the elite troops which would provide the most likely candidates for a praetorian role—the foreign legion, the parachute or marine battalions, the gendarmerie—traditionally have recruited all or most of their members as volunteers. They judge the military professionals' social integration satisfactory; the dependence of the military on civilian support is sufficient to avert the danger of a coup. At any rate, a coup would stand little chance of success in a complex society secure in its democratic political culture and institutions. Also, the new international context is hardly conducive to absolutist values among the officer corps.

17. Surveys regularly show that those who have served as draftees hold more favorable opinions of the armed forces as they grow older than those who have not. Also, no great analytical skills are needed to predict that the benefits to the less than 10 percent citizen-soldiers serving in the new voluntary national service scheme will be a poor substitute for the broader deferred benefits of legitimacy inherent in the old universal/egalitarian conscription system.

18. In fact, the legion's public image is fairly good. Better still is its attractiveness to young males, French (about one-third) or foreign. The rate of nonprior service selection is now 1 in 7.

19. Defense industries now account for 2 percent of the gross domestic product, 5 percent of industrial employment, 7 percent of total industrial output, and 5 percent of exports (10 percent of the world market).

20. The more drastic reforms announced by the Chirac administration (steeper cutbacks in the materiel procurement side of the defense budget and lower requirements in keeping with the reduction in force) will accelerate and deepen

the trend: French defense industries are now due for a complete shakeout, and over two years will go through a contraction process that Britain, Germany, and the United States have taken five years to accomplish. Europeanization, forced mergers (such as that between Dassault and Aérospatiale), and plant closures are the order of the day. The social pain is certain to be great: Military manufacturing is densely concentrated, with three regions counting on defense jobs for up to 20 percent of employment, and another three for 10 percent. (See Joseph Fitchett, "French Military Cuts Could Inflict Big Wounds," *International Herald Tribune*, Jan. 31, 1996.) These cutbacks come on top of base closures that will affect the revenues of as many as 150 towns and cities, including some of those affected by industrial restructuring. The political element is likely to be paramount in determining which state plants and military installations will close; this fact does not guarantee the greatest possible effectiveness.

21. Women are not drafted into the forces. Most enter the services directly as officers or noncoms. Those in the rank and file have the option of serving initially as "national service female volunteers." Very few do so, however: 400 in 1978, 800 in 1990, and 1,000 in 1993, two-thirds of them in the army and the medical service.

22. Emmanuel Reynaud, *Les femmes, la violence et l'armée* (Paris: FEDN, 1988).

23. It may well be that in the longer term the American example will exert some influence, just as it did in the case of sexual harrassment. This was a nonissue ten years ago but has come to the fore recently in civilian society (and, to a much lesser extent, in the armed forces). Lately, a movement has been afoot in political circles, calling for male-female parity in the political class.

24. Military females' marriage rates are lower than military men's (two-thirds overall): slightly over half among officers, two-thirds among noncoms, and about one-fourth of the rank and file. These figures reflect the fact that the women are two years younger than the men on average, but probably also (and more important) indicate a woman's difficulty in reconciling a military career with family life. Women account for 7 percent of volunteers or professionals; the number of military females married to civilians represents only about 2 percent of all career or contract personnel.

25. "Observatoire de la condition militaire," in *Enquête mutations* (Paris: Ministère de la Défense, 1985).

26. "Observatoire social de la Défense (OSD)," in *Enquête Environnement social des militaires, Conjoints-Enfants* (Paris: Ministère de la Défense, 1994). Corresponding figures for women aged 25 to 49 in the general population are 76 percent and 12 percent.

27. It now includes two children on average, as opposed to 1.87 for civilian families. Interesting disparities are apparent, however: There are more childless couples, especially among young service members, than in the population at large, and larger-than-average families among officers.

28. OSD, *Enquête*.

29. Gilles Robert and Louis M. Fabre, "Homosexualité et armée." Unpublished document, Paris, Centre des Relationes Humaines, 1993.

30. Though homosexual associations are much less aggressive in France than in the United States, gay pride marches have come to be part of today's French scene.

31. See, for instance, Alain Finkielkraut, *Défaite de la pensée* (Paris: Gallimard, 1987).

32. See, for instance, Gilles Lipovetsky, *L'ère du vide* (Paris: Gallimard, 1983); and D. Cohn-Bendit and F. Guattari, "Contribution pour le mouvement," *Autogestion, l'Alternative*, Nov. 24, 1986. For a useful discussion presenting Postmodernism as an unanticipated consequence of the 1960s' philosophical and student movements, see Luc Ferry and Alain Renaut, *La pensée 68: Essai sur l'anti-humanisme contemporain* (Paris: Gallimard, 1985) and *68-86, Itinéraires de l'individu* (Paris: Gallimard, 1987).

33. Laurent Joffrin, *La régression française* (Paris: Seuil, 1991); Alain-Gérard Slama, *La régression démocratique* (Paris: Fayard, 1995).

34. Régis Debray, *Que vive la République* (Paris: Seuil, 1991).

35. See note 17.

36. For this reason it was decided that beginning in 2002, all males and females turning eighteen would spend a full week in government precincts for registration; mental, physical, scholastic, and vocational aptitude testing; evaluation of remedial schooling needs; and indoctrination into the meaning of citizenship (*"rendez-vous citoyen"*). This procedure has a functional rationale (as the basis for a standby draft should emergency needs arise), as well as a sociopolitical basis (symbolically keeping alive the idea that the state can summon and mobilize its citizens for the common interest). However, the new leftist government has just decided, for budget reasons mostly, that this "citizen week" would actually be curtailed to one day.

37. See note 8.

38. In the longer term, another possibility must be considered: Will current general economic trends such as globalization, "reengineering," restructuring, outsourcing, and downsizing mean that in the future less and less labor will be required to produce the goods and services offered through the market? In that case, will a "moral equivalent of work," along the lines of what Amitai Etzioni or the Club of Rome have suggested recently, become necessary to avert a profound societal—indeed civilizational—crisis of rising structural unemployment and exclusion? A large-scale voluntary scheme of youth and adult community service funded by the taxpayers then might appear to be the only solution, giving the national service idea the vigorous political momentum it has lacked so far. We have not yet reached that point, however. The outcome will probably hinge on the result of the international debate between those who draw on the American or British example and see the source of such unemployment in too much state interference and overgenerous welfare benefits, and those who observe that the millions of jobs created in the United States and (to a lesser extent) in Britain are mostly menial service jobs that deny their holders security and the dignity equal to their educational attainments. As a result of the latter situation, societies become more sharply polarized between rich and poor, and are at odds with their democratic ideals.

5

Germany: Forerunner of a Postnational Military?

BERNHARD FLECKENSTEIN

Since 1990 the Bundeswehr has undergone the most comprehensive reform in its history. The first phase saw the buildup of the Army of Unification to replace the disbanded National People's Army (NPA) of the former German Democratic Republic (GDR), the establishment of the Bundeswehr in the new federal states, the reduction of the federal armed forces to 370,000 (a cut of roughly one-third), and the reorganization and redeployment of troops. Many problems had to be solved in a short time. This phase was completed early in 1995, with the assignment of the units in the new federal states to NATO.

In the second phase, which is scheduled for completion by 2000, Bundeswehr capabilities, size, and organization will be further adjusted and optimized for an array of new tasks arising from changes in the national security situation and in the personnel and financial resources available. And this is not the end of the reform process. The German government that took office in autumn 1998 decided to set up what is to be called a "commission for the future." It will investigate the Bundeswehr mission and deployment, manpower strength, the training and equipment of the armed forces, and the issue of whether mixed volunteer and conscript forces are to be retained, and will develop structural options for the Bundeswehr beyond the year 2000. As a result of these reorganization processes, the country will have a new Bundeswehr, which will be tied completely to supranational structures. The Bundeswehr is becoming a truly postnational military.

The major factors governing German foreign and security policy are memberships in the European Union, NATO, and the United Nations. These ties are constants in German policy, and the German public takes this view as well. The great international organizations are supported and still liked. The country's political commitment to these three institutions has been amply demonstrated by its financial contributions: Germany supplies almost one-third of the European Union budget, roughly one-quarter of NATO's budget, and nearly 9 percent of the UN budget.

Membership in the European Union has brought great economic prosperity to Germany. Also, NATO has guaranteed Germany's external security for four decades and has contributed substantially to German unification. Finally, Germany, although not a member of the Security Council, has played a major role in the United Nations. The German political and social contract ensures that these pillars of German foreign and national security policy will not be shaken. As one perceptive observer stated,

> Multilateralism has become second nature to Germany. One can assert with a clear conscience that German public opinion, with only a very few exceptions that hardly matter at all, is united in the conviction that our foreign policy must, of necessity, be anchored in a European-Atlantic framework.[1]

The new hazards and challenges facing Germany can be met only with partners and allies. Germany now may not embark on any ventures on its own. Reversion to the classic nation-state would entail falling back on an obsolete model. Instead, Germany is trying to find a "postnational identity," in which integration and community orientation are the key concepts. In a federal European Union, sovereign power is to be relative and wielded jointly by the community.

The political authority entrusted to the state determines the role and tasks assigned to the armed forces. Therefore, a multilateral orientation is essential for the Bundeswehr as the instrument of national security policy. A major tenet of German policy is the repeated declaration that Germany will never act alone in deploying the Bundeswehr; the force will be deployed only in the framework of the Alliance or jointly with partners and allies on missions serving the community of nations. The Bundeswehr soldiers also frown on the idea of the German military's engagement in unilateral operations: Roughly three-quarters advocate military assignments for the Bundeswehr above and beyond territorial defense, or support purely humanitarian missions, only if they are done in cooperation with other countries.[2]

Even at its inception in 1955, the Bundeswehr was tied to a supranational structure. Germany integrated her armed forces completely into the Atlantic Alliance, whereas other nations—such as England, France, and the United States—retained the military capability to assert their national interest. Even after Germany regained full sovereignty as a nation, German policy was designed explicitly to prevent the renationalization of national security and defense. Germany is the prime supporter of the concept of multinational armed forces in central Europe; the Bundeswehr has assumed the lion's share (at division or corps level) of all large European multinational forces.[3] The principle of multinationalism also applies to the air force and the navy: Of the sixty maritime exercises that took place in 1996, only four were conducted exclusively by German participants.

The two core elements of sovereignty are a nation's armed forces and its currency. For that reason one should not take integration and a multinational orientation for granted. It is not easy to change old ways of thinking: National vanity and sensitivities play a part here, as shown by the debate on establishing a German-Dutch Corps. Yet such integration must be included in the agenda if a distinctive European security and defense identity is to emerge.

Structuring the armed forces along multinational lines is only a beginning, however. The next logical step is to standardize weapons, equipment, training procedures, and principles of command.[4] No state, apart from the United States, can deal single-handedly with the new tasks that have emerged since the end of the Cold War. For the Europeans, military capabilities such as satellite reconnaissance and surveillance, tactical ballistic missile defense, long-range air transport, in-flight refueling, and medical supplies and care can be achieved only if national resources are pooled.

The Bundeswehr is a committed member of the NATO Partnership for Peace (PFP) program. In 1997 and 1998 the German armed forces participated in more than 50 percent of all PFP exercises and related activities. The postnational orientation of the Bundeswehr is promoted and reinforced by programs of bilateral cooperation with military organizations outside Germany. On a level lower than the NATO Partnership for Peace program, bilateral agreements have been signed with central and eastern European countries, the Baltic states, and the Commonwealth of Independent States (CIS). Following these agreements, more than 750 joint activities were carried out in 1998, almost 20 percent of them with Poland alone. In addition, individual units have been sponsored primarily to foster personal contacts. The idea behind such undertakings is that all those who bear arms in Europe should come to know and trust one another.

It is pointless to ask when Germany once again will begin to conduct herself in foreign affairs like a "normal" state. A return to national sovereignty and power politics in a world marked by increasing national interdependence would be a one-way street. Germany lost two world wars waged under the aegis of overblown nationalism; this experience was enough to make the country avoid the path taken by "normal" nation-states. As a power at the hub of Europe and a state with numerous industrial and commercial links, Germany has opted for a postnational foreign policy. This decision is also the foundation for its armed forces.

PERCEIVED THREAT

The end of the Cold War has benefited Germany more than any other country. In addition, however, Germany has been required to deal with the ensuing political change, not least through the peaceful revolution in the former GDR. Since October 1990, the country has been reunified. In August

1994 the last Russian soldier left German soil; Germany is now a fully sovereign state. The country is no longer on the front lines and, for the first time in her history, has neighbors who are either allies or partners. Germany's geostrategic situation has improved immeasurably because the country is no longer within reach of a military power capable of a strategic offensive and territorial conquest. In central Europe there is little danger of such a conflict. This type of threat would be conceivable only if current developments changed radically.

Today, however, security can no longer be defined in the narrow territorial terms applicable to the nation-state. Germany is both a member of the Atlantic alliance and a major economic and commercial power. Therefore her security interests are not simply national; they are those of her partners in NATO and the European Union. Moreover, because transcontinental and global links are steadily growing closer, there is a vital interest in maintaining peace and security across the globe.

Security policy studies outline five widely agreed-upon areas in which security risks can be perceived.

First are the risk factors related to the still-uncertain outcome of the political changes in the former Soviet Union, particularly Russia. The country is still undergoing transformation; even when the process is complete, Russia will still have Europe's greatest military capability at her disposal. Russia will remain the largest conventional land power, and will possess the greatest nuclear military capability well into the twenty-first century.

Second are the risk factors caused by the many unresolved ethnic conflicts in Europe. All central and eastern European states have minority populations, some of them quite considerable. Border disputes between neighboring states are numerous, and these could easily turn into armed conflicts.

Third are the risk factors connected with the crisis-ridden arc on the southern and southeastern periphery of Europe. From the west coast of Africa to the Indian Ocean stretches a zone fraught with domestic and external instability, in which religious fundamentalism is increasingly influential. In this region a hidden war is being waged against Western values, Western institutions, and nationals of Western countries.

Fourth are the risk factors stemming from the proliferation of modern armaments, particularly long-range ballistic missile and launch systems outfitted with nuclear, chemical, and biological weapons technology. The means of mass destruction are becoming more accessible, and there is a growing danger that political adventurers or religious fanatics might use them.

Fifth are the risk factors resulting from poverty, overpopulation, environmental deterioration, and political anarchy. Any of these could cause waves of migration that would affect Europe.

In the opinion of the German public, the greatest threats to their security are the conflict in the Balkans, religious fundamentalism, the uncontrolled proliferation of weapons of mass extermination, and potential ecological catastrophes such as the destruction of the ozone layer and climate change.[5] The concept of security now has few military connotations in the public mind. Today security means, first of all, job security and an assured income. It also means protection from crime and violence. Whether or not someone feels secure has little to do with defense and the Bundeswehr; even traffic safety ranked higher than military security in 1996 polls. In the popular view, the military threat may be minor, but other dangers loom large, and these cannot be addressed by military means.

FORCE STRUCTURE

After unification, Germany first had to disband the National People's Army of the GDR while simultaneously building up the Bundeswehr in the new federal states. Of the 50,000 career regulars and fixed-term volunteers who once served in the NPA, roughly one-fifth were taken over by the Bundeswehr. At the same time, the German armed forces as a whole were to be reduced by roughly one-third, restructured, and partially restationed.

Other steps began in 1996 and were implemented gradually. These included a further reduction in peacetime troop strength to about 340,000, the establishment of crisis-reaction forces, and the reorganization of conscription along more flexible lines, with terms of service ranging from ten to twenty-three months. The cuts in peacetime troop strength by a total of 32,000 soldiers reduced the active-duty army to 233,400, the air force to 77,400, and the navy to 27,200. The crisis-reaction forces include 37,000 in the army, 12,300 in the air force, and 4,300 in the navy, a total of 53,600 troops or 16 percent of the entire German armed forces.

The new structure increased the proportion of temporary-career volunteers and regular servicemen by 3 percent at the expense of the conscript contingent. Conscription has not been abolished, despite growing criticism, but it has been reorganized. The basic term of service for conscripts has been shortened to ten months, followed by a two-month period during which they are liable for recall to active duty. Conscripts also may serve on a volunteer basis with higher pay for as long as twenty-three months. In 1996, more than 19,000 conscripts volunteered for a longer term of service averaging seventeen months in the army, which takes more than 80 percent of all those eligible for conscription. That figure represents more volunteer conscripts than had been expected and more than were actually needed at the time. However, after the authorized strength for conscripts volunteering for longer service had been raised, the planned new goal was not met: In 1998, applications from conscripts for a longer term of service fell about 25 percent short of the desired 23,000.

In times of crisis, the peacetime Bundeswehr of 340,000 soldiers can be rapidly augmented to 370,000 without mobilization by calling up conscripts as discussed above and by conducting additional reserve exercises. If re-servists are mobilized, the peacetime Bundeswehr can be increased to its au-thorized wartime strength of 650,000 to 700,000 men.

This new structure has made the Bundeswehr much more strongly de-pendent on mobility than before. With the exception of the crisis-reaction forces, no unit can be made fully operational without reservists. Therefore, a new Bundeswehr reservist concept was enacted in 1994. In the future, ac-cording to this plan, priority will be given to reserve-duty training of indi-vidual command personnel and specialists—that is, officers and noncom-missioned officers. This will be achieved through reserve-duty training periods and command-post exercises. Individuals who participate volun-tarily in reserve-duty training will receive better pay. In contrast, during the period of East-West conflict, priority was given to unit-mobilization exer-cises. Because the advance warning time was so brief, entire units had to be made operational as soon as possible. Now, because the expected advance warning period is much longer, essential training can be conducted even while a crisis is pending. In this situation, the greatest immediate need is for commanders, trainers, and specialists from the reserves.

The new Bundeswehr guidelines for manpower strength provided for 3,000 reservist training positions in 1998 (2,100 in 1995, 2,350 in 1996, and 2,500 in 1997), of which 2,400 were allocated to the army. In 1997, 58,000 reservists took part in exercises for an average of fifteen days. The Bundeswehr's deputy chief of staff is also the commissioner for the reserves, a fact that underscores the growing importance of the reserves in the Bundeswehr.

DEFINITION OF MAJOR MISSION

The mission of the Bundeswehr has changed fundamentally. In the era of East-West antagonism, it was confined almost exclusively to deterrence and defense against potential large-scale military aggression from the East, es-pecially nuclear deterrence. The Bundeswehr's mission was to defend Ger-man territory at the eastern border of the old Federal Republic against an immediate military threat. Therefore, although some of the forces were ear-marked to defend NATO's flanks in Europe, the Bundeswehr's area of op-erations was essentially Germany and central Europe. Detailed military plans had been made for the conduct of defensive operations.

A broad and diffuse array of risks has replaced the one-dimensional threat of the Cold War era—what formerly was the worst case is now an unlikely scenario. At the same time, however, the international responsibil-ities of a unified Germany have grown. Germany formerly was an importer of security; today it must contribute more to the security of others.

This state of affairs has created new tasks for the armed forces. In the future, the Bundeswehr must have the following capabilities.

- To defend Germany and its allies as part of the NATO alliance in NATO's area of operations.
- To furnish military support within the Atlantic alliance area of operations, should this be necessary for collective defense, or within the framework of crisis-management through NATO or the Western European Union (WEU).
- To participate in international crisis-management and conflict-prevention.
- To help in disasters and to conduct search-and-rescue operations in emergencies.

In the decidedly improved security environment, the primary functions of the German armed forces are territorial defense within the alliance framework and effective participation in international crisis-management. These missions determine what military capabilities are necessary and how they will be structured quantitatively and qualitatively. At the 1993 Bundeswehr Commanders' Conference, the Bundeswehr chief of staff succinctly described the future Bundeswehr as "capable of fighting, prepared to help." The "citizen in uniform," whose main mission formerly was the territorial defense of his country, is becoming the "citizen of the world in uniform," whose assignments will embrace all types of peace-support operations.

DOMINANT MILITARY PROFESSIONALS

A quarter-century ago the Bundeswehr introduced the concept of the "soldier-scholar." Since 1973 an academic course of study leading to a university degree has been compulsory for officer candidates applying for a fixed term of service lasting at least twelve years. For this purpose, Bundeswehr universities have been established under civilian management in both Hamburg and Munich. Consequently, the Bundeswehr probably has the world's most highly educated officer corps. Now the Bundeswehr is enhancing the concept of the "soldier-scholar" by adding the ideal of the "soldier-diplomat."

Prompted primarily by the changes in security policy objectives, the army is revising and rewriting its service regulations governing the conduct of operations (HDv 100/100). These regulations are the canon of army operations in wartime; they are intended to ensure that the training received by all military commanders meets a uniform standard. The army chief of staff intends that they should lay the intellectual groundwork for 2000 and beyond. A draft of the new army service regulations went into force for use in 1997. These regulations expand the concept of the conduct of operations. In addition to traditional wartime deployment, the regulations now deal with the conduct of "operations other than war." Such operations present a different challenge to the military command. This expansion of the Bundeswehr mission entails a new conception of the conduct of operations and (necessarily) of the troop commander.

The field on which the future military commander must operate can be described as follows.

- On the one hand, combat under extreme conditions; on the other, peace missions as well as support and rescue operations in crisis areas under conditions of strict neutrality.
- In the area of operations, war, emergencies, poverty, and chaotic conditions; at home, peace with live television reports from the theater and the need to care for families.
- On the tactical level, victory or destruction of the enemy; on the operational level, minimizing collateral damage.
- On the one hand, command based on mission-oriented tactics; on the other, the imposition of constraints on troops due to political conditions in the area of operations.

Other demands as well will be made on future military leaders' *Leitbild* (roughly, "concept of leadership"). Basic principles of command will include multinational cooperation, understanding and taking account of the political reasons of the military operation, considering public opinion and the media, knowing and observing international law, protecting the environment, and observing the United Nations' Rules of Engagement in military operations.

Although the Conduct of Operations regulations have a long history in the German army (they were first issued by General Field Marshal Helmuth von Moltke in 1869), the head of the Ministry of Defense section responsible for the revision writes as follows: "In accomplishing these tasks we will take as much advantage as possible of British and American experience and will not hesitate to simply translate and borrow whatever has proved its worth there."[6]

The new requirements for the future military leader caused the Bundeswehr's chief of staff to issue new regulations for conducting political information activities. Effective January 1, 1996, they give priority to the political education of commanding officers and noncommissioned officers. As stated in the introduction:

> The mission of the Bundeswehr requires that soldiers know what is involved in the political aspect of military decision making and conducting operations. Because of political and military responsibilities, soldiers also must be intellectually prepared for their future assignments. They must master

their assignments in a professional manner but also must be able to fit them into the political context. Every soldier must know and understand what he has been trained and deployed for, should the situation arise.[7]

PUBLIC ATTITUDES TOWARD THE MILITARY

The debate on foreign and security policy has come to a near standstill since German unification. The feeling that Germany faced an immediate military threat has evaporated. For most German citizens, the depressing security dilemma of many years has been resolved and other problems now have priority. Young people in particular have little general interest in politics and even less in security-related issues.

Nevertheless, the Bundeswehr has gained acceptance as an instrument for defense and for maintaining peace. The Bundeswehr (along with the Federal Constitutional Court and the police) is one of the fifteen state and societal institutions most trusted by the public.[8] Approval ratings for officers have risen noticeably in recent years. The need for armed forces is seldom questioned: NATO's approval ratings are high, even in the former East Germany. In view of the adversarial propaganda to which GDR citizens were subjected for decades, this outcome is not to be taken for granted.

On July 12, 1994, the Federal Constitutional Court declared it constitutional to deploy the Bundeswehr outside the NATO area of operations. This decision assured a secure legal framework for the forces. The public as a whole takes a positive view of this development: As of June 1998, 64 percent of the citizens supported the Bundeswehr engagement in Bosnia-Herzegovina and only 30 percent were opposed.[9] These figures mark an astonishingly rapid shift in public opinion. Three factors have contributed to this shift: (1) the major parties in the German Bundestag largely agree on this issue; (2) media coverage has been resoundingly positive; and (3) heavy casualties fortunately have not occurred so far.

The peace movement no longer exists; the dream of Germany as a "civilian power" at the heart of Europe has vanished. Eight out of ten German citizens believe that the Federal Republic should assume more responsibility in global affairs. Hardly anyone supports the idea that Germany should exercise extreme restraint in military matters for historical reasons. No one may be pressing for military assignments, but "checkbook diplomacy" of the kind practiced in the 1991 Gulf War is a thing of the past. Acceptance of the Bundeswehr, however, is not the same thing as willingness to make a personal contribution to peace and security by serving as a conscript. There is a growing trend toward leaving military tasks to the professionals—that is, temporary-career volunteers and regular servicemen. Most young people subscribe to the philosophy "Yes to the Bundeswehr, but without me!"

The trend toward seeking conscientious objector status remains strong,

although a majority of the population at large and a considerable proportion (46 percent) of young males aged between 16 and 20 support universal
conscription.[10] National military service and civilian alternative service are
both regarded as valid options for conscripts. It is no longer simply a matter of conscience to choose conscientious objector status: Cost-benefit considerations are of primary importance. Many view civilian alternative service as entailing less risk and fewer constraints on freedom. It is considered
better to be close to home, to live with one's parents, and to have more free
time and better pay than to be separated from one's girlfriend and family,
to live in cramped quarters, to obey orders, and to undergo military drill.

MEDIA RELATIONS

In addition to youth officers who deal with the younger generation, the Bundeswehr has always included full- and part-time press officers who are
charged with maintaining contact with the mass media. In 1990 the Academy for Information and Communication was established; this organization
is directly accountable to the press and information staff at the Federal Ministry of Defense. The academy's main task is to teach "communicative competence" in dealing with the media and the public.

The experience in Somalia exemplifies how the mass media can strongly
influence foreign-policy decision-making. The new army service regulations
on the conduct of operations (HDv 100/100), discussed above, reflect the
conclusions drawn from that experience; they make the correct handling of
the media an important task of the commanding officer. The ability to con-
vey the right information at the right time in the right place has been ele-
vated to a basic quality of leadership.

In 1993, Bundeswehr 2000 Public Information Activities was launched,
whereby the increased media presence is to enhance public acceptance of
the Bundeswehr and promote recruitment. For the first time, the Bundeswehr is using commercials in an annual autumn advertising campaign
on both public and private television, with the slogan "We are there. Bundeswehr." Analyses confirm that this campaign has influenced public opinion in favor of the Bundeswehr.

CIVILIAN EMPLOYEES

The Bundeswehr comprises the armed forces and the Bundeswehr administration. Article 87a of the Basic Law of the Federal Republic of Germany
governs the armed forces; Article 87b assigns responsibility for administrative tasks to a Federal Defense Administration independent of the armed
forces. This body, which is responsible for personnel matters and provides

the materiel needed by the armed forces, is divided into the Territorial Federal Defense Administration and the Armaments Organization. The Defense Administration has been structured in this way to relieve the armed forces of all tasks that are not purely military.

The Territorial Federal Armed Forces Administration meets the armed forces' military and civilian personnel needs. It is responsible for conducting induction examinations, calling up recruits for military service and reservists for reserve-duty training, procuring food and clothing, and recruiting and training civilian personnel for its own staff and for employment with the armed forces. In addition, this organization is responsible for maintaining barracks, ensuring that force-expansion manpower and materiel from civilian sources are available upon mobilization, calculating and disbursing pay for Bundeswehr personnel, interpreting and translating, operating data-processing facilities, and conducting vocational advancement programs for military personnel.

The civilians employed in the Armaments Organization ensure that the armed forces receive the necessary weapons and equipment. These civilians work in the Federal Office for Military Technology and Procurement in Koblenz and at agencies accountable to that office both in Germany and abroad. They study operating performance, conduct technical research and development, and determine how projects are to be carried out. In addition, they contract with industry for development, procurement, and maintenance, and ensure the standard of industrial products through technical evaluations and quality-control checks.

Civilians working in military units and installations include aircraft mechanics, ammunition workers, clerical staff and other office personnel, nurses, auto mechanics, firefighters, electricians, shoemakers, tailors, storekeepers, and guards. More than two hundred trades and professions are practiced in military units and installations.

Before 1989, when troop strength averaged 480,000 soldiers, the Bundeswehr employed about 180,000 civilians, or one for every 2.7 soldiers. To parallel the armed forces' reduction to 340,000 soldiers, a reduction of civilian personnel to slightly under 140,000 (one for every 2.5 soldiers) is scheduled for 2000. The reduction in civilian personnel will be proportionately smaller than the cuts in military manpower because greater demands now are being made on the Bundeswehr administration. The compulsory service system has become even more complicated. Environmental protection is another responsibility, which will continue to grow in importance. The amount of money the Bundeswehr has spent each year on environmental protection has risen from some 500 million DM in the mid-1980s to over 1.2 billion DM in 1997. A great deal of money will be needed to clean up the damage to the environment in the new federal states and to bring environmental protection up to the standard of the former West German.

WOMEN'S ROLE

Women have never had full status in the German military, with one exception: In the former GDR, women could join the National People's Army, either as volunteers for a fixed term of at least three years or as regulars serving for at least ten years. Their training included handling light weapons. In addition, in wartime women could be inducted into special service under the terms of the GDR service regulations. During the process of unification, nearly all female soldiers who had served with the National People's Army were discharged. Neither the media nor the women's associations, much less the general public, took any notice.

Earlier German military organizations employed women in numerous auxiliary functions. Especially during the two world wars, the military used women's services extensively. Still, German women never were mobilized to the same degree as their Anglo-Saxon counterparts. Even during World War II, women were only "civilians employed in the Wehrmacht sector." In both 1914 and 1939, they were classified merely as part of the military entourage.

Before the Bundeswehr was built up, the years were filled with domestic debate in which even the smallest details were disputed vehemently. Yet it was agreed almost unanimously that women in uniform would have no place in the new West German armed forces. Germany would not follow British or American precedent on this issue. Although the Bundeswehr represented a deliberate break with German military tradition, no one was willing to emulate the Atlantic allies in this regard.

This situation did not change until 1975, and even then the change was due mainly to a severe lack of medical officers. At that time, the Bundeswehr lacked almost half of the 2,100 doctors it needed. To permanently remedy this problem, the federal minister of defense oversaw the creation of the legal framework which, from 1975, governed the employment of women as medical officers if they qualified as doctors, dentists, veterinary surgeons, or pharmacists. Beginning in 1989, women were also employed as Medical Corps officer candidates. In 1991, careers were opened to women as noncommissioned officers and soldiers in the Medical Corps and the Corps of Musicians. Despite the constitutional provisions limiting women to service in these two branches, the number of women serving as Bundeswehr soldiers tripled from 1,300 in 1993 to 4,000 in 1998. Women make up 20 percent of Medical Corps personnel, and this proportion shows signs of increasing.

Women serving as soldiers in the Bundeswehr do not receive combat training, although they are trained to use handguns for self-defense and rendering emergency aid. Therefore even women who serve as medical orderlies are armed. Women are not allowed to stand guard duty or to serve in any protective capacity. The federal minister of defense wants to change this situation, however, and the legal possibilities are under investigation. According to the ministry's reasoning, standing guard duty in peacetime does not constitute military combat deployment but is a policing task in accordance with the Constitution.

The large number of female applicants to the Bundeswehr Medical Corps indicates that young women are increasingly interested in serving in the armed forces. In a survey conducted in November 1998 among young people between fourteen and twenty years of age, 33 percent of male but 42 percent of female respondents approved the unrestricted access of women to the Bundeswehr—including service in combat units.[11] Yet what has long been accepted practice in other countries' military organizations is making only slow progress in the Bundeswehr. In 1997, for the first time, a court found it unconstitutional that women may serve in the Bundeswehr only in the Medical Corps and the Corps of Musicians, and referred the decision to the Federal Constitutional Court. The court found that the existing regulations infringe on the basic constitutional right of equality between men and women. Further, they violate the basic right to choice of profession and the constitutionally guaranteed right of all German citizens to hold any public service office according to their aptitudes, abilities, and professional qualifications. The German Federal Armed Forces Association, which interprets the law similarly, is taking legal action in three additional cases. The final decision of the Federal Constitutional Court is still pending. Another case is currently before the European Court of Justice (ECJ). Should the European Court judges decide that the German regulation conflicts with council directive EC 76/207 concerning the equal treatment of men and women, a new situation would arise: EU law would take priority over national law, and even over the German Constitution.

SPOUSES AND MILITARY FAMILIES

In the past, the Bundeswehr implicitly expected members of military families to recognize that service had priority. Wives and children were expected to subordinate their individual needs and wishes to the requirements of the military. They were supposed to make as few demands on their husbands' and fathers' time as possible, and to function as sources of encouragement so that the men could do their duty. A "staunch little military wife" stood beside her soldier husband, who was committed to a lofty ethic of selfless service. She not only shielded him from all the minor annoyances of family life but also showed a positive commitment to the military system.

Such role sets were maintained largely intact until well into the 1970s. As long as they prevailed, relations between soldiers' families and the military remained largely uncomplicated and attracted very little attention. Soldiers' families did not undergo scrutiny by researchers and the administration until social change finally began to affect relations between the military and military families. These relations became increasingly complicated as families began to be revealed as a "disturbance factor."

A growing number of soldiers' wives hold jobs, and both husbands' and wives' approval of wives' employment has increased. Wives are becoming less willing to orient themselves exclusively toward military demands. Family affairs are now rated as more important than demands made by the service, and the amount of leisure time available to families is gaining importance.[12]

Soldiers' families are becoming less willing to move constantly. According to the 1994 report by the parliamentary commissioner for the federal armed forces, the percentage of married soldiers taking their families along when they were transferred declined from 56 percent in 1985 to 16 percent in 1994.[13] The most important criteria for soldiers' willingness to be transferred are decreasingly those involving promotion and career and, increasingly, "compatibility with family life" and other societal factors. The social groups with which soldiers interact are increasingly civilian, and the groups to which they relate most strongly are consequently more heterogeneous today than in the past.

The Bundeswehr is considering an array of policies to deal with these problems; one possibility is extra pay for those who are willing to be mobile. Such measures, however, cannot be described as a military family policy of the type implemented by other countries. The basic reason for this is that the Bundeswehr does not regard soldiers' families as part of the military community, but as part of society as a whole. Wives and other family members are not viewed as belonging to the military. The "paternalistic" welfare services that cover almost all areas of life in many military organizations outside Germany have a strong side effect: They exercise a great deal of control over soldiers and their families both on and off active duty. Such a state of affairs seemed neither politically desirable nor socially feasible when the Bundeswehr was established.

HOMOSEXUALS IN THE MILITARY

There are no official figures or percentages for homosexual soldiers; the Bundeswehr respects soldiers' right to privacy. Homosexual soldiers are not listed as such, and statistical evidence on the incidence of homosexuality in the armed forces has not been collated. Although sexual orientation is a criterion when conscripts are called up and when volunteers' fitness for service is being assessed, virtually nobody except the doctors concerned hears anything about it.

The military is still a community of men in close quarters, and military personnel policy tries to prevent problems that could be caused in a unit by homosexual soldiers on duty. Young men eligible for conscription are asked during induction about possible homosexual tendencies, if any appear evident. The same is true during the medical examination given to volunteers. Most homosexual recruits disclose their sexual orientation if the doctor examining them steers the conversation around to the subject. The doctor then must decide (if necessary, on the basis of a separate medical examination conducted by a specialist) whether and to what extent the conscript involved is "capable of fitting into a community"—that is, whether he can be integrated into a male military community without attracting notice because of his sexual orientation. If the question cannot be decided unequivocally, he is discharged as "mentally unfit for service" in accordance with military examination regulations.

In practice, recruits who have disclosed a homosexual orientation are usually discharged on the grounds of personality traits attested by the medical specialists consulted. Everyone seems to be satisfied with this solution. It is in the interest of the recruits, who are exempt from compulsory service (and also from civilian alternative service), and it is equally in the interest of unit leaders, who do not want such men in their units.

Homosexual orientation does not render a regular serviceman or a temporary-career volunteer unfit for military service, nor is it grounds for discharge. Nevertheless, it affects the assessment of a soldier's fitness for service because it restricts his assignments. Homosexual regular servicemen and temporary-career soldiers are not considered suited to be superiors. Attitudes toward homosexuality have become more liberal as societal values have changed, but reservations about homosexuals persist. If a commanding officer is known to have homosexual tendencies, conventional wisdom has it that his authority as a unit leader or instructor is seriously impaired. This, in turn, may affect the troops' discipline, cohesion, and performance.

Temporary-career volunteers and regulars advance up a career ladder of various staff and line assignments. On every rung, their assignments may include functioning in some leadership capacity; that is, they will be vested with the power of command. Because commanding officers and noncommissioned officers with overt homosexual tendencies lack credibility in the unit, they cannot effectively be employed and advanced within the framework of command and control systems as required by military structure and planning. Because they are restricted in their exercise of command, the chances of promotion normally open to heterosexual regulars and temporary-career volunteers are generally closed to homosexuals. The normal practice is as follows.

- Homosexual temporary-career soldiers and regulars are relieved of their command if their sexual orientation becomes known or if they admit it themselves. If they are serving in high-security assignments, their cases are handled individually to determine whether they may remain.

- Under military regulations, a lieutenant may be discharged at any time until the end of his third year of service after receiving his commission on grounds of unfitness for service as a career officer. This regulation is applied in cases of homosexual orientation.

- Homosexual temporary-career volunteers and regular servicemen who have served for more than four years are not required to retire prematurely, nor are they discharged before completing their terms of service.

- Volunteers for service as temporary-career soldiers or as regulars are not employed if they are known to be homosexual, and volunteers may not transfer to regular status.

The policy practiced by the Bundeswehr as outlined above has been upheld repeatedly by the courts, specifically in 1978, 1984, and 1990, and again by a decision of the Federal Administrative Court dated November 18, 1997. The court found that homosexuality represents an "aptitude deficiency"; this is sufficient grounds for upholding the right of the military, as an employer, to refuse to allow homosexual soldiers to function in command positions or as instructors and trainers.

The federal German government reaffirmed this position on an occasion offered by a parliamentary query in 1997. Sexual orientation is not a significant criterion for fitness for military service; the decisive factor is whether the conscript is found, on induction, to be "sufficiently capable of adapting to communal conditions so that he can be integrated into the daily training routine." In addition, commanding officers and instructors in positions of authority must expect to be transferred if they make homosexual proclivities known. In justification, the government pointed out that any loss of personal authority which might result could be expected to weaken the operability of the armed forces.

A soldier's homosexual orientation does not constitute an offense against service regulations; consequently it is not punishable as such. What soldiers do off duty and outside the Bundeswehr is their concern. The situation is different, however, if homosexual behavior occurs on duty: Court decisions have confirmed that homosexual acts committed by soldiers on duty cannot be tolerated. This is certainly the case if a superior in his capacity as such molests a subordinate, forcing him to engage in homosexual acts against his will. In a 1988 decision, the Federal Administrative Court defined such incidents as a violation of the inalienable dignity of man as guaranteed by the Constitution:

> The liberalization of the penal code with regard to homosexuality may not, and does not, apply to the relationship between superior and subordinate.

> It would be an intolerable state of affairs if young conscripts serving in the Bundeswehr in compliance with the National Military Service Act were to be exposed to sexual assaults by their superiors.[14]

Homosexuality tends to be a purely academic issue for soldiers in their daily military routine. The incidence of serious breaches of discipline connected with homosexuality is extraordinarily low: From 1981 until 1992, only 5.2 disciplinary court proceedings a year, on average, involved homosexual behavior among soldiers.

In the Bundeswehr the proportion of homosexual soldiers is noticeably less than the percentage of homosexual men in German society at large. One reason may be that very few conscripts known to have homosexual tendencies are inducted, and that homosexual applicants for military service as temporary-career volunteers or as regulars are not accepted. On the other hand, homosexual men may tend to avoid service in the armed forces because they may be made uncomfortable by close contact with others in cramped quarters and by strong social control. Because they have little interest in entering the armed forces, pressure groups representing homosexuals have not lobbied for changes in treatment by military personnel management in the Bundeswehr.

CONSCIENTIOUS OBJECTION

The Basic Law leaves open the question of whether the Federal Republic of Germany should maintain a conscript army or a volunteer army for its defense. When the Bundeswehr was conceived, the Bundestag voted in favor of compulsory military service. The constitutional foundation of such service is Article 12a of the Basic Law; the pertinent statutory regulations are set forth in the National Military Service Act of July 21, 1956, as amended. Since that act came into force, more than eight million young German men have served as conscripts in the Bundeswehr.

There is an inherent contradiction between compulsory military service and conscientious objection. Although it is a constitutional duty to render service involving the use of arms for the public good, the Basic Law also guarantees the right to object to such service on grounds of conscience. It resolves this contradiction by giving precedence to the individual's freedom of conscience.

Recruits must petition for conscientious objector (CO) status; the proportion of petitions granted has recently leveled off at between 88 and 90 percent. Conscripts who receive CO status are required to perform civilian alternative service for a term of thirteen months, in tasks that are primarily social services benefiting the community.

Under the regulations in force since 1983, the state has, in practice, waived its absolute claim to compulsory military service, thus leaving to the individual the decision to serve. Those who wish to serve go to the Bundeswehr; those unwilling to do so stay away. In September 1997, more than 150,000 conscientious objectors were engaged in civilian alternative service. After two years of declining figures, the number rose again to a total of 171,657 applications in 1998. Currently 30 to 35 percent of males eligible for conscription seek CO status. Since 1956, more than two million young men have become conscientious objectors.

A glance at the statistics shows the following development in COs' status: Until the late 1960s (at a time affecting men born between 1938 and 1947), being a conscientious objector deviated from the norm. Conscientious objectors were socially outside the mainstream, and few men petitioned for this status. Civilian alternative service was not established until 1961, four years after the first conscripts had been inducted.

By about 1968, a relatively short time span, the number of petitions for CO status had doubled, although the wider society still regarded compulsory military service as part of a normal man's biography. Viewed in this light, the men born between 1948 and 1950 can be considered the vanguard of a broad-based conscientious objector movement.

In the following years the number of petitions for conscientious objector status rose dramatically. This development established conscientious objection as a social phenomenon, despite (or perhaps because of) the numerous administrative regulations governing it. Since then it has become an institution accepted so widely that one may call it a mass phenomenon of social normalization.[15]

Although conscientious objectors engaged in civilian alternative service were initially considered shirkers, their approval ratings now "are on a par with those for doctors," according to Dieter Hackler, the commissioner for civilian alternative service. The work done by COs engaged in civilian alternative service contributes substantially to maintaining the social safety net.

From the standpoint of social psychology, civilian alternative service ensures that unwilling recruits are immediately filtered out of the armed forces. It is an outlet for social pressure because conscription has long been rejected by many members of the younger generation, and advocates of a professional military are represented there in large numbers. Without the right of conscientious objection and civilian alternative service, conscription would receive significantly more criticism on social grounds. As matters now stand, civilian alternative service actually supports conscription.

ORGANIZATIONAL FOCUS

Today the Bundeswehr must operate with less funding than at any time since it was established. At the same time, because of the new tasks it faces, increased investment in materiel is urgently needed. In addition, because of

German unification, investment in infrastructure is necessary. Market-economy methods and tools must enhance the quality and efficiency of resource deployment so that a target of 30 percent investment in the defense budget may be met once again.

In March 1993 the federal minister of defense established the Work Group for Limiting Operation Expenses. Since that time the group has developed proposals for limiting or reducing operating expenses in the armed forces and in sections of the Federal Defense Administration, in order to release financial resources for needed investment. It found a substantial potential for economizing.

To exploit this potential effectively, a dual approach is needed. On the one hand, it is necessary to think in terms of business management, down to battalion and company levels. In November 1993 the Federal Minister of Defense took steps to set this long-term process in motion, ordering the development of a "cost and performance responsibility system" to establish transparency and to tap the forces' creativity in improving procedures. In this sense the Bundeswehr is following in the footsteps of large industrial enterprises that consider a gradual but steady improvement in performance and the decentralization of responsibility the best ways to rationalize operations. On the other hand, competition must be encouraged, within both the Bundeswehr and industry. This approach is being tried in the British armed forces, where it is known as "market testing."

Since mid-1993, the Federal Ministry of Defense has discussed privatization options with the German defense industry. As a result of comparisons with industry and assessing what the Bundeswehr can accomplish with its own resources, cost-cutting proposals have been made by the Armaments Organization, particularly the Naval Arsenal, and by the armed forces themselves. Using this approach, the army, the air force, and the navy are exploring ways to make better use of their logistic and technical facilities and to reduce total manpower strength by centralizing and by eliminating duplicate capabilities.

All of these considerations are based on the assumption that the changed security situation will allow the further downsizing of logistical units, the transfer of functions to industry, and the pooling of stocks and facilities.

The objective is to tilt the current ratio between investment and operation expenses toward investment so that the Bundeswehr can be reshaped. For this purpose, the savings made by the Bundeswehr through economizing and rationalization measures must be available for investment.

The entire peacetime armed forces organization, including the Bundeswehr administration supporting it, is expected to operate economically. In the past, performance received priority without consideration of expense. In the future, thinking in terms of performance must be combined with economical operation. Operating economically will become essential in conducting military affairs.

CONCLUSION

In general, the model underlying this book applies well to the German experience. The variables of a Postmodern military are applicable to the Bundeswehr, with certain exceptions due to national peculiarities. In particular, the model's expectations concerning conscription, the role of women in the forces, and the place of homosexual servicemen are not borne out. Because the military forces of democratic societies tend to reflect the societies they defend, changes in these areas will come from German society as a whole rather than from within the Bundeswehr.

This seems quite unlikely at the present time. On the contrary, approval ratings for conscription are higher than ever before: Two-thirds of Germans want to keep conscription. In practice, universal conscription has become universal public service for men. Conscription not only meets the armed forces' manpower requirements; it also satisfies a broad array of important social and political needs. "Fairness" in induction is not a problem: Roughly 86 percent of the pool of young men eligible each year are approved as fit for service. Of these, all but 2 percent are inducted into active military service or alternative civilian service.

In addition, conscription most closely embodies the ideal of the "citizen in uniform." A conscript army is considered a more intelligent army. Also, because the Bundeswehr is becoming more conservative, conscription is generally regarded as socially and politically more desirable. Nonetheless, the possibility that conscription might be abolished cannot be ruled out. If Bundeswehr manpower strength is further reduced in the face of a diminished threat to European security and if the Bundeswehr is changed into an intervention force to meet the requirements of a new NATO strategy, it will grow increasingly difficult to justify universal conscription convincingly to the public and to operate it effectively.

The idea of admitting women to the Bundeswehr without restriction is gaining ground. Women are not needed to maintain troop strength; currently there are enough male applicants. In the early months of 1998, the ratio of applicants to places available was 3 to 1 in the ranks and as noncommissioned officers, 5 to 1 for officers, and 11 to 1 for Medical Corps officers. The last of these ratios includes female applicants; as mentioned earlier, women are admitted as officers in the Medical Corps.

In addition, the German public has reservations about incorporating women fully into the Bundeswehr. Skeptics' opinions tend to be confirmed by reports of sexual harassment suffered by female soldiers in other countries' armed forces. Neither women's associations nor homosexual interest groups have exerted pressure on politicians and the Bundeswehr to alter the existing recruiting practice. Indeed, homosexual men seem to be avoiding the armed forces.

Multilateralism is the most notable feature of the postmodern Bundeswehr. For centuries, armed forces embodied the nation-state and symbolized national sovereignty. Today, however, it is difficult to find even one German soldier who is serving exclusively under national command. Multinationalism has become a fundamental structural principle of the Bundeswehr. To ensure the legitimacy of military missions, Bundeswehr soldiers consider it important that operations be conducted multinationally— that is, jointly with soldiers of other nations. This perception underscores the postnational orientation of the Bundeswehr and its soldiers.

NOTES

1. Arnulf Baring, "Wie neu ist unsere Lage? Deutschland als Regionalmacht," *Internationale Politik*, Vol. 50 (Apr. 1995), p. 13.
2. See Georg-Maria Meyer and Sabine Collmer, *Zum Einsatz bereit? Bundeswehrsoldaten und ihr neuer Auftrag* (Wiesbaden: Deutscher Universitäts-Verlag, 1997), p. 91.
3. The following multinational corps are stationed entirely or partially in Germany: (1) the Allied Command Europe Rapid Reaction Corps (ARRC), (2) the EURO-CORPS, (3) the First German-Dutch Corps, (4) the Second German-American Corps, (5) the Fifth American-German Corps, and (6) the (old) German-Danish Corps (LANDJUT). With Poland's entry into NATO on March 12, 1999, this last has been enlarged to become the tri-national German-Danish-Polish Corps (with three divisions). Renamed NORTHEAST, its headquarters have been moved from Rendsburg, Germany, to Stettin, Poland.
4. *Standardization* is the general NATO term for a dynamic process that can reach different levels of efficiency. These levels, in ascending order, are compatibility, interoperability, interchangeability, and, finally, commonality.
5. INRA, November 1998; SINUS, November 1998.
6. Hubertus Muehlig, "Truppenfuehrung bleibt eine Kunst," *Truppenpraxis/ Wehrausbildung*, Vol. 39 (March 1995), p. 197.
7. Department of Defense, *Weisung zur Durchfuehrung der politischen Bildung in den Streitkraeften ab 1 January 1996* (Bonn, July 12, 1995), p. 1.
8. INRA, Nov. 1998.
9. EMNID, June 1998.
10. EMNID, July 1998; SINUS, May 1998.
11. SINUS, Nov. 1998.
12. See Georg Maria Meyer and Siegfried Schneider, "Die belastete Soldatenfamilie," *Working Paper 24* (Munich: German Armed Forces Institute for Social Research, June 1989).
13. Parliamentary Commissioner for the Federal Armed Forces, *Annual Report 1994* (Bonn: German Bundestag Printed Matter 13/700, 1995), p. 25.
14. Federal Administrative Court–Wehrdienstsenat, "Decision of 11 November 1988" (2 WD 69/87), *Dokumentarische Berichte*, Edition B, 9, 37 (1989), p. 122.
15. See Hans-Georg Raeder, "Kriegsdienstverweigerung im neuen Deutschland: Eine empirische Bestandsaufnahme," *Working Paper 92* (Munich: German Armed Forces Institute for Social Research, June 1994).

6

The Netherlands: The Final Professionalization of the Military

JAN S. VAN DER MEULEN

The Berlin Wall had only recently been torn down when Saddam Hussein, president of Iraq, offered the world an opportunity to enforce a new international order. Like many other countries, The Netherlands contributed its share during the Gulf War. A number of ships, medical units from the navy and army, and Patriot and Hawk squadrons from the air force participated in the coalition led by the United States and legitimized by the United Nations. After Desert Shield and Desert Storm, a marine company and some army units took part in "Provide Comfort," an operation intended to safeguard Kurds in the north of Iraq.

The country's political willingness to make military units available during the Gulf War was rather conspicuous, and involved debate and some dissent. NATO partner Turkey even was forced to politely refuse a squadron of Dutch F-16s which it did not need for its defense. At the same time, it was recognized that the country did not stand up to the "real" test of international commitment, namely sending ground troops. There was a growing awareness that the army was not especially well prepared to react quickly and adequately to this kind of out-of-area operation—not only because for forty years it had been focused on preparation for warfare in the plains of northern West Germany, but also because more than half of its personnel were draftees and could be sent out of area only on a voluntary basis.

Although the Gulf War did not lead directly to abolishing the draft, it gave rise to the Defense White Paper, published in the spring of 1991. The White Paper contained extra arguments for raising an airmobile brigade consisting exclusively of professional soldiers.[1] The rationale for this brigade stemmed from the air-land battle doctrine formulated in the context of the Cold War, but soon it grew into a symbol of a new army made fit for new missions. Nobody could foresee that four years later Dutchbat, a battalion from this elite unit, would play a tragic role during a UN peacekeeping mission in the former Yugoslavia.

In writing about the Dutch military during the watershed period after the Cold War, one must discuss Srebrenica. The fall of this "safe area" in

July 1995 evoked emotional and sometimes bitter debate in The Netherlands. The fate of thousands of Muslim men, slaughtered in probably the worst war crime of post-1945 Europe, created doubts about whether more could and should have been done. Whether or not The Netherlands "lost its innocence,"[2] support for sending professional armed forces on new missions was diminished—if not in the eyes of the public, then certainly among politicians. From the start, the military had been somewhat skeptical about next-generation peacekeeping. It remains to be seen whether the line between civilians and the military is blurring or hardening in this respect.

In this chapter I discuss the period from 1989 to 1999. During this time, crucial decisions and painful experiences changed the Dutch military to a degree unprecedented in the previous forty-five years. To clarify these changes and occasionally to put them in perspective, I set them against the background of the Late Modern (1950–90) as well as the Modern period (pre-1950). I will refer to the Modern period mostly in brief glimpses. I will treat the Late Modern period somewhat more precisely because it cannot be regarded as a single time span. A number of elements did not survive the cultural revolution of the 1960s undamaged, even if the effects of that period were delayed.

In this chapter, the topics treated in this book are grouped into four sections. Under "Assessing Security" I discuss perception of threat, definition of mission, and force structure. "Managing Change" covers the dominant military professional, organizational identification, and civilian employees. In "Opening Up Military Communities," I address spouses, women, and homosexuals. "Mobilizing Support, Coping with Criticism" is concerned with public attitudes, media relations, and conscientious objection. In the concluding section, "Civilianization, Professionalization, Marginalization," I review the general theme: the blurring of lines between the civilian and the military in the Postmodern period.

ASSESSING SECURITY

Perception of Threat

In the Modern period, enemy invasion was the worst-case scenario in international security. Neutrality was the foreign policy option used by The Netherlands, from the beginning of the nineteenth century until World War II, to protect itself from this threat. This period was ended by the German invasion of May 1940 and, in late 1941, by the Japanese occupation of the Dutch East Indies. In August 1945 another threat materialized in the latter theater: an anticolonial uprising that resulted in the independent Republic of Indonesia.

During the East-West confrontation, nuclear war came to be the ultimate threat, although the fear of this possibility passed through stages. Also, the possibility of enemy invasion did not disappear. Certainly during the 1950s, "The Russians are coming" was a half-joking expression hiding real concerns. In later stages of the Cold War, invasion sometimes was described rhetorically as preferable to nuclear or even conventional war, both of which would have spelled doomsday for Western Europe. Doubts, debate, and dissent, evoked by the paradoxes of deterrence in general and the cruise missile issue in particular, reached a peak around 1980. The coming to power of Mikhail Gorbachev, the INF Treaty of 1987, and several other "historical moments" were decisive in reducing the fear of nuclear as well as conventional war. Indeed, these events marked a political and psychological "retreat from doomsday."[3]

After 1990 The Netherlands, like every other state, had to radically redefine its security interests. Short of invasion and major war, other diffuse, indirect threats were identified. Though neither term is the ultimate in conceptual clarity or policy guidance, *subnational* and *nonmilitary* are apt categories for summarizing the way the new threats have been labeled. Civil wars on Europe's periphery (and elsewhere) fall into the first category. As emphasized in the Defence Priorities Review of 1993 and its 1999 update,[4] these conflicts have the potential of triggering involvement by neighboring states, including members of NATO. Nonmilitary threats include crime, terrorism, and ecological disaster. It has been argued that a broad concept of security should not be allowed to obscure hard-core military scenarios, even if these are far from imminent in the foreseeable future or are far out of area.

Theoretically, a vast, direct military threat to Western Europe, up to the level of a strategic breakthrough, could come from the Russian Federation. According to the official assessment, the Russian armed forces will not be capable of that kind of military deployment in the center of Europe for years or even decades to come.

From the Dutch defense and foreign policy perspective, purely military threats are not strong or unequivocal enough to define a mission in themselves. Some would contend that this situation makes the military a luxury.

DEFINITION OF MISSION

Defense, deterrence, and *crisis management* are the mission-defining labels that correspond to the successive stages of threat. As implied above, defense of homeland in the pre-1950 period included the Dutch East Indies. During the Cold War, deterrence did not exclude the notion of territorial defense. During this period, support of the alliance became crucial, no matter what was emphasized in mission definition. The Netherlands became a dedicated member of NATO, convinced that the United States was indispensable for Europe's security.

Since 1990, a twofold task has been defined for the military: to conduct crisis-management operations as part of Dutch security policy and to protect the integrity of national and allied territory. These tasks are on an equal footing; the former is more urgent, and the latter has priority in case of concurrence. The difference between the two may be fading. Crisis management is the official, overarching concept for new missions: preventive deployment, humanitarian intervention, peacekeeping, peace building, and (if necessary) enforcement of peace. The elaboration of these concepts, from a political as well as a military perspective, is an ongoing endeavor.

Though peacekeeping tasks are not completely new—during the 1980s, for example, an Army battalion took part in the U.N. mission in Lebanon— in recent years they have taken the Dutch military all over the world. *Qua patet orbis* ("to the ends of the earth") was and still is the motto of the marine corps, but now it could be applied to all of the armed forces. Units from the army, navy, air force, and military police have served from Cambodia to Angola and from Bosnia to Haiti. Routines already have been developed for monitoring elections, verifying weapons agreements, and controlling embargoes; the crucial element of new missions is crisis management proper, where peacekeeping and peace enforcement intersect. When, where, and how Dutch troops should contribute to these kinds of interventions is also a matter of ongoing debate. Fairly precise criteria have been formulated, elaborating on political goals, military means, and public support. The relevance of these criteria is thought to be limited, however, because every mission allegedly is a unique case.

As suggested above, this debate acquired a different tone and weight after the fall of Srebrenica and the fateful role of Dutchbat. The soul searching in society and the armed forces still has not ended. On one level, lessons learned involve the balancing of "narrow" national security interests against the ideal of safeguarding a lawful international order. On another level, identification with and loyalty to the United Nations—traditionally high in The Netherlands—are set against the necessity of sound military mandates and unambiguous command structures.[5]

In sum, three related effects can be identified in the wake of Srebrenica. First, future missions are bound to be accepted more prudently (for instance, in July 1996 there was reluctance to join a possible humanitarian intervention in Burundi, even though another genocide seemed at hand). Second, more emphasis will be placed on the other main task of the military beside peacekeeping and humanitarian intervention: protecting the integrity of national and allied territory. (Though again the difference between defense and crisis management seems to be fading.) Third, greater prudence and a different emphasis have caused some duality in the political and professional business of guiding the military. Depending most of all on the development of international security, the consensus about mission definition might split gradually or suddenly along left-right lines and/or civilian-military lines.

Force Structure

Since August 31, 1996, the armed forces of The Netherlands have consisted exclusively of professional personnel. The new text of Article 98, Paragraph 1 of the Constitution reads: "For the protection of the interests of the state, there are armed forces exclusively consisting of volunteers *and possibly of conscripts*" (emphasis added). The mobilization of draftees is not explicitly ruled out. Formally, conscription has not been abolished, only suspended.

Since 1814 the draft has been one of the two pillars of the system for recruiting what came to be known as a cadre-conscript force. Until 1898, *remplaçants* were the pillar of the militia; thereafter conscription became individual. Draftees were selected by lottery to serve for a short period (five months) and then were added to the reserves. From the beginning, it was constitutionally forbidden to send draftees overseas. Instead, a colonial all-volunteer force was used to pursue imperialistic and constabulary policies in the East Indies. In 1946, the Constitution was changed so that a conscripted expeditionary force could be sent to fight the Indonesian Republic.

During the Cold War the cadre-conscript force became a true standing mass army. Never before had so many served for such a long time—as long as twenty-four months in the 1950s. Gradually the length of service decreased to twelve months in the 1980s. Although the percentage of men actually serving diminished as well (only one out of two was declared fit), the concept of a mass army was followed until the end. Contrary to cultural and technological predictions, the draft survived, though not without debate, dissent, and frustration. A historical, strategic change in international relations was needed to break its logic and legitimacy. In the spring of 1993 The Netherlands became one of the first countries in continental Europe to reach this conclusion.

The end of the East-West conflict and especially the disintegration of the Soviet Union served as important reasons for suspending conscription. The projected size of the armed forces by 2000 (an overall reduction of 40 percent, and 50 percent in the Army alone) is such that it would be virtually impossible to distribute the burden of the draft in any fair way. Calling up a minority of draftees could be justified under the conditions of threat that the Cold War entailed. Continuing with this policy in the new international context could no longer be legitimized, not only because this minority would shrink even further, but also because of the second principal task given to the military: participating in worldwide crisis-management. Politicians as well as the public felt that draftees could not be sent on faraway missions only faintly related to national security. These missions, it was argued, required professional soldiers, well trained and immediately deployable. Whether enough of these soldiers can be recruited, not only in quantity but also in quality, has been one of the main practical concerns of the debate. During the transition years, recruitment results have been rather positive,

but also somewhat biased because of substantial numbers of volunteers motivated to avoid the draft. In 1997, the first post-draft year, immediately
shortages in recruitment made themselves felt, in particular at the sharp end
of the combat arms, but also in functions which require specialist expertise.
Both kind of vacancies cause concern and have elicited extensive recruiting
campaigns.[6]

For the present, conscripts constitute the bulk of the reserve force; phasing them out in that capacity will take about fifteen years. By 2010, all reservists will be former professional soldiers. In principle, they will be called
to duty only in extraordinary circumstances. Most probably these would relate to major conflicts threatening allied and national territory. Except for a
very small number of specialists, reservists will not be used for crisis-
management, humanitarian intervention, or peacekeeping—in short, for
new out-of-area missions.[7]

MANAGING CHANGE

The Dominant Military Professional

During the 1970s, "identity crisis" became a common diagnosis in the military profession. Whether or not substantial numbers of officers experienced
such a crisis, there was reason to believe that the paradoxes of deterrence
and modernity put them off balance. Today there is again talk of a crisis.
Certainly the profession is in flux: Its contours are losing their sharpness, its
coherence is dissolving.[8]

The degree to which new missions call for a different kind of military
professional is a matter of lively debate in journals and at conferences.[9] The
evolving official line appears to be that although blue-helmeted missions require additional qualifications, the soldier's identity derives from his or her
green-helmeted competence.[10] In other words, he or she must be combat-
oriented in training and in attitude, and must master new skills in addition,
not instead.

To the notion of the combat leader, another layer of secondary roles has
been added. After the manager and the technician, the diplomat and the
rescue worker are emerging. The diplomat generally is situated in the
upper part of the hierarchy; the rescue worker, who quite often performs
constabulary-type tasks, is found at the grassroots.

Although the soldier-diplomat and the soldier–rescue worker–police-
man can be said to dominate public perceptions, managers and technicians
probably are equally prominent from an insider's viewpoint. Managers are
prominent because of the process of downsizing and restructuring. The
Dutch military is making an unprecedented move toward cost-effectiveness,
like many other large-scale organizations today.[11] Technicians are promi-

nent because of the consequences of the information age, which are felt throughout the organization and are making the updating of expertise essential.

Both of these roles relate to the scientification of armed forces, a long-term trend that dates from the Modern period and accelerated during the Cold War. If the overall level of managerial and technological sophistication is taken as a measure, from the curricula of military academies to the increase in university degrees, the soldier-scholar indeed can be viewed as a military role model. The term *scholar* is used here not in the sense of researcher or intellectual (though those types are present) but rather as a scientifically educated professional.

Like *scholar*, the term *statesman* must be qualified in order to depict a dominant kind of military professional. As suggested above, *soldier-diplomat* is more fashionable and more suitable in the context of new missions. If not for its unconstitutional connotations, one might gain the impression that the "soldier-politician" is on the rise on the home front. Downsizing and restructuring, together with peacekeeping practices, have increased the relevance of military advice as well as the possibility of conflict with political interests. Some disagreements have arisen concerning what can and cannot be said in public, and by whom. This situation is hardly new: During the Cold War, in the 1950s as well as the 1970s, military contributions to crucial defense debates seldom went unnoticed and occasionally led to involuntary dismissals of generals. Today, however, the question is whether new missions will lead to a structural change in professional advice, and the degree to which it is made public. The unpredictable mix of theater, mandate, and risk could make change in this area unavoidable.

The crux of professional advice relates to what is still defined as the core business of the military: the application of force. Whatever his other competencies, the typical military expert still claims a position somewhere on the continuum from combat leader to manager of violence—maximum violence, if necessary, or minimal violence, as required by constabulary roles. In the latter context, however, the risk of becoming a witness to atrocities, almost appearing to be an accomplice, would certainly damage personal and professional self-esteem. Another Srebrenica would no doubt push the military profession into a crisis. On the other hand, nobody knows how the military will stand up to any future battlefield test, short of high-tech performance in the air or at sea.

Organizational Identification

In the Dutch armed forces, certainty about functions and jobs has been faltering since the end of the Cold War. Until now (and probably for some time to come), professional flux has gone hand in hand with occupational turbulence. At the same time, military personnel confront the prospect of deployment on some kind of new mission and must face the possibility, in the worst case, of compulsory dismissal. This harrowing situation is under-scored by the political promise that nobody will be sacked within half a year after returning. Although in reality only a rather limited number of persons will be let go, the fact of layoffs constitutes a break with the past. It did not happen even during the 1930s, when the economic crisis strongly affected the military. The alternatives to dismissal, however—salary cuts and dead-end careers—caused hardship in their own right. In 1933, as a consequence, a semimutiny took place aboard a Navy ship in the Dutch East Indies, and was violently crushed. In the aftermath of this incident, unions of military personnel were severely curtailed.

Today large unions, which are combining more frequently with their civilian counterparts, are important again in personnel policies, negotiating salaries, and all kinds of work- and career-related issues. Even if they have not been able to rule out the possibility of involuntary dismissal, they in-fluence and guard the quality of management methods used in downsizing. They do so on behalf of their membership: 80 percent of Dutch defense per-sonnel are union members.[12]

No matter how tactful, responsible, or even generous any negotiated policy is with respect to the shrinking numbers, such a process cannot fail to influence overall organizational identification, especially because years will pass before its effects subside. Logically, the identification will tend to become more occupational than institutional. When the organization loosens its institutional ties and takes away career security, the employees them-selves will adopt a more calculating outlook: Take the hint and run for (just) another job, internally or externally. In fact, for more than a decade the in-dividualizing of career patterns has been considered crucial for up-to-date human resource management. The move away from collective promotions, among other things, began officially with the end of the Cold War and has intensified the occupational orientation and turbulence caused by downsiz-ing policies.

Other factors also emphasize the occupational side of professional cul-ture. Of necessity, since the end of the draft, the recruitment appeals for short-term soldiers have become competitive in the labor market. The extra allowances for operational deployments are accordingly generous.

At the same time, however, the character and frequency of new mis-sions emphasize the institution, not only in terms of claiming members but also in terms of taking care of them. Postmission personnel policies have be-come a sensitive issue. As experience shows, the veteran of peacekeeping cannot be left to himself, and the responsibility of the organization does not end with the first debriefing. In an ironic twist of history, this lesson was learned from the veterans of the war in the East Indies. These men, ap-proaching their sixties and having numerous axes to grind, mobilized vet-erans of World War II and Korea and forced a kind of ex post facto institutional care. They wanted recognition, and achieved it to some degree. Most had been conscripts at the time of their deployment; the military never had meant anything to them as an occupation. In fact, their organizational identification may have been the most "civic" in recent Dutch military history. It remains to be seen whether the "civic," which in Modern and Late Modern times represented an additional motivation, will need and find a new anchor. The "world citizen in uniform" already has been proposed in that capacity. It seems too far removed from occupational considerations, however, just as the "UN mercenary" makes a caricature of those considerations.

Civilian Employees

As surveys show, those who feel most uncertain about their occupational future in the army are sergeants and civilians.[13] The former, who have been the backbone of the mass army, see the disappearance of many of their functions related to training conscripts. The latter always have felt like second-class employees, and their overrepresentation at the bottom of the organization makes them especially vulnerable to downsizing. The overall number of civilians probably will shrink even further, insofar as some of their functions and some of the employees themselves will be militarized.[14] This tendency will be strengthened by (among other things) the dominance of new missions calling for maximum deployability of personnel. This is not to say that civilians are categorically exempted from such missions; sometimes they will be granted temporary military status.

In the army, for example, the number of civilian employees as a percentage of voluntary enlistees declined gradually during the 1950s and 1960s, and stabilized around 1970 at roughly one-third. The projected number of civilians for about 2000 continues this trend, although not to a great extent. Overall, this development tends to contradict the prediction of a growing civilian component unless one makes another kind of comparison: between civilians and *all* uniformed personnel, whether volunteers or draftees. Eventually the disappearance of draftees due to downsizing could make a psychological and professional difference for civilian employees, although occupational pressure prevails at the present.

Surely operational considerations help to explain the position and percentage of civilians, but so do the career structures of professional soldiers and the differences in bureaucratic power and status. The differences between services cannot be overlooked: By 2000 the army is expected to have 29 percent civilian employees, the navy 26 percent, and the air force 13 percent. This point suggests that technology is too crude a predictor of the number of civilian employees, though no doubt it has been and remains an important variable in the distribution of functions.

These rough figures mask processes and changes that are not always detrimental to civilians. Moreover, civilian employees occupy essential positions at the top of the Defense Department, supervising personnel management and weapons procurement as well as budgetary issues. Balancing the (civilian) leaders in the central department with their (military) counterparts in the services has been the subject of regular reorganization, during which matrix structures come and go.

Two additional points must be made in this connection. First, since the 1960s, seeking management advice from civilian agencies on an array of topics has been standard practice at various levels of the organization. This practice has been strengthened by the continuing downsizing and restructuring. Second, the general trend toward privatization and outsourcing of tasks also affects the military in areas ranging from communication to education. It is still unclear how important this trend will become and how to appreciate its effects on the core business of the military (which presumably will not be privatized).

OPENING UP MILITARY COMMUNITIES

Spouses

In Modern times, noncommissioned officers had to ask permission from their superiors if they wanted to marry. Many years later, in Late Modern times, officers often refused promotion because of the toll it would take on their families in general and on their wives' career prospects in particular. Interpreting these facts in their respective historical frameworks would no doubt clarify the changing relationship between two greedy institutions. If we focus on the role of spouses and take into consideration the differences between services and ranks, a shift from integration to partial integration and then to segregation appears to be a plausible working hypothesis; the second of these phases would have lasted through the 1950s and into the 1960s.

Since the Late Modern period, functional segregation between family and the military has become the norm, with the notable exceptions of an army brigade stationed in Germany and naval units in the West Indies. For these units, various degrees of integration still apply to housing, schooling, and medical care, among other things. For the majority of personnel, however, medical care is a reliable indicator of spouses' (and children's) removal from military communities: Until recently they were eligible for free care by military doctors and military hospitals.

Concentrating the military in certain parts of the country (the army in the eastern provinces, the navy in Den Helder) probably generates networks of military personnel stretching beyond the workplace. Military communities, however, tend to intersect closely with civilian communities, not only because partners tend to have jobs outside the military, but also because the children attend "civilian" schools. Anecdotal evidence and parsimonious research data suggest that soldiers are active citizens in all kinds of settings, including sports clubs, Rotary, and city councils.[15]

One observation must be added to the general trend toward functional segregation between family and military. For obvious reasons, new missions have enhanced the partners' *emotional* involvement. Home-front committees, with meetings and magazines, have been organized. These initiatives and networks, which take institutional responsibility, are supported by the armed forces. In addition, the military makes sure that families have telephone access to information about ongoing missions, around the clock if necessary. The possibilities of direct communication between soldiers and families—whether by electronic means or by going on leave during missions—are far greater now than in earlier conflicts. The operational effects of soldiers taking leave sometimes cause concern; evidently the relationship between two greedy institutions still has an element of competition. Another area of concern is the hypothesized effect of soldiers' small nuclear families on the acceptance of casualties.[16]

Women

In principle, conscripts constituted a cross-section of young males from about eighteen to twenty-five years of age. Their "representativeness" was legendary and legitimating. Being all male, however, the conscripted population was utterly gender-biased; this was puzzling for feminists, among others. The end of the draft has changed this situation; women now can apply for a wider range of soldierly occupations than in the past.

Women's participation in the Dutch military is entering its third phase. The first was the period of separate corps, from World War II to the beginning of the 1980s. The second was the period of partial integration—partial not only because the draft applied to men only, but also because some units, notably the marine corps and the submarine service, remained closed to women. Partial or not, integration policies in the 1980s received a great deal of attention.

Women's entrance has been stimulated at different levels and in different ways. The military academies opened up to female cadets; lower in the organization, all kinds of corporal specialists were attracted by short-term contracts. Probably most important, men's general reluctance regarding female colleagues, not to mention superiors, gave way to matter-of-fact acceptance. In the beginning, the presence of women caused controversy (including some organized protest by spouses), but this situation gradually became normal.

During the 1980s and the first half of the 1990s, however, women's overall participation has constantly fallen below projected recruitment figures. Eight percent was the official target, but in the summer of 1998 the actual actual proportion of women, while on the rise, was 7.4 percent. This disappointing figure has puzzled everyone involved, and the causes are uncertain. Is it due to a failure of recruitment and retention policies? Is it still, behind a mask of political correctness, an effect of masculine mentality? Or is the figure low because Dutch women's work habits and preferences simply do not match those of the military?

In the summer of 1997, a bold policy move set the target at 12 percent—to be reached in 2010! A number of measures related to combining parental and soldierly roles aim at much higher retention figures for women. It seems certain, however, that whatever figure is reached, women still will be represented very unevenly throughout the organization. Until now, their absence has been as conspicuous among higher-ranking NCOs as among officers at the rank of lieutenant colonel and above. Time (among other things) will be needed before women's present representation among cadets and second lieutenants (15 percent) makes itself felt at the higher ranks. (The only female full colonel in the Dutch military is a physician.) In the navy and the air force a rather more substantial proportion of the enlisted personnel are female than in the army.[17] The combat arms (infantry and cavalry) are not formally closed to women, as is the marine corps, but their physical standards for entrance are so high that women normally cannot meet them.

Three related factors will influence women's further integration during the postconscription period: recruitment outcomes among young men, the saliency of gender diversity as an issue in its own right, and the prevailing image of organizational culture. In regard to the last of these factors, discipline, uniformity, and toughness are making a comeback in the Dutch armed forces. Such a correction of the "excesses" of conscript culture makes some sense, but it might be overdone and unintentionally might contribute to the impression of a macho community. This would be counterproductive for gender diversity.

Homosexuals and Ethnic Minorities

Gender, ethnicity, and sexual preference are often grouped together in discussions of diversity. As members of "minorities," women, ethnic minority members, and homosexuals tend to be viewed as related, even though they differ greatly from a sociological perspective. Ethnic minorities in the Dutch military have received somewhat less policy and research attention than women and homosexuals. This is bound to change, however, given their evolving demographic status. Recruiters will have to target them, and their integration may become a major issue. In fact, since the end of the draft, their presence in the military has risen from below 2 percent to almost 6 percent.

Homosexuals have been officially accepted in the military since the beginning of the 1970s. Active integration policies started in the mid-1980s, not least because of pressure from homosexuals themselves—soldiers, NCOs, and officers. They argued that official acceptance, no matter how important as a first step, was not sufficient and did not put an end to discriminatory practices. An extensive survey proved them right: The prevailing attitude in the armed forces could be described as "tolerance at a distance." As in the population at large, a virtual consensus about equal rights for homosexuals coexists with considerable uneasiness about the prospect of working closely with homosexual colleagues.

Policy measures include counseling programs for homosexuals and diversity training for heterosexuals—measures that are still in effect. It is justifiably feared, however, that budget cuts that affect educational programs may have consequences for lessons in diversity management. Aside from that, one can only speculate about the effects of the postconscription period on homosexual-heterosexual interaction. The percentage of declared homosexuals among draftees was higher than among professional soldiers. That situation was not changed even by the visibility and the symbolic effect of homosexual commanders, whether of a battalion or of a frigate.[18]

Just as with gender integration, if new disciplinary styles set a psychological premium on macho uniformity, the military may become even less attractive to gays and lesbians. Thus, in a sense, their coming out remains a measure of the organizational climate and of the openness of military communities.

MOBILIZING SUPPORT AND COPING WITH CRITICISM

Public Attitudes

Generally the major decisions about the Dutch military—reducing the forces, eliminating the draft—have been backed by substantial majorities of public opinion. Surely the fact that both decisions reduced the burden on society, in money and in personnel, encouraged a favorable response. Presumably there would not be much protest if additional financial cuts were announced.

Positive reasons, however, have been equally important. Participation in new peacekeeping missions is generally welcomed; so are specific deployments, with some nuances. The roles of rescue worker and diplomat have come to be viewed as normal and desirable for soldiers. At the same time, the public has not forgotten the possible need to defend allied territory, including their own country. NATO is as indispensable as ever; eastern European countries are welcome to take part; binational military arrangements with the Germans, the Belgians, and the British are acceptable. The notion of a European military has gained increasing support over the last few years, and a UN brigade at the disposal of the secretary general and the Security Council is also regarded as a worthwhile idea.

This short summary of public opinion surveys suggests that *apathetic* and *indifferent* are not the right terms to describe the country's post–Cold War mood toward the armed forces.[19] The public may not express as much support as supposedly prevailed during the most threatening phase of the Cold War, until the early 1960s. On the other hand, we do not find the critical, even hostile climate which reputedly predominated in much of the 1970s and part of the 1980s, and which culminated in the upheavals concerning the issue of cruise missile deployments. Public attitudes in the 1990s, and not only in opinion polls, could be labeled pragmatic, with an undercurrent of idealism. The most severe test so far—the deployment of troops in Bosnia—showed that public opinion does not simply turn negative when things go bad and that the public can tolerate at least some casualties.

To be sure, the initial strong support for participation in UNPROFOR gradually gave way to growing doubts about the wisdom of staying on. The fall of Srebrenica seemed to tip the balance between risks and outcomes. A month after the event, however, public support for staying in and going on had recovered. Evidently public morale had been boosted by the international community's more aggressive stance; this was symbolized by the French-British Rapid Reaction Force, which included a company of Dutch marines. Eventually the public even obtained what it had wanted initially: major NATO air strikes, in which a squadron of Dutch F-16s took a highly praised part. To the public, the participation in IFOR and SFOR was a foregone conclusion. NATO's intervention in Kosovo in spring 1999 received clear-cut support.

The ambivalence and prudence toward new missions, which have influenced political decision-making to some degree, have not affected the general public until now. Two latent structural strains, however, which in combination constitute a paradox, have the potential for eroding the support and the new legitimacy of the military. One involves the widely paraphrased hypothesis that tolerance for casualties is limited in the West. As suggested above, Dutch public opinion accepts some casualties, but would it be prepared to accept many? If so, under what circumstances and for what causes?

The second potential strain derives from one of the possible effects of political and military reluctance to deploy ground forces in risky, highly violent settings. If idealistic expectations are disappointed too often for that reason, the result might be skepticism about the role of military intervention in crisis-management and in preventing gross abuses of human rights. Rather logically, the public puts quite less emphasis on the classical task of defense, whether of allied territory or of the home country. From the perspective of crisis management and peacekeeping, NATO is seen as indispensable as ever. Of course, a bad turn in European security would make a difference and allied and territorial defense could once again become the only source of legitimacy.

Media Relations

It has been said (not without exaggerating and generalizing) that the typical military professional has a "particular dislike of two things: media and politics."[20] While the primacy of politics remains uncontested in principle, despite clashes of perception and interest, the "intrusions" of the media have been managed in different ways and with varying success. During the war in the East Indies, the military could and did manipulate and censor media coverage. Some degree of manipulation may have spilled over into the 1950s, but only insofar as the press itself played by the defense authorities' rules. Although in retrospect the harmony of this period should not be overestimated, *incorporated* is probably the most accurate term. Each service had its own access to radio broadcasting. At the end of the decade, however, some people in defense circles were complaining that newspapers were too keenly interested in scandals.

In the mid-1960s a second period of media relations began, which lasted until about the mid-1980s. The terms *defensive* on the part of the military and *offensive* on the part of the press suggest the lack of congruency that became typical. This situation was characteristic of the general change in journalists' approach to authorities and institutions, and also represented an overall polarization of society. The mass media in a democracy are a diverse group, however; in the latter process, the military had advocates as well as opponents.

In the 1980s a third phase gradually began when the Defense Department professionalized its public relations policies. Not without some mutual courtship, soldiers and journalists worked out a relationship that can be labeled businesslike. The end of the Cold War contributed to a more relaxed relationship, and the importance of new missions generated sympathetic reporting. (Journalists do not mind being shown around in faraway places.)

Srebrenica, however, was a rude reminder that the media follow their own instincts and interests, especially in the case of "bad news." Journalists did their job as they saw fit; they exposed and explored every presumed mistake they could find, whether military or political. In the process, the media provided a forum for numerous experts and commentators, sorting out causes and pointing out culprits from battalion commanders to the secretary general of the UN.

One of the policy conclusions reached in the aftermath of Srebrenica has been that soldiers at different levels of the organization should be better prepared to deal with the press. Media training should become a standard part of educational courses throughout the organization. At the same time, during deployment, control of who tells what to whom, and at what moment, should be strengthened. The effects of these measures will depend partly on the theater and the mission, and they will not prevent the press from muck-raking when events turn sour. In regard to relationship with the media, another lesson might be that a maximum of openness at the earliest possible moment could help prevent a continuing series of scoops and semiscoops.[21]

A sobering note in this context is the degree to which public opinion has evaluated the debacle of UNPROFOR. Although the public has not been blind to faults and frictions at the interface of the political and the military, and although it has not shed its doubts about whether the utmost was done to prevent genocide, public opinion has not crucified Dutchbat to the same degree as have some of the media. Evidently public opinion is not unequivocally under the influence of the mass media.

Conscientious Objection

Compared with the massiveness of public opinion and the prominence of the press, conscientious objection seems to be a minor story. Even in their immediate context—conscript culture—conscientious objectors in The Netherlands always have been very much a minority. Ironically, when their numbers were greatest, just after the end of the Cold War, their moral impact was at its smallest: Evidently conscientious objection was being used increasingly as a devious way of avoiding not only military but also alternative civilian service. In fact, the smallness of objectors' numbers accounted for the strength of conscientious objection; occasionally it evoked the image of the morally motivated individual standing up against the bureaucratic legalism of the state as well as the compliance of silent majorities. This position made it possible not only to appeal at times to public opinion and the mass media, but also, in a more structural sense, to infiltrate the motivational discourse of conscripts. The latter process won support especially in the 1960s and 1970s, when conscientious objection became more secular and more political.

Before that, beginning in 1924 with its first legal codification, conscientious objection had been regulated strictly by religiously inspired formulas, safeguarded by stern committees and long terms for alternative service. During the 1960s and 1970s this regime became much more relaxed, though not without conflict (the individual versus the state), and that relaxation attracted attention. Conscientious objection in The Netherlands, however, never implied easy, automatic exemption from service. To some degree, motivation was kept under surveillance; on the one hand, this regularly provoked new (symbolic) fights, but on the other it kept the numbers relatively low. During the 1970s the number stabilized at about 3,000 applications each year, while some 45,000 men served their time in the military.[22]

After 1989, the option of making the draft part of a full-fledged civic service was addressed. Although this idea drew public sympathy and seemed appropriate for dealing with vacancies in several sectors of society, it stood no chance against the eagerness to eliminate conscription and the dominance of economic discourse. Labor-market incentives were generally judged more effective than civic morality.

In the meantime, new missions have been a reminder that military professionals also encounter ethical dilemmas, sometimes including the need to make decisions in which individual conscience is crucial. These dilemmas may relate to neutrality, to the use of violence, to dealing with risks, or to providing humanitarian help. Codes of conduct have been formulated which, among other things, intend to match professional and ethical guidelines.[23] With or without such a code of ethics, a professional military will include critics and dissidents among its members. Occasionally someone may wish to be viewed as a conscientious objector, and may succeed in bringing public opinion and media under the spell of this powerful label.

CONCLUSION: CIVILIANIZATION, PROFESSIONALIZATION, MARGINALIZATION

Since the mid-1960s, civilianization has been the master concept for evaluating civil-military relations in The Netherlands. "As civilian as possible, as military as necessary" became a semiofficial motto for a policy of integrating the armed forces more fully and more quickly into society. Conscription was regarded as a crucial mechanism for triggering this policy. Certainly draftees caused winds of change to blow through the military. In retrospect, one could argue that because of their prominence they tended to overshadow the effects of other processes and mechanisms in civil-military relations. In one way or another, old and new indicators of integration can be viewed freshly without the draft.

Even though professionalization already has a long history of its own, it has grown quickly into a timely catchword for striking a new balance between the civilian and the military. On the one hand, professionalization is regarded as a correction of draft-related deficiencies in discipline and of the bureaucratization typical of the mass army. On the other, professionalization leads the way into the twenty-first century by adopting the ultimate technological advances for its operations at sea, on land, and in the air, in a "third wave" of civilianization.

Against this background and in light of the factors considered here, the Dutch case seems to confirm the hypothesis that civilian-military lines have been blurred. Yet even if blurring (in the sense of convergence) prevails, some shifting lines, typical of divergence, should not be overlooked.[24] In fact, because the indicators and variables are so diverse, one could argue that it makes sense not to calculate them into a single overall civilian-military score but to view them as heterogeneous arrangements, fit for different environments and changing situations. *Civilian* and *military* mean different things at different times: the interweaving of the Navy with the maritime sector, the subordination of military judges to civilian courts, and the mutual adaptation of national idiosyncrasies in the German-Dutch Corps, to name a few. From one perspective, it seems very Postmodern, like an array of civilian-military arrangements, and also compatible with the diversity of missions and the necessities imposed by diffuse threats.

From another angle, however, one can ask whether such a Postmodern state of affairs is not another indication of the marginalization of the military. In terms of presence, purpose, priorities (regarding nonmilitary issues), and budget (a 20 percent reduction between 1990 and 2000), such marginalization can be considered the real macro-trend following the end of the mass army.[25] That this trend continues was shown when the new cabinet, elected in the summer of 1998, announced yet another round of reductions and savings vis-à-vis the military. Their primary motivation was to fund policy initiatives in other areas they considered more important. No matter how logical it may have been to end the draft, and despite its old-fashioned aura, the draft constituted a formidable civilian-military arrangement capable of mobilizing society to the utmost.

It is still very unclear what alternative commitment and consensus can be reached in the Clausewitzian triangle of politics, the military, and society, now that the final professionalization of the armed forces is at hand. In the words of J. A. A. van Doorn, one of the most influential theorists on the end of the mass army:

> It looks so logical. Division of labor in the entire society is based on specialization. Professionalism is the norm in all sectors: Our best soccer players are professionals and even our worst members of parliament are professional politicians. Isn't it self-evident that our military consists of professionals as well? It is, but it also goes against reason. A soccer player can ruin his knee and a politician his reputation, but their lives are not in danger. Who will risk his life professionally nowadays for a moderate income? Will the avoidance of mortal danger not become customary? Will the public not sympathize with that? But if this is so, what use will the military be at the hour of truth?[26]

Of course, such worries may prove unnecessary. If the "Hollandization of the world"[27] continues, the civilian-military arrangements of the 1990s may have more and more opportunities to prove their relevance, their effectiveness, and their efficiency. From the perspective of The Netherlands, the very concept of "Hollandization" has a special appeal. Occasionally it might create again the sense of being a country bound for extraordinary missions—hopefully with a sharp memory of lessons learned in the Balkans.

NOTES

1. "Herstructurering en verkleining. De Nederlandse krijgsmacht in een veranderende wereld." *Defensienota 1991* (Den Haag: Tweede Kamer, 21991, 1991).
2. *Verloren onschuld. Nederland en VN-operaties* (Den Haag: Adviesraad Vrede en Veiligheid, 1996).
3. John Mueller, *Retreat from Doomsday: The Obsolescence of Major War* (New York: Basic Books, 1989).
4. "Een andere wereld, een andere defensie," *Prioriteitennota* (Den Haag: Tweede Kamer, 22975, 1993).
5. D. A. Leurdijk e.a., *Nederland op vredesexpeditie* (Den Haag: Instituut Clingendael, 1996).
6. J. S. van der Meulen e.a., *Dienstplicht nieuwe stijl: enkele beschouwingen over het rapport van de commissie-Meijer* (Den Haag: Instituut Clingendael, 1992). Also *Prioriteitennota*; see note 4. On the issue of recruitment see S. Duindam and J. Schoeman, "Werven voor een vrijwilligersleger. De slag om de beroepssoldaat," *Bestuurskunde*, Vol. 7 (1995), pp. 317–326.
7. *Nota Reservistenbeleid* (Den Haag: Ministerie van Defensie, 1996).
8. G. Teitler, *Grensbeveiliging en grensverlegging. Een verkenning van een grensgebied* (Breda: Koninklijke Militaire Academie, 1993), p. 11.
9. A number of professional periodicals have been used as a general source for the sections on organizational identification and the dominant professional, especially *Militaire Spectator*, *Carré*, and *Marineblad*.
10. C. H. P. Vermeulen, "Humanitair optreden als militaire missie," in *Werelden Apart*, ed. Ted van Baarda and Jan Schoeman (Den Haag: SDU, 1996).
11. R. Moelker and N. P. Mol, "De krijgsmacht: taken, financiering en bedrijfsvoering," *Bestuurskunde*, Vol. 7 (1995), p. 305–316.
12. Paul Hartman, "Koninklijke Landmacht: in de overgang naar een tweede jeugd," in *Een unieke samenwerking. Het Duits-Nederlandse Legerkorps*, ed. P. H. Kamphuis e.a. (Den Haag: Sectie Militaire Geschiedenis Koninklijke Landmacht, 1996), p. 162.
13. *Panel Personele Kengetallen Koninklijke Landmacht* (Den Haag: Afdeling Gedragswetenschappen DPKL, PPK-14, 1996).
14. W. J. M. Bunnik, "Defensie en haar burgers," *Armex*, Vol. 80, No. 5 (May 1996), pp. 9–11.
15. Charles Janssen, *Beroepsleger in of naast de samenleving?* (Nijmegen: Studiecentrum voor Vredesvraagstukken, 1991).
16. Jan van der Meulen, "Post-modern Societies and Future Support for Military Missions," in *The Clausewitzian Dictum and the Future of Western Military Strategy*, ed. G. C. de Nooy (The Hague: Kluwer Law International), pp. 59–74.
17. Marion Andersen, "Trends: defensievrouwen en organisatiecultuur," *Maatschappij en Krijgsmacht*, Vol. 17, No. 5 (Oct. 1995), pp. 7–13.
18. Marion Andersen and Jan van der Meulen, "Homosexuality and the Armed Forces in The Netherlands," in *Gays and Lesbians in the Military*, ed. Wilbur J. Scott and Sandra Carson Stanley (New York: Aldine de Gruyter, 1994), pp. 205–216.
19. Public opinion surveys on defense issues are regularly conducted by Stichting Maatschappij en Krijgsmacht and are published in *Maatschappij en Krijgsmacht*.

20. J. A. A. van Doorn, "Tussen ervaring en wetenschap," in *De draagbare Van Doorn*, ed. Gerry van der List (Amsterdam: Prometheus, 1996), p. 39.
21. Jan Schoeman, "Beelden, berichten, blauwhelmen. Media en krijgsmacht in de jaren '90," *Atlantisch Perspectief*, Vol. 20, No. 3, pp. 23–26.
22. Jan van der Meulen, "Full-Circle and Farewell: Conscientious Objection in The Netherlands," in *Conscientious Objection: From Religious Pacifism to Political Protest*, ed. Cynthia Lee Grudo (Zikhron Ya'akov: Israeli Institute for Military Studies, 1992), pp. 73–87.
23. A. H. M. van Iersel, *Dulce bellum inexpertis* (Tilburg: Tilburg University Press, 1995).
24. J. Soeters, *Verschuivende en vergruizende grenzen* (Breda: Koninklijke Militaire Academie, 1995). Also see H. Born and J. van der Meulen, "Convergentie en divergentie. Naar een civiel-militaire balans," *Bestuurskunde*, Vol. 7 (1995), pp. 326–335.
25. G. Teitler and B. Timmer, "De toekomst van Defensie. Taakverschraling en marginalisering," *Bestuurskunde*, Vol. 7 (1995), pp. 296–304.
26. J. A. A. van Doorn, "Vechten als beroep," *HP/De Tijd*, Vol. 9, Feb. 1996, p. 12.
27. Mueller, *Retreat from Doomsday*. Also see William R. Thompson, "The Future of Transitional Warfare," in *The Military in New Times: Adapting Armed Forces to a Turbulent World*, ed. James Burk (Boulder, Colo.: Westview, 1994), p. 84.

7

Denmark: From Obligation to Option

HENNING SORENSEN

The historical distinction between the Modern period (pre-1950), the Late Modern period (1950–90), and the Postmodern period (after 1990) is quite relevant for Denmark, because eight of the twelve issues fit the paradigm: threat perception, major military mission, force structure, the dominant military professional, civilian employees, women's integration, spouses, and life in a military organization. With respect to conscientious objectors and homosexuals, Denmark has pursued a smooth "one-step-ahead" policy in comparison with the paradigm. As a result, in public attitudes toward the military and in media relations, the Danish military is enjoying greater acceptance, contrary to the expected decline in prestige.

The gentle treatment of homosexuals and conscientious objectors in the military, one contrast to the paradigm, can be explained by the overall attitude toward minority groups in the society. In regard to the other exceptions to the paradigm, relations are calm today, but changes in the public attitude toward the military may only be a matter of time because the Danish military so far has avoided severe reductions, investigative research and reports, critical questions from politicians, and in-depth analyses by the media. However, more pressures are imminent in the Defense Commission's 1999 report *Frem Tidens Forsvar* (*Defense for the Future*), and in proposals of reduction in military manpower and expenditures by the Danish defense minister, Hans Hækkerup. In short, Denmark is most likely to pass through the same critical phase of public reaction to its engagement abroad as other Western countries.

PERCEIVED THREAT

Over time, Denmark has reduced its geographic definition of the enemy. In the Viking era, from 700 to 1050, Denmark had neither specific allies nor particular enemies. Since enemies were expected from all directions, Scandinavian Viking expeditions can be perceived as preemptive attacks. This universalistic, "all around the compass" era was followed by a period in which threats toward Denmark came mostly from German cities and monarchs in northern Europe. A third, Nordic-oriented period lasted from the mid-1400s to 1814, when threats emanated mostly from Sweden.[1] The Swedish threat ended with the Swedish victory in 1658, and was followed over the next 150 years by several Danish attempts at revenge, all unsuccessful. A fourth period, from the beginning of 1800 to 1945, came again from the south (i.e., Germany). A fifth period began in 1949 with threats from the East: The Warsaw Pact countries were enemies and the NATO countries were allies. In the 1980s, the threats again became more universalistic; they stemmed more from fear of all nuclear weapons. Another universalistic era began in 1990: Denmark has no specific enemies, only allies, while risks are identified all over the globe.

The present situation, involving no specific enemy but many allies, has enabled Denmark and other NATO countries to select their own security problems from all threats and challenges in the world. In short, NATO has moved from collective to selective security.[2] Therefore the security policies of Western countries now are influenced less by former enemies and present allies than by national preferences. For instance, Denmark chose to deploy troops in the UN mission to the former Yugoslavia for the protection of that population, but declined to do so in Somalia. Germany meanwhile did the opposite. Small Postmodern societies now have more room for security policy maneuvering than in the past.[3]

In the Modern and Late Modern periods—from 1948 to the beginning of the 1980s—Denmark feared a Soviet invasion.[4] In the 1980s, however, Danish fears shifted from actor to armory, from fear of a Soviet attack to fear of nuclear weapons regardless of their possessor. Thus in the Late Modern period (1950–90) both the characteristic Modern fear of an enemy invasion and the Late Modern fear of nuclear war were present. Today Denmark has the Postmodern fear of unintended risks of all types: political, economic, environmental, and social as well as military threats.

FORCE STRUCTURE

Danish armed forces from 1945 to 1949, in the Modern period, were characterized by uncertainty about size and organization.[5] In the beginning of this period, Denmark believed in a peaceful world governed by the statutes of the United Nations, and her military was thought to be less necessary than in the past. Also, before joining NATO in April 1949, Denmark pursued (in vain) three different security arrangements:[6] an isolated, Danish-guaranteed security from 1945 to 1948, a Nordic Defense Union involving Denmark, Sweden, and Norway in 1948–49, and finally a Danish-Swedish Defense Treaty in 1949.

The uncertainty of this security policy is reflected in the low level of Danish military expenditures from 1945–46 to 1949.[7] Since the beginning of its membership in NATO, Denmark's military expenditures have remained stable in relation to the gross domestic product, with a modest decline from the 1950s to the present. Danish military consumption equaled more than 3 percent of the GDP in the 1950s, about 3 percent in the 1960s, about 2.5 percent in the 1970s, about 2.2 percent in the 1980s, and about 2 percent, or less, in the 1990s. The highest level was 3.5 percent in 1953; the lowest, 1.7 percent in 1995–98. In the decade from 1949 to 1959, Danish military expenditures were higher because of Marshall Plan assistance from the United States.[8]

Two aspects of the structure of the Danish armed forces shall be described: the organization of the three services and the personnel balance (i.e., proportions of officers, NCOs, conscripts, and civilians). In the Modern period, the Danish armed forces consisted of the army, headed by the War Ministry, and the navy, headed by the Marine Ministry; each of the two services had its own air force.

In 1950, under the *Lov om Forsvarets ordning* (Law on the Organization of the Armed Forces), the two military ministries were combined into a single defense ministry and their air force units into an independent air force. In addition, it was decided that the Defense Ministry should have a civil servant as chief and that the three services should be headed by a single officer. Then, in 1952, the new position of chief of military operations in war was established to fit the cooperative structure of NATO.

In short, the shift from Modern to Late Modern times entailed increased centralization and internationalization, as in organizations such as Commander Baltic Approaches (COMBALTAP), Standing Naval Forces Atlantic (STANAVFORLANT), and NATO Air Defense Ground Environment (NADGE), but no profound organizational changes were made except those relating to NATO membership. In the Postmodern era a new military unit, Den dansk internationale Brigade (The Danish International Brigade, or DIB), has been established to deliver Danish peacemaking and peacekeeping forces for UN missions, NATO's Rapid Reaction Force, the Organization for Security and Cooperation in Europe (OSCE), and similar undertakings. This period demonstrates Denmark's increased military engagement "all around the compass" and its shift from collective to selective security.

The personnel structure of the Danish armed forces in the Modern era is difficult to trace because, according to the Defense Laws at that time, the size of the armed forces was calculated only in round numbers.[9] Thus no official figures from 1945 and 1950 exist, and data from announcements by the three services are used here to make only rough estimates.[10]

Throughout the period from 1945 to the present, the Danish armed forces have employed all four personnel groups: officers, NCOs, conscripts, and civilians. In the Modern period, however, the Danish armed forces were under reconstruction. In the earlier part of the Late Modern period, from 1950 to 1971, the composition of the four personnel groups seems to have been rather stable, but it changed between 1971 and 1990. In the Postmodern period, all four groups have been reduced.

The smallest group, the officer corps, has remained the most stable, accounting for 9 to 13 percent of all personnel in the armed forces. In absolute figures, however, the officer corps shrank from 7,100 in 1970 to 4,200 in 1998. NCOs accounted for 15,100 soldiers in 1970 but this number was reduced to 13,000 by 1996. The number of conscripts remained stable from 1959 to 1971 at about 25,000 soldiers,[11] but was then sharply reduced. From 1946 to 1971, almost 50 percent of all soldiers were conscripts; in 1989, however, conscripts made up only 27 percent of the force, and in 1998 they were reduced to 7,900 or 23 percent. The number of civilian workers followed the same trend as the NCOs, increasing from 1970 to 1989 and then decreasing slightly from 1989 to 1998 (to 9,100). (See the discussion of civilian employees below.)

As a result of the new Defense Law of 1973, the Danish armed forces were reduced by 27 percent in the Late Modern period and by 12 percent in the Postmodern period. The reduction of the whole Danish mass army began in the middle of the Late Modern period, later than expected in the paradigm, with the decrease in conscripts beginning as early as 1971.

In addition, we find two more exceptions to the paradigm. First, most of the reduction in the Danish armed forces occurred before the end of the Cold War. Second, the reserve forces were not increased; on the contrary, the number of reservists was cut from 72,000 to 60,000.

Some trends were the same for all three services throughout the entire 1970–94 period.[12] First, their absolute strength was reduced. Second, as mentioned above, the absolute and relative strength of conscripts to all personnel (civilians included) was reduced drastically, especially in the air force (from 39 percent in 1970 to 6 percent in 1998) and in the navy (from 41 percent to 8 percent); the reduction was smaller in the army (from 51 percent to 35 percent). Third, the proportion of NCOs increased, especially in the air force (from 30 percent in 1970 to 51 percent in 1998) and in the navy (from 31 percent to 47 percent). This increase was less evident in the army, where the proportion changed from 26 percent to 33 percent.

In other respects, the three services have followed different paths. The navy and the air force fit the increasingly "professional" profile of the Late Modern period, as mentioned in the paradigm, while the army relies on conscripts for a third of its personnel (35 percent). Even though all three services have become more professionalized, with relatively more officers, NCOs, and civilian workers and fewer conscripts, the army at the same time has become more civilianized, with relatively more conscripts and civilian employees. Almost half of the army personnel are civilians, in contrast to only one-third of navy and air force personnel.

In short, conscripts and civilian workers are concentrated in the army, while officers and NCOs are concentrated in the navy and the air force. The two smaller services reflect the Postmodern era; the army still seems to belong to the Late Modern period.

DEFINITION OF MAJOR MISSIONS

Major military missions are regulated in accordance with a nation's security policy. Beginning early in the nineteenth century,[13] Denmark avoided deployment of armed forces outside its borders. It did not believe in military power as an means of resolving conflict, even in matters such as territorial disputes, independence, and ethnic upheavals, when wars normally would be waged.[14] This security policy of stopping aggression, defending democracies, and protecting human beings verbally rather than forcefully was pursued in the Modern as well as in the Late Modern period.[15]

Since 1990, Denmark has been in a new phase, prepared to apply military power to realize its security goals. The significant shift from a Late Modern to a Postmodern definition of mission can be illustrated by recalling the restrictions on Danish military units over time.

Until 1990, Danish armed forces were kept inside the country[16] except for participation in NATO exercises abroad or in peaceful UN missions. The only Danish military unit charged with border-crossing missions was the Jyske Division; this unit's operational area, however, was restricted to Denmark and northern Germany. Since 1990, Danish soldiers have been deployed out-of-area, even in areas such as the Gulf War and the internal war in the former Yugoslavia.

Accordingly, since 1990 the number of Danish soldiers for UN missions has tripled to 1,500[17] and the above-mentioned new Danish International Brigade of 4,500 soldiers was established for this purpose. In fact, in proportion to the size of its population, Denmark contributed more troops than any other nation to the UN mission in the former Yugoslavia.

In the Late Modern period, Denmark pursued a cautious, nonprovocative NATO policy of avoiding nuclear arms on Danish territory, including Greenland and the Island of Bornholm in the Baltic Sea. Another difference between Late Modern and Postmodern times is that before 1990, Danish UN soldiers were deployed only if "the country to which Danish troops are being deployed has at least accepted the UN operation and our participation in it."[18] Today Denmark keeps its UN soldiers in Croatia, even though that government occasionally has asked the UN soldiers to leave the country.

This successive expansion of the Danish military from national to collective to selective defense fits well into the historical distinctions between the Modern, Late Modern, and Postmodern periods. In the Modern period, the military missions of Danish armed forces were national; that is, they were intended to ensure Denmark's protection and security.[19] The geographical area was confined to Denmark. There was no doubt about what the military function of the armed forces would be if Denmark were attacked. There is almost no room for any interpretation of what to do. This national military mission was formulated in the Standing Operational Procedure of 1953, and remains in operation today.

In the Late Modern period, Danish armed forces extended their military missions of mutual assistance to NATO allies attacked without provocation, but the assistance was mostly verbal.

A further expansion took place in the Postmodern period, as documented in the new Law on Defense Personnel of 1993:

> [A]rmed forces personnel [will] participate abroad in the solution of tasks connected to the mutual defense cooperation in NATO after request from international organizations UN and OSCE . . . and the solution of other tasks, including future tasks initiated by international developments.[20]

The last phrase, "including future tasks initiated by international developments," gives very broad and flexible power to the Danish defense minister; it almost states his right to deploy Danish soldiers abroad on his own initiative. Granted, this cannot be done without the agreement of the Danish Parliament. Even so, on paper the Danish defense minister has received an unprecedented right to use Danish armed forces out-of-area whenever warranted by the situation.

In the Postmodern period, Denmark has accepted a much broader security responsibility than in the past. The out-of-area military operations now encompass the world. There is a great deal of room for interpreting the direction of "international developments," what is in the Danish national interest, and especially what kind of military action should be taken. The Danish Parliament and government today have a broad range of military, economic, social, and environmental choices, depending on how they perceive the challenges.

In conclusion, changes in the major military missions since 1900 include new tasks ranging from military to humanitarian/environmental missions, acceptance of "management of organized violence" missions, deployment of many more Danish soldiers than ever before, worldwide involvement in out-of-area operations, and less concern about the belligerent parties' acceptance of a Danish role.

THE DOMINANT MILITARY PROFESSIONAL ROLE

Because of a lack of data and research, it is difficult to trace the dominant military role in Denmark in the Modern and most of the Late Modern period. In a 1980 study, 54 percent of all officers and NCOs were said to work in operational functions, 18 percent in technical positions, and 28 percent in administration.[21] In a 1983 study, only 27 percent of all officers described their jobs as operational; 37 percent identified their work as administrative, 16 percent as technical, 14 percent as teaching, and 7 percent as other functions.[22]

The same 1983 study shows no significant documented differences in the proportion of officers occupied with operations for each of the three services. In the army, 24 percent declared that they performed this function; in the navy, 30 percent; in the air force, 31 percent. Rank, however, plays a significant role in functions: 61 percent of the junior officers (lieutenants) perform operational functions, but this proportion declines to 35 percent for captains and to 30 percent for majors. So, the dominant military role is nonoperational: managerial, technical, or teaching, as expected for the Late Modern period.[23]

No explicit research on the dominant military role is found for the Postmodern period, but the media have defined the Danish soldier in a positive, heroic role.[24] This view is supported by statements from Danish officers such as Col. Carl Kops of the Danish Operational Forces:

> Danish soldiers . . . are doing well compared to soldiers from other countries. And [they] do better than American soldiers, who, in situations where they have been deployed, had to go through a learning process which Danish soldiers have gone through many years ago.[25]

This statement—relating to the Somalia incident in 1993 where seventy-six U.S. Rangers were ambushed—may be correct, but it lacks international and independent analysis for its support.

To conclude, I have identified two different roles, as expected: a managerial officer role in the Late Modern period and a heroic/soldier role in the Postmodern period.

PUBLIC ATTITUDES TOWARD THE MILITARY

Since 1949, when the first Danish public opinion surveys were conducted by a Danish affiliate of Gallup, questions have been asked conistently on three topics concerning the Danish military: support of Danish membership in NATO, level of military expenditures, and the "defense will."[26]

The extent of public support for NATO membership has been surveyed annually. In 1949, in the Modern period, the first survey showed 47 percent in favor of membership and 26 percent against. In the Late Modern period the average level of support was 50 percent in 1960–69, around 60 percent in 1970–79, 70 percent in 1980–89, around 80 percent in the 1990s, and 82 percent in March 1999. This consistently fairly positive attitude toward one aspect of the Danish military stands in contrast to the expected change from supportive (Modern) to ambivalent (Late Modern) to apathetic (Postmodern).

Questions about the level of military expenditures are the second most asked questions after the issue of NATO membership: This topic was included in more than twenty surveys from 1950 to 1999. Even if the questions were formulated in various ways, the findings consistently can be summarized as follows: About 40 percent are in favor of the current expenditure level, another 40 percent want reductions, 10 percent prefer more expenditures, and 10 percent don't know. These attitudes are influenced neither by international tension nor by the actual level of military expenditures. The findings do not correspond to the expected changes in public opinion in the three periods.

The "defense will" of the Danish population[27] actually includes eight questions on the armed forces combined into one score. These questions were asked thirteen times from 1975 to 1998 and (unlike findings on the other two topics) show a significant change over time. In 1975, the average score on a scale from 0 to 10 was 3.9. Then, until 1988, the "defense will" gradually increased to 5.2. In 1990 it decreased to 4.8, but it reached 5.9 in 1998. One of the eight questions was "Do you think the armed forces contribute to peace in Denmark?" In 1975, 53 percent of the public did; in 1998 this figure reached 76 percent. Thus the armed forces are believed to play an increasingly important role for peace in Denmark, despite the absence of enemies. The increased belief in the Danish military as contributing to peace is connected with its greater participation in the UN, NATO, EU, and OSCE missions.

So, the expected decline in the positive attitude toward the military is not found in Denmark. Only one of the questions about "defense will," however, showed a modest increase in skepticism toward the military. In 1986, 56.4 percent answered "yes" to the question "Is it necessary for Denmark to have a military defense so that the country can promote its points of view internationally?" In 1990 this proportion declined to 53 percent; in 1992, to 52.3 percent; but in 1998 it rose to 66 percent.[28] Thus, in this short period only, the Danes have become more critical—i.e., less sure about the necessity of the armed forces.

In general, the Danes have a more positive attitude toward NATO and a stronger "defense will" today than before, and they hold a status quo opinion about the level of military expenditures. In conclusion, the Danish surveys do not substantiate the expected decline in the prestige of the military.

MEDIA RELATIONS

From 1949 to 1980, in the Modern and most of the Late Modern period, the Danish mass media touched only marginally on defense issues. At that time, military matters were held in low esteem and attracted little interest. Accordingly, most of the media covered defense issues only irregularly and superficially.[29] In the Late Modern period (from 1960 to around 1980), only two defense issues appeared on the agenda: treatment of conscripts and level of military expenditures.[30]

In the 1980s, other subjects arose, such as nuclear weapons, the deployment of cruise missiles, and nonoffensive defense (NOD). Thus the relations between the media and the military expanded throughout the Late Modern period, but did not necessarily improve.

Manipulation is the expected media–armed forces relationship for that period, but it is difficult to prove that the mass media manipulated the military, or vice versa. Nevertheless, a Danish study of NOD included a survey about possible manipulation by Danish newspapers. It was found that newspapers contained more material in agreement with their own editorial line than in opposition,[31] but such a policy is to be expected. Thus no clear answer can be given.

From the beginning of the Postmodern period in 1990, however, the Danish media have become more courteous and less critical toward the military, probably due to the increased Danish participation in UN, NATO, EU, and OSCE peacekeeping missions.[32] In the summer of 1993, for example, Denmark, as the only UN participant in the former Yugoslavia, decided to deploy tanks in Tuzla, but the Serbs blocked the deployment for six months. At that time the Danish mass media reported continuously but uncritically on the ten tanks and their difficult journey from Denmark to Bosnia rather than questioning the wisdom of this decision, its strategic implications, or the overall functioning of Danish UN soldiers in that theater. Actually, the Danish UN soldiers in Bosnia were characterized in *Time* Magazine (June 12, 1995) as "probably the most aggressive gunners" of all UN soldiers due to the presence of the Danish tanks. Here, in the Postmodern period, we find both manipulation and courtesy.

In short, just as expected, the relationship between the media and the military has moved from critical treatment in the Late Modern period to a more manipulative, more courteous treatment in the Postmodern period.

CIVILIAN EMPLOYEES

According to the paradigm, an increased number of civilian employees is expected over time, and this is the case for Denmark. The proportion of civilian employees to all military personnel (including officers, NCOs, conscripts, and civilians) increased from 11 percent in 1945 to 21 percent in 1950 and 1970, 24 percent in 1989, and 26 percent in 1994.[33] The increase in civilian employees occurred earlier than expected according to the paradigm (that is, in the Modern period). Since that time, this component has grown only slightly.

In the Late Modern and Postmodern periods, the proportion of civilian employees differed across the services. The proportion in the army increased from 37 percent in 1970 to 43 percent in 1994. In contrast, the proportion of civilians in the air force declined steadily from 40 percent in 1970 to 27 percent in 1994. In the navy, civilian employees increased from 23 percent in 1970 to 29 percent in 1989, and then declined to 19 percent in 1994.[34] Thus only the army reflects the expected increase of civilian employees over time; the navy and the air force actually reduced their concentrations of civilian personnel.

WOMEN'S ROLE

In the Modern period, women were excluded from the Danish armed forces except in positions such as nurses, doctors, dentists, and clerks. In 1946, however, the Home Guard was established. The backbone of the Home Guard was two separate organizations, one for men and one for women, based on the former Danish resistance movement. These private defense organizations were dissolved in 1948 by the Home Guard Act, and the women's Home Guard was reorganized into three sections: Danmarks Lottekorps (for the army), Kvindeligt Marinekorps (the Women's Naval Home Guard), and Kvindeligt Flyverkorps (the Women's Air Force Home Guard).

In the Late Modern period, women's strength in the combined Home Guard increased. In 1957, 14 percent of all Home Guard personnel were women; in 1981 the proportion was 17 percent. Their importance in the hierarchy declined, however: In 1957, 7 percent of the women were officers; in 1981, only 3 percent.

In 1962, during the Late Modern period, legislation established the legal basis for employment of women in the armed forces. It was renewed in 1969 but not implemented until 1971. Thus, in 1972, women accounted for 1.4 percent of all personnel in the Danish armed forces; in 1981, 1.9 percent. In 1997, 5 percent of all volunteer soldiers in Denmark were women.[35] This level has not changed for the last decade. For this reason, it has been decided politically to try to increase their number. This attempt has been in vain, because the military organization still wants female soldiers to meet the same physical recruitment standards as their male counterparts. Before 1994, enlisted women had the same rights, obligations, and conditions as equivalent male personnel,[36] but were not attached to combat units or accepted as pilots.

Today, in the Postmodern period, women are fully integrated in the armed forces. Since 1994 they have been eligible for recruitment as pilots, for combat units, in submarines, and even (since 1995) as enlisted soldiers for the Danish International Brigade. On top of all this, female conscription has been introduced.

Female participation in the Danish military has followed the expected paradigm of separation in the Modern period, partial integration in the Late Modern period, and full integration in the Postmodern era.

SPOUSES

Neither data nor research on spouses' integration into the Danish armed forces are to be found. Yet on the basis of the increasing participation of women in the labor market since the early 1960s (at present almost at the same level as that of men—that is, around 80 percent), it is reasonable to argue that in the Late Modern period more Danish women married to officers now pursue careers of their own. Fewer women, therefore, can concentrate on the career of their husbands. For that reason—and because almost no Danish officers live at the garrison with their families—the few spouses left to do so will live in isolation. Consequently, officers' families will normally relate to civilian families in their neighborhood.

In the Postmodern period, spouses' connection to the military community has almost ended because, as mentioned above, Danish women's employment rate is 78 percent—almost equal to the men's rate of 82 percent. Moreover, dual careers in the family have become a problem for the military: Many a qualified officer has refused promotion and transfer to a career post at another location in the country because his wife, pursuing her own career, is unwilling to move.

In short, high employment rates of Danish women since the 1960s indicate that spouses' separation from the military community occurred in the Late Modern period, not (as expected) in the Postmodern era.

HOMOSEXUALS

From 1939 to 1954, homosexuals were neither recognized, registered, nor recruited for military service.[37] A draftee was rejected, however, if he stated voluntarily that he was gay.

In 1954 the Home Office decided to ask draftees about their sexual orientation. From 1955 to 1978, gays were registered; some were even drafted, although only for the Home Guard. Generally, however, homosexuals could avoid the draft by declaring themselves as such before a judge, with two witnesses.

In the 1970s the Landsforeningen for Bosser og Lesbiske (the National Association for Gays and Lesbians) criticized the automatic rejection of homosexuals; the group wanted gays to be drafted and to serve on equal terms with other conscripts. Since 1979 the draft board has asked no questions about sexuality; therefore Danish gays and lesbians are drafted and recruited on equal terms with heterosexuals.

The Danish policy toward homosexuals differs from the treatment expected on the basis of the paradigm, which entails punishment in the Modern period, discharge in the Late Modern, and acceptance in the Postmodern.

In the Modern period, homosexuals were not punished but were merely rejected for service if they came out of the closet. In most of the Late Modern period, homosexuals were not rejected but were drafted, although only for the Home Guard. Since 1979, homosexuals have been accepted as soldiers on equal terms with heterosexuals.

In short, the Danish policy toward homosexuality was never harsh and was one step ahead of the expected stages of the paradigm.

CONSCIENTIOUS OBJECTION

Denmark introduced universal compulsory military service in 1849. The first case of conscientious objection was recorded in 1884; the case involved religious objection. The objectors, however, were not treated harshly, and in 1917 Denmark was one of the first countries in the world to recognize conscriptions objection and provide public civilian service as an alternative.[38] In applying for conscientious objector (CO) status before 1950, the objector was required only to state a reason for his status. Two witnesses for a "revising board" had to confirm the application of the CO by their signatures and to testify to the local police.

In 1968, in the Late Modern period, the policy was liberalized further: CO status was available to anyone who asked for it, without any investigation or sanction. No CO was required to state his reasons. Today any young man can avoid military service simply by deciding to register as a CO and then performing alternative civilian service.

The trend expected on the basis of the paradigm—prohibition of conscientious objection in the Modern period, permission in the Late Modern period, and presentation of civilian and military service as equal alternatives in the Postmodern era—was not followed in Denmark. Once again, as in the case of homosexuals, Denmark seems to have been in the vanguard regarding conscientious objection, granting exemptions as early as 1917 and beginning in 1968 to permit individual decisions about the issue.

LIFE IN A MILITARY ORGANIZATION

In the Modern period, the Danish armed forces were divided into the army and the navy, each with its own ministry, budget, installations, and bureaucracy. Military life for almost all personnel was "institutional": Education, work, and social networks took place within the confines of the institution.

In the Late Modern period, life in the Danish armed forces can be described not only as an occupation but even as a "free supermarket." Recruits are offered all products (conscription, equal treatment of COs, a militia for the Home Guard, and liberal procedures for homosexuals) at no cost at all; military expenditures and budgets seem fairly equal across the (now) three services. Military life is influenced more strongly by national than by international factors, and in various respects (pay negotiated by unions, education, work, and career) is increasingly conforming to civilian standards. The basic reason for this "free supermarket" model is society's wish to let each employee decide for himself or herself whether, when, and how to live in military garrisons; thus, civilian and military standards are converging.

This continuing individualization is the prevalent characteristic of the Postmodern period and has been confirmed by a survey.[39] Danish army cadets were asked "Which of the following items do you feel most related to?" Seventy-one percent answered "yourself," and only 14 percent "your native city." In contrast, 33 percent of Italian army cadets answered "your family," 27 percent "your country," and only 26 percent "yourself." These responses indicate that Danish army cadets perceive themselves as individualists guided by private beliefs and norms, and support the "heroic," self-conscious dominant military role discussed above. As Janowitz argued, the modern military professional requires a broad liberal education rather than narrow technical and vocational training to prepare for the political and social complexities facing the armed forces today. In addition, as Weber observed, a shift from a bureaucratic to a volunteer armed force is accompanied by a decline in organizational importance and thus by an increase in individualism; this point is illustrated in the Danish survey, in which honor is ranked above discipline.[40]

In short, military life in Denmark follows the expected development from "institutional" in the Modern period to "occupational" in the Late Modern era and "civilian-individual" in the Postmodern era.

CONCLUSION

As stated at the beginning of this chapter, the Postmodern Danish military fits the paradigm in eight of the twelve issues discussed here, and is one step ahead in regard to homosexuals and conscientious objectors.

In public attitude and media relations, however, Denmark departs from the paradigm because of the increasingly positive public attitude toward the armed forces. Two reasons may be found for the improved prestige of the military. First, Danish armed forces have been credited with the absence of an enemy. Second, Danish soldiers abroad, especially in the former Yugoslavia, have been presented as heroes. Neither of these two reasons is guaranteed to endure: the increased prestige of the Danish military may decline in case of casualities abroad, reduced funding for the armed forces, and increased external research and political control of the military.

Yet the most interesting change in the Danish armed forces over the last half-century has been the shift from obligation to option. The Danish military has no single function or image, but can be perceived more appropriately as a "free supermarket" attracting both peace soldiers and Rambo soldiers, offering a militia defense (the Home Guard), an all-volunteer force, and a conscription army serving as either a lifelong occupation or an exciting short-term job.

This shift calls for increased, not decreased, civilian control of the Danish military. Denmark does not need "peace for the military," as argued by some politicians and many officers, but a debate about the type of soldier— and defense—Denmark wants to develop and use in the years to come.

NOTES

1. In the period from 1430 to 1520, Denmark and Sweden disagreed on how to cooperate (within the Kalmar union of 1397) and from 1520 to 1658 they fought six major wars over which country should dominate the Nordic region.
2. See Henning Sorensen, "NATO and Its New Military Security Position," *European Security*, Vol. 7, No. 1 (spring 1998), pp. 74–79.
3. Here I disagree with Nikolaj Petersen,"Denmark's Foreign Relations in the 1990s," *Annals of the American Academy of Political and Social Science*, Vol. 512, No. 97 (1990), pp. 88–100, but agree with Michael H. Clemmesen, "Efterkoldkrigstidens danske forsvarspolitik" (Danish defense policy after the Cold War period) in *Dansk Udrenigspolitisk Arbog 1994* (Danish Foreign Policy Yearbook 1994) (Copenhagen: Danish Undenrigapolitisk Institut, 1994), p. 44.
4. Udenrigsministeriet, *Dansk Sikkerhedspolitik 1948–1996, I: Fremstilling* (Danish security policy 1948–1966, I: Presentation) (Copenhagen: Ministry of Foreign Affairs, 1968), p. 23.
5. Nikolaj Petersen, *Forsvaret i den politiske beslutningsproces* (Defense in the political decision-making process) (Copenhagen: Forsvarsministeriet, 1980), p. 2:41.
6. Udenrigsministeriet, *Dansk Sikkerhedspolitik*, pp. 21–34.
7. For military expenditure and gross domestic product figures for 1945/46–70, see Hans Christian Johansen, *Dansk Historisk Statistik 1814–1980* (Danish historical statistics 1814–1980) (Copenhagen: Gyldendal, 1984), pp. 392ff, table 9.2i, table 9.2k; for 1970–93, see *Samfundsstatistik 1994* (Societal statistics 1994) (Copenhagen: Samfundsfagsnyt, 1994), p. 81.
8. United States Marshall Plan assistance for Denmark in total is estimated at $4.5 billion Danish crowns (DKK), the equivalent of US $0.7 billion. See Udenrigsministeriet, *Dansk Sikkerhedspolitik*, p. 146.
9. Petersen, *Forsvaret*, p. 52.
10. The figures for 1945 are calculated from *Forslag til lov nr 137 om Aendring i og Tilfojelse til lov nr 301 af 6 Juni 1946 om Statens tjenestemaend* (Bill no. 137 on changes in and appendix to Law no. 301 of June 1946 on public servants) and "An-

nouncements for the Army 1945/46, for 1950" from *Lov nr. 278 af 18. juni 1951* (Law no. 278 of 18 June 1951), pp. s910ff., 162 ff., and from *Report to Bill 134 of 1950/1951*, "Answer from Defense Minister on Question no. 3"; for 1970, from Forsvarsministeriet, *Arlig Redegorelse 1985* (Copenhagen: Danish Defense Command, 1985), p. 9; for 1989 and 1994, from Finansministeriet, Forsvarsministeriet og Okonomiministeriet, *Forsvarets okonomi* (Copenhagen: Auditor General of Denmark, 1994), p. 90, table 3. According to a phone conversation held on September 26, 1995, with Maj. Kaj Hansen, Danish Defense Ministry, Second Office, the ministry has no official data for 1945–46. See also Defense Commission, *Fremtidens forsvar* (*Defense for the Future*) (Copenhagen, 1998), p. 142.

11. Keld Jensen, *Strukturudviklingen i forsvaret—og dennes betydning for regional-geografiske forhold* (The structural development in the armed forces—and its importance for regional geographical factors) (Roskilde: Roskilde Universitetscenter, 1994), pp. 180ff., especially 181, fig. 13.

12. Calculated from Forsvarsministeriet, *Arlig redegorelse* (Annual report), 1985; Finansministeriet et al., *Forsvarets okonomi*, 1994, p. 90, table 3; p. 91, table 4.

13. The last time the Danish armed forces waged war was against Germany. The war ended in 1864 with the defeat of Denmark.

14. Denmark accepted Norway's declaration of independence in 1814, that of the island of Iceland in 1944, the home rule of the Faroe Islands in 1946, and the home rule of Greenland in 1979. In addition, Denmark and Norway accepted the International Court's rule in the case of East Greenland in 1937. Also, in 1916, Denmark sold some Caribbean islands to the United States and accepted the new border with Germany in 1920 after a referendum. This was the only border Hitler respected.

15. For instance, Denmark kept a low profile in NATO by abandoning deployment of nuclear weapons on its territory and concurrently denying allied submarine vessels armed with nuclear weapons access to Danish harbors. For the sake of the Soviet Union, Denmark never accepted deployment of Allied troops on the island of Bornholm, situated in the Baltic Sea. Moreover, it spoke strongly in favor of improved relations with the Warsaw Pact countries and took a specific interest in human rights.

16. Since 1948, Denmark has participated in twenty-two of the thirty-one UN missions, with more than 40,000 soldiers serving mainly as observers.

17. Of 1,500 Danish army soldiers now deployed in various UN missions, 1,000 today (March 1999) are in the former Yugoslavia. Thus, in relation to its size, Denmark is one of the largest contributors to this UN mission.

18. Udenrigsministeriet, *Dansk sikkerhedspolitik*, p. 170.

19. The *Forholdsordren* (Standing operational procedure) of 1953 requires every Danish soldier to join his unit without delay to meet an external attack. Parliament passed this bill to prevent another April 9, 1940, when the Germans occupied Denmark without any central Danish authority ordering the armed forces to resist.

20. *Lov om forsvarets personel* (Law on defense personnel) (Copenhagen: Danish Defense Command, 1991), p. 11.

21. Jensen, *Strukturudviklingen*, p. 176.

22. Henning Sorensen, *Den dansk officer: Fra kriger til administrator* (The Danish officer: From warrior to administrator [with English summary]) (Copenhagen: Nyt

fra Samfundsvidenskaberne, 1988), p. 352. Total does not equal 100 percent due to rounding.

23. Sorensen, *Den dansk officer.*
24. "The New Era of the Soldier," *Berlingske Tidende,* Aug. 23, 1995.
25. *Weekend-avisen,* July 8, 1995, p. 1.
26. Henning Sorensen, "Danish Public Opinion of Foreign Policy Issues after WWII: A Stable Distribution?," in *The Future of Security in Europe: A Comparative Analysis of European Public Opinion,* ed. Philippe Manigart (Brussels: Royal Military School, 1992), pp. 135–60; Henning Sorensen, "New Trends in Danish Foreign Policy and Their Public Support," in *Future Roles, Missions and Structures of Armed Forces in the New World Order: The Public View,* ed. Philippe Manigart (New York: Nova Science Publishers, 1995), pp. 44–52.
27. Forsvarets Center for Lederskab, *Befolkningens forsvarsvilje maj 1975–okt 1998* (The defense will of the population May 1975–Oct. 1998), 1998.
28. *Information,* Sept. 17, 1992.
29. Petersen, *Forsvaret,* Vol. 2, p. 41.
30. Nikolaj Petersen, "Forsvaret i den danske opinion" (Defense in Danish public opinion), *Fremtiden,* Vol. 1 (1976), p. 24–32.
31. Henning Sorensen, "Ikke-Offensivt Forsvar i den danske dagspresse" ("Non-offensive defense in Danish newspapers"), in *Ikke-offensivt forsvar—En introduktion,* ed. Henning Sorensen (Copenhagen: Samfundslitteratur, 1990), pp. 177–189.
32. *Berlingske Tidende,* Aug. 23, 1995.
33. See note 10. In 1998, Danish armed forces consisted of 34,300 employees (officers, NCOs/regulars, conscripts, and civilians). The total number of civilians was 9,200; 7,900 served in the army, navy, or the air force, and 1,300 served in common service units.
34. Calculated from Forsvarsministeriet, *Arlig redegorelse 1985,* and Finansministeriet et al., *Forsvarets okonomi,* p. 90, table 3; p. 91, table 4.
35. *BT,* Mar. 3, 1994.
36. Henning Sorensen, "Denmark: The Small NATO Nation," in *Female Soldiers—Combatants or Noncombatants?,* ed. Nancy Loring Goldman (London: Greenwood Press, 1982), pp. 189–202.
37. Henning Sorensen, *Homosexuals in the Armed Forces in Scandinavia* (Copenhagen: European Research Office, 1993).
38. Henning Sorensen: "The Vanguard of Conscientious Objection," in *The New Conscientious Objection: From Sacred to Secular Resistance,* ed. Charles C. Moskos and John W. Chambers II (New York: Oxford University Press, 1991), pp. 106–113.
39. Giuseppe Caforio (ed.), *The European Cadet: Professional Socialization in Military Academies* (Baden-Baden: Nomos, 1998).
40. H. H. Gerth and C. Wright Mills, *From Max Weber: Essays in Sociology* (New York: Oxford University Press, 1973), pp. 254–264.

8

Italy: A Military for What?

MARINA NUCIARI

To analyze the evolution of the Italian armed forces since the 1950s, one must understand the history of the military of the Italian Republic, which was founded in 1946. Although an institution such as the military cannot be changed completely, goals and normative patterns have been drastically redefined because of the change in the political and institutional premises on which the new Italian Republic was built. Before beginning a systematic analysis, it seems useful to review the current relationships between the armed forces and Italian society.

The Italian armed forces still are based on conscription, although some recurrent changes have led to a mixed structure in which the voluntary component is increasing and will be primary in a few years. A strong will to arrive shortly at a definite abolition of conscription is also openly present at government level. The need for force reductions has been apparent since the end of the 1980s. A progressive reduction was begun before 1989 and has continued: The New Defense Model (NDM) was presented to the Parliament for the first time in 1991, and includes further downsizing.

The evolving structure is based now on conscription and volunteer enlistment at the troop level and on career personnel at the officer and non-commissioned officer (NCO) levels. A certain number of short- or long-term volunteers are now present at the troop level, and fractions of the NCOs and reserve officers are draftees.

Because Italy belongs to NATO, her foreign and defense policies are shaped within NATO agreements. The Italian position was defined clearly in the NATO Constitution, which states in Article 11 that "Italy rejects war as a means to solve international conflicts." This position implies a foreign policy based on nonintervention in operations involving possible troop deployments. Two missions in Lebanon, in 1982 and 1984, interrupted a forty-year tradition and began a new period in which Italian armed forces would be employed militarily beyond national borders.

The structure and mission of the Italian armed forces remained largely unchanged from the beginning of the Republic until the end of the 1980s, despite repeated reductions in force and organizational restructuring linked to budgetary concerns. The principal changes became evident only during the 1990s.

For about forty years, political actions regarding the military were designed mainly to accomplish "democratization," as declared in the NATO Constitution. Article 52 states that the "military institution takes inspiration from the Republic's democratic spirit," in order to place it totally under the control of the civilian democratic state.[1] Specific issues concern internal superior-subordinate relationships, the rights and duties of citizen-soldiers, political control over military activities, and representation of the professional interests of military "employees."

This civilian oversight included some legislative action, such as the 1972 Law on Conscientious Objection and the 1978 law introducing military representative bodies and internal democratic principles of action, as well as complex, recurrent legislation concerning the career development and remuneration of military personnel as public servants.

International geopolitical developments during the 1980s, from perestroika to the fall of Berlin Wall, influenced Italian security and defense policy. They increased the trend toward civilianization of the armed forces' tasks and imposed a new structural design to perform new missions and handle probable threats more effectively.

Throughout this process the defense budget has been reduced constantly. The result has been a progressive downsizing of forces, combined with rationalization and organizational restructuring to adapt the forces to the available financial resources. This reduction was not made without stress, as expressed in a provocative comment by former Army Chief of Staff Gen. Incisa di Camerana: "In a situation like this, it would be better to abolish the army!"[2]

Such attitudes are common in public administrations, which are never satisfied with the amount of financial resources at their disposal. Still, it is true that the percentage of the gross national product (GNP) devoted to defense has always been noticeably lower in Italy than in many other European NATO countries. The forces maintained until now, with current deployment needs in international missions approved at the political level, are constantly endangered by the possibility of a financial crisis.

Thus a dilemma is evident, which can serve as an indicator of political schizophrenia in defense matters. Public opinion supports the idea of using the military in peacekeeping operations, both for national prestige and to employ a structure that should serve some practical purpose. No one, however, is disposed to support the increase in taxation needed to sustain such missions properly.

In the political system, weak and transient governments cannot make the economic policies necessary to achieve prestige by participating in international missions. Therefore the question remains: A military for what?

The evolution of relationships between the armed forces and society and within the military organization itself in the last fifty years can be considered according to the model proposed by Charles Moskos: Modern (pre-1950), Late Modern (1950–90), and Postmodern (since 1990). I organize my discussion into these periods rather than dealing with each variable of the model for all periods together.

THE MODERN PERIOD

Perception of Threat in the Modern Period

This period includes the important break caused by the 1922–43 dictatorial regime and by World War II. Republican democracy did not come to Italy until 1946. As in other countries, such as Germany, recent Italian history is influenced strongly by events occurring between the two world wars.

Except for the early decades of Italian unification (from 1861 to the beginning of this century), the new Italian Kingdom followed the politics of alliances signed at the Berlin Conference in 1878. This guaranteed a peaceful period until 1914, during which a complicated political balance was maintained among the European powers.

In this period, and in the following dictatorship as well, the perceived military threat was an attack on national borders by a foreign enemy or an attack on national interests in the colonies. An example of the latter is the French occupation of Tunis, which Italy intended as a place of expansion but had not yet occupied militarily. Italy's temporary neutrality in 1914 and the change of alliances leading Italy to declare war on the Central Powers can be explained by this prevailing orientation toward the defense of national borders (Trento/Trieste), based on perceived national interests. This orientation remained substantially unchanged until 1943.

Force Structure in the Modern Period

The force structure during this period was based on the conscription of young males. Some legislative changes concerning recruitment methods were caused by the need to maintain a balanced force. From 1870 to 1940, the Italian army was large; the result was a lack of balance between the quantity and the quality of the forces, and planning that was too ambitious for the level of financial resources.[3]

In peacetime the country maintained a force of twelve army corps (1882–1915) or thirty-one divisions (1919–35), with a large number of career officers (15,000 to 25,000), many career warrant officers (9,000 to 17,000), and very few career enlisted men (almost all of whom were in the navy). A balanced force was reached with 160,000 to 250,000 draftees.

For the entire period before the Republic, the Italian army was essentially a "mobilization army," distributed uniformly over the national territory and not concentrated at the borders. This arrangement implied an offensive strategy, based on the assumption that the initiative would be on the Italian side. After 1945, however, the army's role became defensive. In fact, even before Italy joined NATO, all available forces were concentrated for forward defense at the northeast border. This required an army designed to prevent surprise attacks rather than to take the initiative. In 1948, twelve active and three reserve divisions were planned; these soon came to be regarded as too expensive, however, and reductions were imposed progressively beginning in 1956.

Definition of Major Mission in the Modern Period

Until 1945 the prevailing mission of the armed forces could be defined as the interventionist defense of the homeland, guaranteed by an adequate offensive capacity. Defense of homeland became the basis of legitimacy, along with the more realistic support of alliances. The military could accomplish this more successfully in an alliance than by remaining exclusively a national force.

The Dominant Military Professional Model in the Modern Period

The combat leader was the professional model for young officers and a reference model for their self-identity. In their academic education, which was already complex and emphasized science and engineering, the prevailing values were military honor, courage, and loyalty to the mission assigned by the country. Analogies with other sectors of society were rejected. Military command and leadership were based on the leader's example; blind, immediate obedience was expected from subordinates. During the dictatorship between the two wars, Mussolini undertook a secularization of this leadership pattern in an attempt to militarize superior-subordinate relationships in other sectors of Italian society.

Public Attitudes toward the Military in the Modern Period

It is difficult to affirm that public attitudes toward the armed forces were supportive during this period. The ambiguity of Italian public opinion toward the military began with the unification of the state, and varied by region. Support of the army was widespread in the north, where the Royal Army, heir to the traditional Savoy Army and based strongly on its original structure, was perceived as a liberator from foreign domination and as an expression of popular feeling. The army enjoyed far less legitimacy in the south, where the northern monarchy prevailed without substantially improving the socioeconomic situation. In these regions the army became the symbol of a new domination, imposing a new serfdom in the form of the compulsory draft. These attitudes were reinforced by the Italians' tragic experience with the use of the armed forces under fascism.

The new republic included "the refusal of war" in Article 52 of its constitution, but considered "the defense of the country as a sacred duty of the citizen" and military service as "compulsory within limits and ways established by the law." It also stated that "the military institution takes inspiration from the Republic's democratic spirit"; thus it admitted implicitly that the military was something different, even though (like any other national institution) it was subject to the state's legislation.

This peculiarity was controlled politically by adequate democratic tools, to assure the progressive democratization of the armed forces and to reduce not only their heterogeneity but also their supposed capacity to endanger democratic institutions. For these and many other reasons, the public attitude in the Modern period was ambivalent. The reasons were different before and after the birth of the Republic, but the overall attitude never could be called supportive.

Media-Military Relationships in the Modern Period

The relationship between the Italian armed forces and the mass media (in this period, radio and the press) was similarly controversial.

The term *incorporation* means an internal use of the mass media, by internal means. This implies that the diffusion of news and information was highly controlled. News not conforming to, or not coming directly from, the bodies officially devoted to military communication were considered false and often were labeled subversive. In Italy, distrust remained a particular characteristic of military-media relations until the 1980s.[4]

Civilian Employees in the Modern Period

Civilian employees were a very minor component during this period; they were concentrated mostly in central bureaus of the Department of War (later the Department of Defense).

Women's Role in the Modern Period

Women were excluded from military participation unless they were soldiers' wives. Even then, their role did not directly interfere with professional military activities. In Italian society between the two world wars, the female role was limited mainly to home and family. This was accentuated during fascism, when women interacted with the armed forces as "producers of soldiers."

Female participation in the war for liberation, which has not been well recognized, led the Constituent Assembly to consider extending compulsory military service to women after the war, inasmuch as they were entitled to full citizenship with all the attendant rights and duties. After much discussion, the matter was solved by eliminating any mention of gender in the definition of "the defense of the country as a sacred duty of the citizen." Thus the task of defining female participation in military endeavors was left to ordinary legislation. The situation remains unchanged, despite repeated debates and ideological disputes on all fronts.

Spouses and the Military Community in the Modern Period

The military was a typical all-male society, especially for cadres devoted to the institution. Therefore an internal and highly integrated role was designed for officers' wives. Italian society of the period was structurally and culturally very traditional: Until the economic boom of the 1950s, officers' wives were expected to belong to the middle or upper class and to be dedicated to their husbands' careers—and consequently not to work outside the home.

Especially in those residential settings definable as "bases" (which were less common in the army than in the navy or the air force), families were strongly integrated with the military and were correspondingly separate from the rest of society. This situation was intensified by living in service apartments or in state flats assigned to military personnel, or else in true military villages.

Homosexuals in the Military in the Modern Period

Homosexuals were strictly excluded from the military, and punishment was applied when homosexual behavior was discovered.

Fascism introduced particularly repressive measures against homosexuals, including imprisonment, discharge, and internment. The situation changed with the Republic, but repression within the military remained until 1985, when the law was changed to provide exemption from military service because of declared or certified homosexuality. Homosexuality as a crime disappeared from the penal code, and was no longer punished in the absence of violent or obscene behavior.

Conscientious Objection in the Modern Period

Conscientious objection also was considered a crime. During the monarchy it was treated like desertion, disobedience, or the refusal to fight, and was prosecuted strongly under fascism. The new constitution did not specifically recognize the right to object, and conscientious objection was prohibited throughout the period. Those who declared themselves COs were imprisoned.

The Organizational Identification Model in the Modern Period

Organizational identification was mainly institutional; many aspects stressed the distance between military and civilian society, particularly in regard to the career cadres.

A career soldier had a diffuse role orientation; he looked to his superior in rank as his natural defender. The draftee was expected to be ready to perform all tasks required to maintain the military institution.

In summary, the variables for the Modern period largely correspond to Moskos's expectations for armed forces and society before 1950, with some exceptions due to Italian political history in the first half of this century. Subsequent changes originate in this period.

THE LATE MODERN PERIOD

Between 1950 and 1990, many changes occurred in the relationship between the Italian armed forces and society. These can be seen by following Moskos's analytical framework.

Threat Perception in the Late Modern Period

The strategic decision to join NATO in 1949 was accompanied by Italian politicians' reluctance to adhere to a military pact. Doubts were resolved by recognizing that the choice was inevitable and that the treaty would have positive effects in terms of financial aid for reconstruction. Italian foreign policy became more Atlanticist; for many years, one of the themes of political debate was the government's inevitable pro-Atlanticism and the equally absolute anti-Atlanticism of the opposition.

The perception of a nuclear menace and "fear of the bomb" was a more recent phenomenon in Italy, becoming apparent mostly after the 1970s. Until the mid-1960s the true military problem was the unsolved question of the border with Yugoslavia: the question of Trieste and Gorizia and the Italian population of Istria.[5]

On the one hand, relations with Yugoslavia were a bilateral question between neighboring states; on the other, "the door of Gorizia" was the critical point of contact between the two countries on Italian territory. The situation justified the concentration of land and air forces in the northeast; Italian-Yugoslavian relations were considered an example of the military threat from the East. In those years the threat was perceived to be "the communist menace," in which the danger was not only military but also economic and political, affecting national sovereignty. Adhesion to NATO consequently was considered a guarantee not only of a place under a nuclear umbrella, but also (and mainly) of protection from communism.

Definition of Major Mission in the Late Modern Period

Even more strongly than in the Modern period, the prevailing mission was defined within alliances, which were considered a more effective means of defending the country. Italy tried for forty years to avoid the direct involvement of its troops, even while emphasizing its willingness to participate in humanitarian and peace operations.

Force Structure in the Late Modern Period

As noted above, Italian force structure still was based on conscription. Despite the downsizing and the resulting increase in the proportion of volunteers (mainly at the cadre level but also in the other ranks), young conscripts always made up more than 60 percent of military personnel. The debate about the choice of troop composition and then about the change from the draft to the all-volunteer force (AVF) began with the Constituent Assembly in 1946. It continued with many ups and downs throughout the Late Modern period and thereafter.

Reasons favoring one alternative or another were based on both political-ideological and financial considerations. Until the end of the 1980s, the draft seemed less expensive but adequate to provide the number of soldiers needed to meet NATO requirements. After the mission in Lebanon in 1984—and even more so after the Gulf War in 1991—the AVF seemed more efficient and more adequate to Italy's new international responsibilities. The risk of praetorianism appeared to be less. As stated in the New Defense Model, the final choice would be a mixed force with a strong volunteer component. Military tasks would be distinguished by the type of soldier: national territorial defense for conscripts, international missions for volunteers.

The Dominant Military Professional Model in the Late Modern Period

The professional model recognized by military personnel, and especially by officers, cannot be described clearly in terms of the "combat leader/manager" dichotomy. This model surely has changed, but not so drastically as to transform one extreme into the other. Researchers, in fact, have found no clear-cut aggregations around either pole. The model was mixed: Managerial components of professional competence and a spirit of initiative were combined with such combat leader characteristics as leadership, discipline, and readiness to sacrifice.[6]

Junior officers support managerial qualities more strongly than colonels, but without denigrating discipline and sacrifice. For 54 percent of officers overall, the self-image is that of "a leader of men"; only 25 percent define themselves as specialists or staff members. The branch of service is influential as well: 65 percent of army officers describe themselves as leaders, but only 36 percent of navy officers do so (another 36 percent prefer the definition of staff member and specialist), as do only 17 percent of pilots (58 percent prefer the image of specialist).[7]

Academic professional military education changed substantially after the academies reopened at the end of the war, especially in the army. Until the 1970s this education was oriented mainly toward science and engineering (basic engineering in the army, naval engineering in the navy, and aerospace engineering in the air force). Beginning in the 1980s, however, first the army and then the navy modified their education to become more humanistic and social-scientific. This was especially true for the army, where 60 percent of the young lieutenants had degrees in political science, 12 percent in economics, and fewer than one-third in engineering. Some social sciences and organizational studies have been added at the naval and air force academies, but these branches remain more scientifically oriented. This type of basic education may have led the way to the Postmodern professional model of the soldier-student-diplomat.

Public Attitudes toward the Military in the Late Modern Period

Public opinion about the armed forces was divided: The pro-Atlanticists were favorable, while the anti-Atlanticists were less positive or even negatively oriented toward the military. Pro-Atlanticists tended to prevail during that period.

A 1958 opinion poll revealed that 46 percent of Italians preferred a distribution of power in which the United States prevailed over the Soviet Union; only 27 percent preferred parity between the two superpowers. After 1974 the situation was reversed: The majority of Italians favored parity.[8]

During the 1970s and 1980s, the change in the attitude favoring or opposing either superpower was associated with an increased perception of the threat of accidental war between the two. Because of concern with "nuclear overkill," nuclear parity was considered safer. Some sectors of society were increasingly concerned about the presence of nuclear weapons on Italian territory and the possible increase in their number. Public opinion favored NATO overall, but new missile installations were strongly opposed. This paralleled the emergence of ecological issues, which linked 1980s pacifist and antinuclear movements to civilian antinuclear and ecological movements.

Unfortunately, complete data on public support for military spending are not available. National samples are available only since 1977; these show that the proportion of those who favored an increase in military spending was always less than 20 percent (with a low of 6 percent in 1989). The only exception occurred in 1992, when this figure reached 20 percent. Those who supported a constant level of spending generally accounted for more than 35 percent (although they were only 32 percent in 1992 and 1994). More than 40 percent (62 percent in 1989) thought military spending should be reduced.[9]

Media-Military Relationships in the Late Modern Period

Manipulation is the most accurate term for relations between the armed forces and the media during this period. The military was suspicious toward the world of the mass media, and journalists often were considered to be badly informed and antimilitary. In addition, the media attached little importance to military matters. These were rarely debated; when there was debate, it often arose in negative contexts such as the utility of the draft, soldiers' stress, military spending, draftees' suicides, accidents, or harassment.

As a result, the military tended to keep itself at a distance and tried to either control or reduce information to the public. The public was informed only about negative or dramatic events. Very often, information about events inside the military world was openly prohibited, and public information was reduced to official communications.

This situation began to change somewhat with the Lebanon missions, where a new role was envisaged for the Italian military. International prestige was perceived as based on performance, and a new trend began to develop within the military.

Civilian Employees in the Late Modern Period

The armed forces were not civilianized. According to data from the Italian Ministry of Defense, defense personnel in 1967 included 371,083 military and 79,439 civilian employees; civilians made up 18 percent of the total. In 1988 this proportion declined to 12 percent (406,859 military and 54,845 civilians). In 1993 civilian employees accounted for 13 percent (337,940 military and 52,351 civilians); the NDM calls for 250,000 military and 43,000 civilians (about 15 percent of the total). Civilian employees were (and are) a minority component.

Women's Role in the Late Modern Period

In the Late Modern period, many aspects of relationships with minorities such as women, conscientious objectors, and homosexuals reflected changes in the parent society. During the 1950s and 1960s, however, the situation of the Modern period remained unchanged in this regard. The major changes began only in the 1970s, with deep reforms in civil rights.

During this period, the question of female military service gained attention again. The concern was women's right to pursue a military career, inasmuch as this was a form of public service. A 1963 law recognized women's full right to perform every public function; as a result, the question of military careers for women was reexamined. Such access cannot be denied in principle, but it has never been enforced by law and has never been put into practice, despite legislative proposals in 1974, 1981, and 1987.

Military service for women was proposed often, but the issue was not considered seriously until 1987. It arose during a general redefinition of the draft as service to be performed in a military or a civilian organization, which both genders could choose equally. This concept was favored by the military hierarchy, but it was still viewed with hostility by feminists and by Catholics and other religious groups. Even those who favored women in the military supported selective roles for them.

Spouse and Military Community in the Late Modern Period

Transformations affecting Italian society during this period, mainly after the 1970s, influenced the role played by military men's wives.

Women's employment increased steadily during the 1960s and 1970s, and reached 30 percent of the female population at the end of the 1980s. This trend had an effect on military spouses. According to research on Italian officers (discussed above), 46 percent of officers' wives overall were homemakers (42 percent of army officers' wives, 49 percent of air force officers' wives, and 57 percent of navy officers' wives). The remaining 54 percent were employed, mainly as teachers or clerical workers. These percentages varied according to the husbands' age and rank; thus 58 percent of officers up to the rank of captain had employed wives, as did 56 percent of majors and 52 percent of colonels.

Generally the wives of officers, especially warrant officers, were employed at a higher rate than the general female population. Spousal employment did not necessarily mean that the wives were no longer integrated within the military community, but it is plausible to assume that a woman with her own job had interests external to the family and to her husband's profession. In some cases the wife's profession affected the officer's career, not the reverse; thus his mobility was limited. The change to partial integration and to prospective "removal" had become a reality.

Homosexuals in the Military in the Late Modern Period

As stated above, homosexuals' status remains unrecognized in the armed forces.[10] With regard to politics, all questions relating to gays in the military must be considered differently for conscripts and for career personnel. Norms regarding homosexuality in the draft were liberal, although homosexuals in fact were always exempted from service. A more traditionally negative outlook dominated the treatment of career personnel; this included exclusion, discharges, and transfers. From the beginning of the Republic, homosexuality was included among the flaws leading to exclusion from service, and it was treated as a psychiatric disease.

A law passed in 1985 defined homosexuality as a behavioral anomaly. It distinguished between homosexuality as a sexual preference, which is not considered per se a cause for exemption from military service, and a set of behavioral and psychological anomalies relating to some sexual problems. These could lead to exemption of a draftee to avoid problems. Since then, self-declared and/or discovered homosexuality, especially when certified by police records in the case of criminally related behavior, has always led to exemption from military service, either on demand by the subject or on the basis of a decision by a psychiatric commission.

Career personnel were excluded or discharged. No written norm explicitly excludes homosexuals from the military, but career servicemen's cases were treated in accordance with the same law as applied to draftees. This treatment made use of the law's various definitions of sociopathic personality unacceptable in a professional soldier. In practice, however, nothing was asked and nothing was told; the eventual discovery (or declaration) was treated pragmatically according to the case. Homosexuality certainly was not regarded neutrally.

Conscientious Objection in the Late Modern Period

In contrast, conscientious objectors (COs) were treated more leniently than in the Modern period. In 1972 CO status was recognized by a law stating the right to object to military service for "those obliged to serve who declare themselves to be against a personal use of arms in every circumstance for unforgettable reasons of conscience, pertaining to a general conception of life based on deep religious or philosophical or moral beliefs professed by the subject."[11]

Those who chose conscientious objector status were required to fulfill their obligation in unarmed service or substitute civilian service for twenty months—eight months longer than required for military service. In 1989 this period was reduced to twelve months, equal to the length of military service. Alternative civilian service was to be performed in public or private institutions concerned with social assistance, care for elderly or handicapped people, education and culture, civil protection, ecology, and other such functions. Until 1989 there were 8,000 COs per year, approximately 2 or 3 percent of those eligible for the draft, but after the reform reducing the service period these figures increased to more than ten percent (44,342 in 1995).[12]

Since the beginning, the right to object has generally been considered a citizen's right. This implies that the duty to defend one's country in the military is equated with patriotic commitment to one's society. What has been lacking since the beginning is a national structure that can employ objectors efficiently without leaving them to the unpredictable and uncontrolled whims of private institutions, large or small.

Thus, in the Late Modern period, one could say that conscientious objection was permitted routinely and was virtually subsumed into civilian service, although with many contradictory effects and inconsistencies.

The Model of Organizational Identification in the Late Modern Period

At the organizational level, the structure still was based on conscription; assets were targeted only toward voluntary personnel, officers, and warrant officers.

A number of the institutional/occupational (I/O) variables remained institutionally oriented: legitimacy, role commitment, the basis of remuneration (that is, the compensation modalities of the public sector because military personnel are included in this sector), reference group, and performance evaluation. Other variables became occupational: the mode and level of compensation, residence, spouses' integration, social prestige, the legal system, and postservice status.

Some of the aspects mentioned here, however, pertain to individual sociopsychological variables. A recent study employed differently dimensioned variables (although they do not differ totally from those included in the I/O model). In this research, even though some occupational trends were evident among military professionals, the overwhelming majority of officers showed characteristics of radical and pragmatic professionalism, and of divergence from civilian society. This was especially true in the army, with no appreciable differences according to rank.[13]

Because no specific research on this issue was conducted before the end of the 1980s, we can consider only the current situation. The supposed shift from an institutional to an occupational organization has been only partial. The aspects more closely linked to job situation and private life (representative bodies, remuneration levels, seniority, career, retirement situation, defined and paid overtime work, residence) apparently have not affected the role patterns recognized by officers. These remain close to the divergent/institutional type—largely for army officers, and less so for navy and air force officers.

THE POSTMODERN PERIOD

Threat Perception in the Postmodern Period

In the past few years, the perceived threat evidently has become something other than war itself or nuclear war, as it still was in the 1980s. After 1989, the idea that war was possible seemed absurd for a limited period, and this inspired the public to rethink the idea of military usefulness. In this period the question "a military for what?" arose, but the evidence that war had not disappeared also became stronger.

Definition of Major Mission in the Postmodern Period

According to discussion about the NDM, the prevailing mission was the set of "new" missions. Even though the country and the alliance were always recognized, the reform was guided by the idea that the military would be employed in peacekeeping and humanitarian assistance. This does not mean, however, that the Italian military will become a reduced AVF with a large reserve, unless we refer to a mixed force in which a majority of volunteers are combined with a number of conscripts; the latter, at the end of their service, would become part of a large reserve of men more or less militarily trained.

Italian officers agree strongly with the new set of missions. They sustain this attitude with the perception of their increasing importance in the future, and also with the willingness to redesign their military role on new grounds of legitimacy. To some extent, the mix of volunteers and conscripts will also mean a differentiation in mission: internal defense and public order for conscripts, and international missions—peacekeeping, humanitarian aid, or even military operations—for volunteers. If and when such a differentiation goes into effect, it could cause a civilianization of the draftee sector of the military, sustained by the combination of military and civilian service and by an emphasis on militarizing the voluntary sector.

Force Structure in the Postmodern Period

The current situation is transitional. It is difficult to say whether and when the force structure will become a small professional military with a large reserve; a more plausible definition can be found in the implementation of the NDM.

The Dominant Military Professional Model in the Postmodern Period

The professional model of the soldier-diplomat-student is possible, but the future is not clear. Officers directly involved in international missions have emphasized the need for a specific education oriented to diplomacy, bargaining processes, and negotiation, as well as some sociological and anthropological knowledge to deal with cultural variety. The trend evident at the formative educational level seems likely to continue in this direction, with the large majority of cadets becoming university graduates in international politics, sociology, economics, and strategic studies.

Public Attitude toward the Military in the Postmodern Period

Since the Gulf War, the public debate has generated many new questions that merit discussion. In recent public opinion research on the various functions that could be assigned to the military, a slight majority expressed favorable opinions about the "traditional" functions of the armed forces (those which were mentioned explicitly in the Italian law regulating the matter), such as the guarantee of law and order and the defense of national territory. Researchers found much wider support (85 percent) for another institutional function of Italian armed forces—help in case of public disasters—and for the use of the army to ensure public order in areas such as Sicily, Calabria, and now Puglia, in the face of illegal immigration.[14]

The structure of these opinions can be explained by the analysis of threat perception: The respondents apparently foresee a generally stable situation. The likelihood of numerous dangerous possibilities (such as accidental nuclear war, war caused by bilateral conflicts, nuclear blackmail by Third World countries, or nuclear war between Third World countries) is regarded as stable and in some cases even as decreasing. The only threats that are perceived to be increasing are those of involvement in Third World countries' conflicts (here, the effect of Italian participation in international missions such as the Gulf War and Operation Restore Hope in Somalia is strongly evident), and, most of all, covert warfare such as international terrorism or nonmilitary problems such as mass immigration from non–European Community (EC) countries.

In short, a positive evaluation is given to both the old and the new tasks assignable to the armed forces. These tasks include peacekeeping or fighting against nonmilitary dangers: peacekeeping operations under the UN flag or NATO/EC command, international armament-control missions, the fight against the Mafia and the international drug trade, and especially the protection of the environment. The proportion of those expressing support declines to 50 percent in the case of military operations under UN command; this finding gives the impression that defining an operation as "military" reduces the likelihood of approval.

Overall, the public attitude now is more indifferent than ambivalent. Opinions about military service and women's conscription make it plausible to state that the mass army pattern, based on conscription (the citizen-soldier), is undergoing a crisis and no longer corresponds to the views of most Italians.[15] The mixed model and the voluntary army have gained most citizens' support. Women's desire to serve in the military is not dominant at all, but it is growing and openly supported in recent years, especially by the younger generation.

Media-Military Relationships in the Postmodern Period

The media now are courted somewhat by the military, which now understands that military events become media events. Thus the relationship between the armed forces and the media has improved substantially, and better information is supplied from both sides. Meetings, conferences, reports, books, and videos on the Italian armed forces' main operations have multiplied. An "image operation" is recognizable here—a marketing operation conducted by the military in order to gain not only public support but "presence" and greater knowledge.

Civilian Employees in the Postmodern Period

Civilian personnel remain, and will remain, a minority.

Women's Role in the Postmodern Period

The full integration of women is another long-term question. The question now is posed in light of the NDM, whose future and complete realization are not without problems. Among the many various difficulties affecting Italian politics and the Italian military in particular, the matter of women's integration is the least. Some women ask to be allowed to serve in the military as an officer, NCO, or even voluntary soldier, in order to support their claim to full citizenship and to carry out full job integration. A law opening military careers to women in the rank and file, NCO, and officer ranks has already been approved by the Parliamentary Defense Commission. The law would permit voluntary enlistments and applications to the three services academies, but as of this writing (in late 1998), Parliamentary consideration has been postponed. Thus, the future remains unclear in this regard.

Spouse and Military Community in the Postmodern Period

As mentioned earlier, the role of the military spouse is vanishing. Women married to military men are increasingly without special links to their husbands' professional community. This trend will become more evident as the number of young working women increases.

Homosexuals in the Military in the Postmodern Period

When homosexuality is certified, the individual usually is exempted unless a psychological evaluation determines that he has no behavioral problems in addition. Sometimes the gay movement poses the question of acceptance so that gays can gain the right to serve the country as full citizens, openly declaring their homosexuality. These requests have received some attention by the Health Division of the Italian Ministry of Defense, which is considering a proposal to include a distinction in the list of diseases and flaws that cause exemption from compulsory service. This proposal would permit the acceptance of psychologically mature and well-adjusted individuals without regard to their homosexuality, and would exempt or discharge only those who present personality pathologies. Yet this does not mean that homosexuality will be accepted in the military.

Conscientious Objection in the Postmodern Period

The question of conscientious objection has already been resolved—athough without much appreciation by the military—with the recognition of the right to object to military service and to serve in a civilian structure. According to the NMD, this structure will be part of a national service department in which objectors will not be regarded as "objectors," but simply as young citizens who have chosen to serve their country in a service other than the military. The subsumption of conscientious objection under civilian service has already been accepted in principle. What is still lacking (dramatically so, because the number of objectors is growing steadily) is an organized structure that can put into practice what has been accepted in principle.

Organizational Identification in the Postmodern Period

Changes in the structural organization will probably affect organizational identification. Such a situation will cause differences between the voluntary sector, which is far more at risk of occupational changes, and the involuntary sector. This is true for both military and civil service; the latter could be assimilated more successfully into a new institutional organization in which community service is emphasized and legitimization is based on solidarity-oriented values.

SOME CONCLUDING REMARKS

An overall question remains partially unresolved: Are the Italian armed forces becoming a Postmodern military according to the dimensions proposed by Moskos? At the risk of some oversimplification, it can be said that only five of these twelve dimensions can be regarded as already typically Postmodern: perceived threat, major mission definition, public attitude toward the military, media relationships with the military, and treatment of conscientious objection (this last, more in principle than in practice because of organizational inadequacies). Two others—force structure and the dominant military professional model—are in an intermediate position, but they are tending rather clearly toward a Postmodern definition. Seven of the twelve dimensions thus are more or less definable in Postmodern terms.

The remaining five dimensions are more complicated because of national and historical peculiarities. As for as the number of civilian employees in the Ministry of Defense and the level of civilian outsourcing, the former will remain a minor component (as in the Modern phase). Outsourcing and private contracting are expensive options that are not possible under the current financial restrictions. They were never a strong component, and are being reduced as far as possible.

The consideration of women's role in the military has surely changed. In principle, women could achieve partial integration, but so far they are still excluded. Military spouses (all women for reasons discussed above) are partially integrated; the degree of integration depends strongly on whether or not they are employed.

For homosexuals the pragmatic "don't ask, don't tell" solution is preferred, with case-by-case decisions, but it is very difficult even to imagine open acceptance in the near future. With the prospect of reduced conscription and increased volunteerism, a more open view will come only from the society and through the legal system—certainly not from an easy change within the military.

Finally, organizational identification seems likely to remain strongly institutional in the career sector, particularly among officers, and to be somewhat occupational for NCOs and other ranks. For conscripts engaged in the military or electing the option of civilian service, these concepts are not applicable. The occupationalization of the military is not yet appreciable but probably will become a major trait, if we assume that volunteers will become a large component of the Italian armed forces.

The blurring of civilian and military lines in the post–Cold War era does not completely characterize the Italian military. In this period, transition proceeds slowly and the future is highly uncertain. All one can say is that the complete actualization of the NDM could move public opinion toward a civilianized conception of the military—that is, a view of the military as a specialized area left to experts so that civilians need not concern themselves with military matters. If conscription ever offers a true choice between service in the military or the civilian sector, the two positions will be considered equivalent in ethical terms.

As in many other modernization trends, some processes move slowly. This viscosity, coupled with the peculiarities of various traditions, suggests that the Postmodern military model can be applied to the Italian armed forces only partially and with great caution.

NOTES

1. For a brief account of this subject, see M. Nuciari, "The Civil Authorities' Responsibilities and the Military in Italy," in *Democratic and Civil Control over Military Forces: Case Studies and Perspectives*, ed. E. Gilman and D. E. Herold (Rome: NATO Defense College Monograph Series, 1995), pp. 127–137.
2. Interview given to the *Corriere della Sera*, June 24, 1995.
3. See V. Ilari, *Storia del servizio militare in Italia* (History of military service in Italy) (Rome: Ce.Mi.S.S.-La Rivista Militare, 1992), Vol. 5, chaps. 1 and 2.
4. P. Ortoleva and C. Ottaviano, eds., *Guerra e massmedia* (Rome: Liguori, 1994).
5. Centro Militare di Studi Strategici (Ce.Mi.S.S.), *I movimenti pacifisti e nuclearisti in Italia, 1980–88* (Rome: Ce.Mi.S.S.-La Rivista Militare, 1990).
6. Marina Nuciari, "Rethinking Military Profession: Models of Change Confronted," *Current Sociology*, Vol. 43, No. 3 (1994), pp. 7–21; Marina Nuciari and Giuseppe Caforio, "The Officer Profession: Ideal-Type," *Current Sociology*, Vol. 43, No. 3 (1994), pp. 33–56.
7. For these and other data, see Marina Nuciari and Giuseppe Caforio, *Presente e futuro della professione militare in Europa. L'ufficiale Italiano* (Rome: Ce.Mi.S.S.-La Rivista Militare, 1995).
8. B. Russett and R. D. Deluca, "Theater Nuclear Forces: Public Opinion in Western Europe," *Political Science Quarterly*, Vol. 2 (1983), pp. 179–196.
9. Archivio Disarmo, "L'opinione pubblica italiana e l'impiego delle Forze Armate per scopi di ordine pubblico," *Informazioni della Difesa*, Vol. 1 (1993).
10. M. Nuciari, "Homosexuality and Armed Forces in Italy," in *Homosexuals in European Armed Forces: Policies, Practices and Problems*, ed. G. Harries-Jenkins (London: U.S. Army–European Research Office of the U.S. Army, Final Technical Report, April 1996), pp. 97–108.
11. Law n. 772, 1972.
12. M. Nuciari, "Conscientious Objection in Italy: Secularization and Ethical Commitment in the Consideration of Military Service," in *Conscientious Objection: From Religious Pacifism to Political Protest*, ed. C. L. Grudo (Zikhron Ya'akov–Israel: 1992), pp. 62–72; Marina Nuciari, "Italy," in *The New Conscientious Objection*, ed. C. C. Moskos and J. W. Chambers (Oxford: Oxford University Press, 1993), pp. 218–219.
13. Nuciari and Caforio, *Presente e futuro*, pp. 53–58.
14. G. Caforio and M. Nuciari, "Military Profession and Defense Issues in the Italian Public View," in *Future Roles, Missions and Structures of Armed Forces in the New World Order: The Public View*, ed. P. Manigart (New York: Nova Science, 1995), p. 74.
15. G. Caforio and M. Nuciari, "Military Profession and Defense Issues," pp. 73–94.

9

Canada: Managing Change with Shrinking Resources

FRANKLIN C. PINCH

In this chapter I characterize sociological dimensions of the Canadian military at the end of the twentieth century, employing a model of change offered by Charles Moskos. Like all Western nations, Canada is confronting global political, social, and economic change resulting partly from dissolved tensions in East-West relations. Trends in the Canadian Forces (CF) reflect the national response to changing conditions; this response includes the redefinition and/or reemphasis of the military mission and associated roles and functions, as well as significant changes in force structure and in philosophies of material and human resource management.

Until the late 1960s, the Canadian military position was influenced heavily by external pressures. Since that time, pressures indigenous to Canadian society—particularly national politics and the economics of defense—have had the greater impact. This situation is likely to be even more pronounced under post–Cold War conditions. The CF will continue to be involved in peacekeeping and related global activities, and will be an institutional partner under both multilateral (e.g., United Nations, NATO) and bilateral (e.g., NORAD) agreements; budgetary constraints, however, suggest that virtually everything military will be scaled down to the essentials.

Over roughly two decades, the CF have been socially transformed through incorporation of major changes—many of them legislated—in their host environment. They have become more democratized, liberalized, civilianized, and individualized, with significantly greater emphasis on human and equality rights. In addition, in keeping with the multicultural makeup of Canadian society, a more enlightened view of managing diversity is emerging. Global events have caused the government to dramatically reduce defense spending by eliminating infrastructure and decreasing the regular and reserve forces and civilian personnel.

Mainly from necessity, the CF also are being rationalized along corporate management lines, especially in materiel procurement and financial and human resources. The aim is to cut costs by reducing bureaucratic overhead and increasing efficiency of "service delivery." A major element of this effort is to retain only core CF competencies, defined primarily as those positions, jobs, and/or occupations which fulfill operational roles and functions or provide direct support to field operations. The military will purchase more services directly and will hire in experts from the civilian sector. At the same time, the military is attempting to create "renewal" and "cultural change" by promoting management principles such as communication (improvements in information management and technology systems, better dissemination and sharing of information), participation (more involvement in decision-making), innovation (emphasis on creative solutions, "working smarter"), and partnership (emphasis on military-civilian "defense team"). More authority is being delegated to the lower levels, and greater emphasis is being placed on "client" service, empowerment of members, flexibility, and accountability.[1] As these changes occur, the military is becoming more interdependent with institutions and organizations of civilian society. Thus, despite the emphasis on core operational roles and functions, the emerging policy and program infrastructure of the CF are occupational, business-oriented, social, and civilianized.

This trend is strengthened by the CF's predominant involvement in peacekeeping activity and other "substitute" roles and functions in support of the civilian and government sectors, and by a "total force" stance. At the end of the twentieth century the CF are emerging as a smaller, more compact institution that must balance protection of national sovereignty, domestic/civic and international roles, but with increasing accountability to a budgetary "bottom line." The Department of National Defence (DND) and CF will remain—at least in theory—integrated and unified; this will be most apparent at the "corporate" headquarters level. However, the predominant role of the corporate center is defined as that of serving the naval, land, and air operational arms (which have been evolving toward greater functional autonomy since reverting back to three distinctive uniforms more than a decade ago).[2] In this scenario, the dominant military professional must possess not only the skills associated with military operational leadership but also those of civilian management and diplomacy—that is, the ability to operate effectively in military and civilian-oriented roles, nationally and internationally.[3] Therefore, career development and reward structures probably will be designed to encourage the acquisition of military and nonmilitary competencies, perspectives, and orientations for entry into senior/executive management positions of the DND/CF "corporation." This synopsis underlies the discussion in the remainder of this chapter.

PERCEIVED THREAT

Canada has no traditional enemies.[4] The raison d'être or threat for the military has almost always been defined by its allies, notably Great Britain (U.K.)

and the United States. Until the end of the Second World War, the U.K.'s wars were Canada's wars. Canada participated in the Korean War under the United Nations' banner, chiefly in support of the United States. (This was also true of the Persian Gulf War.)

During the Cold War, Canada assumed the strategy and "threat posture" defined by the United States and Western Europe. For example, the CF's formally stated mission, roles, and functions were expressed in terms of multilateral and bilateral defense arrangements under NATO and NORAD, backed by commitment of troops and equipment, in both North America and Europe. (Except for diplomatic representation, all NATO-assigned troops were withdrawn from Europe in 1994.) Recently Canada defined the threat in terms of world instability, especially as related to the creation of large groups of political refugees and the existence of widespread poverty, hunger, starvation, human rights abuses, and denial of basic individual freedom, security, and protection. Regional and subnational conflicts are also viewed as indirect threats not only to democratic and humanitarian values but also to Canada's economic interests as a trading nation.[5]

Domestically, the threat is seen in terms of challenges to Canada's territorial integrity (e.g., overfishing in its territorial waters, the illicit drug trade, terrorism, environmental pollution, and disturbances within its borders that require military assistance to a civil power), as well as potential loss of national defense responsibilities to others (particularly the United States).[6]

Finally, the size of the national debt (second only to that of the United States) has been held up as a threat, mainly as a means of rationalizing defense cuts. Large, uncontrolled debt potentially could reduce confidence in Canada's economic integrity among key figures in the world market, and possibly could undermine long-term national independence and viability. (Politically, the same might be said about Quebec's secessionist rhetoric and actions.)

DEFINITION OF MAJOR MISSION

As suggested above, Canada's military mission statements during the Cold War reflected the need to deter threats of nuclear war from the Soviet Union and its satellite countries. This was true even in the 1987 White Paper on Defence (which now is viewed as somewhat myopic and unrealistic). It also included the need to maintain territorial defense capability, to participate in peacekeeping and humanitarian operations, and, when necessary, to assist the civilian power. A policy statement issued on September 17, 1991, listed defense priorities as defense of sovereignty and civil defense responsibilities in Canada; collective defense under NATO and NORAD; and international peace and stability (peacekeeping), arms control, verification, and humanitarian assistance. These goals were reiterated in the 1994 White Paper on Defence.[7]

The first of these priorities indicates that the CF not only will remain actively involved in continental defense, but also will accept civilian support roles such as assistance to other government departments in coastal, law enforcement, and environment monitoring.

Multilateralism and bilateralism in defense alliances are viewed as affordable and productive options that fit Canada's geography (huge territory), demographics (small population), and economic circumstances. In fact, collective security alliances have as much relation to economic affiliation (e.g., under GATT and NAFTA) as to security threats and defense policy. For these reasons, Canada will remain a participant in both NATO and NORAD, as well as a willing peacekeeping partner in the UN. On the latter point, as the Cold War ended, the CF already had greatly increased their participation in peacekeeping, humanitarian, and related UN-sponsored missions. Thus the shift of emphasis in mission was more evolutionary than abrupt, even though peacekeepers generally have faced more instability and risk in post–Cold War operations.[8]

CONSIDERATIONS OF FORCE STRUCTURE

The reduced national security threat (or at least a threat that is defined as more diffuse and more indeterminate), along with domestic pressures, has led to reductions in defense expenditures and to changes in structure, management, and organization of forces. As a proportion of the gross domestic product, Canadian defense spending is at its lowest point since the 1930s—below 1.5 percent. The 1995 budget was slashed by $2.8 billion; the total expenditure for 1997–98 was $10 billion, approximately the same dollar amount as in 1987–88.[9] (This will dip to $9.2 billion in 1998–99, a 23 percent decrease over 1994.) In fact, the military is moving rapidly toward a reduced professional cadre of full-time members, as well as a smaller number of part-time members or reservists. For example, the 1994 White Paper calls for a reduction in regular force personnel to 60,000 (from 75,000) and a reduction of the primary reserve to 23,000 (from 29,000), both by 1999.[10] Total civilian employees will number 20,000, down from approximately 33,000. The scale of the DND/CF training requirements and associated infrastructure will be reduced to reflect these lower numbers.

National Defence Headquarters (NDHQ) staffs—military and civilian—are being reduced by as much as 50 percent (from 14,000 to 7,000), and one level of command (headquarters) was eliminated 1997.[11] The heads of the maritime, land force, and air commands have been transferred to DND headquarters in Ottawa to become environmental chiefs of staff (ECS). The operational arms of the CF have become regional formations or fleets and groups, though a centralized system for training support personnel remains. The army has reorganized into four area formations; the navy into east and west coast fleets; the air force has reconfigured into eastern and western fighter aircraft bases and air transport bases. Eventually there will be a handful of "super" bases, wings, and garrisons as well as some single-purpose satellite units. Overall a smaller, far less costly total force is envisioned.

The proportions of sea, land, and air forces have been adjusted to reflect additional tasks assigned to the land force. The army retains its general-purpose capability across the full spectrum of operational tasks, including peace-keeping, and will receive 3,000 additional troops. The sea element continues to support an operational fleet on the east and west coasts, and training squadrons on the latter. Antisubmarine warfare activities connected with the protection of shipping have been reduced; participation in UN and multilateral operations has been increased. The focus of air operations has shifted from a Cold War stance to a more balanced set of domestic and international activities, many in support of joint operations in peace support deployments; expenditures have been reduced by 25 percent. The main role of the Primary Reserve will continue to be the augmentation, sustenance, and support of deployed regular forces. Although reserve personnel strength is being reduced, issues of training and operational cost-effectiveness are under review in relation to those associated with the regular force.

The concept of "total force" is still in vogue, but its realization as an effective, operable structure in Canada is hampered in a number of ways. Unlike the United States and other nations, Canada has no formal arrangements between government and industry to support reserve members' participation. Reserve service (like regular force service) is voluntary; therefore, personal motivation to serve is usually insufficient to overcome the conflicting obligations posed by reservists' civilian roles. Consequently, both training progress and operational readiness tend to suffer.

Reservists' continuous obligation to fulfill their commitments has been legally difficult to enforce; it depends mainly on efforts at persuasion at the unit level. The CF have taken steps to bring reservists' pay and benefits into line with those of the regular force, with some positive results. Many reservists, however, tend to participate for noneconomic reasons, whereas most members of the regular force are economically motivated. Therefore, additional incentives (e.g., employee leave, enhanced status in the community) are likely to be required for reservists. In the absence of structural supports, military planners are likely to remain vexed by problems of absenteeism, high turnover (greater than 30 percent a year in many units), recruiting, and training.[12]

Greater dependence on the reserves—which is possible if the government continues to see defense spending as a popular target for reduction—is likely to generate additional pressure on the smaller professional cadre. In the short term, however, deployment of primarily regular-force personnel, with limited numbers of similarly trained reserve augmentees, is considered the most efficient and effective response to crises around the world.[13]

THE DOMINANT TYPE OF MILITARY PROFESSIONAL:
THE SOLDIER-DIPLOMAT/CORPORATE LEADER–MANAGER

As Morris Janowitz recognized long ago, dominant military professional types are produced by the confluence of socialization and the type of problems to be resolved at any given time. Although the "technical specialist" was the modal type during most of the Cold War period, the image and rhetoric of the "heroic warrior" have remained part of the CF combat arms, particularly in the infantry regiments and in some operational training schools. To some, the "warrior syndrome" apparently was perpetuated within a dysfunctional form of tribalism—developed to counter the effects of integration and unification of the armed forces during the 1960s and 1970s—whose norms and values became distorted internally and received neither adequate scrutiny nor sufficient external validation.[14] The most extreme case of this negative evolution occurred in the now-disbanded Canadian Airborne Regiment (CAR), where antisocial norms, values, beliefs, and practices appear to have reached their zenith in the 1980s and 1990s. These documented aberrations—which included individual and group indiscipline, as well as poor and/or inappropriate leadership—led to disastrous results in the deployment of CAR to Somalia. The latter included torture and murder of at least one Somali youth, the alleged unnecessary shooting and abuse of others, and numerous other unsavory and/or illegal acts.[15] (It needs to be emphasized that the vast majority of CF deployees of all ranks conducted themselves in a highly professional and responsible manner.)

Contemporary military professionalism requires transparency and value-integration with the external world; peace support, humanitarian, and domestic roles require social sensitivity, respect for diversity, and a sense of "civic consciousness."[16] Because these roles have moral and ethical implications, military leaders and professionals must model the highest standards of professional conduct, behavior, and judgment. According to the rank and file of the DND/CF, these are basic leadership qualities for the officer corps and senior noncommissioned officers in the post–Cold War environment.[17] This view is buttressed by both the findings of the Commission of Inquiry into the Deployment of Canadian Forces to Somalia[18] and by the recommendations of an independent review panel appointed by the minister of national defense in December 1996.[19] Professional ethics and values are destined to have a prominent place in future training and development of CF leaders at all levels.

The CF, like other post–Cold War militaries, confront rapid change on all levels. They need leaders who can cope with these changes, define military requirements in terms that are congruent with them, and gain acceptance for these requirements from above and below. The DND/CF are making efforts to ensure that awareness of change becomes part of the senior leader's repertoire, but this process is neither easy nor certain, and resistance is widespread.[20]

Political awareness is necessary both for anticipating strategic requirements and for obtaining needed resources; knowledge of technological advances is necessary both to improve military effectiveness and to reduce costs; an appreciation of economic trends and conditions is necessary to determine options that are realistic and fiscally supportable; and knowledge of the probable effects of social change is necessary for an appropriate response to the external public (e.g., lobby and interest groups, local community leaders) and members of the CF.

Virtually all change has implications for the management of human resources, often as direct results. Canadian Forces leaders must be able to understand and handle increasingly complex human resource issues and groups as they work with reduced personnel budgets and attempt to maintain a reasonably effective military. The emphasis is increasingly on business and corporate management techniques, primarily to reduce costs and increase efficiencies. "Postmodernization" is now represented by business process reengineering, supported by a computerized information technology and applications that are responsive to personnel management and administrative problem-solving. Military leaders must preside over replacing people with computers and doing more with fewer military and civilian employees.[21]

A more interdependent, community-based military that incorporates the reserve gives officers additional opportunity for direct contact with the civilian community. This will become a more important prerequisite for more senior appointments, along with other developmental credentials and civilian-related experience. This trend has been endorsed by a career-development board that focuses on (among other things) making the "corporate level" officers more compatible with their public service and other civilian counterparts.[22] An area of deficiency that has been singled out for improvement is the low formal education level of CF officers, relative to other modern militaries. Fully 50 percent of combat arms—including a significant number of senior officers—hold less than a postsecondary degree.[23]

The dominant type of post–Cold War leader will require institutional legitimacy, gained in a series of operational and staff positions. This leader will be rendered effective, however, by strategic elicitation, analysis, and use of knowledge in making decisions and by the ability to move easily between the military and the civilian worlds. Many of these skills can be gained only through extensive education and experience outside the CF. The current changes also may affect qualitatively the relationship of the officer corps to their political masters, the public, and the rank and file.

Thus, knowledge of the factors that create internal pressures—political, economic, and social—will become quite important for the institutional stability and survival of the CF. The dominant leader in this scenario is likely to combine many of the skills and attributes of a soldier-diplomat on the operational side and a corporate leader-manager on the administrative and management side.

PUBLIC ATTITUDES TOWARD THE MILITARY

Public opinion generally has supported the Canadian military's entry into conflict; in the Second World War, this support was maintained throughout. During peacetime the military generally has not been thought to require attention, and the institution has had to work hard to determine the public's perceptions. Attitudes toward the military generally vary by region: The province of Quebec shows a different pattern of support (usually weaker) for the military than the rest of Canada. In 1990, for example, only 54 percent of Quebecers saw the necessity for a military, in contrast to 71 percent of Canadians outside Quebec.[24] As for roles, Quebecers are more likely than other Canadians to support provision of humanitarian aid over defense of the country, and 66 percent of other Canadians (but only 56 percent of Quebecers) view the military as a symbol of national pride. Much of this pride is due to the CF's participation in UN peacekeeping and humanitarian operations, but problems in Somalia and other reported incidents have probably tarnished the military's reputation in the eyes of the public.

Even so, in the absence of a visible enemy, national security and defense barely enter most Canadians' consciousness. Throughout the 1970s and 1980s, fewer than .5 percent of Canadians mentioned defense as one of their major concerns. This proportion increased only to 3 percent during the Persian Gulf crisis (which was supported by decreasing numbers of Canadians as the war progressed) and returned to its traditional level at the end of the conflict.

From the 1960s to the 1980s, attitudes toward the Canadian military can be defined most appropriately as ambivalent. Such ambivalence was reflected particularly among youths, both in their propensity to view the military as a career option and in the turnover patterns of those who enrolled in the CF.[25] Had it not been for severe economic conditions and the massive downsizing and job losses in the public and private sectors during the late 1980s and early 1990s, the CF would have found it difficult to maintain adequate personnel levels. In the words of one analyst, the military organization—which is regarded as limiting individual freedom and restricting choices—is "a tough sell."[26]

The CF's greater emphasis on peacekeeping and humanitarian missions resonates with a significant number of Canadians, who prefer to see the military perform useful social and humanitarian roles.[27] However, this quality probably will not be sufficient to engage most Canadians in defense issues in the medium to long term, especially in light of other preoccupations, such as national unity and the economy.

Despite positive views about the CF expressed by Canadians in an opinion survey carried out by the Pollara polling group in the fall of 1998, indifferent or negative public opinion is likely to remain a recurring challenge. Thus the military must continuously strive to be a visible part of the community and to improve upon its public image. Owing to relatively poor job prospects for young Canadians (especially from those regions and groups that have traditionally seen the military as an avenue for social mobility) and the low projected personnel requirements for the CF, recruitment is unlikely to be a serious problem between now and the early years of the twenty-first century.

Likely exceptions to this projection include professional categories of high demand (e.g., engineers and pilots) and those occupational fields that pose specific barriers to certain categories of potential recruits (e.g., women's entry into the combat arms).

CIVILIAN EMPLOYEES

The primary issues regarding civilian DND employees are the degree to which they will (1) influence military decisions and (2) represent increased civilianization of the military culture. Under the planned cuts, civilian employees will represent one-third of the regular force and slightly less than one-quarter of the total force. Some civilians will occupy the highest bureaucratic positions and will profoundly affect defense policy (not to mention those in key middle level positions). For example, the deputy minister of national defense, whose status is equivalent to that of the chief of the defense staff (CDS), often has been enormously influential, and sometimes has overshadowed a newly appointed CDS.

According to Harriet Critchley,[28] the initial military-civilian integration at the NDHQ level made the military more influential in decision-making. She focuses almost entirely on the committee system in existence since the early 1970s; there is little to suggest that this situation will change appreciably with the current cutbacks. It is not known, however, how strongly the day-to-day work will influence important decisions under the new organizational configuration. We can assume that a civilian incumbent in a middle or senior management position for a significant length of time will develop a great deal of position power. Civilian and military staffs generally have worked well together, and although tension has existed below the surface, serious problems have been the exception. Thus, little change from previous periods is expected.

In regard to cultural influence, the military already has been civilianized. Although most of the civilian personnel are employed in NDHQ, current trends in reducing uniformed personnel may well see greater proportions of civilians, as employees or contractors, at lower levels. The new "defense team" concept suggests that commonalities rather than differences should be the focus of attention among military and civilian personnel. It has also been argued that the civil service ethic and the military ethos, while distinct from one another, are also complementary.[29] One salient issue is that junior ranks (corporals and privates) should not be sent to NDHQ because military socialization is likely to be seriously weakened in the civilianized environment. Overall CF members have had extensive experience in working with civilian employees in an integrated format. Nonetheless, the increased presence of contract civilians, at all levels of the military organization, is likely to make organizational boundaries more permeable and, in turn, may render the maintenance of internal integration more difficult.

GENDER INTEGRATION AND SEXUAL ORIENTATION

Redefinition of missions and roles, adjustments in force structure, and reforms of administrative process are occurring not only under severe economic constraints but also against the backdrop of social change, which has penetrated the CF far more deeply than could have been imagined two decades ago. The principal reason is that trends have been formalized in social (equal rights) legislation; this legislation compels the CF to justify any policies that exclude individuals (who also may claim membership in an identifiable social group) from participation. Such justification must be made on the basis of bona fide occupational requirements. The Canadian Human Rights Act and the Charter of Rights and Freedoms (the Charter), which were enacted in 1982 and 1985, respectively, prohibit discrimination on the grounds of race, national/ethnic origin, color, religion, age, sex (including pregnancy and childbirth), marital status, family status, pardoned conviction, and physical or mental disability (including disfigurement and drug dependency). Exemptions under the Charter are possible only if they are demonstrably justified as constituting "reasonable limits in a free and democratic society"; the burden of proof is placed on the institution(s) claiming exemption. The military has been unable to make a convincing case for exemptions in most areas, and therefore has had to accommodate a number of important changes.[30]

Mixed-Gender Employment

One of the most dramatic changes has been the removal of barriers to women's entry into all military occupations and units except submarines.

(The latest step was their entry into all combat occupations and units, ordered by a human rights tribunal in February 1989. All restrictions on air combat had been lifted before the tribunal ruling.) Women now serve on combat vessels in about one-third of the naval fleet, and in selected artillery and armored environments in the land combat arms; this is in addition to previously integrated combat service support units, supply vessels, and isolated units. Women have exactly the same liability to serve as do men, including service in peacekeeping operations, to which they have been deployed since 1973. They now constitute about 11 percent of the regular force and 23 percent of the reserve.[31]

The major difficulties in achieving gender integration have been encountered in the regular force infantry, where few women have succeeded in completing "battle school" training. While the occasional woman has broken down these barriers and gone on to serve in ground operations (for example, a female infantry captain has twice served very successfully in an infantry company in the former Yugoslavia, and a number of junior-rank women have also served in other overseas combat arms assignments), none have remained employed in combat operations for any appreciable period of time. Once women have demonstrated capability, they generally have been utilized in their appropriate occupational role, but the physical and social odds do not favor their success.

Studies conducted in 1997 show that women who have entered the combat arms have typically confronted an inhospitable environment. Their lives have been made uncomfortable and additionally stressful by the negative attitudes and behaviors of males, whom many women believe have not treated them respectfully, equitably, or fairly.[32] Also, the fact that many male supervisors, instructors, and training staff have stated that they do not feel confident in their ability to deal effectively with women puts the latter at a great disadvantage. Even when women have met the physical standards, they still have had to overcome significant social and psychological barriers that exist in a world of decided male dominance. These have included discrimination, sexual harassment, and various forms of abuse (more of which later). Not surprisingly, women have tended to enter the combat arms in small numbers and cycle out of combat units at a higher rate than males, making little or no social impact on this heightened masculine domain.

It is clear that the regular force combat arms leadership has been less than totally committed to fully integrating women. The results are apparent: very small numbers of women remain in the combat arms at time of writing. This problem, and the responsibility for it, has been publicly acknowledged by the current chief of the defense staff (CDS), an army general, who seems determined to overcome the army's failure to support gender integration adequately. For example, he has stated that he expects any remaining discriminatory barriers against women to be removed from the training and development system. Also, spurred by recommendations from the previously mentioned independent panel review, recruiting targets for women entering the combat arms were set by the CF early in 1997. Whether or not these efforts will appreciably increase women's representation in the regular force combat arms remains to be seen.[33]

Women have been integrated more easily into reserve combat arms, where men's attitudes have—with some notable exceptions—been more amenable to their participation, and where differences in standards and shorter periods of duty have permitted them to compete with men more successfully. However, most reserve women have no desire to transfer to the regular force combat units, in large part because they believe they would not be welcome there.

It is unlikely that women will ever form a significant part of the regular infantry, primarily because of self-selection as well as the physical, social, and psychological barriers mentioned above. Also, the great majority of women are found in support occupations; therefore the current reductions, which aim to decrease nonoperational support personnel, are likely to reduce the overall proportion of women. Nonetheless, as a group and individually, women are gaining acceptance and respect from men for their performance, adaptability, and commitment to their military careers. In some support occupations this is apparent in the rates of promotion, which equal or surpass those of men. Overall, however, women are still well below equal representation with men in the most senior ranks for both commissioned and noncommissioned groups, and they have no senior representation in the combat arms.[34]

Combat arms and infantry aside, in the past, one of the most serious concerns in managing a mixed-gender force was related to women's absence during pregnancy. The CF have developed a policy that permits up to twenty-seven weeks of maternity leave, and the option of requesting additional leave without pay for early child-rearing. Because of the economic squeeze, replacement for maternity-related absences is difficult: Additional trained personnel are required, but are not always available. Even so, replacement reportedly has been managed satisfactorily in most situations.

As more women have entered the CF, the percentage of married service couples has risen to approximately 7 percent and is likely to increase even further over the next decade. Although colocation of service spouses has been well accommodated in the CF (in some years, up to 90 percent of service couples colocated), child care—particularly when both spouses are serving in operational units—is a continuing management challenge.

Research in the early 1990s indicated widespread harassment in the CF;[35] this included personal and sexual harassment (almost one-third of female respondents indicated that they had been sexually harassed by a male) and abuse of authority. Indeed, the harassment problem cited most often by both males and females was abuse of authority by supervisors and superiors. In 1992 the CF adopted a policy of zero tolerance for harassment of any kind. Military units have harassment complaint advisors to accept complaints from members and assist in their appropriate handling. Preventive measures include a broad-based education, training, and sensitization program.

None of the actions taken have prevented harassment and abuse of women by men (incidents of which have been highly publicized and/or have resulted in convictions against males[36]). In this regard, the chain of command often appears to have been part of the problem rather than providing the solution. During May to July of 1998, *Macleans Magazine* ran a series of articles describing various forms of abuse suffered by former CF women members, many of whom alleged they had complained (or attempted to complain) while serving, only to be further victimized and/or drummed out of the military by CF authorities.[37] The graphic details of the alleged abuse, mainly against junior women of both officer and noncommissioned status, occurred across the CF among regular and reserve units. To some extent, this supported previous internal research results which had not been acted upon.[38] They prompted the CDS to order the establishment of a complaints hotline to be staffed on a full-time basis. An avalanche of complaints followed, many directed to the CDS personally at his invitation. Investigations of all complaints were ordered by the CF provost marshall, and as of this writing are being carried out by a newly constituted National Investigation Service.

Moreover, the CDS has personally directed executive leaders to become actively involved in stamping out all forms of abuse and discrimination against women, with the clear implication that inaction is not an option. Many observers agree that such direction and commitment from the top to support the employment of service women is long overdue.

The problems of gender integration described above should be seen in the context of a long-term transition from single- to mixed-gender units. Overall, progress has been made, especially among the support arms of all service elements and components. Also, the presence of women in operations is affecting, and will continue to affect, the units' masculine cultural norms. Supervisors (male and female) will be assessed increasingly on their ability to manage diversity, which includes a mixture of genders. Problems such as sexual harassment will require heightened sensitivity among men; this is only now showing signs of development, as the educational and training programs and experience begin to take effect. Over the next decade, as more women enter senior ranks, the incidence of gender-related interpersonal problems is likely to decrease. With greater emphasis on accountability by executive leaders, as well as closer support and monitoring and a more enlightened complaints process, those incidents which do occur are more likely to be handled in a satisfactory manner.

Sexual Orientation

Since October 1992, known homosexuals have been enrolled and retained in the CF. The CF had actually agreed to lift the ban on homosexuals in October 1991, but members of the Progressive Conservative caucus objected and the move was delayed. A settlement of a complaint registered under the Charter by an admitted lesbian officer who had been discharged rendered all restrictive regulations against homosexuals null and void.[39]

Before the lifting of restrictions, official policies toward homosexuality had created a great deal of uncertainty among supervisors and senior leaders (not to mention homosexuals themselves). Various restrictive policies were in place, from outright prohibition to making it a service member's responsibility to report known or suspected homosexuals. As the policies became more liberal, primarily as the result of social, political, and legislative pressure, contradictions appeared. For example, known gays and lesbians could not be developed, moved geographically, or promoted, but many were seen to be performing their duties well. Many supervisors regarded this state of limbo as unfair and discriminatory; units and commands placed increasing pressure on senior authorities to end the state of uncertainty.

Numerous politicians and the Canadian human rights commissioner saw the policy as violating the terms of the Charter, and a majority of the Canadian public indicated that they did not agree with discriminatory policies against homosexuals. Moreover, research and other evidence were weak and inconclusive in supporting restrictions. Four complaints under the Charter provided the legal impetus for change, but the decision was made on the basis of only one complaint. Although this case was not argued in court, the settlement, in effect, included the lifting of all restrictions on homosexuals.

The removal of restrictions has had virtually no negative impact in any of the predicted areas, including CF recruitment, retention, morale, trust, and confidence. Yet culture-based homophobia persists below the surface, especially among males within some segments of the combat arms.[40] However, there has been no significant increase in declarations of homosexuality by CF members; authorities consider this largely a nonissue. Six years after the policy change, it is clear that much of the earlier concern about an open policy on homosexuality was unwarranted. This development may be due in part to the behaviorally based zero-tolerance harassment policy covering both heterosexuals and homosexuals, which was issued simultaneously with the decision to lift restrictions. Also, in view of the CF's recent difficulties with some straight males, a declaration of homosexuality would now appear quite mild by comparison.

The Canadian Supreme Court has not recognized same-sex partners as entitled to benefits. Yet some commercial enterprises, provincial jurisdictions, and even the CF members' insurance companies are now blind to partner gender when awarding claims and benefits. Moreover, the Canadian Parliament recently has included sexual orientation as protected ground under the Canadian Human Rights Act, and it is predicted that benefits for same-sex partners eventually will follow. Indeed, many federal departments—DND included—are planning for such a contingency.

On the issue of benefits and sexual identification (not the same as homosexuality), in the summer of 1998, CF authorities approved financial support for a sex-change operation for a service member. While this may seem radical to some (and was the subject of international media coverage at the time), this decision is quite consistent with Canada's human rights legislation and with a universal health care system that underwrites the predominant medical expenses of Canadian citizens. There is no prohibition against changing one's sex in Canada and no evidence to indicate that this would in any way impair occupational role and task performance. In fact, given the known negative psychological effects of gender identity confusion, there is reason to believe they would be improved.

Overall Impact

Issues related to expanding women's employment opportunities and lifting restrictions against homosexuals are part of the larger concern of incorporating individual, human, and equality rights, as well as democratizing the military institution. These changes have increased the complexity of management and have created anxiety and concern among the more traditional elements of the CF. Although gender integration has been fraught with difficulties for the women themselves, especially in the combat arms, the changes have had no measurable operational impact on the CF, and many of the concerns have proved to be unfounded. This is even more the case for the changed policy on sexual orientation.

The trend toward greater protection of CF members' rights and freedoms is now well established. Recent examples include improvements in the administration of military justice under the provisions of the Code of Service Discipline (especially in the areas of impartiality and procedural fairness), grievance procedures, initiatives in the management of diversity, and the recent establishment of an organizational ombudsman office. These changes were already underway, but were given further impetus by the recommendations of the independent review panel, which reported to the government in March 1997, and the Commission of Inquiry into the Deployment of Canadian Forces to Somalia, which reported to the government in June 1997. Both have assisted in highlighting departmental and military deficiencies that arose out of problems in post–Cold War peacekeeping operations,[41] and have focused the government's and CF's attention on continuing with necessary organizational reforms. There is also an underlying message in the changes that have taken place in the CF: The chain of command, by itself, cannot deal effectively with all human problems—at least in these difficult transition stages—and leaders at all levels must be willing to look to other assisting mechanisms and supports.

MEDIA RELATIONS

During the Second World War and the Korean Conflict, the Canadian military enjoyed a mainly supportive press. Much of the media focus during the Cold War was on defense budgets (which competed with those of social welfare programs) and on examples of the military's "wasteful" spending practices (usually associated with defense contracts); these were widely reported but soon forgotten. The internal departmental conflict generated by integration and unification in the mid- to late-1960s also drew attention (especially the dramatic resignations of several high-ranking naval officers).

In recent years, the CF have experienced increasing difficulty interacting with the media; currently, they exist in an uneasy relationship. This is partly the result of the secretive manner in which the military has operated and partly due to the perception that the media are interested primarily in reporting the sensational, often embarrassing, aspects of the military. In the late 1970s the Canadian Access to Information Act opened most of the files of the military to the Canadian public and the media. Much of the reporting on the military stems from information obtained by this route, which has not been embraced by the CF organization. In recent years, however, the CF leaders have realized that the media are important in building a positive public image, and through the development of internal communication agencies have attempted to exert some control over what is reported. This effort has been only partly successful.

The so-called Somalia Affair has had a profoundly negative impact on CF-media relations. From the time that the torture death of the young Somali was discovered and reported by a Canadian broadcast journalist in March 1993, the CF have experienced one public relations disaster after another.[42] Several officers and noncommissioned members were implicated in the crime and court-martialed but this did not satisfy the public, least of all the media, since it appeared that officers got off very lightly and the only serious conviction was upheld against one private.

The internal public relations turmoil for the military was fueled by almost daily revelations from the government-appointed Commission of Inquiry into the Somalia incidents, which began to hear testimony in the fall of 1995 and did not finish until March 1997. The hearings and the five-volume commission report point to ethical and professional lapses among CF and departmental leaders at the highest levels, as well as deliberate, illegal attempts to withhold, amend, or destroy information pertinent to the Somalia inquiry and/or sought by the news media. Ironically, the DND's own public affairs agency was implicated by the information commissioner in altering documents (two senior public affairs officers were court-martialed and one was acquitted of alleged offenses). A newly appointed chief of the defense staff resigned after appearing as a witness before the inquiry, partly as a result of self-admissions in his own testimony; however, these were then magnified and reinforced by the intense media scrutiny which attended the proceedings. Previously, relations between the CF and the media were strained by details of hazing rituals, with overtones of racism, performed by members of the Canadian Airborne Regiment and captured on videotape. (These incidents directly precipitated the government's decision to disband the Canadian Airborne Regiment). The destruction of another tape by a battalion commander, who subsequently was promoted, gave the media even more ammunition. During these episodes, several attempts by the minister of national defense and the chief of the defense staff to improve relations with the media either failed or backfired. The situation was not helped by the replacement of these officials, so long as the Commission of Inquiry was sitting; indeed, animosity between the commission chairman and both the minister and the acting chief of the defense staff was reproduced and amplified in CF-media relations. Finally, an additional ingredient in military-media relations has been the public criticism of the military leadership by former serving members, most of them senior officers, who also served as informants for a critical media.

The CF recognize the value of good military-media relations, particularly in peace operations, and officers are trained so as to capitalize on the opportunities for media contact. These recent episodes, however, weakened the trust between these two institutions, and repairs will likely take some time.

In the long term, the military needs the media. Cultivating public and political support, obtaining needed resources, and attracting personnel depend in part on the image that journalists and reporters project to Canadians and to the international public. This will be a challenge for an institution that has had a relatively "closed system" attitude toward informing the public and has often been ineffective in internal communications as well. There are some hopeful signs, however. One of the change initiatives has been the development of better internal communications methods; in fact, both departmental employees and CF members are much better informed of these events than they have ever been. Also, current executive leaders appear more adept at eliciting positive media coverage, which may well be linked to a more open, forthright manner in dealing with the public. Moreover, at times the media have been catalysts in highlighting the need for improved conditions of military members themselves and, in this sense, have acted as unofficial ombudsmen in getting CF members' stories out to the public (see next section). Courting the media certainly must be a part of longer-term military reform, but it would be unrealistic to expect the media-military tension to disappear.

SPOUSES AND THE MILITARY COMMUNITY

The role and place of spouses in the post–Cold War military community may be examined in light of trends affecting families in Canadian society and reflected in the military.[43] These include a great increase in Canadian women's rates of labor force participation (to almost two-thirds in 1995); an increase to over 60 percent dual-earner families among households consisting of husband-wife couples; increasing divorce rates among military couples, with 3 percent of CF families headed by a single parent; a greater number of "blended" or "reconstituted" families and common-law marriages; much more emphasis on males assuming their share of domestic responsibilities, including childrearing; increasing psychological stress for both spouses in meeting conflicting demands of career and household; and CF members' reluctance, for family reasons, to relocate or be posted, even if they lose opportunities for advancement.

Today, wives of CF members (especially officers) can no longer be assumed to be adjuncts to their husbands' careers. Spouses now tend to have their own career aspirations and jobs that are considered essential to the entire family's economic and psychological well-being. The world of the civilian spouse is increasingly independent from that of the service-member spouse, and often is incompatible with the demands of the military institution. Fewer and fewer spouses wish to act as unpaid support staff and/or social directors to further their partners' careers. Even those foreign "diplomatic" postings which are held to require a "supporting wife" may be challenged rather than prized.

At the same time, supports for the military family—social services, day care, and special attention during wartime, peacekeeping, or other absences of the service member—are being improved significantly. This is in addition to the traditionally paternalistic support provided by the regiment, the CO's wife, and other sources. A directorate of military family support was created at NDHQ in 1989, and family support centers were established where warranted by the numbers of military families.[44] This approach permits maximum spousal involvement and provides professional, salaried staff to link the military family to social support networks in the civilian community. Policy is set by a board of directors with only minimum uniformed representation. Moreover, spouses have been given access to military facilities for meetings and other activities that help them resolve problems and voice their concerns more effectively.

The military is expected to be responsive to spousal and family concerns because these concerns interfere with CF members' morale and performance, but the CF is losing influence over military families, including the ability to make demands on the spouse through the member. Greater utilization of reservists simply reinforces this trend. Family requirements increasingly exert pressure on CF decision-making regarding individual members, but the

CF cannot expect to use such decisions to gain control over the spouse or the family.

The inability of the CF to make demands on spouses is most evident in the fact that an association of military spouses has been formed. This group may directly lobby the minister of national defense or other members of Parliament, or may stage other protests for the media, often with support of other interest groups. Therefore military leaders must take account of opposition that may arise when defense policies conflict with family requirements. This development has raised military managers' consciousness significantly.

In addition, CF policy now recognizes the rights of common-law spouses for military entitlement and use of facilities; also, pressure will continue to mount for paternity benefits and other couples' support of a type that is becoming commonplace among civilian employers. Flexibility in postings and deployments already has been affected, and family specialists are asked increasingly for advice and assistance in resolving conflicts between the CF and the military family. A zero-tolerance policy aimed at curbing spousal, child, and elder abuse has been issued and requires the input of helping professionals through local committees. These trends are bound to influence CF members' social attitudes.

Most recently, the parliamentary Standing Committee on National Defence and Veterans Affairs, known as SCONDVA, has taken an active interest in quality-of-life issues of service members in general and the well-being of the military family in particular. Hearings have been held in Ottawa and elsewhere and numerous briefs and submissions have been made by informed professionals and CF members and authorities. Compensation and benefit levels of lower-ranking service members, military housing, and spousal disadvantages vis-à-vis the workforce have been taken up as worthy causes by SCONDVA members. This was precipitated, to some extent, by media reports of military families having to go to food banks because they had insufficient funds to feed their families properly. Service members and their spouses recounted, often dramatically, their financially related horror stories before SCONDVA hearings at CF establishments across Canada. Much of the problem was associated with a wage freeze imposed by the government in 1991 and only lifted in 1997.

As a result of the hearings and systematic analyses of compensation and benefit policies and practices in other organizations—analysis provided by the CF and others—SCONDVA, in October 1998, recommended hefty increases (up to 10 percent) in salary levels for the lower ranks (much less for the higher ranks), along with labor force and other family benefits for spouses. Whether these will be implemented by the government has yet to be determined. There can be no doubt, however, that spouses were influential in helping to determine the SCONDVA decisions.

ORGANIZATIONAL TYPE: INSTITUTIONAL, OCCUPATIONAL, OR CIVIC?

The CF remain unique among militaries of the world in their fully integrated and unified organizational structure—even though the navy, army, and air force components have become more autonomous and their separate identities are now more prominently displayed. Institutional features of the CF are maintained through the regimental model of organization. According to the most recent official declaration, operational roles and functions represent the core competencies that the CF wish to retain, along with support functions directly linked to operational roles. This would suggest a step back into a traditional institutional culture. At the same time, however, business metaphors and modeling are being used to make key changes in the CF organization, with emphasis on developing business plans and cases to support various management initiatives. The reorganization that is occurring within the DND and the CF is designed to produce an "operational layer," consisting mostly of military personnel, and a "corporate layer," which is a fusion of military and civilian positions within the DND and the CF, primarily at the national headquarters level. This corporate arrangement reflects the emphasis placed on the defense team; civilians will be the permanent participants, while the military will cycle through periodically.

The notion of business planning, increased use of civilian consulting and/or alternative delivery of services, and total force arrangements brings the CF much closer to the mainstream of civilian society on the structural, dynamic, and role levels. These changes influence both individuals' orientation and the institutional character of the CF. Business values concentrate on the "bottom line" and tend not to focus on generalized commitments which, at least in theory, have been important to the CF. For example, security of tenure has been the main quality characterizing the professional Canadian military as "more than just a job." Now it is being seriously challenged and could well disappear for most CF members, even though this is not necessarily the choice of the military. There is already evidence that CF members' participation is becoming more calculated and more strictly limited to contract obligations than in the past.

The strong penetration of trends in social values has moved the CF toward a "social imperatives" model of service, based largely on civilian norms.[45] These will remain part of the CF institutional makeup. Total force integration also moves the CF closer to civilian society. Reengineering according to business processes incorporates other civilian aspects into the military system as well. Further, when we consider that most of the "perk" supports (e.g., free military travel, accommodation, meals) have virtually disappeared, it is evident that institutional aspects indeed are weak or nonexistent.

As an organization, the military now operates on market principles. There are institutional elements, such as inculcation of a strong mission orientation, but these may be found in nonmilitary organizations as well, particularly those involved in peacekeeping/humanitarian operations or civic emergency roles. Since military service is voluntary, the CF has no real choice but to continue operating according to market principles: a competitive salary and benefits for work done.

Institutional values, espoused in the past by members of the CF, were predicated on performance of the war-fighting role; this role was considered highly probable under conditions that prevailed during the Cold War. Today, peacekeeping, humanitarian, and related missions are defined as "operational roles" and are rapidly becoming the means of assessing command and combat-related capabilities for career purposes. War-fighting, in the conventional sense, is less probable (peace enforcement notwithstanding), and other roles have become acceptable.

Most senior leaders in the CF are not opposed to accepting a wide range of roles; many, however, believe that training and preparation for combat are the basis for effective performance in all roles. Combat training is considered instrumental in developing military professionalism, and differentiates the CF from all other institutions or societal agencies. The important element is to have been exposed to a combat or operational role and to have benefited from the experience in terms of skills, knowledge, discipline, and confidence, gains that may be adapted to other situations. Yet combat/operational training does not provide all the necessary skills or knowledge, or the orientation required for the array of peacekeeping and civic tasks that could be assigned.[46] Experience and study have shown that additional education, training, and orientation are needed, particularly for peacekeeping and humanitarian operations. Much of this must be integrated throughout the education, training, and development processes. The necessity of combat training for all the various roles remains a perception, not a proven fact.

The effects of performing peacekeeping and related roles, with notable exceptions, have been reported by CF members as largely positive, especially in developing pride in service and country. Also, involvement in tasks that further the public good—and for which CF members receive public approbation—apparently increases their civic consciousness and heightens their sense of military identity and professionalism. In fact, one could argue that both institutional and civic norms become more important under these circumstances. Opportunities for training, development, and employment will remain the major motivation for participating in the regular force, but the performance of civic duties also may justify entering and remaining in the CF, especially for members of the combat arms.

Structurally, the total force has become significantly more civilianized. Much of the training, development, and socialization will take place in contracted civilian agencies, and will tend to weaken the effects of intense military socialization. Even in performing domestic roles, the ability to draw on a well-indoctrinated sense of professionalism is important. If divisiveness between the citizen soldier and the professional soldier is to be avoided, the socialization system of the post–Cold War military must emphasize adaptability in making transitions between roles and must stress the capacity to relate to different reference groups. Already the move to a total force demands this type of flexibility from regular force members; without it, total force is unlikely to succeed.

Thus, in the CF of the future, individual membership identification or orientation is likely to reflect some combination of institutional, occupational, and civic organization; one identity or another will be emphasized, depending on the circumstances and/or the component of the military in which one is serving. This flexibility of identification will be reinforced at the organizational level, which is shaped increasingly by economic constraints and by societal and community influences. To be sure, lessons must be learned and acted on as a result of the Somalia Affair; this is already evident in the changes that are being introduced at all levels of education and training. For example, an additional week is being added to basic training in order to adequately examine issues of ethos and ethics. Senior and executive leadership courses are also being revamped, and subjects dealing with the laws of armed conflict, cultural training, and the like are being added to a number of training and development curricula. The combat arms, however, are likely to remain the crucible of homogenizing institutional influences on the individual, providing strong indoctrination in basic military values and (it is hoped) new, improved ethics. They will not, however, be exempt from accommodating the diversity of gender and ethnicity.

CONSCIENTIOUS OBJECTION

In Canada, conscientious objection was an issue during both the First and the Second World Wars, in the face of pressures for universal adult male service and conscription. Since then, under an all-volunteer system, conscientious objection has become less relevant. Its implications are considered only in times of crisis; at such times the Canadian Emergencies Act, which specifies conditions under which conscription may be enacted, becomes pertinent. (Conscientious objector status is recognized within the act.) Under most conditions, CF decisions regarding conscientious objections would be made informally to prevent forcing the issue; this is made easier under total force arrangements. Conscription in Canada is not considered politically feasible; CF commanders would prefer that "reluctant soldiers" pursue other options, mainly for reasons of reliability. This situation is unlikely to change.

CONCLUSION

The Canadian Forces are constrained domestically by economics, transformed in complex ways by mandated social change, and kept modest in
size and resources by the tenuousness of public and government support.
Apart from the Canadian military's alliance commitments, the CF mission
is focusing more strongly on peace, stability, and protection of sovereignty
and the environment, in keeping with social and domestic change and concerns. The force structure consists of regular and reserve force and civilian
departmental employees, under an integrated total force format. Traditional
military institutional features are becoming progressively weaker as the
CF grows more civilianized, socially representative, individualized, democratized, community-based, and oriented toward business management.
Civilian-military relationships, as they affect civilian organizations, CF members, spouses, and military families, are becoming increasingly reciprocal
through contracts for goods, services, facilities, obligations, and supports.

Relationships with the media are strained; a mutual lack of trust prevails, stemming primarily from Somalia incidents and their aftermath. These
relationships are likely to improve as the CF court the media in the future;
the situation is likely to be helped by the CF's deliberate attempts to com-
municate more openly and effectively with their internal and external con-
stituents.

Command and control of the CF are likely to become more decentralized as NDHQ passes more responsibilities to lower levels (although this
process has limits) and reduces the size of the headquarters accordingly. The
dominant professional is the soldier-diplomat and corporate leader-manager, who, in consultation with reserve and civilian counterparts, will set
the tone for future change. This change will include balancing global demands with domestic constraints, and finding more economical ways of
maintaining a credible military force in the twenty-first century. Part of such
credibility must involve efforts to overcome the scathing criticism of senior
and executive military leadership by the Somalia Inquiry, especially in the
areas of public trust, effective communication, and ethical leadership, and
in personal and professional accountability. At least in their declarations,
both the government and the military appear to be taking these concerns
seriously.

NOTES

1. See *National Defence, Defence 2000: Framework for Renewal*, and *Defence 2000 News*
   (Ottawa: Department of National Defence, 1996).
2. The Royal Canadian Navy, the Canadian Army, and the Canadian Air Force
   were abolished in 1966 by an act of the Canadian Parliament, and replaced by

an integrated unified Canadian Forces. A common, green uniform was adopted across all services. The reversion to three distinctive environmental uniforms (or DEUs) occurred in the late 1980s—ironically, at a time when most CF members had come to accept the common uniform. The impact of uniform color as a friction against unification is assessed as being substantial.

3. Lt. Gen. Romeo Dallaire, assistant deputy minister (Human Resources–Military), in an address to IUS Canada Fellows in Ottawa, May 8, 1998, stated that he foresees military and civilian exchange positions being created to provide military leaders the opportunity for civilian experience so that they may better cope with change in the twenty-first century.

4. This point has been made well by Jerzy Wojciechowski, "Progress of Knowledge, Social Change and National Security," in *Social Change and National Defence: Conference Proceedings* (Ottawa: Department of National Defence, 1990), pp. 143–150.

5. Noted in F. C. Pinch, *Lessons from Canadian Peacekeeping Experience: A Human Resources Perspective* (Alexandria, Va.: Institute for the Behavioral and Social Sciences, 1994).

6. Government of Canada, "Canada–United States Defence Cooperation," in *Defence White Paper* (Ottawa: Supply and Services, 1994).

7. Government of Canada, "Canada–United States Defence Cooperation."

8. See note 3, above.

9. The Hon. David Collenette, *1995 Budget Impact Statement: National Defence* (Ottawa: Government of Canada, Feb. 1995). Figures are in Canadian dollars.

10. Many observers have expressed the view that the number of regular force personnel will be reduced even further if a budget crunch is experienced or it is obvious that large capital outlays are required.

11. Projections contained in *Fact Sheet on Management, Command and Control Re-engineering* (Ottawa: Defence Department of National Defence, Nov. 1995) and in *Defence 2000 News* (Ottawa: Department of National Defence, Apr. 1996), pp. 2–4.

12. See for example T. C. Willett, "The Reserve Forces of Canada," *Armed Forces & Society*, .Vol. 16 (1989), pp. 59–76. There are great differences between the air, naval, and army reserves; the latter are the largest and most problematic for resource management.

13. See note 4, above.

14. This conclusion is drawn from personal observation, media reports, and testimony given by various witnesses at the ongoing Commission of Inquiry into Deployment of Canadian Forces to Somalia, January 1996 to March 1997. See also Chapter 18, "Discipline" in *Dishonoured Legacy: The Lessons of the Somalia Affair, Commission of Inquiry, Volume 2* (Ottawa: Canadian Government Publishing, 1997), pp. 429–462. While this dealt with the Canadian Airborne Regiment, problems of dysfunctional cultural norms and socialization processes have been reported by members of other regiments.

15. A detailed analysis of the Airborne culture is found in Donna Winslow, *The Canadian Airborne Regiment in Somalia: A Socio-cultural Inquiry* (Ottawa: Canadian Government Publishing, 1997). Among other things, this study explains the process leading to hyperinvestment in a maladaptive culture by· members of the Airborne.

16. *Civic consciousness* is used here in the sense used by the late Morris Janowitz and found in Pinch, *Lessons*. Members of contemporary militaries from democratic

societies should be imbued with national sensibilities and should conform to international standards of conduct expected by the publics of civilized nations.

17. See for example The Phillips Group/The Wyatt Group, *Military and Civilian Employee Feedback Survey* (Ottawa: Department of National Defence, 1995).

18. See *Dishonoured Legacy: The Lessons of the Somali Affair (Executive Summary)* (Ottawa: Canadian Government Publishing, 1997), pp. ES33–34, ES52–53.

19. See The Hon. M. Douglas Young, *Report to the Prime Minister on Leadership and Management of the Canadian Forces* (Ottawa: Government of Canada, March 25, 1997), pp. 1–3, 16–17.

20. For areas of resistance to change, see Maj. Gen. Bill Leach, "Yet Another Point of View," in *Defence 2000 News* (Ottawa: National Defence, April 1997), pp. 4–7.

21. This is based on observations, discussions, and projections made by Canadian defense planners. Business process reengineering of the DND Personnel Group is predicated on the introduction of electronic information technology and management techniques that will eventually reduce the amount of human effort now required for many of the routine functions. This sentiment is captured by Lt. Comdr. Guy McQue in "CFB Esquimalt: Costs Down, Productivity Up," in *Defence 2000 News* (Ottawa: National Defence, 1997), pp. 1–2.

22. Recently, this trend has been reinforced by the current assistant deputy minister (Human Resources–Military; see note 3, above) and, more formally, built into the revamped executive leadership educational courses being conducted at the Canadian Forces College, Toronto, Ontario.

23. Information provided by Directorate of Land Personnel, National Defence Headquarters, Ottawa, November 1997.

24. CROP, Inc., *Analysis of Omnibus Questions for the Department of National Defence* (Montreal: CROP, Inc., 1990).

25. F. C. Pinch, *Youth Motivation and Military Service in Canada* (Munich: SOWI, Forum 6, 1986).

26. R. Bibby, "Canadian Youth: Values, Attitudes and Lifestyles," in *Social Change and National Defence* (Ottawa: Department of National Defence, 1990).

27. Pinch, *Lessons*, pp. 78–99.

28. W. H. Critchley, "Civilianization and the Canadian Military," *Armed Forces and Society*, Vol. 16 (1989), pp. 117–136.

29. This is the position taken by the current assistant deputy minister (HR-Mil), Lt. Gen. R. Dallaire.

30. F. C. Pinch, *Perspectives on Organizational Change in the Canadian Forces* (Alexandria, Va.: U.S. Army Research Institute for the Behavioral and Social Sciences, 1994).

31. Information provided by Directorate of Personnel Policy, National Defence Headquarters, February 1997.

32. For a summary of detailed analyses of the problems faced by women in so-called mixed-gender units (contained in three studies conducted in 1997), see Lt. (N) K. D. Davis, *Gender Integration in the Canadian Forces: The Army Challenge*, a paper delivered at the International Military Testing Association Conference, Sydney, Australia, October 14–16, 1997.

33. Based on personal communication with National Defence Headquarters Personnel Group authorities, November 1997.

34. Information provided by Directorate of Personnel Policy, National Defence Headquarters, November 1997.

35. R. J. Hansen, *Personal Harassment in the Canadian Forces: 1992 Survey* (Willowdale: Canadian Forces Personnel Applied Research Unit, 1993).

36. Two of the most publicized involved an air force colonel, who was tried and convicted by court-martial in 1995 for an incident involving a female staff officer while both were on deployment during the Persian Gulf War; the other involved a female infantry captain, who was reportedly physically abused and otherwise discriminated against during infantry phase training. For a variety of reasons, no disciplinary action was taken in this case and the captain resigned from the regular force.

37. Articles were carried in *Macleans Magazine,* Volume 111, Nos. 21 (May 25, 1998), 23 (June 8, 1998) and 28 (July 13, 1998).

38. See Davis, *Gender Integration.*

39. Virtually all of the section on homosexuality is taken from Pinch, *Perspectives* (1994).

40. See Donna Winslow, *The Canadian Airborne Regiment: A Socio-cultural Portrait* (Ottawa: Canadian Publishing, 1997).

41. However, the Commission of Inquiry became embroiled in a squabble with the minister of national defense and the cabinet and was terminated (actually, its mandate was not extended when requested) prematurely by the government. Thus the commission was unable to examine the details of the torture-murder of the young Somali, Shidane Arone, and other incidents that occured in Somalia and the former Yugoslavia, but it did examine a broad range of issues surrounding the deployment to Somalia in 1992–93. The report, in five volumes, is a stinging indictment of the executive leadership of the day as well as of the inadequacies of the organization and preparation for deployment. The government has accepted or acted upon many of the 170 recommendations made, but has not accepted those relating to reform of the military justice system or recommending the establishment of an extraorganizational ombudsman. The independent review panel's recommendations also covered a broad range of topics and were more favorably received. They were synthesized with those emanating from within the department and many received attention.

42. Widespread coverage in the electronic and print media beginning in 1993 documents both the tension between the Canadian military and the media and the difficulties faced by the latter in communicating effectively with the media and the Canadian public. For recent examples in the print media, see D. Jenish, L. Fisher, and E. Kay Fulton,"Charges of Coverup over Somalia Rock the Military: What Did He Know? Missing Documents and Cries of Coverup Mark the Most Serious Military Scandal since the War," *Maclean's Magazine,* Apr. 15, 1996.

43. J. L. MacBride-King, *Families, the Labour Force and the Future: Social Change and National Defence* (Ottawa: Department of National Defence, 1990).

44. Personal communication with Maj. Linda Tyrell, Directorate of Military Family Support, October 1995.

45. Pinch, *Perspectives,* pp. 2–5.

46. Pinch, *Lessons,* pp. 78–99; *Dishonoured Legacy: The Lessons of the Somalia Affair. Report of the Commission of Inquiry into the Deployment of Canadian Forces to Somalia (Executive Summary)* (Ottawa: Canadian Government Publishing, 1997), pp. ES26–ES29.

10

Australia and New Zealand: Contingent and Concordant Militaries

CATHY DOWNES

The ending of the Cold War constitutes as significant a watershed in the domestic environment for armed forces as it does for international security affairs generally. Its ending has also occurred in a period of significant technological change affecting, to varying degrees, the socioeconomic foundations of most nations. The confluence of these two forces of change has varying effects upon the purposes for which armed forces are maintained and for their legitimacy, structures, composition, and culture. How armed forces are affected by these forces of change depends upon how closely bound up they were in the prosecution of the Cold War, and how far advanced their societies are in transiting from Industrial Age to Information Age socioeconomies.

Profound changes have occurred in the international security order that governed relations between most nations since 1945. For those nations dominated by the nuclear relationship between the superpowers, and with forces tailored to fight a high-level war in Europe, the ending of the Cold War is having a substantial influence on the size and shape of contemporary and future military forces. This may be seen in the adoption of Postmodern defense strategies and postures and through shifting national priorities in response to peace dividend pressures to redirect resources into domestic programs.

The changing sociological makeup of these military forces and their relations with their parent societies are also the result of a number of domestic socioeconomic and cultural variables. Many of these are unrelated to, or only indirectly influenced by, the ending of the Cold War. It may be that there is only an indirect causal link between the ending of Cold War and many changes which are currently being experienced in Western military organizations. In this case, the effect of the ending of the Cold War may be more to hurry the pace of ongoing changes, generated by socioeconomic and political causes, rather than to initiate new directions in military culture and organization and relations with civil societies.

Therefore, the importance of distinctions drawn between Late Modern and Postmodern militaries will depend upon the balance of influence between changes in military cultures and models of organization that can be related to the ending of the Cold War, as opposed to those that are likely to occur as a consequence of ongoing social, economic, and political change in parent societies.

One way to assess this balance of influence is to look at armed forces and societies which, to all intents and purposes, have been at a distance from the Cold War and determine whether the trends in military organization are the same there as for previously Cold War–oriented militaries and societies. If the types and pace of change are basically similar in both sorts of society, then it would be reasonable to suggest that the ending of the Cold War is less important for the shape and character of future military organizations than are domestic social, economic, and political change. Australia and New Zealand, and their militaries, constitute just such a control situation against which to measure the extent of the influence of the ending of the Cold War.

THREAT PERCEPTIONS

The nature and types of military forces found acceptable to the public reflects their perceptions of the intensity and proximity of violent threats to their security. Where threats are overt, immediate, and geographically close, the desire for protection is usually translated into the maintenance of large standing and reserve armed forces, support for medium to high levels of defense expenditure, and even the conscription of civilians to serve the cause of national defense. When threats are perceived as distant, vague, and infrequent, substantially smaller military forces, less well supported, are more likely. Of course, cultural, strategic, political, and historical circumstances and affiliations, in addition to extant threat perceptions, will also influence a preference for conscript or all-volunteer forces, for standing or militia forces, for alliance or independent defense strategies, etc.

In the case of Australia and New Zealand, threats to security have almost invariably concerned the "tyranny of distance" and the inherent vulnerability of long lines of communications and trade with Northern Hemisphere alliance and trading partners. It is interesting that this geographic isolation has been interpreted by Australians and New Zealanders differently, leading to different perceptions of threat. In the former, as Anthony Bergin and Hugh Smith remark:

> . . . a sense of insecurity has long been a feature of Australian society. It began with fear of the hostile and dangerous land itself, with concern about the ambitions of European colonial powers such as France, Russia and Germany, and with anxiety about the immigration of Asian and non-European

settlers. . . . Even at a time when government policy is to proclaim the absence of major threats to Australia for the foreseeable future, it is unlikely that this long-standing, if underlying, sense of insecurity has disappeared from Australian society.[1]

While New Zealanders have demonstrated at times a similar level of insecurity, it has been partially offset by a perception that at times geographic isolation is no bad thing—it has served to keep the ills of the world at bay. At the same time, this attitude is not inconsistent with the committed willingness with which New Zealanders have joined their Australian counterparts in volunteering their forces for wars overseas.[2] This merely reflects the logic of forward defense—it is preferable to fight elsewhere in order not to have to fight at home if conflicts are allowed to spread.

For both countries, these notions of strategic vulnerability and isolation were mixed with strong affiliations with Great Britain and emerging senses of national identity. This resulted in a symbiotic defense relationship with Great Britain. In both nations, the force structures, operating procedures, and organizational culture for the armed forces were all primarily modeled on the appropriate British pattern.

Prior to the Second World War, Britain retained military forces within the greater region to maintain its presence and influence, and for the protection and support of its former colonies. In turn, Australia and New Zealand developed military forces, to the best of their resources, which were available to support Great Britain, either inside the region or farther afield. As a consequence, prior to the Cold War period, Australian forces were sent to New Zealand (1863–72 Maori Wars), the Sudan (1885–86), and the Boxer Rebellion (1900). Australian and New Zealand forces were sent to the South African Boer War (1899–1902), and the First (1914–18) and Second (1939–45) World Wars.

Because of Great Britain's inability in the Second World War to provide sufficient assistance for defense against Japanese aggression in the Asia-Pacific region, both nations turned to a new protector: the United States. Following the war, the United States agreed to join with Australia and New Zealand in a formal defensive alliance, ANZUS. This arrangement was substantially looser than NATO's for example, merely specifying that each party would maintain and develop its force capabilities and exercise together regularly. Recognizing that if the security of one was threatened, this affected the others, each agreed to consult and decide on an individual and collective response to threats or aggression.

While the alliance was initially prompted by the need to respond to a possibly resurgent Japan, it continued its relevance in the Cold War "domino theory" years as a broad expression of commitment to Western concepts of collective security. Throughout this period, the New Zealand and Australian defence forces were routinely committed to force actions with their British counterparts, most notably in the Berlin Airlift (1948), the Korean War (1950–53), the Malayan Emergency (1955–59), and the Indonesian Confrontation (1964–66). However, both war-fighting and logistic support structures shifted to reflect regional forward defense strategies. They combined operations with both the United States and Britain, with Australia and New Zealand making contributions to the United States in the Vietnam War from 1964 onwards.

After the Vietnam War, and prompted by the 1969 Guam Doctrine, each nation moved at its own pace to embrace a more independent defense policy. Forward defense was replaced by more territorially based defense postures. These policies reflected a more realistic assessment of the nature of superpower rivalry in the Asia-Pacific region and the level of threat this posed. Policies also reflected a commitment to address the distortions which had been created in force structures by reliance on solely allied-based defense. As a result, the force structures and force planning of both the Australian Defence Force (ADF) and New Zealand Defence Force (NZDF) have, over the last two decades, been characterized increasingly by a regional and territorial focus. Levels and direction of threat perception, particularly in the Australian case, have been substantially disconnected from thermonuclear war or scenarios of high-level war in Europe.

This is not to infer that the region, and Australia and New Zealand, were unaffected by the Cold War. Indeed, for much of the 1970s and 1980s, both nations were demonstrably concerned about Soviet initiatives to gain influence in the Asia-Pacific region and the inability of international security organizations such as the UN to function effectively because of it. Both also put forth well-intentioned initiatives to control the nuclear arms race.

In terms of a shift in threat perceptions over time, Australia and New Zealand do not conform to the transitions indicated by the typology of change proposed for Western militaries. Also, there is a qualitative difference in the type and significance of threats perceived. Thus, for example, since nationhood, threat perceptions have always been concerned with the possibility of external invasion or the severing of lines of communications and trade. The prospect of a Japanese invasion in the Second World War served as a constant reminder afterwards, and influenced defense strategy into the late 1970s. The response, in addition to home defense, was the predominance of forward defense and alliance-based strategies until the early 1980s. From the 1950s until the mid-1980s, Australia and New Zealand supported both the Western nuclear war deterrent posture and initiatives to limit nuclear arms.

The key watershed in defense thinking occurred in the 1980s, with a focus on the most likely threats to security rather than on the greatest but least likely—the threat of nuclear war. This shift occurred substantially before the ending of the Cold War. It is likely that, if anything, the effect of the ending of the Cold War has tended to confirm this focus on likely regional threats. Moreover, indications are that these threats are more likely to be conventional and intranational than international.

Postmodern threat perceptions in both nations have been influenced by the uncertainty surrounding the nature of the post–Cold War world security order and what this may mean for the region. Unlike in Europe, countries in the Asia-Pacific region have not substantially downsized their military forces and arsenals. There is a continuing trend towards expanding and upgrading weapons inventories. Indeed, European and U.S. downsizing has contributed to this, as arms suppliers are expanding into the region to compensate for declining Northern Hemisphere markets. This trend is somewhat affected by the Asian economic crisis, which has substantially reduced available foreign currency for weapons acquisitions in a number of Asian countries. A number of territorial disputes, which were dormant and deferred during the Late Modern period, remain unresolved. There are also transborder resource and environmental issues which have the potential for violent conflict. While civil war remains a key and ongoing concern for some nations in the region, many others are now procuring limited first-line external power-projection capabilities. This has the potential to reduce the warning time for acts of aggression. This, in turn, can increase the state of readiness of response forces and decrease the margin of error in interpreting ambiguous actions by other powers.

The policy-makers of both countries view their national vulnerabilities and the security uncertainties in the Asia-Pacific region with great concern. On the one hand, the defense policies of both countries recognize the need to shape the Asia-Pacific security environment; on the other, the ongoing Asian economic crisis has brought home to both countries that their security futures, just as their economic futures, are fundamentally bound up in the fortunes of the Asia-Pacific region.

FORCE STRUCTURES

Australia and New Zealand have consistently followed the British force structure design of small, professional, peacetime military forces, reinforced and supplemented by still smaller regular reserve forces, civilian militias, and volunteers. For example, the permanent force of the Australian Army numbered just 3,000 in 1939 (a participation ratio of 0.04 percent), and the New Zealand Army of the time consisted of 510 Regular Force members (a participation ratio of 0.03 percent).[3] Yet, when the occasion has demanded it, both countries have created large military forces. For example, by the end of World War II, some 726,500 people had served in the Australian Army— a participation ratio of 10.2 percent, the highest of the group of nations including the United States, Great Britain, Canada, Australia, New Zealand, South Africa, and India. The New Zealand Army swelled to some 138,000 members during the war—a participation ratio of 8.1 percent, second only to Australia.[4] Both nations substantially demobilized after the war and have maintained small standing volunteer forces with supporting reserve volunteer forces since. Today, the participation rates for the Australian active army, for example, is 0.136 percent and for the New Zealand Army, 0.12 percent.[5]

This mix of standing and reserve service has persisted from nationhood in both countries. Mass armies have only been created on two occasions— the First and Second World Wars—and even these were manned substantially by volunteers. In the First World War, conscription was only introduced in 1916 in New Zealand and rejected in two referendums in Australia. The experience of the manpower requirements of the First World War prompted earlier consideration of conscription in the Second World War. Small standing professional forces, supported by militias and civilian volunteers, have been preferred by both nations.

This mix represented a satisfactory compromise which allowed defense expenditures in peacetime to be held at very low levels—and, in Australia's case, represented an acceptable response to cultural sensitivities about the social and political power potential of militaries. As Bergin and Smith note:

> If Australia had to have a military force in peacetime, it should be one without a military caste, without pretension, without undue authority which might be abused. The new Federation should avoid the evils of militarism which Australians perceived in Europe. . . . Permanent forces were a necessary evil; their role was above all to provide support for citizen armies when the need arose.[6]

While conscription in war has been often rejected, and at best reluctantly accepted, universal military training of one shape or form has been quite common in both countries. However, the underlying reasons for this have more to do with citizenship and social development goals and levels of unemployment than a preference for maintaining military forces by conscription to ward off external security threats.

Like any military force, the shape of the current ADF and NZDF formations and equipments reflects the procurement and manpower policies of the previous twenty years as much as it does recent changes in strategy or international relations. Yet, force structures are changing and more change is planned. However, these are not being undertaken as a direct response to the ending of the Cold War. Rather, force structures are being reconfigured to address the military employment demands of the likely contingencies envisaged in the more self-reliant and regionally focused defense postures adopted in the 1980s, and to address the obsolescence of equipment procured in the late 1960s.

At the same time, the ending of the Cold War has had an indirect effect upon the fiscal environment for defense spending in Australia and New Zealand. There has been considerable temptation for many groups to apply out of context the calls for a peace dividend being expressed in Cold War nations. There was pressure to redirect defense resources into social programs on the grounds that the ending of the Cold War uncritically reduced the requirement for military forces everywhere. In fact, current initiatives to reduce or constrain defense expenditures are a response solely to the recessionary state of both the Australian and New Zealand economies and have little if anything to do with any easing of security circumstances which would warrant a change in government spending priorities.

MAJOR MISSION DEFINITION

According to the model, Modern, Late Modern, and Postmodern militaries are supported by different types of defense policies and strategies. The policy focus and major mission of Modern militaries is the defense of national territory or homeland. Policies and missions of Late Modern militaries are dominated by alliances. Postmodern militaries focus mainly on operations other than war.

As with perceptions of threat, the mission of the Australian and New Zealand armed forces is an amalgam of the three conditions identified above. Thus, for example, Australian defense strategies are influenced heavily by a concept of territorial defense because the government views low-level harassment, raids, and interdiction as plausible security challenges to Australian territory and offshore resources. These threats are managed by maintaining defense forces at least nominally sized and equipped to provide independent responses up to the level of threat perceived. For more significant threats to Australian interests or territory, Australia maintains an array of alliance commitments (principally to the ANZUS alliance with New Zealand and the United States) as part of its defense strategy. At the same time, especially over the last five years, Australia has received and answered UN calls for troop contributions to peace-support operations and those of ad hoc coalitions, including operations in Cambodia and Somalia.

The major military missions of the NZDF are prescribed in the current statement on defense policy, "Defence of New Zealand—A Policy Paper 1991." In this paper, four key roles are recognized for the NZDF: (1) performing tasks associated with national territorial defense for which New Zealand needs independent military capability (these mainly concern counterterrorism, maritime surveillance, and civil support); (2) contributing to regional security (confidence-building measures, multinational military exercises, and interoperability arrangements); (3) contributing to defense alliances (ANZUS, closer defense relations with Australia, and the Five Power Defence Arrangement with Australia, the United Kingdom, Malaysia, and

Singapore); and (4) contributing to collective security (participation at an appropriate level in UN and coalition operations for peace-support and enforcement).

In these respects, the Australian and New Zealand defense forces have not made the transition from one stage of the framework to another. Rather, they have acquired new tasks over time without abandoning previous responsibilities, particularly for territorial defense.

ORGANIZATIONAL TENSIONS

In the typology proposed, Modern, Late Modern, and Postmodern militaries are identified by a dominant type of organizational tension. For Moskos, a defining characteristic of Modern militaries is that the formulation of military policy is heavily influenced by conflicts over defining "the turf" and agreeing on the particular roles of land, sea, and air forces. In Late Modern militaries, Moskos suggests, the focus of organizational tension shifts to a preoccupation with each service seeking to secure what it regards as its fair share of the resources. Finally, Moskos proposes that Postmodern militaries are likely to be preoccupied by another source of tension: the conflict over setting the most acceptable organizational goals in terms of the balance between war-fighting and nonviolent uses of military forces.

The evidence from consideration of Australian and New Zealand defense organizations suggests that the shifts identified may not be as defining as has been suggested. It would appear that all three sources of organization tension are present in comparatively similar proportions, regardless of the particular overall orientation of the forces (i.e., war-readiness, war-deterrence etc.). This is logical because all three address the fundamental relationships and balances between the three operational environments—land, maritime, and air—and, as crucially, how the ubiquity of technology has influenced the relative importance and demands of each. For example, service concerns over securing an acceptable proportion of resources is a perennial preoccupation in defense establishments.

Yet, within the context of these concerns, a key shift in organizational tension has taken place. In the Modern and for most of the Late Modern periods, budgetary fights have tended to be between the three services in a defense organization. Service arguments over role jurisdiction have been one crucial instrument in the fight to justify ownership of the military capabilities upon which resource funding is determined. However, by the end of the Late Modern period, the combination of technological developments and some military failures and marginal successes demonstrated the extent to which jurisdictional battles over roles, to sustain a resource share, were deleterious and inefficient. The response has been to create central and joint defense staffs with varying degrees of authority and responsibility for setting force requirements and arguing resource priorities from the perspective of the whole defense force rather than from that of a single service. The emergence of these staffs has shifted the focus of the organizational tension from being solely between the services to being as much between the three services and defense staffs as with each other. This is primarily because the responsibilities of central staffs act to cut across and erode the individual power bases of the services as the latter seek to secure their funding base.

In the United States, the main manifestation of this response is the 1986 Goldwater-Nichols Act and the substantial expansion in the role and power of the Joint Chiefs of Staff—and especially that of the chairman. In the United Kingdom, this organizational change is reflected in a series of management reforms, started in 1983 under then secretary of state for defense, Mr. Heseltine. Further refinements in 1992 confirmed the trend towards centralization of key policy staffs in operational commitments, policy, and force requirements.

The shift is also well set in place in Australia, with the creation of the Headquarters, Australian Defence Force (HQ ADF) in the early 1980s. Over time, single service staffs have been split off and centralized into joint divisions of the Headquarters. The final move was made in the early 1990s to centralize force-development staffs for major projects into a Development Division of the Headquarters and most recently to bring the civil and military sides of the department closer together in a newly structured Australian Defence HQ. This significantly reduces the staffs of the single services.

By contrast, the NZDF has followed a different path of organizational reform. To conform with a corporate management philosophy being applied across the government sector in the late 1980s, the defense bureaucracy was divided into two separate organizations—a civilian Ministry of Defence and a military Headquarters. The secretary of defense is responsible for civilian policy advice, audit and assessment, and capital procurement. For his part, the chief of the Defence Force is the principal military adviser to the government, chief executive officer of the Defence Forces, and chief resource manager. Also as part of the business-management philosophy, there has been a substantial devolution of financial authority to the single services. In the absence of centralized and unified policy staffs, both actions have served to increase the independence of the services, resulting in the maintenance of organizational tensions between them and the creation of tensions between civil and military organizations. Recognition of the inefficiencies which flow from these tensions has led, in the short term, to a series of ongoing procedural initiatives to at least ameliorate and manage their consequences.

In all these organizational reforms it is evident that various factors have been the driving force—budgetary constraints, fiscal reform philosophies, political intervention, and defense strategies predicated on joint operating frames of reference. In some senses, therefore, it may be argued that the nature of the threat only indirectly influences the types of organizational tension within militaries. The principal cause will always be resources, without which the organization ceases to be able to function. As Kaufman observes in his dissertation on why organizations die:

> Sometimes the required inflows cease because the resources are exhausted. Sometimes the resources are as available as ever, but the organizations are decreasingly successful in attracting them. . . . [S]uch deprivations of essential ingredients [are likely to] prove the most common cause of death.[7]

If anything, the end of the Cold War is likely to heighten rather than change the existing types of organizational tension. This is because post–Cold War peace dividend pressures will reduce the size of the resource pool over which the services compete. The ambiguity of the threat environment will make it significantly more difficult to establish strong cases for preferential treatment, because there is substantially less certainty over the nature and likelihood of credible employment circumstances. This helps to explain the interest demonstrated in the United States in non-war-fighting roles such as drug interdiction, nation building and humanitarian assistance, and peacekeeping.

DOMINANT MILITARY PROFESSIONAL

In the typology of change in military forces, Moskos identifies a dominant type of military professional for the Modern, Late Modern, and Postmodern periods. In this conception, the Modern era is seen to be typified by the combat leader as the predominant role model for officership; in the Late Modern, the manager/technician.

In the Postmodern era, the soldier-statesman and the soldier-scholar are seen as the defining type of military professional. When the experience of Australia and New Zealand militaries and that of other Western nations is examined, it would appear that there is more to the basis for such distinctions than just the shift in international security affairs which is occurring.

At any one point in time, military forces are likely to represent a mixture of role models. The particular balance between them, which demonstrates the dominant type of military professional, is likely to be determined by factors such as long-term trends in military technology and the application of large-scale managerial methods and a managerial/technocratic ethos to military operations and decision-making. At the same time, this determination will be influenced by the prevailing international security environment.

Until the mid-twentieth century, it could be argued that unless military forces were primarily tasked with nation-building, the combat leader model predominated. It did so in the substantial absence of competing models. However, from this point onwards, the impact of technology and managerialism have challenged the primacy of the combat leader with the emergence of an alternative. It is this challenge, as much as the unthinkability of large-scale war generated by the Cold War, which has threatened the place of the combat leader. The influence of particular international security threats has been to forestall such challenges. For example, the manager/technician has been successful in competing with, and even supplanting, the combat leader only in those forces exposed to long periods of relative peace. In militaries which regularly have confronted the credible prospect of warfighting, the influence of the manager/technician model has been constrained and the combat leader's centrality and relevance has been maintained despite the impact of technology, etc.[8]

Therefore, if this relationship holds true, the nature of a Postmodern security environment will influence the most likely balance between role models. If that security order is characterized by an increased probability of violent conflict, then this influences the dominance of the warrior model. Technological and managerial influences will be channelled towards war readiness and preparation. If the post–Cold War order is stable, economically focused, and law-abiding, it may well be that the manager/technician model will be more influential, directing technological and managerial instruments towards the goals of nation-building and nonviolent peacekeeping.

Finally, there are other influences which, in tandem with the ending of the Cold War, may affect the dominant role model of the military professional—for example, the trend towards civilianization of military manpower. For reasons of economy, increasing proportions of the manpower base of many Western militaries are being civilianized either with defense civilian or contract civilian labour. In a war-readiness military, this may have the ultimate effect of allowing the profession to focus more completely on its primary mission of war-fighting. In contrast, in a nation-building and peacekeeping frame, civilianization may serve to further strip away the behavioral norms and practices which define the profession's war-fighting focus.

PUBLIC ATTITUDES TOWARD THE MILITARY

The framework characterizes public attitudes as essentially supportive of the Modern military, ambivalent toward Late Modern armed forces, and apathetic toward Postmodern militaries. Australians' and New Zealanders' attitudes toward their defense forces reflect these stages.

In Australia the ADF generally has enjoyed high levels of public support because of broad public perceptions of threat. This is caused by Australia's geostrategic location, her historical experiences with the region, and the intervention of external actors in the Asia-Pacific region. Yet although this public support is positive, it does not necessarily translate into a high level of commitment to military expenditure or into a willingness to serve in the defense forces. The situation is similar in New Zealand, where comparatively high levels of public support for keeping a defense force are matched by unwillingness to pay for it.

Particularly in New Zealand, the defense debate has often been reduced to a superficial argument over the lost opportunity costs for social expenditures (frigates versus hospitals), in which defense inevitably loses. This situation is created by the limited availability of accurate and factual public information on defense matters. As a consequence, the public often remains uninformed and ill-informed about the realities of defense expenditure.

Despite this reluctance to divert resources to defense purposes (greater in New Zealand than Australia), the public in both countries have demonstrated high levels of support for the commitment of their defense forces to a wide spectrum of peace-support operations. This was evidenced for example, with the commitment of an Australian battalion to Somalia in 1993, and a New Zealand company group to Bosnia in 1994–96.

Both nations' defense forces are vulnerable to media searches for scandals. In recent times these scandals have involved various sensitive points in civilian-military relations, such as sexual harassment (see section on Women in the Military), homosexuality, misuse and abuse of public funds, commercialization of defense assets and functions, and redundancies.

Public attitudes toward defense in both countries are also influenced by the visibility of the defense forces, and relocation trends are a cause for concern. For the past decade the Australian defense strategy has called for a relocation of the ADF to the underpopulated north of the country. This move takes the ADF out of its traditional recruitment base in the southeast, and reduces the ADF's visibility to Australians in general. There is a concern that the public will become more apathetic toward the ADF as it becomes less visible.

The same concern is expressed in New Zealand, although declining visibility is attributable to another cause: The base structure of the NZDF has been severely rationalized over the last decade. Much of the New Zealand Army has contracted onto a single principal location in the unpopulated desert mountain center of the North Island. The air force's presence in the South Island, in the population center of Christchurch, was terminated in 1995. The Royal New Zealand Navy is based almost totally in Auckland, which at least is a significant population center.

In 1997, a further review of basing was conducted to again reevaluate where the NZDF could be most efficiently located. In the search to reduce basing costs, there is a strong pressure to relocate out of expensive urban area bases. Bases that were located on the distant edges of urban areas have been overtaken by urban growth and land expenses have increased commensurately. However, a corollary of moving bases to less expensive locations is a significant reduction in the visibility of the NZDF to its public.

To counter this decrease in visibility and the expected corresponding reduction in public support, both defense forces have undertaken campaigns and strategies to maintain their public profiles. In 1995 the NZDF launched a public information "road show," similar to the British forces' presentation teams. This road show is designed to tour the country and to provide briefings on the NZDF—the purposes of defense, defense expenditure, activities, bases, and issues—to any interested groups in the community. After a period of particularly ill-informed public debate in the late 1990s, another initiative was launched to increase the information available to the public on defense matters and the defense force.

RELATIONSHIPS WITH THE MEDIA

The framework describes the relationship between the media and the military as *incorporated* for Modern armed forces, *manipulated* for Late Modern militaries, and *courted* for Postmodern militaries. The relationships in Australia and New Zealand mirror these stages. Both defense forces fit the Postmodern stage of media relations. Both have recognized the power of media organizations in reaching broad segments of the general public and have sought to develop functional, cooperative relationships with all sections of the media. Yet a significant amount of distrust remains on both sides of the relationship. On the part of the defense forces, it mainly concerns the irresponsibility of sensationalist journalism, which feeds on scandals, seeks a negative and melodramatic angle for every story, and is based on highly selective, unbalanced, and instant reporting of events. Meanwhile, many in the media continue to believe that the defense forces are withholding information from them.

This distrust and its consequences are a matter of particular concern to the NZDF and the ADF. As in most other Western democracies, public opinion is important in any governmental decision to commit forces to military operations, particularly if they are to be conducted in distant locations and if territorial security is not threatened. The government's willingness to support overseas deployment also depends strongly on continued public support. When the press has the resources to report events even before military units on the ground can provide complete information to national headquarters, the potential for dissemination of misinformation is considerable. This situation can have damaging consequences for public opinion—consequences which are difficult to redress. It can also be harmful and stressful for the families of deployed service members.

Over both the Late Modern and the Postmodern periods, the defense organizations in both countries have sought to establish and maintain effective working relationships with media organizations that can address the concerns of both. This mutual need for an effective and consultative relationship is perhaps a better descriptor of the Postmodern military's interaction with the media than the concept of courtship.

CIVILIAN EMPLOYEES

According to the framework, civilian employees in Modern, Late Modern, and Postmodern militaries have different roles. In the first, civilian employees are only a minor component of defense employees; in the second, their proportion is more balanced in relation to military members; in the third, they are a major component of the defense workforce. The Australian and New Zealand defense workforces have passed through these three stages. Another type of defense workforce also has become prevalent, particularly over the past two decades: the defense contractor, as opposed to the defense civilian employee.

In the past, both defense forces maintained workforces with a high proportion of uniformed military personnel. This profile reflected the forces' focus on deploying on out-of-country operations and indicated the nature of those operations. In recent decades, however, financial pressures have forced a reconsideration of this policy, based on the calculation that civilian employees are usually less expensive than military members. Although this reasoning has not always proved accurate, and despite costs in operational flexibility and depth of forces to support sustained operations, both defense forces became significantly more civilian in the 1980s and 1990s

The trend has been to contract both military and defense civilian workforces and to expand the amount and type of defense work outsourced to private sector contractors and suppliers. Over the 1990s, the Australian Defence Organization initiated its Commercial Support Program, which has examined all support areas of the ADF's operations to identify opportunities for outsourcing and negotiate service-support contracts. In New Zealand, devolved financial responsibility has, for example, allowed base commanders to contract out locally for base support services. The trend also has been supported through NZDF-wide or single-service-wide arrangements with private contractors to use defense lands and facilities to provide commercially oriented services.

WOMEN IN THE ARMED FORCES

The model sees womens' role as changing from exclusion or separateness in the armed forces of war-readiness militaries to one of partial integration as these militaries become focused on war-deterrence. The prediction is that full integration will be achieved as militaries move towards Postmodern frames of reference.

Women have served on general service in the Australian and New Zealand armed forces since the Second World War, although specialist nursing corps were formed in both countries in the First World War. Until the 1970s, women were recruited into separate corps or services and were limited in their employment and career opportunities usually to headquarters and static installations and within their corps structure (although many moved into nontraditional areas in WWII). Pay and conditions were also distinctive and unequal with those of their male counterparts. For example, in the early 1970s, Australian female officers only received 80 percent of the male general list salary and in New Zealand, servicewomen pay rates were set at 85 percent of the public service male pay scales.

Over the 1970s and 1980s however, there was a gradual expansion of employment opportunities and an equalizing of pay and conditions of service in both militaries. In 1974, the Australian Committee of Reference on Armed Forces Pay recommended the principle of equal pay, although it was not finally implemented until 1979. Reviews in the 1980s led to a substantial opening up of employment opportunities, but women were still barred from combat support and combat positions. In 1990, a review recommended the removal of the combat-related (combat support) exemption, with implementation to be completed by 1993.[9] This will see the overwhelming bulk of positions within the ADF open to women.

In 1976, an internal New Zealand Defence Department review of the employment of women recommended that all unnecessary discrimination be removed and that, as far as possible, equal employment should be provided for women. It also recommended the integration of women into the mainstream branches and the disbandment of the separate women's services. The principles were confirmed in a 1981 Defence Council Order which affirmed the principle of individual merit without regard to sex in recruitment (apart from those areas where minimum male strength standards have been set), the principle of equal access to training opportunities within employment categories, and the principle of equality in terms of conditions of service (except where specifically provided to the contrary—for example, women cannot be sentenced to military detention). The order also retained the principle that women would not be committed to combat, recognising that it is "not politically or socially acceptable at the present time to deliberately involve women in combat."[10] Subsequent reviews have led to an expansion of employment opportunities to the fullest extent possible under the Defence Council Order.

Clearly, the Australian and New Zealand experiences mirror those of the transitions identified in the typology, which are demarcated by the shifts in threat perceptions and states of military preparedness. The question raised is whether these changes in threat perceptions are the principal catalyst for changes in the role of women in armed forces, or whether the events are merely coincidental in time. Forecast changes in women's roles have taken place in Australia and New Zealand, and can be expected to occur as predicted, despite being essentially on the very periphery of the Cold War and influenced differently by its ending. This would tend to suggest that the changing role of women in armed forces is less connected to changes in international security than to other changes in the military's external environment.

In the case of Australia and New Zealand, the principal catalyst for the expansion of opportunities for women in armed forces has come from shifts in societal attitudes towards women in nontraditional roles, as is the case in most Western societies. In some instances, the defense forces themselves have anticipated this change and amended their own policies before social shifts were reflected in binding legislation. This was the case with the NZDF, which equalized pay and conditions for women members before the Human Rights Act of 1977, which mandated it across the New Zealand labor force. In Australia, the ADF was moving towards integration in the early 1980s, but was then directed to step up the pace as a result of the 1984 Sex Discrimination Act. Also, pressure has come from external agencies and women's lobby groups, many of whom have gathered up the issue of equal employment opportunities for military women as part of their larger agenda on women's issues in society.

In the future, the pressures for full integration are likely to be almost solely driven by societal interest. The one significant pressure generated by the Cold War—the need to sustain a sufficient recruiting base with the smaller-sized male cohorts of the 1990s—is likely to reduce with the ending of the Cold War and the consequential reductions in the size of forces maintained. Yet, the smaller-sized cohorts of the 1990s and 2000s will continue to exert as much pressure (if not more) than did the Cold War on the Australian and New Zealand defense forces to increase their recruitment of women.

While the early stages of integration of women into nontraditional employment in both Australian and New Zealand defense forces proceeded with relatively little difficulty, the 1990s have been a checkered period. Both the ADF and the NDZF have encountered difficulties with sexual harassment and various forms of gender discrimination in managing the integration of women. In New Zealand for example, public revelations of sexual misconduct in the Royal New Zealand Navy led to the 1998 joint commissioning of a gender-integration audit by the New Zealand Defence Force and the Human Rights Commission. The audit was conducted by Dr. Clare Burton, who had just finished a similar task for the Australian Defence Force.[11] The report was critical of the NZDF's personnel policies with regard to equity issues and the attitudes which existed in some areas of the NZDF towards women. While acknowledging the work of the NZDF in

1997–98 to improve its human resource management practices, the chief of the defense force accepted all 122 of the report's recommendations.

SPOUSES AND THE MILITARY COMMUNITY

The relationship between military spouses and the NZDF and ADF military communities has also mirrored the transitions identified in the typology from being one of close integration to one of partial separation. As barriers to career and life aspirations for women in Western societies have been challenged, eroded, or hurdled, significant changes have occurred in the life patterns of women both within and outside marriage and the family. This is the case in Australia and New Zealand. In Australia, for example, the overall participation rate for women in the labor force rose from 36 percent in August 1966 to over 50 percent in 1988, with almost all this increase being experienced amongst married women and women in the ages twenty-five to forty-four.[12] These changes have been reflected in the defense force populations. For example, in the ADF, in its October 1991 Families Census, more than half of all members' partners were in paid employment. An additional 10 percent of members' partners were not working, but actively seeking work.[13]

As the age at which people get married has fallen, the percentage of military forces which are married has increased because of the youthful recruitment base for military service. As a result, the pressures of working spouses can also expect to be more widely felt in the military community than in civilian communities. For example, in the ADF, 21.1 percent of male members aged 20 to 24 are married, as opposed to 18.1 percent of their age cohort in the general workforce. Among 25 29-year-old ADF males, 60.8 percent are married as opposed to 55.3 percent of their age cohorts in the general population. The trend is reflected across all age cohorts.[14]

The circumstance of working spouses and changing social attitudes towards responsibilities in partnership have been the main catalysts for a shift in the relationship between the spouses and the military community. The shift has been from a relationship of mutual support to one of competition. Contemporary working military spouses confront an almost pure example of conflicting demands and divided loyalties. They must juggle child-rearing, household management, paid employment, and the community-involvement demands of the military community. Something has to give in this equation. While most working spouses in civil communities must manage these competing demands, marriage to the military creates extra difficulties, including a range of problems associated with the mobile family. Child-care facilities may be unavailable near military bases. If access to local community child-care is available, it may be limited by constantly having to join the bottom of the waiting list in each new posting location. Spouses may face discrimination from employers who are unwilling to take on a military spouse who can be expected to leave, sometimes with little notice, to move wherever the partner's employer dictates. Regular moves also limit career choices and reduce the opportunities for spouses to develop skills and seniority in a career or occupation.[15]

In the past, militaries have relied upon the mutual support and involvement of spouses to ease the turbulence generated by posting cycles. The quid pro quo has been the military community philosophy, which supported the military family with housing, educational assistance, community recreation, service infrastructure, etc. However, the social contract has been broken by both parties. Working spouses for their part are less likely to have the time or inclination to contribute to community-support activities. At the same time, usually for fiscal reasons (or, in the case of Australia, as part of a conscious policy to bring the armed forces into line with the level of employer support provided by civilian employers), the supports to the military family have been eroded.

The future direction of this relationship is not clear. It is dependent as much upon the social policies pursued by armed forces as upon evolving societal attitudes towards working spouses, economic and employment circumstances, and the career and life aspirations of partners in marriage or relationships. For example, in Australia, the ADF is shifting many defense units to the north of the continent in support of the military strategy of defense in depth. In this move, it is relocating military families to highly underpopulated, underurbanized, and isolated areas. In such locations, employment opportunities are few, and the civilian community infrastructure very limited or a considerable distance away. As a result, greater attention is once again being paid to the needs of the military family in order to ensure the retention of service personnel. These types of circumstances could delay or partially reverse trends towards the breakup of the military community proposed by the model.

HOMOSEXUALITY IN THE MILITARY

The model predicts that in Postmodern militaries, homosexuality will be accepted. The status of homosexuality in the military is another area where changes in societal attitudes have been the motivator for change in military behavior. Also, it is another area where legislative change has been the prompt for armed forces to conform to broader social shifts in norms of conduct.

In the past, in Australia and New Zealand, the need for contrary practices in human rights have been recognized in law with specific exclusions or exemptions to protect the management and employment practices of the ADF and NZDF. This is the case, for example, in Australia's 1984 Sex Discrimination Act and New Zealand's 1977 Human Commission Act with respect to women in armed forces. However, this circumstance is changing. Australia's recent Human Rights and Equal Opportunities Act does not make any exemption for the ADF in regard to homosexuality. This circumstance has prompted the ADF to promulgate a new personnel-management policy to conform with the act. The new policy takes the opportunity to address what it terms "unacceptable sexual behavior" rather than homosexuality. This has allowed the inclusion of policy on sexual harassment, sexual assault, and sexual behavior "inconsistent with or contrary to the inherent requirements of ADF Service."[16]

The change in policy is important in that it brings the ADF into broad conformity with societal attitudes, while still responding to a number of the concerns held about possible consequences of some homosexual behavior in a military environment. The policy is a step towards normalizing the place of sexual orientation in the defense forces in two respects. It implicitly abandons the policy that a person's sexual orientation per se could constitute grounds for dismissal from the service. It also shifts the emphasis to defining the circumstances and types of sexual behavior that are unacceptable in the defense forces (which in most cases are held to be equally unacceptable in civilian society: unlawful sexual harassment, obscene behavior, indiscreet sexual relationships between superiors and subordinates, derogatory sexual remarks, rumors and public discussion with the intention to embarrass). This philosophy is reflected in the preamble to the Defence Instruction on Unacceptable Sexual Behaviour: "The ADF has no concern with the sexual preferences of its members provided they are not unlawful and are not contrary to or inconsistent with the inherent requirements of the Service."

CONSCIENTIOUS OBJECTION

Conscientious objection to military service is primarily an issue of civil-military relations for those nations which have a tradition of raising armed forces by conscription or which currently have a policy of doing so under particular circumstances. As noted earlier, conscription has been used in both Australia and New Zealand in peacetime for various reasons and only with considerable reluctance, if at all, in wartime. This mixture of manning methods, and the rationale for them, provides an interesting example of the possible relationships between conscription and its creator: nationalism. It is an example that offers an insight into the future directions which may be taken in respect of conscription and conscientious objection in other parts of the world where the effects of the Cold War and its passing are more pronounced. These directions are not necessarily consistent, at least in the short term, with the alternative civilian service model proposed by the typology.

Nationalism is a powerful cause which continues to encourage volunteerism and justify conscription. This is demonstrated as much in Australia and New Zealand's experience of war and conflict as elsewhere. In the Australian case, a very significant part of Australia's national sense of unique identity has been forged by a volunteer tradition—embryonic in the Boer War and matured in the First World War with the 1st Australian Imperial Force.[17] This identity—real and perceptual—stresses independence, freedom of choice, innovativeness, egalitarianism, and a healthy questioning of authority. Conscription, as the compulsory enrollment of civilians for military service, cuts across these traits. The importance of these traits to Australians has been such as to place severe restrictions on the circumstances in which support for conscription will be given. Only where there is a strong and widely felt perception that the nation's physical integrity and sovereignty is fundamentally threatened has conscription been supported in times of war. This was the case in the Second World War, when conscription was only accepted after assurances that conscripts would not be used outside Australian territory.[18]

In many countries of contemporary northern Europe, the generalized notion of "service to nation" has evolved to compete with the primary purpose of conscription as "service in defense of the nation." This evolution is consistent with the undertaking of alternative forms of service which have normally been required of those who object to military duties on the grounds of conscience. It is reasonable to propose that in times of prolonged peace, internal stability, and gradually reducing levels of threat perception that "service to nation" could supplant "service in defense of nation" as the rationale for conscription. However, it is not clear that these conditions will prevail in all of Europe. Nationalism appears likely to influence the possibilities for these conditions to a considerable extent as the Cold War ends and with it, the Soviet Union and the Warsaw Pact.

This is particularly the case as much of the political energies released by the former Soviet Union in relinquishing control over its eastern European buffer zone and over its own republics are being focused upon the achievement of independent nationhood by former substates and groups. As Van Evera remarks:

> The demise of the Soviet empire entails risks . . . from three specific sources: the unsettled nature of borders in Eastern Europe and the former USSR; the intermingling of nationalities in the region; and the intense conflicts among these nationalities. These dangers are magnified by the ongoing collapse of the former USSR's economy: this collapse is bound to sharpen inter-communal conflicts. . . . The dismantled Soviet Union will . . . be riddled with national conflicts. These will arise from nationalities' demands to annex territory other republics inhabited by their own members; from complaints against the oppression of national kin who live across accepted borders; and from demands by the small, stateless nationalities, for autonomy or secession from the republics where they reside.[19]

The evidence of violent conflict in the dissolution of Yugoslavia; nationality-driven strife in Georgia, Chechnya, and the southern republics; and the potential for conflict in other parts of the former USSR all suggest that the pressures for formal and expedient conscription for military service may increase in these regions, rather than decrease, in at least the short to medium term. In such circumstances, nationalism is a powerful and emotive force which tends to deal harshly with conscientious objection. Also, there may be little tolerance for civilian alternative service preferences when the state of peace which allows such services to be delivered has not been secured.

CONCLUSIONS

The Australian and New Zealand defense forces and their parent societies offer a control situation against which it is possible to assess whether the ending of the Cold War is the key catalyst in shaping the character of future military organizations. Against most of the parameters of the typology, the changes experienced, and predicted for the future, have taken place and can be forecast for the ADF and NZDF, yet both have been substantially unaffected by the ending of the Cold War. This circumstance suggests that the ending of the Cold War might not be the key variable in determining the shape of future military organizations.

Within this generalization, however, it is clear that those parameters of military organization which are directly related to the nature of the security threat are most likely to be influenced by the Cold War and its end. This is evidenced in the fact that threat perceptions in Australia and New Zealand, which are dissimilar to those held by Cold War nations, have led to different experiences and predictions for the future with respect to the model variables of force structure, dominant type of military professional, organizational tensions, and public attitudes towards defense.

In those variables which characterize the proposed sociological makeup of future military organizations, there has been considerable consistency between Australia and New Zealand and the model. This circumstance supports the case that in these parameters of military organization, the influence of the Cold War may well be subordinate to social, cultural, political, national, and economic experiences and trends of their broader societies. In these cases, it may be of no consequence at all or at most act as an accelerant of change being generated by other causes.

NOTES

1. Anthony Bergin and Hugh Smith, "The Public Perceptions of the Army" in *Reshaping the Australian Army—Challenges for the 1990s,* ed. David Horner (Canberra:

The Australian National University, Canberra Papers on Strategy and Defence No. 77, 1991), p. 202.

2. It is interesting to note in this respect that, for example, in the First World War, the troops sent overseas by New Zealand amounted to 10 percent of the 1914 male population and 41 percent of the 1914 male population of military age. (See Maj. G. C. Clayton, *The New Zealand Army—A History from 1980s to the 1990s* [Wellington: New Zealand Army, 1990], p. 103.) In the Second World War, 25 percent of the Australian male population enlisted for military service, which constituted 80 percent of the eligible male population between ages eighteen to thirty-five. By way of comparison, the Union Armies in the American Civil War constituted just 21 percent of the white males of military age, and the Confederate Armies marshaled 73 percent of white males of military age. (See John Terraine, *White Heat—The New Warfare 1914–18* [London: Guild, 1982], pp. 13–14.)

3. Peter Firkins, *The Australians in Nine Wars—Waikato to Long Tan* (London: Pan Books, 1973), p. 185; and Clayton, *The New Zealand Army*, p. 110.

4. John Ellis, *The Sharp End of War* (London: David & Charles, 1980; Corgi Books Edition, 1982), Appendix 1, pp. 384–385.

5. See *Military Balance 1997–98* (London: International Institute for Strategic Studies, 1997).

6. Bergin and Smith, "The Public Perceptions of the Army," pp. 206–207.

7. Herbert Kaufman, *Time, Chance, and Organizations—Natural Selection in a Perilous Environment* (Chatham, N.J.: Chatham House, 1985), p. 27.

8. See for example, Cathy Downes, "Great Britain" in Charles Moskos and Frank Wood, eds., *The Military—More Than Just a Job?* (Washington, D.C., Pergamon-Brassey's International Defense Publishers, 1988), pp. 153–176.

9. See also Maj. Kathryn E. Quinn, "Servicewomen: Careers into the 1990s," *Australian Defence Force Journal*, No. 87 (Mar./Apr. 1991), pp. 43–49.

10. New Zealand Armed Forces Defence Council Order 9/1981.

11. Clare Burton, *Report of the Gender Intgration Audit of the New Zealand Defence Force* (Wellington: New Zealand Defence Force, New Zealand Human Rights Commission, Crown Copyright, 1998). It was a tragedy that Dr. Burton succumbed to a short battle with cancer shortly after completing her report. The NZDF has accepted all 122 of her recommendations for achieving a fuller integration of women in the NZDF. As her obituary in the front of the report states, "Clare Burton made a difference."

12. Office of the Status of Women, Department of the Prime Minister and cabinet, *Convention on the Elimination of All Forms of Discrimination Against Women— Report of Australia* (Canberra: Australian Government Publishing Service, 1986), pp. 87–88.

13. Greg Snider, *Australian Defence Force 1991 Families Census* (Canberra: Australian Institute of Family Studies, Final Report, 1991) pp. 29–30.

14. Greg Snider, *Australian Defence Force 1991 Families Census*, p. 27.

15. See for example Cathy Downes, *High Personnel Turnover: The Australian Defence Force Is Not a Limited Liability Company* (Canberra: The Australian National University, Canberra Paper on Strategy No. 44, 1988), pp. 29–38; and Parliament of the Commonwealth of Australia, Joint Committee on Foreign Affairs, Defence and Trade, *Personnel Wastage in the Australian Defence Force—Report and Recommendations* (Canberra: Australian Government Publishing Service, 1988), pp. 217–240.

16. Headquarters, Australian Defence Force, *Unacceptable Sexual Behaviour By Members of the Australian Defence Force* (Canberra: Defence Instruction [General], 1992).

17. See for example Jane Ross, *The Myth of the Digger* (Sydney: Hale & Iremonger, 1985); and Patsy Adam-Smith, *The ANZACS* (Melbourne: Nelson Publishers, 1985).

18. This experience was repeated during the Vietnam War, where antiwar protests were as much directed against the policy of sending national servicemen to Vietnam as to the war itself and Austalia's participation in it.

19. Stephen Van Evera, *Managing the Eastern Crisis: Preventing War in the Former Soviet Empire* (Cambridge, Mass.: Massachusetts Institute of Technology, Center for International Studies, Defence and Arms Control Studies Working Paper, Jan. 6, 1992), pp. 5–7.

11

Switzerland: Between Tradition and Modernity

KARL W. HALTINER
EDUARD HIRT

Switzerland is one of the few countries in Europe to be free from war over the last 140 years. Although it was threatened more or less directly by this century's two world wars, it was not involved in war activities. Switzerland is unlike most European countries, where wars caused a crucial break in both political and military tradition. Nevertheless, the two world wars left deep traces on the country's national identity. They confirmed the Swiss in their opinion that the existence of their small Alpine republic could be guaranteed only if they were able to avoid areas of tension in regard to changing European interests. Neutrality, practiced and internationally guaranteed for 200 years, became the constant basis of Swiss foreign and security policy. Switzerland has joined neither the United Nations nor the European Union. It approached NATO only recently by joining the Partnership for Peace program. The myth of neutrality still determines the Swiss national identity. Switzerland still defines and legitimizes its statehood and identity as a historic special case.

In less than ten years, the geopolitical environment has undergone fundamental change. Today Switzerland is located in the middle of a Europe where nations are about to unite into a federation, where old lines of conflict have vanished, and where a common European security structure is under discussion. Toward whom should Switzerland be neutral today? This change jeopardizes the centuries-old basis for Swiss security and defense policies.

This question also concerns the armed forces. Switzerland still maintains a mass army of the old type. According to its constitution, every Swiss male is liable for military service. To date, no other country except Israel has applied the principle of universal conscription as emphatically as Switzerland. No Swiss male can avoid close contact with the armed forces during his lifetime. He either renders military service or, if unable to serve for medical reasons, pays a "substitution tax." This equality has been called "military socialism." The Swiss self-concept, however, preserves the idea that everybody must share the burden of defense in a democratic society.

Worldwide, the Swiss armed forces are considered the purest form of a regular militia system. The constitution forbids the federation from keeping standing troops. The armed services exist in a continuous state of mobilization and demobilization of individual troops throughout the year, with only a small basic organization of military personnel. The militia consists of all male citizens between ages 20 and 42 (age 50 before 1995) except those with handicaps. After undergoing basic training for 15 weeks (17 weeks before 1995), a male citizen must serve up to 28 (32) weeks in two-week refresher courses extending over 22 (30) years, for a total of 10 (11) months.

The militia does not constitute a reserve army: During his total time of service, the militiaman remains a regular member of a war formation, with personal equipment and automatic rifle and ammunition at home, and constant compulsory target practice. He is in training throughout his years of eligibility. Except for a small corps of professional soldiers, all officers and NCOs have the same status as the rest of the troops. A career-minded person begins as a soldier and then must pass through the ranks by serving as trainer and commander in basic training courses. These voluntary services add up during a military career.

After one and one-half centuries in which Switzerland practiced a policy of strict neutrality and deterrence with its mass army, this small state in Europe's heartland is now at a turning point; it is considering a radical redefinition of its national and security policies. What will be the consequences of the new geopolitical situation? More importantly, what will be the consequences of the new consolidated European peace order for the military structure and for the social and political position of the armed forces in Switzerland? What changes may be anticipated in the near future?

The following purely empirical analysis is based on Moskos's paradigm of change regarding a Postmodern military. We examine the extent to which the Swiss development supports or refutes this paradigm. In doing so, we investigate each variable in the model of change to determine how fully the postulated developments affect the Swiss armed forces. Because military doctrine and the organization of the militia forces have always been closely interdependent with the country's political and social developments, we include the latter in the analysis as well.

PERCEIVED THREAT

The Modern Era

As the Alpine bottleneck between northern and southern Europe and an important passage from eastern to western Europe, Switzerland has always been strategically very important to the large western European nations. During the European conflicts of the nineteenth century and this century's two world wars, invasion and/or occupation by a direct neighbor was a real danger. This threat prevailed until 1945. The fear of involvement in European conflicts has been so strong an element in the Swiss people's collective identity that even today, at a time of European integration, their defensive reaction regarding neutrality makes a natural relationship with the European Union impossible. The policy of neutrality practiced by Switzerland today is a result of the centuries-old perceived threat.

The Late Modern Era

Developments in arms technology during World War II and the subsequent establishment of alliances (NATO, the Warsaw Pact) resulted in a reassessment of the national threat. Because of the emergence of nuclear weapons and the large number of casualties in the civilian population due to air raids, a civil defense and protection organization was created after World War II, with nationwide construction of bomb shelters able to withstand a nuclear attack. Today, 90 percent of the population have places in a shelter in case of emergency. In 1958, the military seriously considered the development of its own nuclear weapons, but the federal government decided against nuclear armament.

The analysis of official threat was reflected in the defense concept of 1973. Military, civilian, political, and economic aspects of national defense were to be coordinated within the framework of a common defense doctrine. A high degree of willingness to defend the country should signal to any potential aggressor that a violation of Swiss neutrality would not be feasible from a cost/benefit viewpoint. The aim of this policy, officially called *dissuasion* (i.e., deterrence), was to guarantee Switzerland's neutrality in case of high-level East-West conflicts.

As shown by investigations from the 1970s and 1980s, the threat, as perceived by the population at the time, corresponded to the official idea of threat: A majority of the population thought a major armed conflict in Europe would be fought with nuclear weapons.

The Postmodern Era

In reaction to the collapse of the communist East, the Swiss government submitted to Parliament a report on security policy, known as *Security Report 90*.[1] That report reassessed the threat analysis after the end of the Cold War and reevaluated the defense concept of 1973. The report concluded that a major war in western Europe with Swiss involvement had become unlikely and, mainly because of the European integration process, would remain improbable.

Whereas the defense concept of 1973 dealt exclusively with military risks, *Security Report 90* provides integrated and interrelated analyses. It discusses the worldwide changes in balances of power and covers social, economic, demographic, and ecological developments as well as procedures in case of natural or manmade disasters. With direct reference to the change in the spectrum of threat and the new nonmilitary risks, security policy is now considered a comprehensive policy assuring the state's existence.

In the reformulation of threat priorities, *Security Report 90* reflects the change in the Swiss people's awareness of threat. The persons interviewed attach less importance to military threat than to ecological and economic concerns, to aspects of foreign infiltration as a consequence of international migration, and to lack of internal security.

In general, the developments of the military threat perceived by politicians and the Swiss population conform to the three-stage modernization hypothesis in content and timing. A civilian threat periodically has substituted for the military threat. Yet the example of Switzerland also shows that the collective awareness formed by previous threats, particularly military threats, is still strongly affected by fear.

FORCE STRUCTURE

As stated above, Switzerland does not have standing forces, but only a militia. From this fact it follows that the Swiss army cannot correspond to the mass army, whose end is postulated by the modernization hypothesis. A more detailed analysis of the military's structural change and the political and technological conditions in Switzerland shows that developments in the Alpine republic conform somewhat to the trend postulated by the model in regard to timing and general direction. They occur, however, in milder form and with a time lag.

Until 1945 the Swiss citizen army corresponded to the prototype of a rather undifferentiated and static mass army, with not much division of labor and little sophisticated high-tech weaponry. In 1945 the strength of the infantry, almost 800,000 persons, was roughly two-thirds of the army's total number. The heart of the static defense concept was the Alps, which had been transformed into an enormous fortress during World War II.

After 1945 the infantry doctrine was partly replaced by a concept of increased operative flexibility. The static defense lines were supplemented increasingly by mobile armored units prepared to strike back. In addition, the air force was strengthened. Both the army and the air force were armed with the most modern equipment available, mostly bought from NATO states. Today, militia soldiers operate the modern German Leopard II tank, and militia pilots fly a slightly modified version of the Mirage IIIS and the F-5 Tiger II. In 1990 the proportion of infantry had declined to one-third of all troops. The segment consisting of technical, logistical, and special troops, however, had grown to about two-thirds. In regard to armament and operative capability, today's Swiss armed forces hardly differ from the Western European standard.

In light of the rapid technological advances in weapon systems, it has become important to ask whether at least a partial professionalization of the militia is necessary. So far, however, only a few specialists have raised the subject. It has seldom been discussed in public. In view of the almost mythical public admiration for the ideal of the citizen-soldier, it could not be achieved anyway. Today, Swiss military experts agree that developments in arms technology have made the handling of complex arms systems easier. Maintenance and repairs, however, have become so complex that professionalization in logistics and training organization is absolutely necessary if military efficiency is to be ensured in the future. The recently acquired F/A 18 fighters represent the limits on adaptation imposed by the militia. In spite of protests by militia pilots, these planes can be flown only by professionals.

A close look at the structural change in the Swiss military suggests that latent trends toward professionalization may be observed in addition to the manifest trends.

- *Manifest*: In addition to the "regular" militia air force, a permanent air surveillance squadron consisting of professional pilots and maintenance crews was formed as early as 1941 and was expanded until 1990.

- *Manifest*: A professional corps of soldiers for maintaining and operating the Alpine fortresses was created in World War II.

- *Latent*: The original small instructional corps of professional officers and NCOs responsible for training militia officers and NCOs, as well as supervising the troops' training, grew steadily from about 500 in 1945 to 2,000 in 1995. In addition, the number of NCOs in charge of technical missions rose faster than the number of officers.

- *Latent*: Since World War II, the positions of corps and division commanders have been professionalized so that militia officers striving for two- or three-star rank have had to give up their civilian professions. Only a few have done so since 1970. Not only the highest ranks of the army but also the commands of regiments have been taken over increasingly by members of the professional instructional corps.

- *Latent*: The number of civilian employees needed to operate and maintain military arsenals and installations in order to guarantee minimal standby in case of militia mobilization has increased since World War II.

The professional core increased from 1 percent of the total strength of the militia in 1940 to 3.5 percent in 1995. This percentage is very low in comparison with conscript forces of other nations; it indicates the unbroken militia character of the Swiss armed forces. It also shows, however, that in today's society, minimal military standby can no longer be guaranteed without a professional core.

In 1995 the armed forces were reformed and reduced under the heading "Army 95" as a consequence of the shrinking threat and the increased internal opposition to the armed forces; this opposition included a referendum to abolish the army in 1989 and, in 1991, political attempts to reduce military expenditures by 50 percent and codify them in a constitutional amendment. The principle of militia thus remained intact. The size of the armed forces was reduced by roughly one-third, to 400,000 militia members. Length of conscription was reduced from ages 20 to 50 to ages 20 to 42, and the duration of initial training was shortened. According to the government's intention, increased technology was to compensate for the reduction in troops. "More muscle, less fat" was the defense minister's slogan. The determination to reduce "fat" was demonstrated by the acquisition of F/A 18 fighters in the context of comprehensive modernization of the air force.

More interesting than the Army 95 reform itself was the accompanying public debate. Three different types of criticism and suggestions can be identified.

First, immediately after the referendum to abolish the army was rejected in 1989, a proposal was made to create a national civic service whereby military service would be only one option among various forms of service. The proposal, submitted in 1990–91, is supported by clerical circles and sporadically by the middle class center. The government has taken up the proposal and has charged a commission to investigate the option seriously. Simultaneously it has questioned whether a national civic service, which could make citizens also liable for services of a nonmilitary type, would be compatible with a liberal and democratic constitutional state.

Second, with a view to the changed threat and the new military tasks (and for the first time in Swiss history), since 1991 some experts advocate doing away with universal conscription and creating a small professional army or a mixed system consisting of a standing professional core and a territorially organized militia. The latter would be entrusted only with secondary and supporting tasks. These people criticize the Army 95 reform because they do not believe it goes far enough; they view it as a mere reduction within the present framework. The critics, mainly economists, call for a higher value to be placed on efficiency than on institutional tradition and political aspects. In 1993 a study reflecting such arguments caused a stir because well-known members of the Swiss Parliament and security experts had contributed to it.[2] In 1998 the same parliamentarians restated their claims in a new position paper.[3]

A third group criticizes the Army 95 reform because Switzerland's disarmament is not sufficiently evident to them. They doubt whether Army 95 is an adequate response to the end of the Cold War. This form of criticism is expressed mainly in a study published by the Social Democrats in 1995. They advocate disarmament in the form of "militia army light," with a static character and only light armament, and want to manage on half of today's budget.[4] The initiators of the referendum to abolish the army, which was rejected in 1989, think along the same lines: In 1997, they announced that they would soon launch a referendum to do away with the army.

The government and the great majority of the political and military establishments reject such criticism. The official side emphasizes two arguments for keeping a militia as the organizational basis of the armed forces. First, it would be impossible today to finance a professional force large enough to defend the country effectively. In contrast, the militia is cost-effective.[5] Secondly, the traditional link between the people and the army is a strong argument for maintaining the present militia system.

Switzerland is prevented from seriously considering alternative defense models not by reasons relating to greater military efficiency, but by the lower costs and the long tradition of the citizen-soldier. The present defense minister, however, has hinted that Army 95 may be only a transitional model. The 1998 *Report of the Study Commission on Strategic Issues* insists on maintaining the militia model, but pleads strongly for a substantial reduction in size in the near future and for supplementing the smaller militia more and more with professional units.

At first sight, the structural development of Switzerland's armed forces does not conform at all, in content or in timing, to the modernization hypothesis. To date, Switzerland has adhered firmly to the principle of universal conscription and the institutional tradition of the militia. On further examination, however, subtle tendencies toward professionalization in the period after World War II are apparent. Moreover, it is not inconceivable that Switzerland will change to a semiprofessional or militia volunteer force in the future. The political debate that has continued increasingly since 1990 leaves all options open for the time being.

DEFINITION OF THE ARMED FORCES' MAJOR MISSION

The inquiry about the major military mission is bound up with Switzerland's political self-concept and foreign policy.

From 1815 to 1990, Switzerland followed a strict policy of neutrality that did not permit it to participate actively or passively in any military or political alliance. To demonstrate how deeply the idea of neutrality is embedded in the collective Swiss identity, Switzerland does not belong to the United Nations, nor has it institutionally joined the European Union. The major mission of the armed forces from the founding of the federal state to 1990, despite changes in military doctrine, was principally the same: defense of neutrality, and thus of Swiss territory, against any aggressor. The policy of neutrality compels the armed forces to follow a single mission: to defend all of its territory. Even during the Cold War, official Switzerland tried to keep equal political and military distance from both East and West, although the people's mentality always clearly favored the West.

Since 1990 the geostrategic upheaval has called into question not only the centuries-old political concept of a neutral Switzerland, but also the traditional mission of the armed forces. Toward whom should Switzerland be neutral in an increasingly integrating Europe? Toward whom should national defense be directed in a Europe about to unite? Does a costly mass army with a doctrine of defense all around still make sense? Can Switzerland afford economically, politically, and militarily to be neutral and solitary without isolating itself politically and militarily? The ongoing debate threatens to divide the country, which until now has sought its identity by differentiating itself from others.

Since 1990, the government and parts of the political and economic establishment have been pleading for Switzerland's increased cooperation in the European integration process. The traditional neutrality is thought to be a thing of the past, and should be given up in favor of international cooperation. *Security Report 90* contains a principal reorientation of security policy matters, as follows:

> One of the main goals to which Switzerland intends to contribute is a stable and secure Europe. The security of our country depends largely on the security of our geographical environment. Therefore we want to take part in creating a European security system based not on deterrence but on trust and on cooperation.[6]

This principal intention is expressed in the careful reformulation of the major mission of the armed forces: They should not be an immediate part of the European defense system, but (a new feature) should be entrusted with international peacekeeping. Their priorities are stated as follows in *Security Report 90*.

1. *Promotion of peace*: Participation in peace-promoting UN operations, delegation of observers, advisory functions for a defensive military doctrine and militia structure, protection of conferences, verification activities performed by specialized military personnel.

2. *Prevention of war and defense of Swiss territory*: Defense of the country against any aggressor, combat only within the country, no engagement in operational cooperation with other countries;

3. *Assistance as a contribution to generally safeguarding our means of existence*: Relief in case of major disasters caused by nature or man, im-

migration control in the event of a major influx of refugees, police functions.

In contrast to the concept of 1973, much more importance is attached to promoting peace and safeguarding the Swiss people's existence. In 1989–90, Switzerland for the first time dispatched an unarmed medical unit to Namibia; in 1991–92 it sent a unit to the western Sahara. Furthermore, about twenty-five Swiss military observers are on duty worldwide in various theaters of war. Swiss army specialists participate in UN verification missions in Iraq. The parliamentary study commission report of 1998, mentioned earlier, recommends the establishment of a Swiss Solidarity Corps. This unit would consist of specially trained and equipped professional and militia personnel able to undertake rescue and peace-support operations, as well as actions in support of civilian authorities.[7]

The government's recommendation for opening foreign and security policy, however, meets stiff opposition from that part of the population which still sees Switzerland's well-being as depending on "splendid isolation." Since 1992, concrete projects calling for international participation have been rejected in several referendum votes. Among others, these projects concerned economic integration into the European Union and the creation of a Swiss blue-helmeted battalion for the UN or the Organization for Security and Cooperation in Europe (OSCE). In fact, the internationalization sought by Swiss security policy and the Swiss armed forces is rather restricted. The Swiss government at least obtained in 1996 parliamentary approval to join NATO's Partnership for Peace.

The same points apply to the change in the armed forces' mission as to force structure. In content and in timing, Swiss development differs considerably from the predicted trend toward modernization. A sequential change in the military mission is out of the question. At most, a change may be noticed in the array of tasks in which tendencies to embark on new missions become evident.

THE DOMINANT MILITARY PROFESSIONAL

Only 1,000 of the more than 30,000 Swiss officers are professionals. They function primarily as instructors, and only secondarily as leaders of the militia. The same applies to the roughly 1,000 professional NCOs. In view of the conditions set by the system, the question implied by the modernization hypothesis may be applied only conditionally to Switzerland.

There are indications that until World War II or even until the 1960s, some professional officers pictured themselves as combat leaders in their military identity and their potential role rather than in their explicit role as military instructors of militia officers. Thus Switzerland's few aristocratic families were overrepresented in the corps of professionals until the 1960s.[8]

Apparently the military tradition was honored there. A recent survey shows that the older professional officers, in contrast to the younger ones, perceive themselves primarily as soldiers when defining their roles.

In the course of the rapid technological advances and the increase of noncombat segments in the militia in the 1960s and 1970s, the officers' self-concept apparently changed so that their identities as teachers and trainers now dominate. In a survey conducted in 1991, more than half of the Swiss professional officers regarded themselves as teachers, one-tenth as managers, and one-third as soldiers and leaders.[9] The professional NCOs in particular viewed their profession as essentially technical.[10]

A possible indication that their profession might be reinterpreted again is the training reform for professional officers introduced in 1991 by the Swiss Military College in Au-Zürich. Before that time, professional officers underwent a largely military and technically oriented basic training. Now, for the first time, the young officers-to-be must complete a three-year education in which studies in social sciences, psychology, and politics at a public university account for fully half of all training time. Apparently the officer's education will be more scientifically oriented, and the officer will approach the status of a soldier-statesman or a soldier-scholar.

In summary, in regard to the role of the Swiss army's professionals, one may notice a change that at least approaches, in content and in timing, the postulated trend toward modernization.

PUBLIC ATTITUDES TOWARD THE MILITARY

Until 1970 the militia concept applied not only to the military system in Switzerland, but also to political institutions. Many cantonal governments and all parliaments, including the Federal Assembly, were organized on the basis of a militia. Because of the centuries-old tradition of the militia in Swiss society, the symbolic functions normally assumed by citizens' armies could develop early and strongly in the relationship between the military and society. These functions included the role of the military as the "school of the nation," the symbol of civic honor and national identity. The militia military served not only as an instrument of national security but also as an important factor for national cohesion in this ethnically heterogeneous country. Ever since the establishment of the militia, the degree of military participation has determined the degree of civil integration and closeness to the social and political core of Swiss society. As John McPhee commented, "If you understand the New York Yacht Club, the Cosmos Club, the Century Club, you would understand the Swiss Army."[11]

This close and supportive relationship between society and the military reached its climax during World War II, when Switzerland was surrounded by fascist governments and was virtually left on its own. At that time the "army myth" crystallized, and it formed public opinion until the 1970s.

During the accelerated change of values in the 1970s and 1980s, the valuation of the military began to change as well. The militia lost its former central position as an essential symbol of Swiss national identity, as an ideal of civic participation, and as a site of passage into manhood. In public opinion, the army began to be viewed increasingly as a necessary evil.[12] Especially for the young, it became the preferred target of political opposition, embodying traditional, antimodern Switzerland.

This process of desymbolization came to a climax in November 1989, when a referendum, a constitutional initiative to abolish the army, received 36.5 percent of the votes. Analyses show that a majority of 20- to 29-year-olds approved the referendum. This erosion of traditional legitimization is an example of what Max Weber called disillusionment by modernization.

Since 1990, public opinion has changed once more. The military is less an object of internal political criticism and argument today than in the 1980s. In 1998 its acceptance rate reached more than 70 percent[13] in surveys, although the social and political valuation of the military's role has changed. Today's attitude is characterized by a certain apathy. Although most people realize the necessity for national defense, they wish to have nothing to do with it personally. This "without me" attitude manifests itself in the increasing attempts to avoid individual conscription with the help of a medical certificate, and in the increasing difficulty of recruiting voluntary militia NCOs and officers in sufficient numbers and quality. In 1997 more than one-third of the persons interviewed favored a professional army; in the 1970s and 1980s only 10 percent did so.

The change in Swiss public opinion toward the military conforms to the modernization hypothesis in content but not in timing. After many discussions about the social valuation of the military between 1970 and 1990, the earlier support has changed to an attitude characterized largely by apathy and indifference. Today Switzerland's militia military is an institution of secondary importance.

MEDIA RELATIONS

Switzerland has a great variety of media, especially print media. Therefore it is difficult to establish dominant trends. It makes sense to assume that a correlation exists between media and public opinion; thus the attitude of the media toward the armed forces may be similar to that of public opinion.

Until the mid-1970s, a rather uncritical and positive coverage of military matters prevailed. For its information policy, the military relied on an almost automatic support by the leading Swiss media.

In the 1980s this close relationship changed to tension when individual media began to report, with apparent enjoyment, about young people's growing opposition to the military. In the eyes of the army, the media granted the opposition too much space to express their criticism of the army before the referendum of 1989. They were blamed for negatively influencing the outcome. Since that time, mutual accusations of manipulation have marked the relationship between the armed forces and the media.

Since the 1990s the military has abandoned its rather passive attitude toward the media and has tried to pursue a media and public-relations policy on its own behalf. Thus in the spring of 1993 it succeeded in influencing a referendum on the acquisition of F/A 18 fighters, in spite of initial unfavorable public opinion. A year later, however, it failed in the referendum against the introduction of a blue-helmeted UN battalion. At present, the media pay no special attention to the armed forces. On the other hand, some of them push for a new return of the forces.

The development of the relationship between the media and the military in Switzerland corresponds only partially to the postulated modernization trend. Media relations typical of Modern and Late Modern times may be observed, but not those postulated for the Postmodern phase.

CIVILIAN EMPLOYEES

The military administration tries to avoid recruiting professionals to perform tasks that can be performed as well by temporarily conscripted civilian specialists. As fully as possible, the citizens liable for military service are entrusted with tasks that resemble or correspond to their civilian work. Apparently the greatest compatibility between military and civilian activities can be achieved in the noncombatant technical troops; the lowest, in the combat troops. According to a recent study, the average degree of affinity between civilian and military activities is 66 percent.[14] That is, about two-thirds of the citizens serving in the militia are given tasks that are similar to their work in civilian life. The number of civilian employees can be kept small if the civilian professionals' potential is used optimally.

Civilian employees are to be found almost exclusively in arsenals and maintenance stations. The percentage of civilian employees was higher during World War II than in the postwar period. Today, without an obvious trend and with few fluctuations, it amounts to about 75 percent of the full-time professional personnel or less than 3 percent of the total militia. The very low and currently steady number of civilian employees plays a key role in the preparedness of the militia army, one far more important than the percentage would lead us to imagine.

The small number of civilian employees appointed to the permanent staff of the armed forces may be explained by the adherence to the militia system. If we assume that Switzerland retains the militia system, the proportion of civilian employees will not increase considerably. Therefore this aspect of the modernization trend postulated in the hypothesis may not be substantiated in Switzerland.

WOMEN'S ROLE

As early as 1903 women, especially nuns, were able to assume voluntary charitable duties in the armed forces under the Red Cross. An army branch for women, however, was not formed until the beginning of World War II. The separate Women's Corps was part of the army but had only the status of an auxiliary service (in German: Hilfsdienst—HD). This HD branch of service, created mainly for men whose fitness was limited due to medical reasons, had its own ranking system different from the regular order and was low in prestige.

In 1945 women began fighting for equal status in the army; they achieved this goal in 1985. Although these volunteer members of the militia were subject to less duty than their conscripted male counterparts, they could now attain all regular NCO and officer ranks up to one-star general. The auxiliary service statute was abolished; women served alone and in mixed units or headquarters, as well as in exclusively female units in logistical and medical branches. Since 1990 they have had the option of carrying a pistol for self-defense.

With the Army 95 reform the exclusively female units were abolished, and women's status and length of voluntary service became more similar to men's. Moreover, the array of tasks that women could perform was enlarged considerably. In 1993 the first women were trained as helicopter pilots. Since 1995 Switzerland has had its first female UN military observer.

Women's participation in the Swiss militia has always been minimal and has decreased over the last few years, possibly in connection with growing criticism and the loss of the army's social importance. About 100 women apply each year for voluntary service. Presently about 5,000 women belong to the armed forces.

Apart from the fact that women still are not admitted to combat activities, their integration into the Swiss army has largely succeeded. In this respect, Switzerland largely conforms to the postulated modernization trend.

SPOUSES AND THE MILITARY COMMUNITY

The militia lacks the elements of a standing army. The troops do not train over a single long period but in relatively short periodical courses. Service often takes place in a civilian infrastructure rather than in garrisons. As a result, few militia members are housed in barracks. Switzerland has never had any real military communities. The corps of professional officers and NCOs usually lives close to where the conscripts are trained, and all instructors have a car at their disposal. Because of high personal mobility and the smallness of the country, professionals may work at almost any place in Switzerland without the need to change their places of residence. Thus the question about spouses and the military community implied by the modernization hypothesis may not apply to Switzerland.

HOMOSEXUALS IN THE MILITARY

The Swiss armed forces have always had a liberal attitude about homosexuals. This may be the case because the short periods of militia duty spread over a longer period in an individual's life and the limited degree of isolation in barracks have never made homosexuality a problem, as it would be in standing armies. Homosexuality alone has never been a reason for discharge from the military or an obstacle to a military career; no explicit legislation forbids it. If social or psychological problems ensue from homosexual behavior, a medical or psychiatric discharge is possible but not imperative.

In 1985 the highest-ranking military judge remarked laconically, "Le problème de l'homosexualité ne se pose pas dans l'armée suisse" ("There is no homosexual problem in the Swiss army").[15] An indication of this statement is the lack of statistical documents and the nonexistence of any discussions of the subject in society or the armed forces. It does not seem that this situation will change.

In the militia system, the line between civilian life and the military is more diffuse and more permeable than in standing armies. As a result the change in society's attitude toward homosexuality, from social stigmatization through tacit toleration to explicit acceptance, may be transferred directly to the military. The modernization trend postulated in the hypothesis is largely proved correct, but has no relation to the time periods.

CONSCIENTIOUS OBJECTION

The federal constitution of 1848 states: "Every Swiss is liable for military service" and "[R]eligious belief does not exempt anyone from his duty as a citizen."[16] Traditionally, universal conscription in Switzerland not only had to make maximum use of the military potential; it also served the ideal of distributing the national defense burden equally across the population. Furthermore, in Swiss democracy the citizens have always had the right to a direct voice. This fact, however, has always been linked to the duty of all citizens to defend their democratic rights, by force if necessary. Therefore conscientious objectors (COs) traditionally have been considered state objectors. In fact, in 1976 and again in 1983, the Swiss people refused by referendum the introduction of alternative civilian service.

In the past two decades, however, the rejection of COs has softened gradually as individualistic values have gained importance. Both the political elite and the public have shown increased understanding toward the COs, who even today are a small minority compared with the country's mass army. In 1991 a decriminalization act was approved by national referendum.

This gradual shift in public opinion encouraged the federal Parliament to make a new attempt to change the Constitution. The clause "Every Swiss is liable for military service" was to be supplemented by an amendment stating, "The law will provide for the organization of a civilian service." In May 1992 this amendment was accepted by 83 percent of the Swiss who voted on the issue.

The principle of universal conscription is still followed strictly. Conscientious objectors must defend their position before a commission. Under the provisions of a law passed in 1996, conscientious objectors whose ethical or religious motives are recognized by this commission may be subject to a term of civilian service one and one-half times longer than military service. Those who object for other reasons will continue to receive prison sentences. No free choice between military and nonmilitary service is offered.

As mentioned above, some people are calling for a more generous solution because, in their view, the military threat has vanished. They favor the introduction of a universal civic service, which would include military service as one option among other, civilian services.

With a time lag, it becomes obvious that Switzerland will pass through the same stages of development as already exist at a higher level in other democracies. In that respect the country follows the general modernization trend.

ORGANIZATIONAL FORMAT: INSTITUTIONAL VERSUS OCCUPATIONAL

The format of the Swiss armed forces, based on the militia principle and on universal conscription, is fundamentally and predominantly institutional. The existence of the organization is legitimized by patriotic ideals: Motivation to participate is based on values such as honor, duty, and sacrifice.

An indication of change toward an occupational format may be found only if the armed forces are exposed, entirely or in part, to the market. As shown above, this is not the case in the Swiss armed forces, where the number of professionals is small. Yet there is every indication of change if the occupational trend is defined not only as a development within the military but also as a reflection of a modernization process embracing the society as a whole.[17]

In the past, the Swiss public perceived the military as a citizen ideal, a symbol of national identity, and an important social and political reference group. Since the 1970s, however, this has been less and less the case. Today, as mentioned earlier, the military is viewed increasingly from an instrumental and utilitarian perspective. It is now considered a necessary evil, and service is regarded by many people as a nuisance to be avoided if possible.

Although a military career in Switzerland has never yielded any material profit but has always required a great deal of energy, there were always enough qualified volunteers available until the 1970s because the position of a militia officer or NCO always entailed high prestige. Since the 1970s, however, it has been harder to recruit enough volunteers for cadre positions. More often than before, NCOs must be forced to take a higher rank. Traditional values such as prestige and honor no longer motivate officers to pursue a military career; instead they seek instrumental goals such as profit for the civilian profession or individual challenge. Personal involvement no longer focuses on social and political values, but on individual motives.[18]

A similar change of motivation may be observed in the small corps of professional officers. According to an international comparative study,[19] the proportion of Swiss officers with a predominantly occupational attitude is 38 percent. In Great Britain's voluntary armed forces it is a mere 29 percent; in France, 21 percent.

Although the Swiss military system is still based largely on institutional criteria and values, we see indications of a shift toward an occupational format. If we include the above-mentioned political discussion about introducing civilian service as an alternative to universal conscription, the indicators point toward the modernization hypothesis. The development in Switzerland seems to follow the general trend, though hesitantly and with a time lag.

CONCLUSIONS AND PERSPECTIVES

Are the Swiss armed forces becoming a Postmodern military? Many of the criteria set forth in Moskos's modernization model apply to Switzerland only partially or not at all. Obviously, insofar as Switzerland follows the principles of militia, universal conscription, and mass army, it is bound up with Modern military structure. Within this tradition-bound context, however, modernization processes are evident. They include the change of threat perception and of public attitude as well as the professionals' altered self-concept and the integration of women, and approach the postulated trend in these respects. Today the Swiss armed forces have attained a modernization status that may be assigned equally to the Modern and the Late Modern periods.

The Swiss development is ambiguous because the geostrategic situation has largely changed the requirements for Swiss security policy and the militia military system, but Switzerland has not yet produced institutional solutions. The armed forces have been reduced and the defense expenditures cut by almost a third since 1990, but the defense system has not yet found a new concept. Public and political debate continues in regard to Switzerland's position in Europe, with possible consequences for the tasks to be performed, and future structure.

The outcome of the discussion is difficult to forecast because in a direct democracy, with the collection of signatures, plebiscite pressure can always be applied in one direction or the other. Furthermore, the development of a new military doctrine and the structure of future armed forces in Switzerland depend strongly on whether the country joins the European Union. They also depend on the possible form of a future pan-European security system.

Switzerland has two basic options. One option is to expand the elements of professionalization and voluntariness, as is currently occurring in many Western European states.[20] In the extreme case, universal conscription would be abolished in favor of a small volunteer army entrusted with largely international tasks. The second option could be called "national guardization." In this model, a voluntary militia would replace universal conscription. Military service would be a part-time option as in the U.S. National Guard. This model would obliterate even more fully the line between military and civilian life, a situation that exists already in the current conditions of the militia based on universal conscription.

On the basis of Swiss military tradition and the present situation, the following trends seem plausible.

1. Because of the long and unbroken tradition of a militia army, a transition to a standing professional army seems unlikely. It is far more probable that Switzerland will, in a first step, come to rely on a strongly reduced militia army with an extended core of volunteers. In a second step, conscription might be abolished in favor of a militia of volunteers. That is, it will be based on principles similar to those of today's conscription-based militia but will have the characteristics of a reserve force such as the U.S. National Guard, which may be mobilized only in emergencies.

2. A small corps of volunteers, made up of a few thousand men, will constitute the mobile hard core of the new militia. These professional soldiers, mainly officers and NCOs, will continue to be in charge of the training but will increasingly take over leadership functions. This corps will support the militia even more strongly than today and will become a recruiting pool for special tasks and international missions.

It is very likely that the future military will no longer be every citizen's concern, but will become the business of militia volunteers and a few career soldiers in the military branch of a national civic service. The corps of officers will be identified far less closely with the country's civilian elite than today. This situation will alter the future forces' social legitimacy: As a small corps, they will have status similar to that of the police or a government service. The political influence of these forces will be smaller in the future than today. National defense will no longer be a primary state mission, as it is today, but tertiary at best. There is every indication of a modernization trend in Switzerland, which conforms partially to Moskos's hypotheses.

NOTES

1. "Swiss Security Policy in Times of Change," in *Report 90 of the Federal Council to the Federal Assembly on the Security Policy of Switzerland* (Berne: EDMZ, 1990).
2. *Sicherheitspolitik und Armee*, a position paper edited by the working group Sicherheitspolitik, Zurich, Oct. 4, 1993.
3. *SIPO 2000—Expectancies for a New Security Report*, position paper of the working group Sicherheitspolitik, Zurich, August 1998.
4. Lutz Unterseher, *Die Landesverteidigung der Schweiz: Ein praktisches Modell fur die Zukunft* (Bonn: Social Democratic Party of Switzerland, 1995), mimeographed text.
5. "Armeeleitbild 95," report by the Federal Council to the Federal Assembly on the concept of the armed forces in the nineties, (Berne: EDMZ, Jan. 27, 1992).
6. "Swiss Security Policy," p. 7.
7. Report of the Study Commission on Strategic Issues, p. 17.
8. E. Wetter and E. von Orelli, *Wer ist wer im Militar?* (Frauenfeld: Huber, 1987).
9. Karl W. Haltiner, "Berufs-und Arbeitszufriedenheit der Instruktionsoffiziere," *Forum*, Vol. 8 (1992), pp. 5–13.
10. Eric Signer, *Arbeits-und Berufszufriedenheit der Berufsunteroffziere der Schweizer Armee* (Lausanne: IDEHAP, 1994).
11. John McPhee, *La Place de la Concorde Suisse* (New York: Farrar, Strauss & Giroux, 1983, 1984).
12. Karl W. Haltiner, "Switzerland," in Charles C. Moskos and Frank R. Wood, eds., *The Military: More Than Just a Job?* (Washington, D.C.: Pergamon-Brassey, 1988), p. 255–275.
13. Karl W. Haltiner, "Sicherheit '98—Aussen—und sicherheitspolitische Meinungsbildung im Trend," *Beiträge und Berichte der Militärische Führungsschule ETHZ*, Vol. 1 (1998), pp. 57–58.
14. Beat Kocherhans, "Der richtige Mann am richtigen Platz?—Zur militarischen Nutzung des zivilen Berufspotentials in der Schweizer Milizarmee," in *Diplomarbeit* (Au-Zurich: MFS, 1994).
15. Raphael Barras, Exposé du discours lors du "Congres de la sociéte internationale de droit penal militaire et de droit de la guerre," *Garmisch-Partenkirchen*, Oct. 2–8, 1985, mimeographed text.
16. Article 18 and 49 of the Federal Constitution of 1848 (revised 1874), in force today.
17. Karl W. Haltiner, "Switzerland," pp. 255–266.

18. Karl W. Haltiner, "Sicherheit 95—sicherheits—und verteidigungspolitische Meinungsbildung im Trend," *Beiträge und Berichte der Militärischen Führungsschule ETHZ* Vol. 4 (1995), pp. 64–68.

19. Giuseppe Caforio and Marina Nuciari "The Officer Profession: Ideal-Type," *Current Sociology*, Vol. 42, No. 3 (winter 1994), p. 37.

20. Karl W. Haltiner, "Reform of Europe's Armed Forces," *The Officer, ROA National Security Report* (June 1994), pp. 37–47.

12

Israel: Still Waiting in the Wings

REUVEN GAL
STUART A. COHEN[1]

Measured by the paradigm of this volume, the Israel Defense Force (IDF) is
a mixed case. Some areas of societal-military relations in Israel began to show
signs of Postmodernism as early as the mid-1970s; in others, change has been
retarded by a residue of Late Modern and even Modern traits. We begin by
reviewing the principal factors that account for this blend of accelerators and
brakes, and then examine their respective manifestations.

THE IDIOSYNCRASIES OF SOCIETAL-MILITARY
RELATIONS IN ISRAEL

Societal-military relations in Israel traditionally have been determined by a
combination of strategic and cultural circumstances, none of which are Postmodern. This situation reflects the fact that Israel was born into war and has
confronted constant military threats to its survival since 1948. Despite
progress in the Middle East peace process, a deep sense of military insecurity remains a hallmark of Israeli life, private as well as public. This sense
of danger is not comparable to attitudes prevalent in Western society since
the end of the Cold War.

The persistence of this perception of threat has also nurtured a singular
cultural heritage, which helps to perpetuate Israel's status as a "nation in
arms." The structure of the IDF is changing substantially. Even so, it remains
a people's army, in which long-service career professionals are greatly out-
numbered by compulsory conscripts and reservists, both male and female.
Another indication of Late Modernism is the extent to which the IDF remains part of Israel's entire social fabric; civilian-military boundaries remain
porous[2] or, according to some views, virtually nonexistent.[3] Above all, service in the IDF retains its ritualistic public status as the most meaningful of
all civic obligations.[4]

Although still powerful, the pressures which thus place a Late Modern
imprint on the IDF are increasingly undermined by Postmodern tendencies.
This development is due in part to circumstances similar in kind to those

affecting the armed forces of many other nations. Like those other forces, the IDF has been forced to come to terms with rapid changes in its geopolitical situation. The Israeli-Egyptian peace agreement concluded in 1979 was supplemented by a treaty with Jordan in 1994 and by several interim accords with the PLO, signed between 1993 and 1997. Moreover, since 1991 Israel has conducted intermittent negotiations with Syria, and in 1992 began to participate in the Multilateral Working Group on Middle Eastern Security and Arms Control. Such regional shifts reflect the global realignments caused by the end of the Cold War. These realignments also have created public expectations of a "peace dividend." Particularly evident are pressures to reduce the proportion of national resources devoted to defense.[5]

Simultaneously, Israel has experienced some dramatic domestic transformations, notably (1) an influx of Jewish immigrants to Israel from the former Soviet Union and from Ethiopia, which increased Israel's Jewish population by more than 15 percent between 1991 and 1995 and caused a sharp increase in the size of the conscript cohorts available for military duty; (2) the Palestinian intifadah (uprising), which erupted late in 1987 and with whose implications Israeli society continues to wrestle; (3) the 1991 Gulf War, which exposed the entire country to the twin traumas of ballistic missile attack and unprecedented IDF inactivity in wartime; and (4) the assassination in November 1995 of Prime Minister Yitzchak Rabin, followed by two changes in government (the election of Binyamin Netanyahu as prime minister in a Likud-led coalition in June 1996 and of Ehud Barak in a coalition headed by the "One Israel" party in May 1999).

Other shifts in Israeli society, however (themselves accelerated in part by the experiences cited above), warrant consideration as local expressions of a wider international phenomenon. Particularly relevant are the gradual appearance of a far less deferential public attitude toward values once considered unquestionable, and a decline in the quasi-totemic status previously accorded to national symbols and collective memories. Such demonstrations of what is sometimes called *post-Zionism* are comparable to shifts toward cultural Postmodernism in other Western societies. Moreover, and again in line with trends observed elsewhere, they have impinged on public attitudes toward military service as an individual rite of civilian passage. In surveys conducted in 1980, 1984, and 1988, prospective recruits consistently expressed great willingness to enlist (90 percent, 88 percent, and 94 percent respectively), even if conscription were voluntary.[6] In 1995, however, Lt. Gen. Amnon Lipkin-Shahak, IDF chief of staff, stated in public that recruitment motivation was being weakened by what he called "a preference for individualism over the collective in the age of liberalism."[7]

It is impossible to assess the precise strength of the pressures thus prodding Israel toward Postmodernism. The unprecedented flux characterizing relationships between the military and society in Israel creates the impression of a palimpsest, in which older patterns of behavior are still visible beneath the new. By examining the individual components of the paradigm, we reveal the extent of this situation.

PERCEIVED THREAT

Israel has always faced three distinct categories of military threat.[8] One consists of perimeter (i.e., cross-border) incursions. In addition to large-scale attacks launched by the conventional armies of Israel's immediate Arab neighbors, these could take the form of low-intensity raids conducted by groups of Palestinian marauders stationed in Arab lands. A second category of military threat consists of intrafrontier insurgent activities and guerrilla attacks on civilian as well as military targets, emanating from inside the borders of the state or from regions behind the lines held by IDF troops. The third category of military threat is remote; it consists of long-range aerial or missile bombardment launched by foes with whom Israel shares no geographical boundaries.

Progress in the Middle East peace process has largely assuaged Israel's perimeter fears. Treaties with Egypt and Jordan reduce the danger of a large-scale two-front invasion, such as was threatened in 1967 and conducted in 1973. Moreover, the dissolution of the Soviet Union, which until the late 1980s was Syria's principal patron, has restricted Syria's ability to attempt anything more than a small-scale landgrab on the Golan Heights. Also diminished is the challenge once posed by low-intensity perimeter incursions, such as those conducted by the fedayun in the 1950s and by Palestinian guerrilla units organized within the framework of the FATACH in the 1970s. At present, this threat is limited almost exclusively to the Lebanese border; there IDF units, supported by the South Lebanese army (which Israel funds and trains), confront Hizbollah paramilitary groups in a prolonged and occasionally costly struggle.

In contrast, the intrafrontier and remote threats to Israel's security have increased substantially over the past decade. The former, which were long relegated to what the IDF refers to as "current security" concerns, first became a serious operational burden during the Israeli occupation of southern Lebanon (1982–85) and assumed unprecedented proportions during the intifadah. Despite the 1993–97 agreements with the PLO (if anything, precisely because of those accords), terrorist attacks within Israel increased during that period. Radical Palestinian groups, many of whom subscribe to extreme forms of Muslim fundamentalism, such as Hamas and the Islamic Jihad, now seek to sabotage the peace process by often suicidal bus bombings and knife attacks in major centers of Jewish population. It remains to be seen how the transfer of constabulary duties to the Palestinian Authority on much of the West Bank will affect the suppression of such missions. Nevertheless, for both political and military reasons, the preservation of security there (as elsewhere) remains a primary IDF commitment.

This commitment ranks alongside the need to counter the danger posed by long-range air or missile attack. Before the 1980s, this was not considered a major threat; in fact, Israel's major cities were spared massive bombardment in the wars that erupted in 1956, 1967, and 1973. That perception was changed radically by the ease with which Iraq directed more than thirty SCUD missiles onto Israeli targets in 1991. Notwithstanding the overwhelming defeat inflicted on Iraqi forces by the allied coalition in Operation Desert Storm, the possiblity that Iraq might retain a ballistic (and possibly nonconventional) capability continues to generate deep public anxiety— especially at moments of high regional tension.

Iraq, however, is not the sole focus of Israel's "remote" military concerns. Since the mid-1990s, increasing attention has been concentrated on the potential threats posed by hostile countries still further afield. Iran arouses particular concern. Quite apart from providing such guerrilla organizations as Hamas and Hizbollah with logistical support and ideological inspiration, Iran is also known to have developed and tested a long-range missile (Shihab-3) capable of striking deep into Israel. Reports that Iran might also rapidly be approaching the nuclear threshold serve merely to enhance the virtually demonic stature which she now assumes in Israeli minds, both public and official. Looking toward the twenty-first century, senior sources in the Ministry of Defense categorize the development of a technological and doctrinal response to the threat of a massive missile bombardment from Iran, as well as from Iraq and Syria, to be Israel's primary strategic concern.[9]

The atmosphere generated by this change in threat perception is as important for its novelty as its substance. Over time, Israel's military and society had grown accustomed to a regional milieu that was menacingly antagonistic but reassuringly familiar. This permitted the retention of a relatively stable set of strategic and operational formulae that emphasized (in an ascending order of violence) deterrence, preemptive attacks, and short wars. The complexity of present circumstances is widely believed to mandate a reconsideration of that menu. One indication of possible change was supplied in 1991, when the IDF established an entirely new Rear Command (Pikud Oref), specifically in order to coordinate home defense in the event of missile attack. By 1998, further revisions in the national security doctrine were reported to be under consideration.

DEFINITION OF MAJOR MISSIONS

In contrast to the process generated elsewhere by the end of the Cold War, changes in Israel's security concerns have not led to formal redefinitions of the IDF's major missions. With regard to war aims, the basic formula remains "disabling attempts on the part of the Arabs to defeat Israel by military force."[10]

Yet when we extend the analysis beyond the strictly military realm to the IDF's relationship with society at large, major shifts are evident. Throughout the first three decades of Israel's existence, the state's armed forces undertook several essentially civilian major missions.[11] Indeed, they were explicitly instructed to do so by David Ben-Gurion, who was both Israel's first premier and defense minister (1948–53 and 1955–63) and the man principally responsible for creating the IDF and defining its character. Insisting that the military become an instrument for new Jewish nation-building, Ben-Gurion envisioned the IDF as "a pioneering educational force for Israeli youth, both native-born and immigrants."[12]

Ben-Gurion's credo defined several of the IDF's early missions. The IDF not only was projected as a symbolic focus of national sentiment; it also functioned as a melting pot in which new immigrants were socialized and became full members of the polity. Therefore, military networks often were tailored to meet civilian needs. One example is the NAHAL (Youth Pioneer Fighting) Corps, established in 1949 to set up and sustain agricultural settlements in remote and insecure regions. Another is the establishment, within the Education Corps, of a special subsection mandated to provide supplementary instruction to schoolchildren and new recruits in underprivileged communities. As a third example, the Engineering and Medical Corps were required to make provisions, in the 1950s, to construct and service the camps established for new Jewish immigrants.

Israel's development into a more mature, more self-sufficient state has transformed this situation.[13] Most of the national projects with high civilian content once conducted under IDF auspices are now carried out either by the relevant government ministries (e.g., Education, Immigrant Absorption, Social Welfare) or by voluntary citizens' associations. Concurrently the IDF has steadily reduced its participation in nonmilitary enterprises. Thus the NAHAL corps, for which public esteem has declined in any case, is now a declared target of reform. Similarly, the organization that provides supplementary education to underprivileged recruits—once considered the flagship of the IDF's commitment to national welfare—has been deprived of funds.[14]

To further illustrate how strongly the IDF still focuses on what Moskos calls "defense of their homeland," it participates only modestly in humanitarian operations overseas. In this respect, too, Israel's armed forces are still at the Modern stage. Granted, IDF medical units participated in the multinational rescue missions dispatched to aid victims of the 1989 Armenian earthquake and the 1994 Rwandan civil war. Moreover, government ministers occasionally have raised the possibility that Israeli troops might regularly join UN forces in similar operations.[15] Such proposals, however, are still considered premature: In 1994, Israel's parliament acceded only hesitantly to a request from the United States that an Israeli police contingent participate in Operation Uphold Democracy in Haiti. Indeed, such ideas are unlikely to be implemented as long as Israeli society feels the need to conserve its military energy for traditional force missions closer to home.

FORCE STRUCTURE

The IDF has adhered essentially to a militia structure since it was established in 1948. The great majority of troops are either compulsory conscripts (male and female, drafted for periods of up to three years at age eighteen) or reservists (principally male and liable to further duty of about one month per year until middle age).[16] Professional soldiers are a third component.

Although the IDF's three-tier structure in part was a response to Ben-Gurion's commitment to forming a people's army,[17] it primarily reflected military assessments of Israel's prospective force requirements. The system was predicated on two hypotheses. One was that Israel's principal military commitments were chiefly perimeter in nature. Because of the short distances involved, only a brief period of time would elapse between the mobilization of reservists and their participation in combat, even in emergencies. The second hypothesis was that the great majority of troops would be able to reach the required level of battle readiness during their conscript service, and could maintain that level thereafter through short annual refresher courses and training exercises.[18]

Both assumptions are now questionable. Senior IDF officers currently emphasize the need for what Lt. Gen. Dan Shomron, chief of staff from 1987 to 1991, called "a leaner and smarter force." In part, this reform is justified by the growing complexity and sophistication of Israel's new battle systems, whose efficient maintenance and successful coordination require greater specialization than the traditional militia structure allows. In a wider sense, however, the call for increasing professionalization also reflects an awareness of the changes in the IDF's prospective commitments. A semiskilled system geared primarily to supplying the manpower required for intermittent bursts of intense activity near the borders is unlikely to be appropriate for conducting either remote missions or persistent intraborder operations. Both types of combat are thought to demand an order of skill and stamina that few conscripts can attain, and even fewer reservists can maintain.[19]

At the most superficial level, changes in IDF force structures amount simply to an upgrading in the caliber of the personnel assigned to tasks that once received relatively low priority. In January 1992, for example, civil defense duties in the face of air and missile attack were reorganized within the framework of an entirely new IDF Rear Command designed to replace the notoriously primitive home guard (HAGA), whose inadequacies were exposed during the Iraqi missile attacks of 1991. Counterinsurgency units have been similarly overhauled. The Lebanon campaign and the intifadah provided harsh reminders that intrafrontier duties cannot simply be rotated among formations not specifically trained for the delicate, often distasteful tasks that they entail. As a result, constabulary missions have been transferred increasingly to more specialized formations: the Border Guard, masquerader squads,[20] and (since the 1994 Cairo accords with the PLO) patrol squads explicitly trained to operate with the Palestinian authorities in joint peace-enforcement missions.

This development has important sociological implications. Unlike the regular IDF combat divisions, which are composed of conscripts or reservists, most of the "special forces" are staffed by professional career servicemen. Moreover, because their duties demand fluency in the Arabic language, many of these troops are either Jews from an oriental background (Sephardim) or members of Druze and Bedouin non-Jewish minorities who serve in the IDF.

The overall order of battle also shows how strongly the transformations in mission commitments affect the IDF's force structure. In the past, and especially during the wars of 1967 and 1973, Israel's ground forces were organized mainly into armored brigades and territorial commands (North, Center, and South, reflecting respectively the Syrian, Jordanian, and Egyptian fronts). These formations still exist, but their status has been modified by two developments. One is the creation, in the late 1980s, of a combined-arms field command (Mafchash). The other, due largely to the prolonged intifadah, is the creation of smaller regional units such as the Gaza Brigade and the Bethlehem Brigade, most of whose missions are constabulary.

Still more fundamental are the changes taking place in IDF personnel.[21] Slowly but apparently inexorably, the principle of across-the-board conscript and reserve military duty is being relaxed. Indeed, in a high-powered review of Israel's manpower requirements prepared for the chief of staff in 1993, the Shaffir Committee recommended more discriminatory personnel procedures; if adopted, these will result in a selective form of service. In brief, the new program proposes three basic reforms, parts of which are already in progress. One is a reduction in the overall size of the reserve and conscript complements. This goal is to be met by liberal exemptions and/or discharges for males and (especially) females who fail to pass the IDF's educational, physical, and psychological screening tests. A second is the expansion of predraft training courses for conscripts with technological skills and aptitudes. A third is the provision of greater professional and material incentives to talented junior and senior officers, especially those with proven technological expertise, to contract for extended periods of career service.

THE DOMINANT MILITARY PROFESSIONAL

As early as the mid-1980s, before pressures for a reform of Israel's force structure had gathered momentum, Reuven Gal discerned an attitude of "professional pragmatism" among IDF career personnel.[22] More recent changes substantiate that observation. The IDF has not yet substituted an occupational ethos of military service for an institutional ethos. Even so, the dominant character of the military professional has changed greatly.

One indicator is the increasing emphasis on material remuneration rather than symbolic rewards as appropriate compensation for military service. This development has even affected the reserve complement, as indicated by suggestions that tax rebates be granted to reservists summoned for especially long tours of duty. The change is most obvious, however, among professionals. Over the past decade, successive chiefs of staff have waged persistent public campaigns to raise military salaries and to expand the array of fringe benefits (e.g., housing and car allowances, bonuses, pensions) to career personnel of all ranks. Supported by a cohesive veterans' association of former professionals, this campaign has enjoyed considerable success. Despite incremental cuts in the overall defense budget, increases in professional military incomes have consistently surpassed those granted in other public service sectors.[23]

More difficult to audit, but still apparent, is, the simultaneous transformation in the image of the Israeli soldier, especially at senior levels. In keeping with the paradigm of a Modern force, senior IDF officers traditionally took the stance of combat leaders.[24] They presented themselves as warriors, whose primary duty was to lead from the front in the swift battles of maneuver that the force always preferred to wage. Moreover, a distinguished record of active service in the field was the primary criterion for promotion; even Late Modern roles such as manager or technician were invariably considered subordinate to this standard.

This is still largely the case. Yet traditional attributes of senior IDF personnel are complemented quite noticeably by the Postmodern qualities of the soldier-scholar and the soldier-statesman. This development initially was stimulated by the Israeli administration of the territories conquered in 1967 (which until 1981 were under direct military government), and was encouraged by the intifadah (1987–93). Both experiences necessitated the involvement of senior IDF personnel in local civilian engagements with clear political connotations; as a result, these soldiers assumed administrative as well as constabulary roles in the public domain.

The protracted Israeli-Palestinian negotiations that began in 1993 added another dimension. Several officers, including brigadiers and even colonels, were prominent in the Israeli delegations. Indeed, the team that conducted the talks which resulted in the 1994 Cairo accords was headed by Gen. Lipkin-Shahak, then the deputy chief of staff, who attended meetings wearing a civilian suit. In many ways his appearance typified the soldier-statesman position cultivated by the highest IDF echelons; this is distinct from the warrior mold in which they were cast and even from the manager-technician role required by their command of a large, sophisticated force.

PUBLIC ATTITUDES

Israeli public attitudes toward the military have undergone changes comparable to those simultaneously generated elsewhere by the end of the Cold War. According to a survey conducted in 1995, the IDF enjoyed the "full confidence" of 77.5 percent of young Israelis approaching military enlistment. Although high by most international standards, that figure represented a noticeable decline from the 91 percent, 90 percent, and 92 percent recorded respectively in 1980, 1984, and 1988.[25]

Nevertheless, and for reasons mentioned earlier in this essay, Israeli public attitudes toward the military are still Modern. Israelis remain overwhelmingly supportive, are seldom ambivalent, and are never apathetic. The IDF continues to head the list of institutions for which the society expresses the highest regard. Still more striking is the public support enjoyed by voluntary agencies that provide service members with recreational and material amenities which the IDF itself cannot afford. Organizations with public-spirited names such as The Committee for the Soldier and The Fund for Israel's Security (known by its acronym LIBI, which translates as "my heart"), annually raise considerable sums from individual and corporate contributors. In doing so, they give material expression to a degree of societal empathy with the military that deviates markedly from the Postmodern paradigm.

The public attitude toward the IDF perhaps is best described as one of involvement. It can be critical as well as complimentary, however, and over the past two decades the former tone has become more pronounced.[26] Signs of this development first emerged during the 1973 war, when the entire Israeli defense establishment swayed dangerously on the pedestal of invincibility triumphantly mounted in 1967. Thereafter, the pace of change was increased considerably by evidence of operational deficiencies during the Lebanon War (1982–85) and the intifadah. The IDF's reputation was tarnished further by reports of training accidents, abuses of human rights in the occupied territories, and financial corruption at some senior military levels. Those revelations steadily demythologized the IDF, which no longer receives the virtually automatic public veneration that it once enjoyed.

One particular expression of the shift in public attitude is evident in the Jewish settler community on the West Bank. (We discuss this point in greater detail under "Conscientious Objection.") There it takes the form of charges that the IDF no longer deserves respect as the custodian of "the national spirit," and is expressed in a dramatic rise in the frequency and violence of physical confrontations between settlers and IDF troops.[27] Elsewhere and more widely, the new attitude is reflected in the degree to which the force is subjected to judicial scrutiny. Since 1973, military conduct has been the subject of three major legal tribunals: the Agranat Commission on the 1973 War, the Kahan Commission on the 1982 Sabra and Shatila massacres, and the Shamgar Commission on the 1994 Hebron killings. During the same period, Israel's Supreme Court conducted increasingly stringent reviews of IDF activities, particularly during the military occupation of the West Bank and the Gaza Strip.[28]

MEDIA RELATIONS WITH THE MILITARY

The media have played a crucial role in articulating changes in public attitudes toward the IDF. They have also facilitated that process, not least by encroaching on what was once considered the sacrosanct domain of military affairs. This shift from compliance to intrusion is a variant on the "incorporated-manipulated-courted" trajectory proposed in the paradigm.

Throughout the first three decades of Israel's existence, the local media exercised considerable discretion about all information pertaining to national security. In addition to acquiescing in strict military censorship, the media honored the gentleman's agreement, framed as early as 1949, whereby newspaper editors refrained from citing the confidential briefings that they received regularly from senior officers and cabinet ministers. Individual military correspondents invested the IDF Spokesman with virtually oracular prestige, and dutifully awaited his authorization before publishing items of military information; most of these, in any case, were initially broadcast by the army's own public radio network.

The institutional apparatus designed to ensure military control over the media remains in place. Nevertheless, the IDF's ability to manipulate (much less incorporate) the media has been curtailed considerably. One reason is that electronic communications have provided greater license to foreign press representatives in Israel. As amply demonstrated during the Lebanon War,[29] and even more so during the intifadah and the 1991 missile attacks, foreign correspondents no longer depend on government-controlled Israeli facilities to transmit their reports. Instead, they employ their own satellite and cable systems. The domestic media have learned to exploit this situation: Israeli correspondents now regularly circumvent the censor simply by quoting reports already published by their foreign colleagues (to whom, it is often alleged, they themselves supplied the relevant information).

Transformations in Israel's own media exert a similarly liberalizing influence. As recently as the late 1980s, the Israeli public had access to only one domestic TV station, itself largely dependent on government funding. During the past decade, however, that monopoly has been broken by the establishment of additional local and national TV and radio channels and by satellite links to international cable stations. Many of these networks cover military affairs extensively and vie with each other in providing novel, sometimes sensationalistic perspectives on the content of their reports. Thus, although most media coverage of the IDF remains laudatory, it is no longer collusive. Several of the judicial inquiries into military misconduct were conducted in response to pressures generated by media revelations.

The increased media intrusion into Israeli military affairs has created a distinctive form of the "courtship" relation suggested by the paradigm. Especially since the intifadah, escort officers attached to the IDF Spokesman's Unit have been more forthcoming with the press. Their position, however, is defensive, as senior IDF sources themselves acknowledge, particularly with regard to television correspondents.[30]

CIVILIAN EMPLOYEES

Contrary to the hypothesis of the model, civilian employees have not become a major component of Israel's armed forces. Instead, the civilian workforce employed directly by the military is currently being reduced in both numbers and proportion.

This development reflects in part the overall drive to cut IDF manpower costs. It is also facilitated by greater flexibility in the compulsory reserve system. In the past, reservists remained attached throughout their military careers to the military formation in which they were trained, but the IDF is now making more rational use of their abilities. The current surfeit of personnel permits the transfer of older reservists to units in which their civilian qualifications and experience can be employed most gainfully.[31] Although this arrangement is not yet applied throughout the IDF, it has already produced a net gain. It provides the IDF with a pool of cheap, expandable talent that is utilized only as the need arises.

The number of civilians employed directly by the Israeli military has declined, but the range of civilian tasks performed by military personnel has increased. This situation presents an interesting variant on the model, and can be explained largely by reference to two trends already noted above. One is the modification in Israel's military manpower requirements; the other is the continued (although weakening) adherence to compulsory conscription. Together these two factors have produced a surfeit of male and (especially) female troops, whom the IDF is prepared to release for duties in nonmilitary sectors such as schools, hospitals, the police force, government offices, and the nature-preservation society.

The IDF's interest in perpetuating this arrangement is clear. It permits the armed forces to retain first call on human resources. At the same time, it eases financial pressures on the IDF because the government ministries to which surplus troops are released must reimburse the military for the services they receive.

WOMEN'S ROLES

Compulsory conscription in Israel always has included females as well as males. Thus women have made up a large proportion of the IDF's complement. Moreover, the fighting roles played by many women during the War of Independence (1947–48) fostered an impression that Israeli female soldiers continued thereafter to share combat duties with males.

Closer analysis, however, largely nullifies this impression of gender equality.[32] A large gender discrepancy in the duration and scope of service has existed for a long time. That gap is now widening because the current program of overall force reduction is affecting women far more strongly than men. In 1994 the term of mandatory female conscript duty was reduced from two years to twenty months (and probably will be cut even further), whereas males still serve for three years. Similarly, twenty-four is generally the age ceiling for female reservists (of whom there are very few); for males, it is usually at least twenty years higher. Draft statistics, where available, tell an even more striking tale: Despite the current move toward more selective conscription, over 80 percent of the annual cohort of male Jewish youths is formally enlisted. Because the policy of exemptions for females is more liberal, the comparative figure for women is just under 70 percent.[33]

Other indicators confirm that Israeli women are still far less fully integrated into the IDF than the paradigm of a Postmodern military would demand. One is the maintenance of a separate Women's Corps, which is responsible for the needs and welfare of female troops. Another, more salient indicator is the character of the service performed by women.

The image of the Israeli woman warrior is a myth.[34] Although female conscripts are commonly assigned to combat units (increasingly as technicians and trainers as well as clerks), IDF regulations preclude women from combat roles. Polemicists debate the meaning of this policy. Some say that its persistence reflects the pervasiveness of male chauvinism in the IDF (and, for that matter, in Israeli society at large). Others attribute it to continued perception of the IDF as a combat-oriented force whose troops still face constant danger.

Whichever is the case, the role of women in the IDF remains subordinate. In November 1995, in a majority decision, Israel's Supreme Court applied the principle of sexual equality when instructing the air force to accept a young woman for pilot training; the military authorities previously had rejected her application to the aviation school. Nevertheless, it remains to be seen whether that ruling, in itself, can alter the male bias that permeates the IDF.[35]

FAMILY AND MILITARY COMMUNITY

In the conventional sense, the families of IDF personnel have always been removed from military life, largely because of the special characteristics of unit mobilization and housing arrangements in the Israeli military. Barracks communities of families do not exist except on air force bases.[36] Moreover, most spouses of professional IDF members are employed independently, reflecting the high proportion of two-career families throughout Israel.

Informally, however, service members' families are part of the military community in which their children and spouses serve. In this respect the IDF remains a Modern military. If anything, this characteristic has become even more pronounced of late: Wives of reservists in combat units now publicly voice their complaints about the length of their husbands' tours of duty. In addition, conscripts' parents exert pressure on individual unit commanders, and on the IDF as a whole, regarding the conditions of their children's service. In fact, mothers and fathers, often organized into parent associations, constitute an assertive lobby which, as the head of IDF personnel has acknowledged, impinges on training exercises and combat operations alike.[37]

The increase in parental involvement (indeed, intervention) in military matters can be attributed in part to the general erosion of deference toward the IDF. It also reflects the fact that a large proportion of today's parents are themselves veterans—unlike their own mothers and fathers, who had no experience of duty in the IDF. Many reservists, especially men, still perform their duty while their sons or daughters are serving as conscripts. This proximity of parents to offspring, combined with the permeability of Israel's civilian-military boundaries, results in a bonding of the family to the military unequaled anywhere in the Western world.

HOMOSEXUALS IN THE MILITARY

Israel Defense Force policy and practice regarding homosexuals in uniform has been discussed elsewhere by Gal.[38] The record exhibits some variations on the three phases of this area as delineated by the model. The IDF has moved from an early stage (before 1980), in which homosexuals usually were discharged from military duties, to a phase in which they were drafted selectively and on a restricted basis (1983–93). Current policy neither restricts nor exempts gays and lesbians who are drafted or who volunteer their services.

This progressive shift toward Postmodernism is not necessarily related to the emergence of new military threats or a new force structure. Probably it owes much more to the foresight of several senior IDF officers, who sought to forestall in Israel the sort of public and intrainstitutional controversy that accompanied President Clinton's attempts to change policy on homosexuals' service in the U.S. military.

CONSCIENTIOUS OBJECTION

Conscientious objection as understood in Western societies is virtually unknown in Israel. Blanket refusals to perform any military duty whatever for specifically pacifist reasons are so rare as to be statistically irrelevant. This phenomenon is due largely to the exceptionally sturdy soldier-citizen ethos fostered by Israel's sense of strategic insecurity. It also owes much to the absence, in the Jewish religious tradition, of anything comparable to the pacifist strain that runs through much Christian teaching.

Even so, two trends deserve comment. One is an extension of the arrangement whereby Jewish citizens are granted exemptions from military duty or deferments of service on religious grounds. The other is an expansion of what might be called "selective" conscientious objection, invariably for political reasons. These two phenomena, although concurrent, are distinct and warrant individual attention.

With the exception of Arab citizens, who have never been subjected to the draft, wide-scale exemptions are granted only to the ultra-orthodox (haredi) Jews in Israel. As early as 1948, haredi leaders petitioned David Ben-Gurion to defer the conscription of full-time male students in their rabbinic academies. On the grounds that military and religious lifestyles are incompatible, they also asked that all haredi females be exempted from service. Ben-Gurion wished to include the religious parties in his parliamentary coalition, and perhaps also was persuaded by the argument that Israel had a national duty to revive a traditional way of life that the Holocaust had largely destroyed. Thus he sanctioned both requests, although on a limited scale.[39]

Since the late 1970s, the exigencies of party politics have become even more acute. Largely for this reason, both portions of the original arrangement have been expanded considerably. Each year, some 20,000 ultra-Orthodox males now receive deferments on the understanding that "the study of the Torah [Jewish law] is their profession." Most of that number perform no military duties at all. Moreover, religious women claiming exemption from the draft are no longer required to have their applications approved by a rabbinical board; they simply submit a pro forma declaration. Over 20 percent of all potential female recruits presently take advantage of this option.[40]

Selective conscientious objection is an entirely different phenomenon. It does not imply a contradiction between all military service and a sectoral vocation or way of life. Rather, it articulates opposition to a precise type of military duty or to service in a particular place at a particular time. As such, it constitutes a form of political protest against the government's use of the armed forces for particular missions.[41]

A rare occurrence before 1982, selective conscientious objection (as defined here) first became significant during the Lebanon War and the intifadah. In both instances, small numbers of individual conscripts and reservists refused to take part in the campaigns on the grounds that they constituted unnecessary (and hence unjust) wars. In most cases, this refusal resulted in what Moskos calls "grey" conscientious objection: Unit commanders generally preferred to reach personal accommodations with the individuals concerned, who were transferred to other duties. Even so, a few hundred troops, mostly reservists, were tried in military courts and sentenced to terms of military imprisonment.[42] Almost all of these COs identified with the left wing of the Israeli political spectrum; they received vocal encouragement, and in some cases legal aid, from organizations such as Shalom Akhshav (Peace Now) and Yesh Gevul (There Is a Limit, a nonpartisan protest group founded during the Lebanon War to denounce the campaign).[43] When the activities of IDF "masquerader" squads were publicized in 1992, Yesh Gevul exhorted high school students not to enlist in such units.[44]

Since the conclusion of the first agreement between Israel and the PLO in 1993, selective conscientious objection has increasingly assumed a right-wing tone. It has become especially evident among members and supporters of the Jewish settler community on the West Bank, many of whom are identified with the national-religious segment of Israeli society.[45] Unlike the ultra-orthodox haredim mentioned above, members of the national-religious camp traditionally have portrayed service in the IDF as a religious obligation as well as a national duty. Nevertheless, soon after the first Oslo accords, a number of settler reservist officers announced their intention to resign their commissions.

A still more symbolic threshold was crossed in July 1995, when rabbinic proponents of the "Greater Israel" ideology, to which many settlers subscribe, called on conscripts to refuse any order they might receive to dismantle either IDF installations or Jewish settlements in regions designated as part of the domain of the Palestinian Authority. The assassination of Prime Minister Rabin in November 1995, by a reservist who claimed to follow Greater Israel teachings, has hitherto moderated the aggressive tone of public debate caused by such proclamations.[46] As a prominent form of political protest, however, selective conscientious objection seems likely to remain a part of Israel's societal-military landscape.

One other recent development is noteworthy. Public attention is being focused increasingly on the need to expand the existing system of national youth civic service in Israel.[47] In the past, most volunteers for such programs were religious females exempted from military duty. Recently, however, it has been suggested that several other segments of society might be encouraged to participate, especially Arab youths and the increasing numbers of Jewish males and females whom the IDF chooses not to enlist. If implemented, a nationwide civic service program also could provide an alternative route for conscientious objectors.

CONCLUSIONS

The realities of the Israeli military are more fluid than might be suggested by the strict logic of the Postmodern hypothesis. In response to transformations in the regional and domestic environment, the IDF has divested itself of some of its earlier characteristics. In significant respects, however, it retains Late Modern and sometimes even Modern attributes. Israel conforms to the Postmodern hypothesis in only two elements of the paradigm—the character of the dominant military professional and the place of homosexuals in the military—and even then not entirely so. Shifts in attitude can be observed in the other variables, but in most instances the dominant pattern still deviates markedly from the Postmodern norm. This is clearly the case with respect to major mission definitions, civilian employees, and female roles. To only a slightly lesser degree, it is also true of perceived threats, force structure, public attitudes toward the military, media relations, the symbiosis between families and the military community, and the status of conscientious objection. Therefore, on the whole, the IDF resists classification as a Postmodern military. It is still waiting to join that category.

NOTES

1. Stuart Cohen's research for this paper was funded by the Israel Science Foundation, administered by the Israel Academy of Sciences and Humanities.
2. Moshe Lissak, "Civilian Components in the National Security Doctrine," in *National Security and Democracy in Israel*, ed. Avner Yaniv (Boulder, Colo.: Lynne Rienner, 1993), pp. 55–80; Moshe Lissak, "The Permeable Boundaries between Civilians and Soldiers in Israeli Society," in *The Military in the Service of Society and Democracy*, ed. Daniella Ashkenazy (Westport, Conn.: Greenwood Press, 1994), pp. 9–19.
3. Rebecca Schiff, "Israel As an 'Uncivil' State," *Security Studies*, Vol. 1 (1992), pp. 636–658.
4. Ya'akov Ezrachi and Reuven Gal, *General Perceptions and Attitudes of High-School Students Regarding the Peace Process, Security and Social Issues* (Zikhron Ya'akov: Carmel Institute for Social Studies, 1995) (in Hebrew).
5. As a proportion of the GNP, Israel's defense budget was reduced from some 18 percent in the early 1980s to about 9 percent in the late 1990s.
6. Ofra Mayseless, Reuven Gal, and Effi Fishof, *General Perceptions and Attitudes of High School Students Regarding Security and National Issues* (Zikhron Ya'akov: Israeli Institute for Military Studies, 1989) (in Hebrew).
7. Clive Haberman, "Israel Deglamorizes the Military," *New York Times*, May 31, 1995, p. A9.
8. Stuart A. Cohen, "Israel's Changing Military Commitments, 1981–1991: Causes and Consequences," *Journal of Strategic Studies*, Vol. 15 (1992), pp. 330–350.
9. "Strategic Challenges to Israel in the 21s Century," unpublished lecture by Maj. Gen. (reserves) David Ivri, senior advisor on strategic affairs to the minister of defense, Tel-Aviv, June 9, 1998. See also the interview with Maj. Gen. (reserves) Ilam Biran, director-general of the Ministry of Defense, *Ha'Aretz* (Tel Aviv daily), Jan. 12, 1998, p. A5 (in Hebrew).
10. Gen. Israel Tal (Ret.), *National Security: The Few Against the Many* (Tel Aviv: Dvir, 1996), p. 55 (in Hebrew).

11. Daniella Ashkenazy, ed., *The Military in the Service of Society and Democracy: The Challenge of the Dual-Role Military* (Westport, Conn.: Greenwood Press, 1994).

12. David Ben-Gurion, "Address to IDF Officers," in *Uniqueness and Mission*, by David Ben-Gurion (Tel Aviv: Am-Oved, 1971), p. 81 (in Hebrew).

13. Dan Horowitz and Moshe Lissak, *Trouble in Utopia: The Overburdened Polity of Israel* (Albany, N.Y.: SUNY Press, 1989).

14. Ashkenazy, *The Military*.

15. Yossie Beilin, interview in *Ha-Aretz* (Tel Aviv), Sept. 14, 1994, p. A3 (in Hebrew).

16. The IDF itself never publishes manpower data. The International Institute for Strategic Studies (IISS) gives the following figures: conscripts, 139,000; regulars, 37,000; reserves, 430,000; see IISS, *The Military Balance, 1995–1996* (London: IISS, 1995), p. 118.

17. Mosheh Nativ, "IDF Manpower and Israeli Society," *Jerusalem Quarterly*, Vol. 32 (1984), pp. 140–144.

18. Reuven Gal, *A Portrait of the Israeli Soldier* (Westport, Conn.: Greenwood Press, 1986).

19. Ran Goren, "Advancement of the Weak versus the Promotion of Excellence in the IDF," *Sekirah Hodshit*, Vol. 37 (Nov. 1989), pp. 3–6 (in Hebrew); Emmanuel Wald, *The Gordian Knot: Myths and Dilemmas of Israeli National Security* (Tel Aviv: Yediot Aharanot, 1992), pp. 166–171 (in Hebrew); Shemuel Gordon, "In Favor of Selective Conscription," *Ma'archot*, Vol. 328 (1993), pp. 32–37 (in Hebrew).

20. Stuart A. Cohen, "'Masqueraders' in the Israel Defence Forces, 1991–1992: The Military Unit and the Public Debate," *Low Intensity Conflict & Law Enforcement*, Vol. 2 (1993), pp. 282–300.

21. Stuart A. Cohen, "The IDF: From a 'People's Army' to a 'Professional Military,'" *Armed Forces & Society*, Vol. 21 (1995), pp. 237–254.

22. Reuven Gal, "Israel," in *The Military: More Than Just a Job?*, eds. Charles Moskos and Frank Wood (Washington: Pergamon Brassey's, 1988), pp. 266–277.

23. Cohen, "The IDF."

24. Gal, *Portrait*.

25. Compare Ezrachi and Gal, *General Perceptions . . . Regarding the Peace Process* with Mayseless, Gal and Fishof, *General Perceptions . . . Regarding Security*.

26. Glad Barzilai, *A Democracy in Wartime: Conflict and Consensus in Israel* (Tel Aviv: Sifri'at Poalim, 1992) (in Hebrew).

27. Stuart A. Cohen, *The Scroll or the Swords? Dilemmas of Religion and Military Service in Israel* (London: Harwood Academic Book, 1997).

28. Menahem Hoffnung, *Israel: State Security versus the Rule of Law, 1948–1991* (Jerusalem: Nevo Publications, 1991), pp. 326–336 (in Hebrew).

29. Evyatar Ben-Tzadaf, "Have We Forgotten That We Are Living in a Global Village?" in *Yearbook of Association of Israeli Journalists*, ed. Dov Atzmon (Tel Aviv, 1985), pp. 64–68 (in Hebrew).

30. Eitan Ben Eliyahu, "The Media As a Front in War," *Ma'archot*, Vol. 322 (1991), pp. 16–19 (in Hebrew); Ran Goren, "The IDF and the Media: Can the Clock Be Turned Back?," *Ma'archot*, Vol. 322 (1991), pp. 20–23 (in Hebrew).

31. Yair Saroni, "A Reform in the Summons," *Ma'ariv*, Sept. 15, 1995, p. B3 (in Hebrew).

32. Natalie Yuval-Davis, "Front and Rear: The Sexual Division of Labour in the Israeli Army," *Feminist Studies*, Vol. 11 (1985), pp. 647–675; Reuven Gal, "The Israeli

Female Soldier: Myth and Reality," presented to the 1987 biennial conference of the Inter-University Seminar on Armed Forces and Society, Chicago; Hedva Almog, "The Integration of Israeli Women in Today's Israel Defense Forces," in *Women in Armed Forces*, ed. H. Hurni (Effingerhof: Druck und Verlag, 1992).

33. Brig. Gen. Yisraela Oron, personal communication, 1995.

34. Gal, "The Israeli Female Soldier."

35. Mosheh Wieinfeld, "The Supreme Court in a Majority Decision: The Exclusion of Women from Pilot Training—Sexual Discrimination," *Ha'aretz* (Tel Aviv), Nov. 9, 1995, p. A5 (in Hebrew).

36. Helena Syna and Reuven Gal, *Coping with Stress by Israeli Families: Searching for "Win-Win" Solutions to a Conflict between Two "Greedy" Institutions* (Zikhron Ya'akov: Israeli Institute for Military Studies, 1995).

37. Yoram Yair, interviewed in *Ma'ariv*, Jan. 14, 1994, p. A7 (in Hebrew).

38. Reuven Gal, "Gays in the Military: Policy and Practice in the Israeli Defence Forces," in *Gays and Lesbians in the Military: Issues, Concerns and Contrasts*, eds. W. J. Scott and S. C. Stanley (New York: Aldine de Gruyter, 1994).

39. Menachem Friedman, "This Is the Chronology of the Status Quo: Religion and State in Israel," in *The Shift from Yishuv to State, 1947–1949: Continuity and Change*, ed. Vera Pilovsky (Haifa: Haifa University Press, 1990), pp. 62–64 (in Hebrew).

40. Daniella Ashkenazy, "Education in the IDF: Alienation as the Enemy and the Anomaly as the Norm," *Nativ*, Vol. 6, No. 1 (1993), pp. 49–54.

41. Cynthia Grudo, ed., *Conscientious Objection: From Religious Pacifism to Political Protest: Proceedings of International Seminar, Caesarea, Israel, 1992* (Zikhron Ya'akov: Institute for Military Studies, 1993).

42. Ruth Linn, "Conscientious Objection in Israel during the War in Lebanon," *Armed Forces & Society*, Vol. 12 (1986), pp. 489–512.

43. Reuven Gal, "Commitment and Obedience in the Military: An Israeli Case Study," *Armed Forces & Society*, Vol. 11 (1985), pp. 553–564; Aryeh Shalev, *The Intifada: Causes and Effects* (Tel Aviv, Jaffee Center for Strategic Studies, 1991), pp. 123–128.

44. Cohen, " 'Masqueraders.' "

45. Ehud Sprinzak, *The Ascendancy of Israel's Radical Right* (Oxford: Oxford University Press, 1992).

46. Cohen, *The Scroll or the Sword?*, pp. 65–66.

47. Emily Silverman and Reuven Gal, "Developing a Civic Youth Service in Israel: A Summary Report of the International Seminar," in *Proceedings of the International Seminar on National Civic Youth Service*, ed. Cynthia Grudo (Zikhron Ya'akov: Carmel Institute for Social Studies, 1995).

13

South Africa: Emerging from a Time Warp

JAKKIE CILLIERS
LINDY HEINECKEN

In civilian-military terms, South Africa emerged from a time warp in the 1990s. In this chapter we attempt to illustrate that by the late 1980s, the South African Defence Force (SADF) still had many of the characteristics of a Modern armed force as portrayed by the Moskos paradigm. The SADF was not a large professional military, nor did it act in support of an alliance, nor was the dominant self-image of the military professional that of a manager or technician, although a discernible trend in this direction had become evident during the 1980s, especially in the navy and the air force.

In certain areas, such as those relating to the media, the role of women in the military, and conscientious objection, some correlation is evident, but on the whole the South African military under white minority rule ran counter to international trends during the 1960s, the 1970s, and most of the 1980s. Then, in tandem with the political transformation taking place in the wider South African society, a very rapid transition from the Modern to the Postmodern occurred. In the process, South Africa literally skipped the Late Modern period.

Some of the reasons for this peculiar development are to be found in the international isolation of the Republic of South Africa from the late 1960s to 1990, during the period when the African National Congress (ANC) was unbanned. Other reasons relate to the dominant ideology of racial separation and to black resistance politics. Afrikaner politics trapped the South African military in the Modern period; black nationalist politics triggered the transformation from the Modern to the Postmodern. Finally, it is debatable whether the paradigm is really universal and not simply the characteristic and the product of the Cold War, limited in its applicability to so-called Western armed forces or to proxy forces of the two major Cold War antagonists. Even so, the paradigm provides useful benchmarks for measuring the comparative status of civil-military relations among various countries within broadly discernible historical periods.

By the late 1980s the force structure and thinking of the SADF was still oriented toward conventional armed invasion. It was a military based on (white) conscripts fighting in defense of the white homeland and value system, generally supported by the white populace in its fight against the black (communist) threat from the north. Through massive covert and overt methods of censorship, disinformation, and manipulation, the media were used as part of a total strategy to counter what had become known as the "total onslaught." As we argue below, although civilian employees played an important supportive role within the Department of Defence, their role was little more than a supportive and administrative one.

PERCEIVED THREAT, FORCE STRUCTURE, AND DEFINITION OF MAJOR MISSION

In South Africa the army had always been the dominant and the largest service in the SADF, and had always been more Afrikaans and conservative than the other services. The air force and the navy had a much larger component of white English-speaking officers, had a more functional approach to discipline, and were more occupational in their approach to service in the military. This pattern is apparent to this day, although it is changing rapidly. Also, apart from the occasional protestation by the odd naval officer, South African defense policy always has been oriented toward a landward threat. Nor was the country especially concerned with air power apart from the dominant (if unstated) view that air power supplements ground forces in the extended African battlefield, not the other way around. This view, incidentally, was found to be essentially sound in southern Angola, where the SADF could operate in an almost continually hostile air situation in conducting what could best be termed semiconventional operations.

During World War II the Union Defence Force (the predecessor to the South African Defence Force) contributed its fair share to the Allied Forces, most conspicuously in east and north Africa and in Italy. At the end of that war, South Africa was relatively strong. An inevitable process of retrenchment followed, despite the involvement of the South African Air Force in the Berlin Airlift from June 1948 to September 1949, and in the Korean War from August 1950 to October 1953 under the auspices of the United Nations.

Until 1960, the Union of South Africa was a member of the British Commonwealth. The South African armed forces were oriented and structured for defense standardization and cooperation; they also acted as part of, and in support of, British forces. This was particularly true of the South African Navy, which had "the lion's share in safe-guarding the extremely strategic Cape sea route on behalf of the West"[1] and therefore had a preponderance of antisubmarine and mine-clearing capacity rather than general-purpose warships. In fact, the South African Navy was little more than an extension of the British Royal Navy.

The Union Defence Force was drastically reduced after 1945 and relied on World War II equipment until the 1960s, having been relegated to a subsidiary role in national affairs. The navy, for example, a force composed of some ninety-six ships by 1945, was reduced within a few years to three frigates, two boom defense vehicles, one minelayer, and a small number of motor launches. In 1961, when South Africa decided to become a republic outside the Commonwealth, the only noteworthy defense acquisitions in the previous fourteen years were several Centurion tanks in 1952, two comparatively modern destroyers between 1950 and 1952, and two squadrons of Sabre aircraft in 1955.

From the period after World War II until 1961, when the country became independent, South African military equipment and obligations therefore reflected the commitment to guard the Cape sea route and to provide one armored division and an air force ground support group for the defense of the Middle East according to the terms of membership in the Commonwealth. In the words of the SADF, "Commonwealth countries left most of the planning, strategic policy, military intelligence and the provision of armaments to Britain, and in the interests of standardization member countries obtained their armaments mainly from British sources. Furthermore in Africa no real threat (for instance terrorism) against South Africa existed."[2]

When a defiant National Party government under Prime Minister Hendrik Verwoerd decided to proclaim a republic outside the Commonwealth on May 31, 1961, the South African Defence Force entered a period of steady, if unspectacular, growth. Defense expenditures rose from .9 percent of the gross national product in 1960–61 to 2.4 percent by 1969–70. Although South African defense expenditure was never excessive in relative international terms (that is, as a proportion of the gross domestic product or the gross national product), it far outstripped the combined defense expenditures of potentially hostile countries farther to the north—a group of countries that eventually became known as the Front-Line States.

Relying now on their own resources, South African defense planners thoroughly revised the threat environment. According to an official Department of Defence Review published in 1971:

[T]he following signs were unmistakable [by 1960]: . . . Communist Imperialism and the Cold War thrived, while the West withdrew post-haste from Africa to avoid the stigma of colonialism. . . . This resulted in a rapid deterioration of the position of Whites in Southern Africa whilst Communism increasingly exerted its influence in the remainder of Africa. The continent of Africa would play a key role in the strategy traditional to the Soviets, and an attack would be concentrated against the White governments in Southern Africa.[3]

During the Sharpeville riots in March 1960, the military was called in to support the police in containing demonstrations against the harsh movement-control laws on black South Africans. Yet the focus remained on an external aggressor in the form of a conventional assault by the combined forces of the Front-Line States, supported by proxy forces from the Soviet Union and its allies. Far-fetched as that threat analysis appeared to be, by the mid-1970s Cuban forces, with massive Soviet support, were deployed en masse in Angola to halt the advance of South African armored columns. In this Operation Savannah, the South Africans eventually came within sight of the outskirts of Luanda and only turned back when American executive support for the invasion ran afoul of the U.S. Congress.

From a very small command and training nucleus in 1960, the SADF manpower demands on the white segment of the population grew rapidly in the years that followed. The number of white males called up through the ballot system increased from 11,759 in 1962 to 19,513 in 1965. Conscription was introduced soon thereafter, and 26,357 young white men were being conscripted annually by 1970. This annual intake figure could not be increased without extending conscription to nonwhites. Consequently, the initial period of uninterrupted service was increased from three months to nine months, then to twelve months, and eventually to two years. After completing this initial period of service, conscripts were allocated to units in the Citizen Force reserve of the territorial force, the Commandos. Both systems increased steadily during the period of subsequent compulsory service: In 1990, when national service was reduced from twenty-four to twelve months (conscription for white males was abolished in 1994), the Citizen Force and the Commandos each had an active strength greater than 120,000 men. Various other categories of reserves boosted the total to almost a half-million white men and women in a population of roughly 4.5 million whites and a total South African population of 34 million.

This large expansion in the part-time component of the military had obvious implications for organization and equipment. New units had to be established and the organization of headquarters elements modified and enlarged accordingly. Training units also had to serve now as operational units. Only in the 1990s, after the abolition of conscription, did the SADF move toward a smaller professional military in which the majority of the combat force were reserves. Caught in its own time warp, the South African military did not become a regular military in keeping with the Late Modern phase of the paradigm when, in the 1950s and 1960s, conscription was replaced with all-volunteer forces in most Western nations.

Within a few years, from 1990 to 1994, the mission of the military changed profoundly. Originally the military was oriented toward forward defense in depth to counter any enemy invasion and to weaken the neighboring countries' ability to support the ANC's low-level insurgency campaign. It now became a military in search of a mission, but still heavily involved in supporting the police in internal law-and-order duties, engaging in border control, and preparing for involvement in peacekeeping operations.

In this period, the military, which had been central to state power under the belligerent authority of President P. W. Botha, was rapidly relegated to the fringes of South African power politics. A budget that had peaked at 4.3 percent of the GDP in 1989 was slashed to 2.2 percent by 1995—a reduction of almost 66 percent in real terms within six years. Under an ANC-led government, civilian control and accountability—notably absent until 1994—were instituted with a vengeance. By 1999, the defense budget stood at 1.6 percent of the GDP.

The SADF had always been essentially a part-time force, relying on its Citizen Force and Commando Forces for the bulk of its combat power. White conscription was abolished in 1994, and by 1995 the newly named South African National Defence Force (SANDF) had committed itself to a level of 70,000 full-time regular uniformed members with a part-time component of 200,000—and even these figures were soon to prove financially unaffordable. In the late 1980s, the force had consisted of almost 110,000 uniformed conscripts and full-time soldiers, 240,000 part-time soldiers, and 180,000 reserves.

In 1995, the minister of defense, Joe Modise, summarized the force composition of the SANDF as follows: "South Africa's basic defense strategy is to have a relatively small affordable 'core force', consisting of elements of the full-time and part-time components . . . backed by a sufficiently large part-time component."[4]

To give an idea of the numbers, in April 1999 the full-time component of the SANDF numbered 87,036. This included 34,593 (38 percent) in the permanent force, 16,233 (19 percent) in the medium-service system (five to fifteen years), 16,610 (19 percent) in the short-service system (two to six years), 19,400 civilians (22 percent), and 200 in the auxillary service.[5]

The racial representation of the full-time force has changed dramatically in recent years. The number of blacks in particular has increased significantly, although the racial breakdown of the SANDF's full-time force does not yet reflect the wider South African population. Most important, the numbers of black officers and NCOs have increased dramatically as a result of the integration of the various opposing armed forces in 1996–97. By 1999, blacks make up some 58 percent of the full-time force, coloreds (persons of mixed-race descent) 12 percent, Asians 1 percent, and whites 27 percent.[6]

As with the full-time forces, the reserve is also a volunteer force. As of April 1999, this component consisted of 54,108 members,[7] serving in both the conventional and territorial part-time forces. With the end of conscription the SANDF is an all-volunteer force and there is no ability for former conscripts to serve in the military. Current and future volunteers in the SANDF would only be able to serve after completion of their term of service during a state of emergency or a state of national defense declared in terms of the Constitution. Both qualitative and quantitative research reveal that former part-time-force white conscripts would in any case not respond to a call-up.[8]

PUBLIC ATTITUDE TOWARD THE SOUTH AFRICAN ARMED FORCES

Public attitudes toward the military must be viewed against the backdrop of the ethnic and cultural divisions in South African society and the historic differences between English and Afrikaner conceptions of patriotism. Before the National Party's election victory in 1948, Afrikaans-speaking whites strongly distrusted the pro-British Union Defence Force. Subsequently, when Afrikaners came to dominate South African politics in the years after World War II, more and more Afrikaners were appointed to senior positions in the Union Defence Force; this trend was intensified after the Nationalist Party came to power in 1948. Eventually the white segment of the population increased its support for the military: The public attitude no longer was clearly split between English and Afrikaans but along racial lines, as the Nationalist Party's policy of separate development of racial groups (apartheid) was implemented.

In the 1970s, public support for the military increased as the threat of communism and communist-inspired insurgency in Africa appeared to escalate.[9] In a public opinion poll conducted in 1982, 35.1 percent of the white populace indicated that they were "inclined to disagree" and 44.8 percent that they "definitely disagree" that the government exaggerated the communist threat to the country.[10] Through the education system and the media, white South African society became increasingly militarized, and most white South Africans came to support the endeavors of the military. Inevitably (and we say this at the risk of overgeneralization), white conscription bound civilian families to the military and contributed to the militarization of white society. Those who disagreed generally emigrated, although there was a small but vocal anticonscription movement.

This support for the military was absent in the black populace, which openly displayed resentment toward the military after the repeated deployment of SADF troops in the townships to curb the rising tide of black resistance.[11] This negative attitude is reflected in a statement by Archbishop Desmond Tutu: "[A]s a black person I know we don't regard the police and army as our friends. No, let me put it more strongly. We regard them as our enemies."[12] Not surprisingly, many blacks regarded the SADF as a racist system that sought to maintain white supremacy.

Support and opposition to the SADF therefore were polarized along racial lines: Afrikaans-speaking whites were most supportive of the military, blacks most strongly opposed, and English-speaking whites, coloreds, and

Asians somewhere between. The meager attempts at increasing the SADF's representativeness were due to personnel shortages rather than other considerations. In 1963, for example, the SADF established a volunteer unit for coloreds, and in 1973 the first unit for black members of the various ethnic groups was established. Yet the supply of recruits for these units always far exceeded the demand, and the SADF never experienced politically motivated disaffection within these units.

It is still too soon after the 1994 integration of the guerrilla armies into the new South African National Defence Force to accurately measure how a more representative composition has affected the legitimacy and public support of the military. There is little doubt, however, that the SANDF is perceived to be more legitimate than the former SADF, although public support among whites has declined. Public attitudes have shifted from either support or opposition (depending on the racial group) to a position approximating ambivalence. According to surveys conducted in 1990 by the Human Sciences Research Council, whites, coloreds, and Indians were more positively disposed toward the military, while blacks displayed both negative and positive attitudes. English speakers were significantly more negative toward the military than Afrikaans speakers (a trend already identified during the 1980s), and Xhosa speakers (the traditional support base of the African National Congress) were more negative than any other ethnic group.[13]

By the end of 1993, before the military integration process began, all population groups in South Africa seemed to have a more positive attitude toward the military, even though black respondents were still the most negative.[14] Because of the SANDF's important role in support of the police in maintaining law and order and the ongoing deployment of the military in the black townships to help curb crime and ethnic conflict, the populace has not yet become apathetic toward the military, in keeping with the conception of the Postmodern era in the Moskos paradigm. Yet the debate about the future of the armed forces is no longer at the center of South African politics and general interest. Without conscription, with a much smaller budget, and with no clear perception of external threat, it is only a matter of time before ambivalent attitudes change to apathy.

MEDIA RELATIONS

The South African press historically has been divided between strongly progovernment printed media (until 1994, corresponding to the Afrikaans-controlled segment of the media) and the opposition press (generally English-controlled newspapers). A vocal, alternative, black-controlled press did not develop until the nineties. The most powerful of the media, television and radio, were virtually government monopolies and slavishly followed the National Party line from the 1950s onward. During the 1970s and 1980s, the SADF attempted to co-opt the media to promote the image of the military and to support government policy—an endeavor generally successful in the Afrikaans press, but generally unsuccessful in the English and the small black press. Particularly during the "total onslaught" era, the media were not only manipulated but in fact were controlled by the SADF in regard to security issues. Section 118 of the Defence Act of 1957 (as amended) prohibited pamphlets, articles, or radio broadcasts on military activity that could prejudice or embarrass the government, or alarm or depress members of the public. Furthermore, all reports on military movements, counterinsurgency activities, or related acts had to be cleared by military authorities before publication.

This control over the media was increased by an agreement signed between the minister of defense and the Newspaper Press Union in 1967 and amended in 1986. The spirit of this agreement was that the media would be subject to restrictions and obligations with respect to reporting. As a result of the prior censorship laws and postpublication penalties, the defense force was seldom mentioned in unfavorable terms. In a 1973 survey of newspaper articles, for example, 245 of 258 media reports were positive toward the SADF; only thirteen were negative.[15]

In addition to the support and cooperation received from the state-controlled media, the SADF's own internal media promoted its image in the military community. According to K. W. Grundy, part of the positive image of the SADF was due "to outright intimidation and legislative control, part to self-restraint, part to conscious public relations and, of course, part grows out of genuine admiration for the effectiveness and professionalism of the SADF."[16]

From 1979 onward, as the internal situation in South Africa deteriorated, even this relationship was undercut by the National Party's increasingly heavy censorship and intimidation of the opposition press. The breakdown in trust began when the public realized how extensively the SADF and the government were lying and withholding or distorting information (for example, with regard to the SADF's involvement in Angola in 1976). In 1986, in the face of the massive unrest that was sweeping across South Africa, the media began to reveal how deeply certain elements in the SADF were involved in illegal and criminal activities, including murder. The public image of the military was seriously harmed by the SADF's admission of the existence of a secret unit, the Civil Cooperation Bureau (CCB), which was involved in hit-squad actions against left-wing activists, and by the admission of similar activities of the Military Intelligence Division within the SADF.

With the acceptance of an interim constitution for the Republic of South Africa during 1993 in preparation for elections in 1994, the media and the military entered a new relationship. Section 16 of the Constitution of the

RSA, 1996, states that "every person shall have the right to freedom of speech and expression, which shall include freedom of the press and other media and the freedom of artistic creativity and scientific research." Section 32 states that "everyone has the right of access to any information held by the state and any information that is held by another person and that is required for the exercise or protection of any rights." Because Department of Defence information is considered public information, no information relating to national security may be kept from public scrutiny, except when it could cause identifiable harm to national security if disclosed. The limitation clause in the Constitution, Section 36, furthermore stipulates that any limitations imposed on the release of information must be necessary, reasonable, and justifiable.[17]

These constitutional provisions have necessitated a revision of media policy. In the new era of media relations, the SANDF has grudgingly come to accept responsibility for providing information as freely as possible and for cooperating with the media. When security checks are necessary, they are conducted in cooperation with newspaper editors to achieve a fair system. A new media policy based on the agreement reached between the British ministry of defense and the British media was submitted to all parties for their comment. In the process the tables have turned to effect a situation in which the military is now courting the media.[18]

In summary, during the 1960s and 1970s one could speak of the incorporation of the Afrikaans-controlled media by the military. During the 1970s and 1980s, one could speak of the manipulation of the media as a whole as the National Party government's perception of threat increased. Throughout this period the government press was controlled and manipulated politically. The English-language press was much more ambivalent in its reporting on the armed forces. In the present relationship, however, the press corps clearly is finding, to its amusement and surprise, that it is no longer cajoled but courted. In this aspect of the paradigm, South Africa therefore finds that it has undergone a staggered but rapid transition from the Modern to the Late Modern and Postmodern periods.

CIVILIAN EMPLOYEES[19]

Two criteria can be used in measuring the civilianizaton in the Department of Defence. One is quantity—merely the number of civilian employees in the department. The other is their relative power and influence. Without policy influence and access to power, an increase in the number of civilians in the armed forces does not necessarily translate into civilianization. In South Africa the role and impact of civilians in Department of Defence declined, particularly from the 1950s through the 1980s, although their absolute numbers increased throughout that period.

According to early white papers, the civilian component of the Union Defence Force was small. The largest civilian component belonged to the Civilian Defence Secretariat, an earlier version of the newly created secretariat, which was abolished in 1967 as the military consolidated its uniform control over the Department of Defence. Until that time "the Secretary for Defence [was] the permanent departmental head and accounting officer, directly responsible to the minister of defense for the implementation of ministerial policy in respect of financial administration and control, and discipline, training and efficiency of the civilian personnel of the Department of Defence."[20]

According to the SADF:

> As the executive military function is inextricably interwoven with the financial and general administration of the Department, the division of functions and responsibilities between the Commandant General [the previous designation for what is now the chief of the South African National Defence Force] and the Secretary for Defence created problems. . . . With this in view a Ministerial Committee of Investigation was appointed in 1966. After acceptance of the Committee's findings, the overhead control of the Department was entrusted to the Commandant General as Departmental Head . . . and the official designation of Secretary for Defence was finally abolished.[21]

Thus, before 1994 the armed forces were not subject to civilian supervision, although there was firm executive control. No civilians outside the executive had influence over the military, and civilian employees were restricted to mundane clerical and other administrative functions. Parliamentary supervision existed in principle; by the late 1970s, however, it had become all but nominal, as paranoia and lack of information swept through the National Party and legislative supervision gave way to executive dictate.[22]

Yet even while the civilians' influence waned, their numbers increased. During World War II the civilian component of the defense force was increased in an effort to release regular military personnel for operational service. In the years that followed, the civilian component of the SADF grew from 1,298 in 1955 to 29,000, or 38 percent of the full-time forces, in 1993.[23] This figure later declined slightly to 20,719 in 1997 as a result of rationalization that affected both uniformed and civilian personnel. It is estimated that in the future, civilians will make up 30 percent of the full-time forces.

As stated above, however, the relatively large numbers do not imply influence. Civilians employed in the permanent full-time force serve primarily in supportive roles in the administrative, financial, technical, and medical branches. Although the civilians' duties are integrated with uniformed personnel functions, civilians and uniformed personnel are treated as two separate components. Uniformed members are governed by the Defence Act, No. 44 of 1957; civilians are generally managed in accordance with the Public Service Act, No. 111 of 1984, as well as the Labor Relations Act, No. 66 of 1995. Civilians are public servants and are under a different administration with respect to service conditions as well as personnel concerns and labor relations.

The recent increase in the civilian component of the department also reflects the greater sophistication of systems and the more intensive support for these systems required from the defense industry. By the 1990s the South African Navy had the largest percentage of civilians: 50 percent of its full-time component and almost the entire dockyard. We also see a trend toward employing civilian contract workers to render specific services, particularly in the navy and the air force.

The civilian component of the Department of Defence has increased since the establishment of a civilian Ministry of Defence and Defence Secretariat in March 1995. The secretary now acts as the accounting officer of the Department of Defence, a function previously performed by the chief of the SANDF. The implication of this is that as of January 1999 the entire "uniformed" finance division has civilianized. The secretary also acts as the principal advisor to the minister of defense on matters relating to defense policy, human resource policy, and fiscal and administrative duties as delegated by the minister.

A strong joint standing committee of Parliament has been established, modeled on that of the German Bundestag and "competent to investigate and make recommendations regarding the budget, functioning, organization, armaments, policy, morale and state of preparedness of the National Defence Force and to perform such other functions relating to parliamentary supervision of the Force as may be prescribed by law."[24] Under the National Party and the previous Westminster parliamentary system, the select committee on defense had proved little more than a rubber stamp for the executive. Now, with its powers enshrined in the Constitution, Parliament has taken an active and vigorously independent role in monitoring defense relations and the military as a whole.

In the new situation the defense committee views itself as an active participant in the major decisions of the Ministry of Defence. The chief of the SANDF, previously in virtual command of the entire Department of Defence, presently still commands the four service arms (the army, navy, air force, and medical services) but has a greatly reduced advisory and policy role that is limited to doctrine and strategy issues. Most important, he no longer controls the purse strings. Within only a few years, the relative power and influence of civilians in the Department of Defence will be comparable to that in most Western armed forces.

To place this discussion in the framework of the paradigm, the civilian component of the armed forces in South Africa has increased steadily over time, although their political influence decreased. Particularly during the 1960s and thereafter until the 1980s, the need for more highly skilled technical personnel led to civilian defense contractors' increasing involvement in logistics, maintenance, and support. Beginning in 1993, as the debate about civilian control of the armed forces intensified, South Africa entered the Postmodern era energetically, complete with a defense secretariat and related civilian political control measures. Henceforth the civilian employees in the Department of Defence will be a major component of the military, both numerically and in power and influence.

THE ROLE OF WOMEN

South African white women have always played some role in the country's defense. During the battles against the indigenous black tribes, for example, the *Voortrekker* women assisted by loading rifles and rendering other support functions. Afrikaner history contains many examples of their involvement in such battles; many have reached near-mythical status.[25]

More recently, women served in supportive roles during World War II in female auxiliary corps such as the South African Military Nursing Service (SAMNS), the South African Women's Auxiliary Army Service (SAWAAS), the South African Women's Auxiliary Naval Services (SAWANS), the South African Women's Auxiliary Military Police (SAWAMP), and the South African Women's Auxiliary Air Force (SAWAAF). Most were disbanded shortly after the war; only the women in the nursing services were retained.[26]

Although women served in a limited capacity thereafter, white women were not appointed on a permanent basis in the SADF until 1970. As in previous years, the main incentive for allowing women to serve in the defense force was to release men for operational duties. Although women were no longer enlisted in separate corps, they were excluded from training and employment in combat specialties (in armor, infantry, artillery, and air defense artillery, and as pilots or operational medical orderlies) or any other combat role. They were limited to supporting specialties such as finance, personnel, logistics, intelligence, medical services, and welfare.[27] A college to train "young ladies in civil defense techniques" was established at George and commenced its activities on February 1, 1971.[28]

While women in the SADF were limited to noncombat roles, women serving during this period in the armed wing of the African National Congress, Umkhonto we Sizwe (MK), were integrated into the guerrilla force. Despite initial reservations about women's serving in the liberation struggle, specifically in a combat role, women soon proved their worth as scouts, messengers, and couriers, bringing ammunition in and out of the country.[29]

In view of the racial, gender, and cultural discrimination faced by black women in South Africa, the role of women in the MK contrasts sharply to that in white Africa. According to Jackie Cock, "[T]he female soldier, the MK Guerrilla, is a popular mass image of the strong, liberated woman."[30] Consequently, with the integration of the armed forces since 1994, the ANC has come out strongly in support of women's full integration into the armed forces, based on their guerrilla army experience.

In 1994, in agreement with the constitutional provisions forbidding discrimination on the grounds of race or gender, military policy guidelines were issued to allow women to be trained and employed on the same basis as men. Previously the dominant attitude among Afrikaners had been strongly patriarchal; no consideration was given to an increased role for women in the armed forces apart from administrative, nursing, and other supportive services. Therefore, the change in official policy regarding women's role in the armed forces represented a radical shift.

Today the career path of a woman in the SANDF is the same as that of her male counterparts: She faces the same selection and training procedures, and no posts are reserved exclusively for men. In addition to the traditional support specialties, all combat specialties are now accessible to women. A concerted effort is being made to increase the number of women in combat positions and at decision-making levels throughout the armed services. Recently, women have been integrated into the infantry, artillery, and armored corps of the South African Army, and now serve as pilots in the air force and on ships in the navy.

Despite these formal provisions, both the military and the general population still express strong resistance to women's serving in combat positions. In a recent public-opinion survey, 59 percent of respondents felt that women should not be allowed to do combat duty or serve on the front line. Because of ingrained cultural attitudes and stereotypes in South African society, women still are regarded as unsuited for positions that may involve risk or danger. Some time will therefore pass before the women serving in the South African military are really and fully integrated into all combat functions.[31]

The gender composition of the SANDF by rank as of April 1999 still reflects a small female representation, starting as it did from a very low base. Only five general officers (out of 152) are female, as are 6 percent of the colonels, 12 percent of the lieutenant colonels, 22 percent of the majors, 34 percent of the captains, 25 percent of the lieutenants, and 32 percent of the second lieutenants. In the enlisted ranks, women account for 15 percent of the warrant officers, 16 percent of staff sergeants, 18 percent of the sergeants, 16 percent of the corporals, 13 percent of the lance corporals, and 6 percent of the privates.[32] Women in uniform therefore made up 13 percent of the full-time forces.

In summary, in the 1970s the South African armed forces adopted a policy of limited integration of women into the military, but generally at much lower levels than (for example) in the United States. Yet until 1993, combat roles for women in the SADF were not considered. Since then this policy has changed dramatically. The armed forces have moved to full integration at all levels. South Africa underwent a delayed but rapid transition to the Postmodern military; the correlation regarding this variable in the Moskos paradigm is greater than for most of the others.

THE ROLE OF THE SPOUSE IN THE MILITARY COMMUNITY

In South Africa, the white military spouse has played an integral role in the military community and in support of her soldier-husband. Under the Union Defence Force, soldiers' wives sought to improve conditions in the training camps and to tend to the men's physical welfare.

This supportive role continued, though to a lesser extent, until the end of the counterinsurgency or "bush war" in northern South West Africa (Namibia) in 1989. The Defence Force Ladies Association played an especially important role in the military community by rendering support to spouses during times of separation and relocation, and when husbands were deployed on border duty in South West Africa. As a semi-welfare, social, and cultural organization, the Ladies Association also worked to broaden the understanding of military life, and in doing so played an important socialization role. They arranged briefings and visits to military units to incorporate spouses into the military organization and expose them to the military culture.

With the end of regular wartime deployment far from home, the exact role of the Ladies Association was less clearly defined. Activities shifted from a supportive to a more social role in which entertainment and social outings were organized for military spouses. Various projects still are undertaken to enhance military life and upgrade facilities at military units, but not to the same extent as in the past.

Beside involvement in the military community, spouses are still expected to take part in the array of social functions characteristic of military life, such as attendance at formal functions and parades. In recent years, however, wives have become increasingly reluctant to participate in the customary military unit functions, largely because of the increase in dual-income families, but also because many military families now live off base. In exceptional cases, where members live in isolated areas, work and social life are still centered on the military base. This situation was much more prevalent during the so-called border war when the SADF was deployed in northern Namibia. Although military spouses are still partially integrated according to the Moskos paradigm, there are definite trends toward greater separation from the military community. Therefore, even in this sense, South Africa has undergone a delayed transition to the Postmodern period.

HOMOSEXUALS IN THE MILITARY

There is little documentation on the treatment of homosexuals in the South
African military before the 1970s; thus it is difficult to determine how severely soldiers displaying homosexual tendencies were punished during this
period. Indeed, the treatment of homosexuals in the armed forces has not
been an issue of public debate in South Africa. Part of the reason is the
strongly conservative Calvinistic ethic of the Afrikaner, until recently the
dominant political group.

Past policy pertaining to the treatment of homosexuals was outlined in
the SADF personnel code, which classified homosexuality as sexually deviant and immoral behavior. A person would not be selected to become a
member of the permanent force if he or she were suspected to be homosexual. Members found guilty of homosexual acts were subject to disciplinary
action and, depending on the gravity of the misconduct, discharged if found
guilty by a court-martial. If a member of the permanent force admitted guilt
but there was no evidence of misconduct, the person was sent for rehabili-
tation. This policy applied only to permanent force or service volunteers,
not to conscripts; it was believed that false claims of homosexuality would
be used to avoid national service. Thus, gay conscripts had to be accommodated, but were not appointed to leadership positions or posts where
they had access to sensitive information. The general trend was to place such
persons in posts considered more suitable, such as in catering or as medical
orderlies.

The comparative lack of public discussion does not imply that this was
not a sensitive issue once conscription became obligatory for white males in
South Africa. In an internal 1992 Chaplains Services document, members
were cautioned not to discriminate against those perceived to be homosexual because "the very nature of the defence force, its emphasis on discipline,
physical hardness and the standards of an (almost) all male military world,
make it extremely difficult for a homosexual male to feel at home or to enjoy army life and training."[33] Homosexuals, in turn, were warned not to declare that they were gay or to display an aggressive "gay lib" attitude because "this is the quickest way to invite anger and opposition." Even though
homosexuals were (and largely still are) viewed with disapproval, they were
tolerated if they did not openly display their sexual preference.

The current SANDF policy, formulated in 1995 and a virtual reversal of
former policy regarding the treatment of homosexuals, is consistent with international trends and with the provisions stipulated in Section 9 (3) of the
Constitution: "No person shall be unfairly discriminated against, . . . on one
or more of the following grounds in particular: race, gender, sex, ethnic or
social origin, color, sexual orientation, age, disability, religion, conscience,
belief, culture or language."[34] At least at the level of formal policy, persons

are recruited and appointed according to the job requirements for a specific service, regardless of sexual orientation.

Although no action will be taken against a member of the SANDF for being homosexual, the policy still stands: Any sexually atypical or immoral behavior that could be detrimental to esprit de corps or morale, or could cause emotional stress, thereby affecting military discipline or effectiveness, is subject to disciplinary action. The perpetrator may be punished with detention, reprimand, fine, or discharge. Even so, the South African Military Discipline Code is currently under comprehensive revision to ensure that it complies with the new Constitution.

In view of the growing social and political tolerance of homosexual behavior, it remains to be seen how the SANDF will cope with the full acceptance of homosexuality, including aspects such as homosexual marriages between soldiers. In this respect the South African armed forces have been thrust very rapidly into the Postmodern era.

CONSCIENTIOUS OBJECTION

Conscientious objection to military service is generally associated with compulsory military conscription. In South Africa, national service in either the military or the police was obligatory for all white males over age eighteen until 1994. As mentioned earlier, the length of conscription varied from three months to two years, depending on the intensity of the external threat or the degree of internal political instability.

Exemption or deferment (but not exclusion) from military service could be obtained from an exemption board when justified. Grounds for such exemption included study, domestic obligations, physical defects, ill health, mental incapacity, or any other reason deemed sufficient.

Even though the original Defence Act 9 (Act 13 of 1912) accommodated religious objectors in a limited sense, conscientious objection did not become an issue until 1961, when compulsory military service was introduced. The original narrow definition of religious objectors was broadened in 1983. Those applying for exemption or exclusion from performing military service on religious grounds were classified by the Board of Religious Objectors according to three categories: (1) those who refuse to serve in a combatant capacity; (2) those who refuse to render service in a combatant capacity, to perform any maintenance tasks of a combatant nature, or to be clothed in a military uniform; or (3) religious objectors whose religious convictions are in conflict with any military service, training, or tasks connected to the armed forces. Persons classified in the first category served in noncombatant capacities in the defense force for the same period as other conscripts; those classified in the second category served for one and one-half times as long in prescribed noncombatant tasks; those classified in the third category rendered community service equal to one and one-half times as long as the aggregated period of service (including reserve service) that otherwise would have been applicable. This period amounted to six years during the two-year conscription era and reflected a punitive attitude.[35]

The Defence Act (Act 44 of 1957) made no provision for objection to military service on moral, ethical, humanitarian, or political grounds; a penalty of up to six years in prison was imposed on those who refused to render military service. Yet as the SADF became increasingly involved in operations inside and outside the country, conscientious objection on political grounds gained prominence. Formal resistance during this period emerged under the banner of the End Conscription Campaign, established in 1983, which aimed to broaden the rights of conscientious objectors and to create a system of alternative national service without additional punishment.[36]

In 1992, on the basis of recommendations by the Gleeson Committee, the Defence Act was amended and the scope of conscientious objection to military service was broadened to include moral and ethical objections. This amendment had hardly come into effect, however, in 1994, when conscription for white males was replaced by a volunteer system. An additional moratorium was applied to members of the part-time forces who were liable for prosecution for failing to respond to call-ups for military service.[37] Now, because of the move to an all-voluntary force, military conscription is no longer obligatory, and conscientious objection has ceased to be an issue of public concern in South Africa.

According to the Moskos paradigm, South Africa has therefore moved directly from the Modern stage, in which conscientious objection was severely circumscribed, to a situation reflecting the Postmodern era, in which the issue has been subsumed into civilian society.

SUMMARY AND CONCLUSION

The final variable in the paradigm is the organizational orientation of the military, described as generally institutional in the Modern period (pre-1950s), occupational in the Late Modern period (1950–90), and civic in the Postmodern period. This variable largely captures the essence of the entire paradigm and thus of all the preceding variables. It reflects the entire shift in the orientation of the military over the three periods. Therefore it is appropriate to examine this variable in summarizing the overall civil-military orientation of the South African armed forces.

Several issues complicate analysis in the case of South Africa. The first, which prevailed until shortly after the end of World War II and the victory of the white Afrikaner-dominated National Party at the polls in the white elections of 1948, was the division between Afrikaans- and English-speaking whites in South Africa. Their mutual antipathy strongly affected civil-military relations in the (then) Union of South Africa. Only after World War II, with the rise of black nationalism and resistance, did race became the dominant factor in South African politics, and therefore eventually a factor in civil-military relations. Black nationalist politics triggered the transformation from the Modern to the Postmodern, a transition delayed by the effects of Afrikaner nationalism and politics.

The race-based character of South African society and politics further complicates analysis and comparison between South Africa and other countries. If white society and white politics are used as a measure, the former SADF was a mass army based on conscription, with a supportive public and with women in a separate corps, virtually until its transformation into the SANDF in 1994 (or at least until the late 1980s). The (white) military leader's self-image was predominantly institutional, partly because of the match in values between a beleaguered white Afrikaner nation and its military defense system. South African society is deeply racially conscious; attitudes, views, and even policy are race-based, even in the post-apartheid period. Therefore, in discussions of civil-military relations in South Africa, the use of racial groups in explaining and reflecting past and current reality is tragically inevitable.

Although the SADF had become the most racially integrated of all National Party government departments by the 1980s, nonwhites' involvement was tolerated only up to certain levels. As recently as 1992, South Africa had only one nonwhite officer of general rank (a brigadier). Conscription was never applied to three-quarters of the South African population (the black, colored, and Indian groups). In fact, the military was disliked, feared, or hated by the vast unenfranchised portion of the South African population (that is, until 1994). Therefore, meaningful comparison is complicated by the exclusion of most South Africans from the military.

Another complicating factor is the continued involvement in operations since the mid-1970s. By the late 1970s the SADF had become a modern military force, complete with modern weapons and computerized command, control, intelligence, and communication systems. It was managerially competent and operationally effective. At the same time, South Africa was involved in an escalating war by proxy. Initially—until the coup in Lisbon in 1973—this war was waged in support of the Portuguese colonial powers in Mozambique and Angola; then it was conducted extensively in the former Rhodesia (Zimbabwe) until the Lancaster House settlement of 1979; also, and most prominently, it was waged in the former South West Africa (Namibia). During 1976 the SADF also became involved in Angola in support of UNITA; this involvement did not end until 1989, when the last South African troops withdrew from across the Cunene River in compliance with the New York Accords.

At the same time, because of escalating unrest inside South Africa after the Soweto riots of June 1976, the military was required to assume an increased support role for the police. By July 1985, South Africa was experiencing its first limited state of emergency; this had become national by June 1986. South Africa was under increased military influence, but the influence was not that of a creeping coup; it was present by the political invitation of Prime Minister P. W. Botha, who later became president.

Angola, South West Africa, and Rhodesia were part of the buffer zone that protected white South Africa from black Africa. Although modern managerial practices and technology had left their mark on the SADF, the dominant self-image of the average army officer was still institutional because the military was fighting in defense of the (white) homeland, not waging a far-off war in another country. (In contrast, the American experience in Vietnam infused the American military with a rampant careerism.)

Although the South African armed forces had many features of the traditional institutional British military, they did not enjoy the institutional centrality in society, nor the professionalism, associated with most armed forces in the period under review. Because of the integration of British with Afrikaner military traditions, South Africa struggled with the concept of military professionalism. In the British tradition the regiment was the basis for loyalty and service, the focus of civil-military relations. The Afrikaner tradition was that of the citizen soldier, the burgher, armed with his own rifle and carrying his own food, and fighting only as long as necessary before returning home.

In the latter years of the SADF, deployment was used primarily in an internal role in support of the police, not in defense of the country or to combat an enemy invasion. Although the Union Defence Force had many features of an institutional military, the South African military did not exhibit clear institutional features until after World War II, specifically toward the 1960s.

Beginning in the 1960s, the main mission definition of the military was the defense of the nation against communist invasion. The entire force structure and the system of conscription were adapted to counter this threat. In 1971, for example, the SADF argued:

> Our enemies receive increasing moral and material aid, not merely from the Communist countries, but also from several organizations and some governments in the West. Hostile African states are mainly armed and organized with aid from Communist countries. The presence of the Russians in the Indian Ocean and the Chinese in Zambia and Tanzania is now an accomplished fact. Terrorists are active in Angola, Mozambique and along the Rhodesian border; their training, organization and armament are improving appreciably.[38]

As the "total onslaught" against the country increased, the legitimacy and public support for the military intensified, particularly in the white population. The media were incorporated to report on defense issues, but at the same time were controlled in order to enhance the stature and image of the military. During the 1970s the civilian component of the military was increased in order to relieve uniformed members for border duty, and women were permitted to serve in a permanent capacity in noncombat roles. All in all, if one analyzes the variables listed by Moskos[39] as institutional/occupational indicators, the South African military displayed many of the features of a traditional institutional military until the late 1980s, not only in regard to the variables already discussed but also in regard to conditions of service.

In the 1990s, with the end of the war and the waning of the perceived threat against the country, a definite trend toward occupationalism appeared. This trend increased as the conscript system was replaced by a volunteer system. Cuts in the military budget necessitated the reduction of the full-time forces, and affirmative action threatened the promotion prospects of the former SADF officers still in uniform in the SANDF.

Since the unbanning of the ANC, the South African Communist Party, the Pan-Africanist Congress, and their armed wings on February 2, 1990, and the negotiated settlement that eventually placed Nelson Mandela in the presidency, the South African military has been involved in a remarkable process of catch-up in moving from a Modern to a Postmodern mind-set. This transition is not yet complete. Still unknown is the extent to which the corporate culture of the conservative SADF leaders, who are still crucial in the new SANDF, can cope with and internalize the transition, or how fully the emerging black officer corps can develop the managerial competency to run the military. Our guess is that the SANDF will experience severe stresses and strains in the years that lie ahead, as institutional memory and modern practice collide. The transition under way in the SANDF is too massive and too ambitious, and is occurring in too short a period, to permit any other prediction. Inevitably it will severely affect operational competence, management, effectiveness, and morale in the armed forces.

The most dramatic event in this period, and one that illustrates the extent of the transition, was the ANC's sweeping election victory under Nelson Mandela's leadership in the April 1994 elections. At midnight on April 25–25, the SADF ceased to exist and was replaced by the South African National Defence Force—a potentially legitimate force to be crafted from the integration of the former SADF, the armed wings of the ANC and the Pan-Africanist Congress, and the armed forces of the four nominally independent homelands: Transkei, Bophutatswana, Ciskei, and Venda. After the ANC election victory, ANC military commander Joe Modise, the archenemy of the former SADF, was appointed minister of defense; Ronnie Kasrils, the Communist Party stalwart and head of the ANC's propaganda and intelligence section, was appointed his deputy. Serving under them as commander of the SANDF was General George Meiring, previously the commander of the SADF and the man who was in charge of the military campaign against the ANC. Yet even as the integration of the seven armed forces began under the watchful eye of a British Military Assistance and Training Team (BMATT), the wider settlement process in South Africa implied far-reaching and much more fundamental changes in the relationship between the SANDF and South African society.

This analysis should confirm that the SANDF is undergoing rapid, far-ranging, and massive transition as it moves from a Modern to a Postmodern military. In addition to the changes in the structure and operation of the military organization itself, forces in society are propelling the military to become more fully in tune with civilian values. The acceptance of civilian control over the defense force and the creation of a civilian defense secretariat and civilian ministry were structural changes ensuring that the defense force would be more accountable to society. The acceptance of a constitution that enshrines certain fundamental rights also means that defense legislation and policy must be reviewed and brought into line with the values of society. Further, the involvement of the public and other stakeholders signifies that the military organization, at least at a formal level, is moving toward a civic organization. How effective this transition will be, and how widely the good intentions of the new South African Constitution will differ from actual practice, only time will tell.

NOTES

1. Republic of South Africa, *Review of Defence and Armaments Production: Period 1960 to 1970* (Pretoria: Defence Headquarters, April 1971), p. 4.
2. Ibid., p. 9.
3. Ibid., p. 5.
4. J. Modise, "Preparing the Army for the 21st Century: New Volunteer Part-Time System," *African Security Review*, Vol. 4, No. 6 (1995), p. 49.
5. Statistics obtained from Directorate Personnel Planning, Personnel Division, SANDF, April 7, 1999.
6. Ibid.
7. Ibid.
8. See for example C. Schutte and B. Sass, "Public Opinion Regarding Part-Time Military Service and Threat Perceptions," *African Security Review*, Vol. 4, No. 6 (1995), pp. 39–48.
9. J. Barber and J. Barratt, *South Africa's Foreign Policy* (Pretoria: Southern Book Publishers, 1990), p. 2.
10. K. W. Grundy, *The Militarization of South African Politics* (London: Oxford University Press, 1988), p. 12.
11. Troops were deployed in the townships after Sharpeville in the 1960s, during the Soweto uprisings in the 1970s, and in the mid-1980s under the state of emergency.

12. L. Nathan, "Troops in the Townships, 1984–1987," in *War and Society—The Militarization of South Africa*, ed. J. Cock and L. Nathan (Cape Town: David Philip, 1989), p. 70.

13. S. Kruger and A. du Toit, *Navorsingsbevinding—Die beeld van die Suid-Afrikaanse Weermag onder blankes, kleurlinge, Indiers en swartes in metropolitaanse gebiede en dorpe in the RSA* (Pretoria: Human Sciences Research Council, 1993).

14. S. Kruger and G. Thiele, *Navorsingsbevinding—Die beeld van die Suid-Afrikaanse Weermag onder blankes, kleurlinge, Indiers en swartes in metropolitaanse gebiede en dorpe in the RSA* (Pretoria: Human Sciences Research Council, 1993).

15. C. Smith, "Die Nuusmedia en die Suid-Afrikaanse Weermag," *Paratus*, Jan. 1974, p. 4.

16. Grundy, *Militarization*, p. 60.

17. Constitution of the Republic of South Africa, Sections 16, 32, and 36, May 8, 1996.

18. G. Opperman, "Relationship between the Military and the Media in South Africa" (paper presented at a seminar, "The Military and the Media," hosted by the Institute for Defence Policy, Halfway House Midrand, Aug. 17, 1995).

19. The definition of civilian employees is limited to persons employed by the military on a permanent basis as part of the full-time forces. It excludes civilians called up for active duty in the armed forces and civilians employed in the vast South African armaments industry.

20. Republic of South Africa, *Review*, p. 17.

21. Ibid., p. 18.

22. Also see P. Frankel, *Pretoria's Praetorians: Civil-Military Relations in South Africa* (London: Cambridge University Press, 1984).

23. L. Heinecken, "The Effect of Industrial Democracy and Unionization on the South African Security Forces" (paper presented to the South African Political Science Association, Broederstroom, Oct. 22–23, 1993), p. 6.

24. Constitution of the Republic of South Africa, Act 200 of 1993, as amended, Section 228(3)(d).

25. Examples include the Battle of Blood River (1938) and Vegkop (October 1938). During the second War of Independence (1988–1992) women followed their men, cooking and tending to the injured. See E. Meyers, "Die Suid-Afrikaanse vrou in landsverdediging-agtergrond en perspektief," *Militaria*, Vol. 16, No. 2 (1986), pp. 36–37.

26. Meyers, "Die Suid-Afrikaanse vrou," pp. 1–19.

27. C. Zietsman, "Operating in a Man's World," *Salut*, Vol. 2, No. 10 (Oct. 1995), pp. 26–28.

28. Republic of South Africa, *Review*, p. 20.

29. According to Maj. Gen. Jackie Sedibe, women were used effectively in clandestine combat operations.

30. J. Cock, "Feminism and Militarism: Some Questions Raised by the Gulf War," *South African Defence Review*, Vol. 1, No. 6 (1992), p. 20.

31. C. Schutte and J. Cilliers, "Public Opinion Regarding the South African Defence Industry, South African Participation in Peace-Keeping and Women in the Security Forces," *African Security Review*, Vol. 4, No. 4 (1995), p. 54.

32. Statistics obtained from Directorate Personnel Planning, Personnel Division, SANDF, April 7, 1999.

33. South Africa Chaplains Services, "Homosexuality" (SADF, Chaplains Services, 1992, internal document).
34. Constitution, Section 9 (3).
35. Over the six years from 1984 to 1989 the Board of Religious Objection received 1,898 requests, of which 124 were withdrawn. Altogether, 1,722 were successful and only forty-four unsuccessful. See Centre for Military Studies (Cemis), "Hantering van beswaardes teen diensplig" (voorlegging aan Lt. Gen. I.R. Gleeson, Pretoria, July 1991), p. 5.
36. J. Cock, "An Overview of Responses to Conscription" (Center for Intergroup Studies, University of Cape Town, Rondebosch, Cape Town, 1990, Occasional Paper 14); L. Nathan, "Marching to a Different Beat: The History of the End Conscription Campaign," in *War and Society*, ed. J. Cock and L. Nathan, (Cape Town and Johannesburgh: David Philip Publishers, 1989), pp. 309–310.
37. Institute for Race Relations, *Race Relations Survey 1992/3* (Johannesburg: Institute for Race Relations, 1993), p. 136.
38. Republic of South Africa, *Review*, p. 26.
39. C. Moskos, "Institutional/Occupational Trends in Armed Forces: An Update," *Armed Forces & Society*, Vol. 12, No. 3 (1986), p. 378.

14

The Postmodern
Military Reconsidered

JOHN ALLEN WILLIAMS

No social institution is more affected by both national and international factors than the military. The case studies presented here show the changes in the military's role and its relationship to society as the international structure underwent two radical transformations: from the Modern to the Late Modern era in 1945 and, especially, to the Postmodern era at the end of the Cold War, around 1990.[1] The theoretical expectations of the model presented at the outset proved a reliable guide to these changes, particularly those incident to the Postmodern era. Although national differences persist, the direction is clear.

Both national and transnational factors affect the relationship of the military to society. Perceptions of the threats and opportunities presented by the international situation shape military forces, military missions, and the relationship of the military to society. Similarly, a nation's political culture and shared memories condition both the military and its relation to the broader society. Military professionalism itself is shaped in a context provided by the state and its relationships with the outside world.

In the second chapter we presented Charles Moskos's typology, which outlined the expected evolution of several important civil-military variables during this century: perceived threat, force structure, major mission definition, dominant military professional, public attitude toward the military, media relations, civilian employees, women's role, spouse and military, homosexuals in the military, and conscientious objection (Table 2.1, p. 15). We predicted that certain trends would be apparent in a variety of national settings as a consequence of the dramatic changes in the international system and national adjustments to them.

Guided by the expectations of the model, chapter authors discussed the situation in their particular countries. The purpose of the model was to enhance the comparability of the cases and ensure that similar and theoretically interesting topics were addressed. The editors did not wish to impose such a rigorous structure on the authors that the peculiarities of their systems would be hidden, but to ensure the greatest possible comparability among cases. Authors were not rigidly confined by the model, and were encouraged to bring out ideas not related to it or to contradict it.

TESTING THE MODEL

The objective situation in which a state finds itself powerfully affects the relations between the military and the society it defends. If national decision-makers are at all rational, their perceptions of threat will be affected by the international situation. This, in turn, will affect the military and its relation to society. Although there are many similarities in how the nations studied reacted to the changing international environment, their adaptations are not uniform.

Domestic cultural and political considerations play a critical role in determining the shape of civil-military relations. States carry their histories around with them and will continue to do so for the foreseeable future. Thus, while there are commonalities among nations, national differences persist. States are unlikely to change at the same rate, even along a particular dimension. There is nothing deterministic about the changes that will occur from one era to another.

There are many common trends in the militaries studied, however, despite the fact that the international situation is interpreted through national lenses by decision-makers and citizens alike. The purpose of the model (Table 2.1) was to highlight these similarities and also to show where the expected similarities were not seen. Since the relationship between the military and society in each social system also reflects national history and culture, the importance of detailed case studies to understand developments over time is apparent.

At this point it may be useful to summarize briefly the degree to which the expectations of the model were borne out by our case studies. Examples are given that seem most appropriate to explain the fit of the model, and no attempt is made to summarize the situation of a particular country.

Threats

Certain trends are apparent cross-nationally as leaders adapted to changes in the world order caused by the rise and fall of the bipolar international system. For the states most directly involved in the Cold War, the concern for national survival that marked the Late Modern period has given way to worry about such lower-intensity (but still potentially deadly) threats as domestic unrest and terrorism. In addition, peacekeeping and humanitarian actions are increasingly seen as firmly in the mainstream of military missions, rather than a distraction from the "real" purpose of militaries.

These actions are not new, but they have moved to the forefront. They also require serious military capability for their success. As recently noted:

In this ugly new order, brutalizers act with impunity and prove daily that a peaceful, humane world is not going to be built with good-governance programs. Force, or a credible threat of force, may be necessary.[2]

It is interesting that Israel exhibits both Modern and Postmodern characteristics with respect to threat. It remains concerned both about enemy invasion and subnational violence and terrorism. To this will be added the Late Modern concern with nuclear attack as unfriendly neighbors develop nuclear capabilities. On the other hand, France's experience follows the model more closely. The Late Modern period began, for France, in the early 1960s, with an increased interest in managing its alliance relationships. There is now no particular enemy, but France remains aware of remaining military threats in the international environment and prepares for them.

Force Structure

Military budgets, already under pressure in response to the rapidly escalating costs of sophisticated technology and a widespread expectation of a "peace dividend" once the Cold War was over, are further vulnerable due to the ambiguous nature of many of the new threats. When one cannot identify a clear enemy, it is more difficult to generate popular support for military expenditures.

Neither the objective threats faced nor the resources available for defense make a return to mass armies or even large professional armies likely. Modern technology renders the labor intensive "industrial" model of warfare obsolete, and even the United States found itself slashing personnel costs as it entered the Postmodern era. France, which traditionally viewed conscription as a mark of patriotism, joins the other industrialized nations in moving toward an all-volunteer force. Germany still has conscription, but relies primarily on a small professional army.

The major exceptions to this trend are Switzerland and Israel, which rely not only upon conscription but robust reserve forces for defense. Indeed, the relationship between reserve and regular forces could be a separate variable in a revised typology. Over the periods discussed, the reserve forces' role would likely be seen to evolve as follows: (1) in the Modern era, a source of relatively unskilled combat replacements; (2) in the Late Modern era, separately organized and structured combat, combat support, and combat service support units; (3) in the Postmodern era, skilled and deployable components of a total force, either separately or integrated with active component counterparts. Reserve components in the Postmodern era do more of the specialized and technical work, with members serving in such capacities as pilots and medical and civil affairs personnel. Certainly that has been the direction in the United States, and it would be interesting to see if this pattern is seen elsewhere.

Major Mission Definition

Most all countries studied were Postmodern in their military missions. The greatest exception, of course, was Israel, which must still focus on defense of its homeland. The Israeli military's earlier involvement with nonmilitary nation-building missions has now largely been superceded by civilian efforts. South Africa's military has made the greatest transformation in this, as with so many other variables, moving directly from Modern to Postmodern and bypassing the Late Modern era. Although South Africa has not yet done much peacekeeping, it views this mission as an important opportunity for cooperative action and integration into the international community.

The importance of military capability and determination for the successful completion of the stability missions endemic to the Postmodern era was underscored by the Dutch experience when they failed to defend the "safe area" of Srebrenica, Bosnia. The missions of the Postmodern era are not all military as traditionally understood, but they still rely on competent and resolute military force for their accomplishment, as much as do traditional warfighting missions. In the United States, a new emphasis on preventing and mitigating the effects of terrorism, including an attack using chemical and biological weapons, has a large military component, much of which is located in the reserve forces.

Dominant Military Professional

In most societies the dominant military professional exhibits characteristics of each era; the roles of combat leader, manager/technician, and soldier-statesman/soldier-scholar are added rather than substituted as the international environment changes. The emphasis may shift toward the Late Modern and Postmodern era expectations, but all roles remain necessary.

Assuming this is true, then the requirements for effective leadership grow dramatically over the years. This is especially the case if multiple roles must be assumed by the same individual. The implications of this for the training and education of military officers are significant: narrow technical training will not be sufficient to produce the officers needed in the Postmodern era. It may be necessary to go outside the formal institutions of the professional military education system and give the best officers a graduate education at the most prestigious civilian institutions.[3]

It may also be that an officer corps that is more broadly educated and more sophisticated politically will seek to influence policy issues of interest to the military or to their particular service. Given the decreased level of political leaders' personal military experience in most Western democracies, this is not necessarily a bad thing. While inappropriate influence must always be guarded against, an improved level of policy advice could be beneficial.[4]

With respect to the case studies, Canada has been a leader in supplying peacekeeping troops and developing a body of theory and experience as to their most effective use. After an unfortunate incident in Somalia, Canadian officers have moved toward the manager and soldier-diplomat roles, rather than that of the combat leader. Perhaps no country has moved further in the Postmodern direction on this variable than Denmark, whose well-trained soldiers have adapted well to peacekeeping missions.

Public Attitude toward the Military

Public attitudes toward the military shift over time, but the evolution from support to ambivalence to indifference is rarely seen. Indeed, public opinion in most countries studied has remained supportive, although citizens are generally not interested in military service for themselves or their families. Public opinion seems to change more as a result of relatively short-term influences, such as the Vietnam War for the United States and the fall of Srebrenica for the Netherlands, than as a result of long-term trends. The continuing high public opinion could be due to the fact that military force remains relevant, even in the Postmodern era. It may also be due to the increasing integration of the military and society, reflected in the increased role for reserve forces.

Media Relations

The expected Postmodern relationship is most clearly seen in this variable. Only Switzerland seems to be a partial exception to the general tendency of the military to court the media. It could be argued that there is more manipulation of the media by the militaries than is apparent, although the media are becoming far more cognizant of such attempts. Video clips of laser-guided munitions destroying Baghdad, played repeatedly on CNN and other news outlets, support the belief that a good deal of manipulation of the press is still occurring in the United States.

Civilian Employees

Britain and Israel are the greatest exceptions to the expected increase in the role of civilian employees in the military. The United States, Germany, Israel, Australia, and New Zealand have moved the furthest toward a Post-modern civilian role. The interchangeability of certain civilian and military skills and tasks makes the decision about job assignment increasingly one of economic rationality rather than military necessity.

Women's Role

The role of women in the military has expanded, but hardly at the same rate and not to the extent that advocates of complete integration see as desirable. Although the principle of full integration is accepted in some societies, such as Canada, the Netherlands, and South Africa, this is not the case generally. Some states, such as Italy and Germany, remain in the Late Modern era of partial—or even minimal—integration.

Popular mythology notwithstanding, the "woman warrior" in Israel is a myth from the days of the war of independence. Women are not currently allowed in combat roles there. Although they are required to serve, they serve for a shorter period and are more likely to be granted a waiver than are men. In South Africa, despite the end of formal barriers to full integration, neither the military nor the general society support the notion of women in combat. In the traditional society of Italy, women have not been integrated into the military despite legislation protecting women's rights in performing public functions. Even advocates of women's military service there tend to think in terms of selective roles, rather than full integration in all functions. Similarly, women's integration into the German armed forces is minimal, and mainly seen in the medical specialties. In Switzerland, women are not yet permitted in combat.

The United States military is more Postmodern than those of most states on the issue of women's integration, despite continuing barriers to their service in ground combat and on certain naval vessels. Unlike less legalistic societies, however, the United States will be more likely to carry out formal commitments to integration once they are made. As just noted, de jure policies do not automatically translate into de facto opportunities, and domestic interest groups know they must use both legal and political instruments to ensure that they do.

Spouse and Military

In civilian life people are less inclined than before to seen themselves as an adjunct of their spouse's profession. This is also true in the military, where the spouses of military members have an existence apart from their husband's or wife's career. Over time, the role of spouses in the militaries of most societies has decreased. Not all have become completely removed, as predicted—indeed, that may not be possible—but there has been a significant reduction over time. Increasingly, spouses have careers, not just jobs, and their tolerance for frequent relocations can no longer be assumed. This is true even in Italy, which remains Late Modern in many other social dimensions. Australia and New Zealand best display the Late Modern expectation of partial involvement of spouses in the military community, largely because of the need to rely on military services at remote locations.

The two small countries defended largely by militias, Switzerland and Israel, exhibit opposite patterns on this variable. Switzerland has always been essentially Postmodern in this respect (the rotational militia can remain near home), while the extreme dangers to Israel have resulted in a very tight bond between the military and military families.[5]

Homosexuals in the Military

The issue of open homosexuals in the military is far from resolved, although the trend toward increasing acceptance is clear. Britain and Italy remain the most conservative on this issue, and open acceptance cannot be expected soon. Other nations have formal policies that permit homosexuals to serve, but in practice they do not achieve real integration. In Germany, homosexuals may serve, but they can be discharged if their orientation affects their duty and they are penalized by a lack of promotion opportunities. The United States' "don't ask, don't tell" policy[6] attempted to find an acceptable compromise between gay and lesbian service members living in fear of witch hunts on the one hand and celebrating Gay Pride Week in uniform on the other. Although this policy has not prevented the dismissal of a large number of homosexuals from the force, it is simply a formalization of a policy practiced informally by individual military members over the years.[7]

The countries most reflective of the Postmodern era expectation of acceptance are Denmark, Switzerland, Canada, Israel, and the Netherlands, although even in these cases the integration of gays and lesbians has not been without incident. Still, the success of Canada, in particular, has been noteworthy. If the full acceptance of openly homosexual service members is only a matter of time, given the increased tolerance for diversity of sexual orientation among the general population, it would be advisable for policymakers in countries where this is true to move beyond wishful thinking or abhorrence and consider how such a transition can be made with minimal negative impact on group cohesion and military effectiveness.

Conscientious Objection

With the rise of smaller professional militaries and the decline of conscription, the issue of conscientious objection becomes less contentious. Without routine conscription, conscientious objection is an issue only in principle in terms of entering military service—although the issue is very real for service members who develop (or discover) pacifist beliefs once they enlist.

Some countries still conscript. In Switzerland, conscientious objection has been equated with objection to the state. Alternative service is permitted, but objectors can be forced into combat roles if their petition is not approved. Israel sees a number of grounds for conscientious objection to service, but generally not pacifism. Certain ultra-Orthodox Jews object to service, and have been granted exemptions from military service since the founding of the state of Israel. These exemptions are beginning to face judicial barriers, and the issue is quickly becoming contentious. There is also an increase in "selective" conscientious objection.[8]

In general, civil-military relations in the states studied have evolved as the model would predict, with allowances for the particularities of each system.

THEORETICAL ISSUES

Analytical Model

The book occupies a middle ground between description and theory. Given the importance of good description in theory-building, we thought it useful to present a number of comprehensive and context-rich case studies. They are all studies of Western-style democracies. The countries outside Western Europe and North America—Australia/New Zealand, Israel, and even South Africa—are still predominately Western in orientation. Whether the similarities apparent in these cases would also be seen in other states, particularly in the developing world, is a matter for speculation. Nevertheless, no country is immune from the transnational influences that shape civil-military relations.

There is an explicitly Western focus of the analytic model and the case studies. We are quite aware that this study is based on a Western—indeed, American—social science model. Constructs and hypotheses grow out of historical experiences and objective situations, and it is possible that a Western-oriented model would miss important elements of interaction if used in places where its assumptions do not apply. It could even be argued that using a nonindigenous model to explain variations in a particular social system is a form of intellectual imperialism.

This is an important research issue, going beyond the matter of cultural sensitivity, but it would be a problem only if the resulting analyses were weakened by the limitations of the model. The best tests of its utility are the analyses produced by the chapter authors. We believe that our decision to use this model was appropriate.

First, no model is ideal. Models generally do not detect, or even illustrate, interactions beyond their scope, and we thought it best to begin with what we know.

Second, the framework was applied by social scientists from the countries in question who have been trained in the appropriate use of such models and are aware of their limitations. Moreover, each author was encouraged to go beyond the model categories, or even to contradict the model entirely, whenever appropriate.

Finally, the model is not a statistical analysis of dependent and independent variables, but a schema to illustrate areas of particular relevance to the historical evolution under study. Given the state of knowledge and theory-building in this area, this approach seemed preferable to one suggesting an illusory certainty.[9]

Postmodernism

In general, the military forces of the countries studied approach the model's expectations for the Postmodern era. In each case, the model highlighted important areas of change in the relationship between their militaries and society. Tailoring the model itself for particular situations would reduce cross-national comparability and weaken its utility.

The position of the study in academic discussions of postmodernism needs to be further discussed. To be sure, the scheme of the book, the framework for analysis, and the contributions of our authors are not postmodern at all. The major contribution of this book is to the literature on civil-military relations, not to the theoretical debates on the nature of postmodernism. The chapters speak for themselves, and the editors and chapter authors are quite orthodox positivists. Far from rejecting empiricism in the search for objective (or at least intersubjectively verifiable) truth, we embrace it. While different observers will have different opinions as to where truth may lie, we hope that this study will expand the body of facts to serve as the basis for further theorizing and policy decisions.

Furthermore, military leaders would make a grave error if they became postmodern in the sense of rejecting empirical experience as a basis for planning and decisions. Combat is an unforgiving teacher, and war is a reality, not a social construct, for those engaged in it. Decisions made on forces, personnel, and missions have empirically verifiable outcomes: casualties suffered or inflicted, objectives met or denied, and victory or defeat.

The era toward which at least the Western world is moving has elements that cause the militaries to structure themselves and to act in similar ways. The Postmodern name for the period derives primarily from its inception after the cataclysms in central and eastern Europe that marked the end of the Late Modern era (in our scheme), around 1990. The direction of military organization, personnel, and missions is away from the comfortable absolutes that defined the military sphere, gave it its purpose, and separated it from things civilian in previous eras.

One area of overlap with academic postmodernism is the book's predictions of cultural relativism and a breakdown of traditional lines of demarcation. In the Postmodern era, the distinctions between the military and society are lessening, as are those between many military functions and civilian equivalents. Military culture is challenged by a relativistic civilian ethos from without and by the increasing civilianization of military functions and personnel orientation from within. Absent a clearly defined military opponent, considerations other than military effectiveness assume a greater importance in making decisions about force structure and personnel. "Chaos" and "disorder" are poor substitutes for an obvious enemy for this purpose.[10]

The degree to which the militaries studied here are becoming postmodern in the academic sense is still an empirical question, as is the degree to which patterns observed in the United States and other developed Western nations are generalizable to other settings. Indeed, the changes observed in Western militaries may well be part of a more widespread reinvention of modern organizations in society and not unique to the military.

IMPLICATIONS FOR POLICY

The variables around which the case studies were organized relate to current policy debates in the United States and elsewhere as leaders try to preserve military effectiveness and fairness simultaneously. Three of these are particularly contentious: women's role, homosexuals in the military, and (with respect to conscripts and those who have postinduction conversions or revelations) conscientious objection.

Perhaps the greatest value of these case studies is as a source of data and experience that hitherto has been largely ignored. Ignorance may be a lesser impediment to wise policy than is a belief that something is true when it is not. Decision-makers in the United States and elsewhere make a grave mistake if they assume that experiences of other militaries are irrelevant to their situation.[11] Granted that no nation approaches the United States in aggregate military power, the capabilities of every nation studied here are relevant to the subnational, low-intensity, and/or stability operations in which military forces will increasingly be engaged in the future. The small-unit forces most appropriate for these operations could come from anywhere and would be similarly affected by the civil-military issues discussed here.

Partisans on all sides of contentious issues would do well to study the experiences of the countries examined here to see what lessons can be drawn.

As seen earlier, conventional wisdom often errs, and beliefs about the experiences of other countries are often not accurate. For example, the United States is sometimes portrayed as lagging behind its allies in certain personnel issues. This is true with respect to sexual orientation (with the notable exception of the United Kingdom), but the United States is much further along in the integration of women into the military. Whatever position one takes on these issues, policy discussions should take account of relevant experiences elsewhere.

CONCLUSION

Five major organizational changes were predicted for the Postmodern era: (1) the increasing permeability of civilian and military spheres; (2) a reduction in differences in armed services based on service branch, rank, and combat versus noncombat roles; (3) a change in military purpose from fighting wars to conducting missions not traditionally considered "military";[12] (4) a more extensive use of multinational military forces authorized or legitimated by supranational institutions; and (5) the internationalization of military forces themselves.

All of these changes are observable to some degree. We began with a model to explain what has happened in civil-military relations and predict what is likely to happen along a number of its most important dimensions. Central to the discussion was the interaction of a common development (the rise and fall of the bipolar world) with factors unique to particular states. National factors may alter, but do not necessarily overwhelm, the effect of the changing strategic landscape on relations between the military and society in the countries studied.

To be sure, the concept of national sovereignty still has plenty of life in it. National factors will continue to influence civil-military relations into the indefinite future. States will continue to respect each other's borders for most purposes, but the range of issues deemed purely domestic is shrinking.[13] Militaries will work increasingly with one another, either side by side in combined operations or as part of the same military unit.

Many factors are pushing in the direction of postmodernism. Global economic integration, telecommunications and advanced information systems, immigration patterns, and international travel all contribute to an increasingly interdependent world. Armed forces after the Cold War reflect and possibly contribute to these forces. Specifying these relationships in an accessible manner has been a main purpose of this book. Over time we expect more nations to display the characteristics identified with the Postmodern era and those nations already identified as Postmodern to move even further in that direction.

NOTES

1. Other dividing lines are conceivable, but these reflect major changes in the international balance of power and the resultant calculations of national leaders and their militaries.
2. Barbara Crossette, "Lost Horizon: The World Expected Peace, but Got a New Brutality." *New York Times*, Jan. 24, 1999, pp. D1,D16.
3. This is argued extensively in Sam C. Sarkesian, John Allen Williams, and Fred B. Bryant, *Soldiers, Society, and National Security* (Boulder, Colo.: Lynne Rienner Publishers, 1995).
4. This point of view is presented forcefully in Sam C. Sarkesian, "The U.S. Military Must Find Its Voice," *Orbis*, Vol. 42, No. 3 (1998), pp. 423–437.
5. It is arguable that the separation between spouses and the military is actually premodern, antedating the categories of the model. If so, the separation seen in the Postmodern era is a case of "back to the future."
6. This policy was proposed by Charles Moskos and has proved more resilient to court challenge than many (including his coeditors) expected. The U.S. Supreme Court will generally not hear appeals of discharges for homosexuality, and as of now has refused five times to overturn the ban on homosexual activity. "Legal Watch: High Court Lets Gay Ban Stand," *Army Times*, Jan. 25, 1999, p. 6.
7. According to Steven Lee Myers, "Military Discharges for Homosexuality Double in 5 Years," *New York Times*, Jan. 23, 1999, p. A13, there were more discharges for homosexuality in 1998 than there have been in any year in the last decade. He notes that the services "discharged 1,145 gay men and lesbians in the last fiscal year, a 13 percent increase over the year before and nearly double the number in 1993, the last year before the 'don't ask, don't tell' policy took effect." Whether this is due to the services inappropriately "asking" or the members "telling" (either to get out of the service or out of personal conviction) remains at issue.
8. For a detailed discussion of the evolution of the grounds for conscientious objection from religious to secular, see Charles C. Moskos and John Whiteclay Chambers II, *The New Conscientious Objection: From Sacred to Secular Resistance* (New York: Oxford University Press, 1993).
9. It is often useful to map relationships onto the tautologies of the numerical system and manipulate them in various ways, but in this case the effort would be both uninformative and misleading.
10. Fortunately for the United States and its allies, recent opponents, such as Muammar Qaddafi, Saddam Hussein, and Slobodan Milosevich, have been easy to demonize and thereby personalize the disputes with their countries in a way that would not be possible otherwise. Future conflicts when "good" and "evil" are more difficult to distinguish will pose a problem in maintaining public support.
11. The United States military's tendency to discount the experiences of nonsuperpowers is very shortsighted. One editor recalls meeting a U.S. Navy officer who had just left a post in Saigon, where his task was to translate the lessons learned from the French experience in riverine warfare when they fought in Indochina. This would be commendable, except that it occurred in 1972, one year before the United States pulled out of Vietnam and after a decade of learning expensive lessons the French might have taught for only the effort of translating them.

12. The term "operations other than war" (OOTW) is losing ground in the U.S. Army in favor of the more descriptive "stability operations." These include humanitarian assistance, peacekeeping, and the more challenging (and most similar to traditional operations) peace enforcement. See Col. Robert B. Killebrew, USA (Ret.), "Deterrence With a Vengeance: Combat Infantrymen Remain the Best Choice for Peace Enforcement Operations," *Armed Forces Journal International*, Vol. 136, No. 3 (October 1998), pp. 76–81.

13. Note the 1999 series of crises in Kosovo, legally a province of Serbia, and the willingness of international actors to intervene in a situation that not many years ago would have been considered purely domestic.

Appendix
Post–Gulf War Military
Roles of Western Nations*

Location	Date	Mission	Participants
USA borders: Joint Task Force Six	1990–	assist in drug interdiction	100–1,500 military plus law enforcement agencies
Turkey: Operation Provide Comfort	1991	Kurdish refugee relief & enforce no-fly zone	U.S. forces and coalition (23,000 peak)
Bangladesh: Operation Sea Angel	1991	flood relief	8,000 U.S. Navy & Marines
Albania: Operation Pelican	July 1991 to Dec 1993	relief work & port patrol	Italian military (1,200 peak)
Phillipines: Operation Fiery Vigil	July 1991	Mt. Inatubo volcano rescue	5,000 U.S. Navy & Marines
Western Sahara	Sept 1991–	observer force	365 UN military with U.S. officers
Zaire	Sept 1991	rescue foreign nationals	French & Belgian troops with U.S. airlift
Former Yugoslavia (Croatia): UNPROFOR	Nov 1991 to Dec 1995	peacekeeping	UN contingents (14,500 peak)
Cuba (Guantanamo): Operation Safe Passage	Nov 1991 to May 1992	Haitian refugee relief	U.S. military and Coast Guard (2,000 peak)
Cambodia: UNTAC	Dec 1991 to Sept 1993	peacekeeping	UN force (19,000 peak)

*Partial listing through mid-1999.

Location	Date	Mission	Participants
Russia: Operation Provide Hope	Dec 1991 to Feb 1992	food relief	Western and U.S. airlift
Chad	Jan 1992	rescue foreign nationals	French contingent
Italy: Operation Volcano Buster	Dec 1991	Mt. Etna volcano rescue	Small U.S. Navy & Marines
United States (California): Joint Task Force Los Angeles	May 1992	restore domestic order	8,000 U.S. Army Marine Corps, 12,000 National Guard
Somalia	Aug–Nov 1992	famine relief 500 Pakistan	Small UN force: military, U.S. airlift
Adriatic: Sharp Guard	1992–	monitor former Yugoslavia	NATO naval force
United States (Florida): Joint Task Force Hurricane Andrew	Aug–Sep 1992	disaster relief	21,000 U.S. Army, Air Force Marines, 6,000 National Guard
Iraq: Operation Southern Watch	Aug 1992–	surveillance	U.S. Air Force, Navy
Somalia: Operation Restore Hope	Dec 1992 to May 1993	famine relief and restore order	UN force (peak 35,000; U.S. peak 20,000)
Former Yugoslavia (Macedonia): Able Sentry	Dec 1992–	monitor border	1,000 UN force: Nordic & U.S. contingents
Mozambique: ONUMOZ	1992–	peacekeeping	UN force (6,700 peak)
Kuwait: Operation Iris Gold	1993–	Kuwait defense	U.S. forces (4,000 peak)
Zaire	Jan–Feb 1993	rescue foreign nationals	French, Belgium troops
Somalia: UNOSOM II	May 1993 to Dec 1994	establish order & humanitarian aid	UN force (peak (15,000)
Iraq	June 1993	Baghdad bombing	U.S. air forces
United States (Puerto Rico)	July 1993–	anti-drug law enforcement	300 National Guard troops with local police

Location	Date	Mission	Participants
Rwanda	Jun 1993 to May 1994	oversee cease-fire & elections	2,200 UN force
Colombia	Jan–Feb 1994	civic works engineers	150 U.S. Army
Bosnia	Feb 1994	downing of Serb planes (first NATO military action)	U.S. Air Force
Rwanda & Burundi	Apr 1994	rescue foreign nationals	Belgium & French troops; also U.S. Marines
Bosnia	Apr 1994	bombing of Serb positions	U.S. planes under NATO
Rwanda/Zaire/ Uganda: UNAMIR, Operation Support Hope	Jul–Aug 1994	relief work	UN force, (2,300 U.S. troops)
United States (Washington state)	July 1994	forest fire fighting	600 active duty; 7,000 reservists
Bosnia	Aug–Sept 1994	air strikes against Bosnian Serbs	U.S. & British planes under NATO
Haiti: Operation Uphold Democracy	Sept 1994 to Mar 1995	secure change of government	20,000 U.S. at peak, token force from 24 other countries
Kuwait: Operation Vigilant Warrior	Oct–Dec 1994	protect Kuwait from Iraq	13,000 force at peak (mainly U.S.)
Bosnia	Nov 1994	air strikes against Serbs in Croatia	U.S., British & French planes (largest NATO military action)
Kazakhstan: Operation Saphire	Nov 1994	removal of uranium	U.S. civilian-military team
Panama: Operation Safe Haven	Sept 1994 to Mar 1995	guarding Cuban refugees	3,000 U.S. military at peak
Somalia: Operation United Shield	Dec 1994 to Mar 1995	aid evacuation of UN troops	1,800 U.S. Marines, 400 Italians

Location	Date	Mission	Participants
Haiti	Mar 1995–	follow-on of American intervention	UN force: 1,500 troops and police
Comoros	Oct 1995	reestablish order	1,000 French troops
Bosnia: IFOR, Operation Join Endeavor	Dec 1995 to Dec 1996	enforce peace agreement	60,000 NATO force (20,000 U.S., including Hungary)
Liberia	Apr–May 1996	evacuate American nationals	U.S. Marines and Special Forces
Iraq	Sept 1996	air attack on missile sites	U.S. Air Force and Navy
Bosnia: SFOR, Stablization Force	Dec 1996–	enforce peace agreement	20,000 NATO force (6,000 U.S.)
Central African Republic	Jan 1997	reprisal for killings of French soldiers	2,000 French troops
Zaire	Apr 1997	evacuate foreign nationals	1,200 troops from U.S., Belgium, France, Britain
Albania: Multinational Protection Force	Apr–Dec 1997	assist in restoring order and protection of humanitarian missions	6,000 European force led by Italy
Sierra Leone	June 1997	evacuate foreign nationals	U.S. Marines
Congo (Brazzaville)	June 1997	evacuate foreign nationals	French forces
Central America	Nov 1998 to Jan 1999	Hurricane Mitch relief work	1,700 U.S. forces
Iraq: Operation Desert Fox	Dec 1998	air attack	U.S. and British air units; U.S. military buildup in Gulf
Yugoslavia: Operation Allied Force	Mar–June 1999	bombardment of Yugoslavia	NATO forces, primarily U.S.

Ongoing Peacekeeping Forces:
    UN Peacekeeping Force in Cyprus (UNIFICYP), 1,500, 1964–
    UN Disengagement Observer Force: Israel/Syria (UNDOF), 1,300, 1974–
    UN Interim Force in Lebanon (UNIFIL), 5,800, 1978–
    Multinational Force and Observers: Sinai (MFO), 1982–

Index

CPSIA information can be obtained
at www.ICGtesting.com
Printed in the USA
JSHW031737120121
10842JS00001B/24